TEACHERS COLLEGE STUDIES IN EDUCATION

RECENT TITLES IN THIS SERIES

PROGRESSIVES and
URBAN SCHOOL REFORM

The Public Education Association
of New York City
1895-1954

SOL COHEN

BUREAU OF PUBLICATIONS
Teachers College, Columbia University
New York   1964

FOREWORD

THE PUBLIC EDUCATION ASSOCIATION of New York City is one of the oldest civic groups in the United States specifically devoted to school improvement. Born of the "triumph of reform" in the city elections of 1894, the organization has stood, for more than a half-century, at the center of New York's educational affairs. It has managed to attract a steady flow of notables to its ranks: Nicholas Murray Butler, Felix Adler, Miriam Sutro Price, Mariana Griswold Van Rensselaer, Charles Howland, Abraham Flexner, and Willard Straight in the early period; Margaret Lewisohn, Adele Levy, Harrison Tweed, Frank Karelson, Winthrop Rockefeller, and William Nichols in more recent years. And it has sponsored an impressive list of exciting educational innovations: the first school recreation program, in 1897; the first school for juvenile offenders, in 1900; the first "visiting teacher" program, in 1906; the first "all-day neighborhood school," in 1935; the Bronx Park Community Project, in 1950; and the "School Volunteer Program," in 1956. Today, the organization plays a vital role in the development of local and state educational policy, and it maintains a comprehensive research program; indeed, it is busily reproducing itself in other cities across the nation.

Dr. Cohen tells the story of the Association with insight and verve. He goes far beyond a narrow organizational account to give us a fascinating sketch of twentieth-century New York politics as seen from the vantage point of those interested in education. And he insists upon venturing appraisals throughout. Thus, he is eloquent in his praise of the Association's effort to expose corruption, mismanagement, and waste in the schools, yet sharp in his criticism of the Association's pedagogical policies. Not all readers will agree with Dr. Cohen's judgment; but none can accuse him of having written a "house" history.

At least two of Dr. Cohen's conclusions strike me as especially significant. First, he has hammered one more nail into the coffin of that old commonplace about education being "above politics." The

v

schools are publicly controlled in the United States; and since citizens inevitably disagree about what they want from the schools, the schools inevitably end up the subject of political controversy. The Association's leaders have known this from the beginning, and have acted accordingly. Thus, Dr. Cohen points out: "Regardless of the impression it prefers to foster, the PEA has been throughout its career involved in politics. Its chief raison d'etre has been to influence the decisions of a department of the New York City government—the Department of Education. In its efforts to influence decision-making in the New York City school system, the PEA has employed all the strategies and tactics available to a skilled and resourceful interest group in city politics. It has been remarkably successful in winning acceptance of its basic program."

Second, Dr. Cohen's study has provided additional data in support of the thesis that progressive education was not merely an isolated pedagogical creed, but rather the educational phase of the broader progressive movement in American life and thought. I advanced this thesis in *The Transformation of the School* (1961), and was privileged at that time to draw upon Dr. Cohen's preliminary data. Now, he has fully documented the relationship between school reform and municipal reform in New York City, concluding that progressive education was simply one facet of progressivism writ large. To understand progressive education in this light is to enable us to appraise its strengths and weaknesses much more rationally and fruitfully than we did in the 1950's, when educational dialogue so often took the form of a medieval morality play, in which angels and devils competed for the souls of men.

Lawrence A. Cremin

PREFACE

ONE OF THE MOST STRIKING ASPECTS of American historiography since World War II has been the resurgence of interest in the progressive movement. Postwar historians have studied the movement more intensively and from a great many more viewpoints than had preceding generations of scholars. With the aid of a spate of new monographs, historians have already produced syntheses radically altering the basic historical interpretations of progressivism. Yet the fact that public school reform was one phase, and an extremely vital phase, of progressivism is still largely overlooked. The history of the Public Education Association of New York City, born in a crusade for municipal reform, helps fill this lacuna. Its founding and subsequent career document the intimate ties among progressivism writ large, progressive education, and public school reform.

The PEA was born in October 1895. It was a direct offspring of New York's great political uprising of November 6, 1894, which saw the ouster of Tammany Hall from control of the city government and the election of a fusion administration sworn to a unique platform of political and social reforms. The reform crusade that culminated on November 6 was a many-pronged and complex affair. Nevertheless, several features stand out. In the first place, the "boss" and his cohorts were to be ousted from City Hall and replaced by the "good people," or the "better element," who would restore decent government to the city. This was the good-government phase of the reform movement: the old Mugwump tradition of reform. But the reform movement of 1894 went beyond Mugwumpery to include a positive concern for the health, welfare, and comfort of the city's inhabitants, to include social reform planks. This was its uniquely progressive phase.

One of the most intriguing aspects of the reform uprising was the central place occupied in it by the city's public school system. The public schools were a major campaign issue; public school reform became part and parcel of the triumph of reform in November. The

Public Education Association owes its existence to the centrality of the public schools on the reform agenda; leaders of the reform uprising believed that an organization of women, ostensibly independent, disinterested, and nonpolitical, under the neutral designation "Public Education Association," might prove a most effective ally in advancing the cause.

Public school reform, or progressive education, meant several things to the New York reformers. In the first place, like the broader reform movement, it had its good-government phase: Tammany Hall and its followers were to be ousted from their positions in city school government, control of the schools was to be placed in the hands of the "good people," and the machinery of school administration was to be reformed along good-government lines. Progressive education was also caught up in the social phase of the broader reform movement. The functions of the public school were to be extended beyond their traditional, formal intellectual concerns in order to conquer the urgent problems posed by the immigrant and the slum, in order to "meet the needs of the city," as contemporaries frequently expressed it.

A more definitive description of progressive education, at least as it emerged in New York City, cannot be assayed at this point. The content and meaning of progressive education shift through the decades. One of the purposes of this study is to describe its different meanings, the various forms which it took, and the connections between them, as seen in the career of the PEA between 1895 and 1954.

Since its founding the PEA has been in the forefront of virtually every important legislative and administrative change affecting the New York City public school system. It has initiated, demonstrated, or lent its support to many instructional practices and procedures which are now established policy. Almost everything the PEA has striven for over the years has come to pass. Assuredly, it is difficult to measure influence. The PEA, like any political interest group in the dynamic world of New York City politics, has had its ups and downs. And decision-making in the field of public education, as in any unit of government, is the end product of complicated and diverse pressures, many of them more or less invisible. Still, with one reservation, the most cautious appraisal of the PEA's career must agree with City School Superintendent John E. Wade, who said in 1945: "The history of fifty years of progress in education in New York is inextricably bound up with the history of the Public Education Association." The caveat may be entered where the School Superintendent acknowledges fifty years of public school "progress" in the city.

This is not a complete history of the PEA. It emphasizes the PEA's public life rather than the intimacies of its private life, which concerns us only to the extent that it has a bearing on the Association's career. This study is not intended as a history of a political interest group as such, nor as a history of public education in New York City, but as a contribution to American social and intellectual history. Through the program and activities of the PEA broader aspects of progressivism may be illuminated, and through progressivism the activities of the PEA may be illuminated.

Study of the PEA will, perforce, throw light on the history of reform in New York City. But only in its setting is this study local history. The essential political and social problems to which progressive education was the response were present not only in New York City. The reform movement came first, among the big cities of the nation, to New York. And New York provided a model for other urban centers. The history of the PEA is thus a case history in urban progressive education. It should shed some light on the sources and meaning of progressive education by asking such questions as: What was it? Who wanted it? Why? How many wanted it, and how did they go about getting what they wanted? Were they successful, and under what conditions? It will not be possible to do more than indicate answers to such questions, but even this may have its uses in so neglected a subject.

The president of the PEA, William B. Nichols, extended every courtesy to the writer. The files of the PEA were thrown open; all documents, all historical materials of any sort in the possession of the PEA were made accessible. Staff members Frederick McLaughlin, Clarence Tompkins, and Mary Hoagland gave assistance and encouragement. Without the cooperation of the PEA this study could not have been undertaken. However, this is in no sense an "official" or authorized biography of the PEA.

I would like also to express my appreciation to those others, people and institutions, who helped me in the course of this study. For access to the manuscript collection at the Little Red School House, I am indebted to Mrs. Milton Tarlau of the Little Red School House. The staffs of the libraries at Columbia University, Teachers College, Amherst and Smith Colleges, and the University of Massachusetts were always cooperative. Thanks to the grant of a Romiett Stevens Scholarship by Teachers College, I was able to begin this study. Thanks to the indulgence of Dean Albert W. Purvis of the School of Education, University of Massachusetts, who lightened my teaching load, I was able to finish it.

This book grew out of a Ph.D. dissertation begun in the winter of 1958 and completed in the spring of 1963. My major advisor was Professor Lawrence A. Cremin, who read and criticized the manuscript at various stages of its preparation and in whose seminars I learned both that progressive education is simply another manifestation of the progressive impulse, and that educational policy-making is the outcome of a political process. Professor Cremin has done the pioneering work in opening up progressive education and public school reform as a new field of historical research, and I am particularly indebted to his path-breaking study, *The Transformation of the School: Progressivism in American Education, 1876-1957.*

I would also like to thank Professor Wallace S. Sayre, whose provocative questions at an early stage opened up new and extremely fruitful perspectives. Professor Sayre also read the complete manuscript at a later stage and saved me from several errors. His and Herbert Kaufman's *Governing New York City: Politics in the Metropolis* has been an indispensable guide to the history, politics, and government of New York.

Professors Frederick D. Kershner, Jr., R. Freeman Butts, and Dwight C. Miner provided helpful criticism and suggestions. I gained many valuable insights through study with Martin S. Dworkin. Franklin and Linda Nash and Professors Morris I. Berger and Ralph R. Pippert gave support and assistance at critical moments in the preparation of this book. I alone, however, am solely responsible for any shortcomings in the following pages.

Sol Cohen

CONTENTS

PROGRESSIVES AND URBAN SCHOOL REFORM

Chapter 1

ROOTS OF REFORM

1880-1895

THE PROGRESSIVE MOVEMENT was heralded in the early 1890's by a nationwide crusade for municipal reform.[1] In some cities by the mid-1890's reformers had already achieved more than negligible changes. But events in New York City overshadowed everything else. On November 6, 1894, the voters of New York overthrew Tammany Hall and elected a city administration sworn to a unique platform of progressive political and social reforms.[2] The "triumph of reform" reverberated throughout the land. To many reformers, it was the most significant event of the civic renaissance.[3]

Shortly after the election, on December 11, 1894, a small group of society women met in Mrs. Valentine Mott's Victorian drawing room to form a ladies' auxiliary to Good Government Club E, one of the most energetic of the numerous anti-Tammany groups in the city at the time. Besides Mrs. Mott, such well-known New Yorkers as Mrs. William S. Rainsford, Mrs. Edward R. Hewitt, Mrs. Oliver S. Teall,

[1] William H. Tolman, *Municipal Reform Movements in the United States: The Textbook of the New Reformation* (New York, 1895). See also Albert Shaw, "Our 'Civic Renaissance,'" *Review of Reviews*, XI (April, 1898), 415–27; Clifford W. Patton, *The Battle for Municipal Reform* (Washington, D.C., 1940), Chap. IV; Frank Mann Stewart, *A Half Century of Municipal Reform: The National Municipal League* (Berkeley, Calif., 1950), Chaps. I–II.

[2] *The Triumph of Reform: A History of the Great Political Revolution, November Sixth, Eighteen Hundred and Ninety-Four*, Introduction by E. L. Godkin (New York, 1895); Gustavus Myers, *The History of Tammany Hall* (New York, 1901), pp. 333–34; Morris R. Werner, *Tammany Hall* (New York, 1928), p. 442; Charles Garrett, *The La Guardia Years: Machine and Reform Politics in New York City* (New York, 1961), p. 38.

[3] Tolman, *op. cit.*, p. 36; Shaw, *op. cit.*, pp. 422–23; Lincoln Steffens, *Autobiography* (New York, 1931), p. 215; Delos F. Wilcox, *The Study of City Government* (New York, 1897), p. 116.

Mrs. Ben Ali Higgin, Mrs. Lorillard Spencer, Mrs. Charles A. Runkle, Mrs. Willard Parker, Mrs. Charles T. Barney, Mrs. Charles Lee, Mrs. Edward S. Mead, Miss Carlotta Lowell, and Miss Martha Lincoln Draper had been invited to join the reform movement. To help Club E reform the New York City school system, they organized the Woman's Association for Improving the Public Schools. In April 1895 the WAIPS formally severed itself from Club E.[4] This step was taken, we are informed,

to sever the Association from even this slight connection with politics, it being generally felt by the men who were on the Committee [Club E's Public School Committee], that they were supposed to be biased in the work by their profession or their politics, from which imputation and its retarding effect the women should be wholly free.[5]

In October the ladies changed their name to the blander and more euphonious Public Education Association of New York City.[6]

The ladies who helped organize the PEA were selected with utmost care. Several were wives of members of the Board of Trustees of Club E. All of them had been active in philanthropic and church work in the city for years. Mrs. William S. Rainsford, the PEA's first president, was the wife of the famous rector of St. George's Episcopal Church and was active in the kindergarten branch of St. George's institutional program.[7] Mrs. Edward R. Hewitt, the daughter-in-law of Abram S. Hewitt, was active in the New York Kindergarten Association and other city charities. Martha Lincoln Draper and Carlotta Lowell,

---

[4] See the following publications of Good Government Club E: *Annual Report of the Trustees for the Year Ending November 26, 1894*, No. 3 (New York, 1894); *Report of the Committee on Schools, November 26, 1894*, No. 4 (New York, 1894); *Education and the Public Schools*, No. 5, Leaflet No. 1 (New York, 1894); "Report of the Committee on Public Schools," *Public School Buildings in New York City*, No. 7, Leaflet No. 3 (New York, 1895), pp. 19-20; "Report of the Committee on Education and the Public Schools," *Progress in School Reform*, No. 9 (New York, 1895). See also J. Augustus Johnson, "Good Government Clubs," *The Triumph of Reform* . . . , p. 153; Mariana Griswold Van Rensselaer, "The Public Education Association of New York," *Educational Review*, XVI (October, 1898), 209; Lillian W. Betts, "In the Interests of Education," *Outlook*, LI (June 1, 1895), 910-11; PEA, *Annual Report*, 1895, pp. 3-4.

[5] PEA, *Annual Report*, 1895, p. 4.

[6] Van Rensselaer, *op. cit.*, p. 209; *New York Times*, January 12, 1896; PEA, *Annual Report*, 1895, p. 8.

[7] In fact, many of the ladies who helped organize the PEA were active in the affairs of St. George's, including Mrs. Ben Ali Higgin, Mrs. Valentine Mott, Mrs. Charles M. Perry, Mrs. Lorillard Spencer, and Miss Cornelia E. Marshall. *Yearbook of St. George's Episcopal Church* (New York, 1894), pp. 73, 77, 135, 143-44.

Josephine Shaw Lowell's daughter, were "friendly visitors" for the
Charity Organization Society and were among the organizers of the
Consumers' League and the Woman's Municipal League.

There was no question that the ladies were a competent group,
nor that they understood and acquiesced completely in their handmaid
status to the reform movement. The ladies had their office at Club E's
headquarters on East 23rd Street; they met weekly with Club E's Committee on Public Schools; and the Rev. William Ware Locke, secretary of the Committee on Public Schools, managed their secretarial
affairs.[8] Men were barred from membership in the PEA (until 1905),
but actually during its formative years the PEA was led by Nicholas
Murray Butler and a carefully selected Advisory Council which included, besides Butler, J. Augustus Johnson, John B. Pine, and Ernest
H. Crosby, all Club E trustees, and also Felix Adler of the Ethical
Culture Society, James B. Reynolds, Head Resident of the University
Settlement, Dr. Edward Shaw, Professor of Pedagogy at New York University, and Dr. Henry D. Chapin, a pioneer in the field of pediatrics.[9]
In short, as Mr. Johnson, president of Club E, stated, "while the
women are independent, they are in official harmony with the club and
aim to cooperate in effective work." [10] Clearly, the PEA was not a center of new thought. Its objectives and program were simply echoes from
the reform movement. What were these objectives?

In the first place the PEA had its good government phase, that
concerned with school administration and school control. The PEA
was called into existence to help lift the subject of public education
"above the dominion of political methods to the independent position
of a . . . scientific treatment." [11] Another of the PEA's earliest stated
objectives was to stimulate public interest in the schools. Again and
again the PEA emphasized that its purpose was to rouse and educate
"the whole population" of New York City on the subject of public
education.[12] Finally, the PEA was to help the reform movement shape
a school system to meet the needs of the city. In the PEA's second an-

[8] Good Government Club E, "Report of the Committee on Education and
the Public Schools."
[9] PEA, *Annual Report,* 1895, p. 4.
[10] J. Augustus Johnson, "Good Government Clubs," *The Triumph of Reform* . . . , p. 153.
[11] Good Government Club E, *Education and the Public Schools,* p. 2.
[12] PEA, *Annual Report,* 1895, p. 7; Betts, *loc. cit.;* Lillian W. Betts, "Women
and Public Education," *Outlook,* LIII (March 21, 1896), 512; *New York Tribune,*
November 21, 1896.

nual report the work of its pioneer School Visiting Committee was
noted. Then, in a remarkable sentence, the PEA observed that the
Committee would pay special attention

to the schools below 14th Street where the system had been longest
at work and where it has had to deal with [a] peculiar environment, an
almost foreign population in some localities—and where, if the system had
not adapted itself to, or conquered, that environment, it was clearly no
system for the city at all.[13]

Thus, inadvertently, the ladies articulated the generally accepted goal
of New York City school reform. The basic core idea of progressive
educational reform in New York was never better stated. Progressive
education arose in an effort to shape a school system to meet the needs
of the "peculiar environment" below Fourteenth Street, to meet the
needs of the East Side. The PEA was not a center of new thought.
Where did it get this notion? From Johnson? Butler? Adler? Reynolds?
No matter. The PEA, to borrow Daniel Coit Gilman's apt remark about
the new Teachers College, breathed the spirit of the times.

Perhaps it would be best to pause at this point. The origins and
program of the PEA can be understood only if we begin our inquiry
at the critical juncture of movements and tendencies in which it was
conceived. Although the PEA was founded in 1895, its story cannot
begin in that year, or even in the reform movement of 1894 which
provided the immediate stimulus for its establishment. Something
more than political expediency accounts for the central position occupied by the public schools in the New York City reform crusade.
The reformers' singular concern with the city's public school system,
their school reform program, the role of the schools in the campaign
proper, and the creation of the PEA have their roots in the 1880's, in
a tumultuous period of social and political crisis in which two factors
stand out: a disturbed awakening to the myriads of poor immigrants
from southern and eastern Europe streaming into the city, and an
equally apprehensive awakening to the growing power and influence
of the Roman Catholic Church. Since the development of public education in New York, no less than the career of the PEA, can be explicated only with these phenomena in mind, it will be necessary to
look more closely at the immigrant and the slum, and at the crisis in
Protestant–Catholic relations.

[13] PEA, *Annual Report*, 1896, pp. 8–9.

I

Disorders and discontents plagued the nation in the closing decades of the nineteenth century: labor uprisings of unprecedented scope and violence in the late 1870's; bloody strikes in the 1880's, culminating in Haymarket in 1886; Omaha and the "coalition of the discontented" in 1892; harrowing depression in 1893; Pullman, Cripple Creek, and Coxey's Army in 1894. The thunder in the West jolted the East. Edwin L. Godkin thought a revolution was bound to come.[14] While Easterners pondered the warnings of Godkin and other venerated seers, they awoke with dismay to the strangely variegated tide of aliens pouring into their cities. The awakening was felt most intensely in New York City, the port of entry for most, the greatest immigrant center in the nation.

The census of 1890 revealed New York to be the home of some 1,500,000 inhabitants. Of this population, 42.8 per cent were foreign-born; 80 per cent were foreign-born or of foreign parentage. The simple fact that New York was the home of a huge foreign population was of itself nothing new (in 1860 about 50 per cent of its population were foreign-born), but in the closing decades of the nineteenth century its composition was undergoing significant changes. New York was the nation's chief center of the "new immigration." The new immigrants began to arrive in the early 1880's. They were predominantly Russian and Polish Jews, but there was also a considerable Italian element. In 1880 the newest immigrants constituted only 10 per cent of the foreign-born population of the city. By 1890 this figure had jumped to about 23 per cent. By 1900 more than 40 per cent of the city's foreign-born were Southern and Eastern Europeans, with the great outpouring from Europe to the New World still not at peak tide. The newcomers landed at the foot of New York and stayed there, pushing the older Irish and German inhabitants northward up the long, narrow island of Manhattan. By 1900 in the wards below Fourteenth Street, where some three-quarters of a million people lived, seven-eighths of the popula-

[14] Russel B. Nye, *Midwestern Progressive Politics: A Historical Study of Its Origins and Development, 1870–1950* (East Lansing, Mich., 1951), Chaps. II–III; Henry Steele Commager, *The American Mind* (New Haven, Conn., 1950), Chap. II; Eric F. Goldman, *Rendezvous with Destiny* (rev. ed.; New York, 1956), Chap. III; Samuel P. Hays, *The Response to Industrialism, 1885–1914* (Chicago, 1957), pp. 37–47; Harold U. Faulkner, *Politics, Reform, and Expansion, 1890–1900* (New York, 1959), Chap. I.

tion were of foreign parentage. The population was mixed, but it might be said that all of the East Side below Fourteenth Street was a Jewish district, the largest Jewish city in the world.[15]

The East Side was conspicuous not alone for its huge foreign population; it had also the evil distinction of being one of the most densely populated areas in the world, an area of unimaginable crowding and squalor. Conditions in the downtown tenement slums were trying for adults; they were stultifying for children. The "filth-soaked, dark, unventilated" tenements were a standing menace to their health. Moreover, the city had made no provision for play or recreation. On the bursting East Side almost every foot of ground was occupied by the ubiquitous tenements, factories, pushcarts, and peddlers. Crowded out of their homes and lacking normal outlets for play, the children drifted into gangs and were exposed to the most openly plied vice and crime.[16] Poverty may have been endemic on the East Side, but the East Side was not inhabited by a passive or apathetic folk. It burst with vitality. The labor union, Socialism, anarchism, Henry George-ism, and countless other varieties of political radicalism and protest movements flourished there. Furthermore, its population was a fluid and highly mobile one.[17] This was the famous East Side, New York's poor and foreign quarter, and it represented, in a special way, *the* educational problem of the city.

New York's traditional reform leadership, Protestant clergymen, civic leaders, and philanthropists, alarmed by the immigrant invasion, greeted the newcomers with fear and repugnance and hostility. Jacob Riis, one of the reform leadership's chief spokesmen, lugubriously warned New Yorkers in 1892, in words that would echo down through the immigration restriction debates of the next three decades, that New York was "the dumping ground where it [immigration] rids itself of its

[15] Moses Rischin, *The Promised City: New York's Jews, 1870–1914* (Cambridge, Mass., 1962), pp. 79ff; Kate Holladay Claghorn, "The Foreign Immigrant in New York City," U.S. Industrial Commission, *Report of the Industrial Commission on Immigration and on Education*, Vol. XV, Chap. IX, pp. 467–77; Milton Rizenstein, "General Aspects of the Population: New York," in Charles S. Bernheimer, ed., *The Russian Jew in the United States* (Philadelphia, 1905).

[16] New York State Legislature, Assembly, *Report of the Tenement House Committee* (Albany, 1895); "New York's Great Movement for Housing Reform," *Review of Reviews*, XIV (December, 1896), 695–96; Jacob A. Riis, *How the Other Half Lives* (New York, 1890); Roy Lubove, *The Progressives and the Slums: Tenement House Reform in New York City, 1890–1917* (Pittsburgh, 1962).

[17] Rischin, *op. cit.*, Chaps. VII–X; Steffens, *op. cit.*, Chap. V; Mary Kingsbury Simkhovitch, *Neighborhood: My Story of Greenwich House* (New York, 1938), pp. 63–64; Howard Lawrence Hurwitz, *Theodore Roosevelt and Labor in New York State, 1880–1900* (New York, 1943), Chaps. I, IV, *passim*.

burden of helplessness and incapacity leaving the procession of the strong and the able free to move on." [18] As they awoke to the Italian and the Jew, New York's erstwhile leaders came to the startled awareness of the squalid downtown section of the city in which the newcomers were so glaringly concentrated. The tenements were assailed at the great Christian Conference of 1888 held in Chickering Hall. "Home is virtually banished by these abodes, and physical and moral misery necessitated. How can Christ reach these people?" the Reverend James M. King queried.[19] The influential Tenement House Committee of 1894, with more secular concerns, was no less dire in its depiction of tenement life:

Keeping children up and out of doors until midnight in the warm weather, because the rooms are almost unendurable; making cleanliness of house and street difficult; filling the air with unwholesome emanations and foul odors of every kind; producing a condition of nervous tension; interfering with the separateness and sacredness of home life; leading to the promiscuous mixing of all ages and sexes in a single room—thus breaking down the barriers of modesty and conducing to the corruption of the young, and occasionally to revolting crimes.[20]

Because the immigrant lived in the slum, immigrant and slum became lumped together. And there they both were, on the East Side. To many uptowners in the 1890's, the East Side came to stand for a vague but alarming threat to everything they held inviolate; a cancer on the body politic of the city.

[18] Jacob A. Riis, *The Children of the Poor* (New York, 1892), p. 2; Riis, *How the Other Half Lives*; Jacob A. Riis, "Special Needs of the Poor in New York," *Forum*, XIV (December, 1892), 492–93, 501. See also *The Religious Condition of New York City: Addresses Made at a Christian Conference Held in Chickering Hall, New York City, December 3, 4, and 5, 1888* (New York, 1888); New York Society for the Prevention of Cruelty to Children, *Eighteenth Annual Report*, 1893, p. 7; New York Kindergarten Association, *Second Annual Report*, 1892, p. 29; and George Haven Putnam, *Memories of a Publisher, 1865–1915* (New York, 1915), p. 169. The Russian or Polish immigrant was an alien figure even to his coreligionist, the well-fixed, cultured, assimilated German Jew, just then stepping forward to join his Yankee Protestant uptown neighbor in civic improvement efforts. Arthur Garfield Hays, *City Lawyer* (New York, 1942), p. 24; Rischin, *op. cit.*, Chap. VI; Samuel Joseph, *History of the Baron De Hirsch Fund: The Americanization of the Jewish Immigrant* (New York, 1935), pp. 7–8, 24, 41–42. For nativism and the new immigrants in the 1890's, see John Higham, *Strangers in the Land: Patterns of American Nativism, 1860–1925* (New Brunswick, N.J., 1955), Chap. IV.
[19] *The Religious Condition of New York City . . .*, p. 131.
[20] *Report of the Tenement House Committee*, pp. 12–13; Riis, *How the Other Half Lives*; Riis, *Children of the Poor*.

The jeremiads pronounced by New York's civic leaders and social critics should have led to the blackest despair. But, typically, optimism prevailed. New York's reformers, like reformers in other urban centers of the land, were buoyed by a sublimely confident faith in the omnipotence of environment in the shaping of behavior. A major corollary of environmentalism is the plasticity of child nature. To go from here to the public school was a short and inevitable step. The school was an environment par excellence to which almost all children could be compelled to submit. It was an environment that could be manipulated or shaped to whatever ends by those who controlled or dominated the public school system.

In the 1890's, against a background of a country shaken by disorders and discontents, New York reformers seized upon education and the public schools as the Great Panacea. The public school was cast as the great immigrant assimilating agency. The school was also cast as the anodyne of the East Side, and the prophylactic for crime, vice, pauperism, juvenile delinquency, and the other social ills of the city. Finally, although those who led the reform movement in New York may have been anti-foreign and anti-immigrant, they were also sincerely concerned with the plight of the slum dweller. The public schools were cast as a major agency in their program for the amelioration of slum life and a major agency in their program of constructive social reform. Instead of generalizing, it may be best to illustrate these remarks through the work of reporter-reformer Jacob A. Riis. It was Riis, more than anyone else, who fashioned the East Side problem and who formulated the educational solution to that problem.

The Danish-born Riis needs no introduction as an anti-slum crusader. His muckraking articles in the *New York Tribune* in the 1880's made him the terror of the downtown landlords.[21] With the appearance of *How the Other Half Lives* in 1890, his reputation was secured.[22] *How the Other Half Lives* was one of the most widely read books of the nineties. It educated a generation of New Yorkers to the section of the city below Fourteenth Street.[23] With unsurpassed skill Riis depicted

[21] Lubove, *op. cit.*, Chap. III, contains an excellent portrait of Riis's life and career. See also Emma Louise Ware, *Jacob A. Riis: Police Reporter, Reformer, Useful Citizen* (New York, 1939); Jacob A. Riis, *The Making of an American* (New York, 1901); John Haynes Holmes, "Jacob August Riis," *Dictionary of American Biography*, XV, 1935, 606–08; and Steffens, *op. cit.*, pp. 203–07.

[22] New York, 1890. This was shortly followed by *The Children of the Poor* and a spate of magazine articles.

[23] E.g., Theodore Roosevelt, *An Autobiography* (New York, 1913), p. 187; Mariana Griswold Van Rensselaer, "People in New York," *Century*, XLIX (Feb-

the full misery and squalor of the downtown section: the infamous
double-deckers and rear-houses, the gross overcrowding, the ubiquitous
saloons and brothels, the children swarming and dying at an appalling
rate. One of the salient facts Riis emphasized about the tenement house
population was that it was composed almost exclusively of the foreign
element. In Riis's hands the newest immigrants suffered because they
were foreign and non-Protestant, and they also had to suffer the opprobrium which he meted out in full measure to the tenement section
which they inhabited. The picture which emerges from *How the Other
Half Lives*, as one contemporary expressed it, was grim; the revelations
were sinister.[24]

This 1890 classic of the muckraking genre was intended to shock.
Riis deliberately chose to depict the blackest and most dramatic aspects
of slum life to awaken New Yorkers to the existence of "the other
half." [25] When he had their attention, he proceeded to point out how
imminent catastrophe might be avoided. Riis has been described by his
good friend, the Reverend William S. Rainsford, as "a lover of, a
believer in the East Side boy." [26] Here is the key to Riis's reform activities. The one ray of light in *How the Other Half Lives* is the child.
Where children were concerned Riis was an environmentalist. Heredity,
he proclaimed, was not so formidable as we used to think. The child
was a creature of his environment and that was that. What made boys
bad were the street, the saloon, and the tenement. It was simply "a
question of getting hold of the child early enough before the evil
influences surrounding him have got a grip on him." [27] Riis called for
the rescue of the children and thereby became one of the nation's chief

ruary, 1895), 547; Raymond B. Fosdick, *Chronicle of a Generation: An Autobiography* (New York, 1958), p. 58; Earnest Poole, *The Bridge* (New York, 1940),
p. 66; Holmes, *op cit.*, p. 606. See also Robert H. Bremner, *From the Depths:
The Discovery of Poverty in the United States* (New York, 1956), pp. 68–69.
    24 Riis, *How the Other Half Lives*, Chaps. V, IX–XI; Riis, *The Children of
the Poor*, p. 2; Riis, "Special Needs of the Poor in New York," pp. 492–93. In its review of *How the Other Half Lives*, the magazine *The Critic* expressed serious
reservations: "There is a lack of broad and penetrative vision, a singularly warped
sense of justice at times, and a roughness amounting almost to brutality. The 'Hea-
then Chinee' and the Russian Jew fleeing from persecution in his own land, find
no mercy in Mr. Riis's creed." XIV (December 27, 1890), 332. However, see
Jacob A. Riis, "The Jews of New York," *Review of Reviews*, XIII (January, 1896),
58–62.
    25 Ware, *op. cit.*, p. 67; Riis, *The Making of an American*, pp. 247, 248.
    26 William S. Rainsford, *The Story of a Varied Life* (New York, 1922), p. 255.
    27 Riis, *How the Other Half Lives*, pp. 185–86; Riis, *The Children of the
Poor*, pp. 4, 5–6. Rainsford held similar convictions. Rainsford, *op. cit.*, pp. 233,
275–76; and the same author's *A Preacher's Story of His Work* (New York, 1904),
p. 141.

apostles of the salvation of society through the public schools. The outline of Riis's school reform program may be found in *How the Other Half Lives* and in his important 1892 *Forum* article, "Special Needs of the Poor in New York." [28] His great educational treatise, however, is *The Children of the Poor* (1892).

Riis had no use for the New York City school system. He scored the compulsory education law as wholly inadequate, unenforced, and unenforceable. Riis estimated that there were some 50,000 children between the ages of five and fourteen who received no schooling at all, except for that of the dread street. And even at that, Riis was not sure who was better off, the "street Arab" or the school child. The schools, he bitterly complained, were terribly overcrowded; the curriculum utterly impractical.[29] In his school reform program Riis anticipated by a decade the future course of progressive education in New York. He called for the strengthening and more effective enforcement of the compulsory education and child labor laws; municipal provision of truant schools, nurseries, kindergartens, manual training, and school playgrounds; and the opening of the schools in the evening for the use of boys' clubs.[30] Finally, when Riis emphasized that "the immediate duty which the community has to perform for its own protection is to school the children first of all into good Americans, and next into useful citizens," he formulated the overarching objective of school reform in New York.[31]

Riis was a synthesizer, not a creator—a great propagandist, rather than a great innovator. Although given to unseemly boasting in his role as slum reformer, Riis freely gave credit to the sources from which he borrowed his school reform program. From London he borrowed school evening play centers.[32] For the rest, he turned to materials close

[28] XIV (December, 1892), 492–502.
[29] Riis, *The Children of the Poor*, pp. 92, 118, 120; Rainsford, *The Story of a Varied Life*, p. 360; Lillian W. Betts, *The Leaven in a Great City* (New York, 1902), p. 7. The Compulsory Education Law at that time required all children between the ages of eight and fourteen to attend school at least fourteen weeks in each year, eight weeks of which had to be consecutive. New York City, Department of Education, *Manual of the Board of Education*, 1894, pp. 48–49; A. Emerson Palmer, *The New York Public School* (New York, 1905), p. 167.
[30] "Special Needs of the Poor in New York," pp. 501–02; *The Children of the Poor, passim*; *How the Other Half Lives*, Chap. XV; "Playgrounds for City Schools," *Century*, XLVIII (September, 1894), 657–66; Lubove, *op. cit.*, pp. 73–75.
[31] *The Children of the Poor*, pp. 8, 51ff, 204, *passim*.
[32] *Ibid.*, p. 238; "Playgrounds for City Schools," p. 665; Robert Archey Woods, *English Social Movements* (New York, 1891), pp. 90, 256.

at hand. *The Children of the Poor* is a Baedecker of city charities: the New York Kindergarten Association, the American Female Guardian Association, the Wilson Mission, the Five Points House of Industry, the Fresh Air Fund, the Baron De Hirsch Schools, and, especially, the Children's Aid Society. In the end the ideal of Americanization which emerges from Riis's writings is hardly distinguishable from the English charity-school ideal. It was enough if the public schools taught the little foreigners the elements of the English language and trained them to be clean, obedient to authority, industrious and truthful, and to revere the American flag.[33]

Riis's school program reflects more, however, than a concern with the training of the young to be proper Americans. For this "apostle of Americanism," the downtown section of the city implied more than the existence of a foreign population which needed urgently to be assimilated. His program referred equally to bitter poverty, reeking tenements, greedy sweatshops, and cruel lack of provision for the welfare of young and old alike. The battle with the slum had to be fought along a broad front: tenement house regulation, construction of parks and playgrounds, and reform of the public schools. "Do you see," Riis cried,

how the whole battle with the slum was fought in and around the public school? . . . The kindergarten, manual training, and the cooking school, all experiments in their day, cried out as fads by some, have brought common sense in their train. When it rules the public schools in our cities . . . we can put off our armor; the battle with the slums will be over.[34]

[33] Riis, *The Children of the Poor, passim; How the Other Half Lives,* Chap. XV. And see also William T. Elsing, "Life in New York Tenement-Houses as Seen by a City Missionary," in Robert A. Woods, ed., *The Poor in Great Cities: Their Problems and What is Being Done to Solve Them* (New York, 1895), p. 59; Children's Aid Society, *The Children's Aid Society of New York: Its History, Plans and Results* (New York, 1893), p. 29; New York Kindergarten Association, *Third Annual Report,* 1893, p. 39; Felix Adler, *The Workingman's School* (New York, 1881). The philanthropic tradition in education was deeply rooted in New York City. It was not until the mid-nineteenth century that the city's public school system was born. William Oland Bourne, *History of the Public School Society of the City of New York* (New York, 1873); Lawrence A. Cremin, *The American Common School: An Historic Conception* (New York, 1951), pp. 96–99, 151ff, 173, 174–75; Palmer, *op. cit.,* Chaps. I–XIV.

[34] Jacob A. Riis, *The Battle with the Slum* (New York, 1902), p. 410. See also Riis, *The Making of an American,* p. 311; Lubove, *op. cit.,* p. 73. Much influenced by Riis, the powerful New York Tenement House Committee of 1894 urged kindergartens and playgrounds as part of its proposals for tenement house reform. *Report of the Tenement House Committee,* pp. 45, 77.

Unquestionably, the conquest of the slum and the Americanization of that polyglot child population below Fourteenth Street were the dominant concern of the school reform movement. But the movement was a broad one, and while there was general agreement on the role of the schools in slum reform, there was less agreement on the meaning of Americanization. The charity-school ideal that informs Riis's work and the work of the city's great philanthropic organizations was strongly challenged by another ideal, one emanating from a wing of reform represented by the infant social settlement movement.

The first social settlements to be established in New York City, the Neighborhood Guild, later to become the University Settlement, the College Settlement, and the Hebrew Alliance, later to become the Educational Alliance, arose in an effort to reform the East Side. In their efforts to meet the needs of the downtown section, they soon found themselves with a sprawling educational program on their hands.

Pioneer settlement residents greeted the immigrant poor with more respect and understanding, and something closer to true Christian charity, than did Riis and the poorhouse masters of New York. Settlement residents were fully aware of the packed tenements with their "tiny apartments, ill-lighted, ill-ventilated, and unfit in every way for human habitation." [35] But they made an effort to keep straight the line between the characteristics of the slums and the character of the peoples who, perforce, had to inhabit the slums.[36] The settlements also gave priority to Americanization. But no educational theory is conceived in a social vacuum. Since settlement residents had a different image of the East Side from Riis's, their school reform program was permeated by different values. For James K. Paulding and James B. Reynolds, Jean Fine and Jane Robbins, and David Blaustein, Americanization stood for the sharing of a common culture and a common citizenship, a sharing of the highest ideals of American *paideia*. "We think no part of our knowledge too precious to be shared with those about us," said Jane Robbins of the College Settlement, "and we hold a communism in intellectual acquirements to be one of the abiding principles of all Settlement work." [37]

[35] College Settlements Association, *Seventh Annual Report,* 1896, p. 15.

[36] Settlement residents in this early period patiently tried to correct the impression rife among uptowners that a morally inferior brand of people inhabited the tenements: *ibid.,* p. 7; University Settlement Society, *Report of the Year's Work,* 1894, p. 8; Mary Kingsbury Simkhovitch, *Here is God's Plenty* (New York, 1949), p. 30.

[37] College Settlements Association, *Fourth Annual Report,* 1893, p. 12; University Settlement Society, *Report of the Year's Work,* 1894, p. 25; Gaylord S.

To recapitulate, reformers in New York City in the mid-1890's turned to the public schools for help in solving the city's social problems. They turned to the public school as the city's chief instrument for Americanizing the immigrant, and as the city's strategic agency for philanthropic effort and neighborhood reform. However, the motives and values of those involved in the school reform movement were not at all uniform. Frequently, as with Jacob Riis, school reformers had many, even contradictory, ends in view. But no matter how varied their goals and special interests may have been, all agreed that with the public schools lay the real solution to the city's problems, and all joined with Riis in condemning the city schools as obsolete, inefficient, and unsuited to the needs of the time.

II

The rise of the great city was a new challenge to American public education. The public school, as John Dewey pointed out in 1899 in *The School and Society*, was more suited to the needs of ante-bellum America than to the needs of the new urban–industrial America emerging in the late nineteenth century.[38] The public schools of New York, like those in other urban centers of the country, went their own way, heedless of the city's new character or its new problems. Bound by tradition to intellectual concerns alone, formalistic in conception, the immigrant and the slum scarcely figured in their calculations. The reformers, therefore, would shape a school system to meet the needs of the city. There was remarkable unanimity, no matter how diverse their objectives or special interests may have been, on the nature of the educational reforms needed. Actually their rallying ground was progressive education.

Although no one did more than Jacob Riis to awaken the public mind in New York to the need for school reform, the spirit of educational protest began to stir in the city in the early 1880's, several years before Riis's emergence as a key spokesman for reform. The concern of leading New Yorkers with a more practical system of education for the city manifested itself first in an organized agitation to persuade the Board of Education to incorporate kindergarten and manual training

White, "The Social Settlement After Twenty-Five Years," *Harvard Theological Review*, IV (January, 1911), 51; Helen Rand Thayer, "Blazing the Settlement Trail," *Smith Alumnae Quarterly*, II (April, 1911), 133; Lawrence A. Cremin, *The Transformation of the School* (New York, 1961), pp. 67, 70.

[38] Chicago, 1899, Chap. I; Morton G. White, *Social Thought in America: The Revolt Against Formalism* (New York, 1949), p. 100; Cremin, *The Transformation of the School*, pp. 117–19.

as part of the city school system. In 1880 the Ethical Culture Society, under Felix Adler's aegis, established the Workingman's School as a model school for the children of the poor.[39] In 1881 Grace Dodge and some like-minded philanthropists organized the Kitchen-Garden Association. Later in the decade the campaign to persuade city authorities to adopt the new education was spearheaded by the Industrial Education Association, formed in 1885 out of the older Kitchen-Garden Association, and the New York Kindergarten Association, organized in 1890. The New York College for the Training of Teachers, organized in 1888 by Nicholas Murray Butler, clothed kindergarten and manual training in the garments of scientific education and lent its own voice to the clamor for public school reform.[40] The "institutional church," that unique expression of the Social Gospel, with the Reverend William S. Rainsford's St. George's Episcopal Church leading the way, joined the school reform movement.[41] Social settlements like the University Settlement and the College Settlement, just getting on their feet in the early 1890's, developed all the features of the new education in their attempt to meet the needs of the downtown section, and they became a powerful lobby for school reform.[42]

By the early 1890's criticism of the public schools of New York and demands for school reform were of such magnitude and intensity as to have no precedent in the history of the city public school system. The Board of Education added manual training and domestic science to the curriculum in 1890 and opened a few kindergartens in the downtown

[39]Adler, *op. cit.*; New York Society for Ethical Culture, *Report of the Workingman's School* (New York, 1880). A recent commentator claims pride of place for Adler in the progressive education movement. Robert H. Beck, "Progressive Education and American Progressivism: Felix Adler," *Teachers College Record,* LX (November, 1958), 77–89.

[40] Kitchen-Garden Association, *Annual Reports,* 1881–1884; Industrial Education Association, *Annual Reports,* 1885–1888; New York Kindergarten Association, *Annual Reports,* 1891–1895; Walter Albert Jessup, *The Social Factors Affecting Special Supervision in the Public Schools of the United States* (New York, 1911), pp. 34–46; Lawrence A. Cremin, David A. Shannon, and Mary Evelyn Townsend, *A History of Teachers College, Columbia University* (New York, 1954), pp. 12–27.

[41] Rainsford, A *Preacher's Story of His Work,* pp. 118, 126, 151, 165, 167; Rainsford, *The Story of a Varied Life,* Chap. XVI; *Yearbook of St. George's Episcopal Church,* 1894, p. 17. St. Bartholomew's, a fashionable Episcopal church in central Manhattan, also carried on a great institutional program. So did Judson Memorial Church, Grace Church, and Calvary Baptist Church.

[42] Cremin, *The Transformation of the School,* pp. 59–65; and two volumes by Robert A. Woods and Albert J. Kennedy: *The Settlement Horizon* (New York, 1922), and A *Handbook of Social Settlements* (New York, 1911). See also Morris I. Berger, "The Immigrant, the Settlement, and the Public School" (unpublished Ph.D. thesis, Columbia University, 1956).

section in 1893.[43] But the board's action was too little and too late. The reformers plunged the schools into the mayoralty campaign of 1894.

Class and religious interests were conspicuously involved in every aspect of the school refom crusade. On the one hand the crusade was the effort of the city's erstwhile dominant classes—well-to-do, cultured, and Yankee Protestant—to shape a school system for the Russian and Polish Jews and the Italians who began to pour into the city in the 1880's. On the other hand, the school reform movement was the effort of the same class of New Yorkers to wrest the school system from the hands of the Irish Catholics who controlled it at the time.

III

The history of government and politics in New York City is largely the history of Tammany Hall, the Democratic party organization of Manhattan. Tammany's resilience and seeming permanence is one of the marvels of American political history. The respectable element in New York thought Tammany was sunk for a long time to come in 1871, the year the gigantic swindles perpetrated by the Tweed Ring were exposed, the "boss" imprisoned, his followers imprisoned or chased from the city, and a reform city administration elected. But under Tweed's successor as "boss" of Tammany, John Kelly (1874–1884), Tammany won the mayoral election of 1874 and began to rise from its burial place beneath obloquoy. Tammany survived two more reform interludes in the early 1880's. Then, when Hugh J. Grant, a Tammany hack, was elected Mayor of New York in 1888, it was clear that the machine was once again in sound running order. Grant was re-elected in 1890. In 1892 Thomas F. Gilroy, another loyal Brave, easily won the mayoralty. Tammany's leader through this long skein of victories was Kelly's protegé, Richard Croker. By the early 1890's, shrewd and taciturn Dick Croker was "Master of Manhattan." Led by this astute businessman, and emboldened by continued success at the polls, Tammany proceeded to turn the city into a fabulous cornucopia.[44]

New Yorkers who considered themselves pre-eminently suited by tradition, education, or wealth to govern the city watched Tammany's

[43] Palmer, op. cit., pp. 178–79, 193; New York City, Board of Education, The First Fifty Years, 1898–1948: Fiftieth Annual Report of the Superintendent of Schools (New York, 1948), p. 27.
[44] The standard histories of Tammany are those by Myers, op. cit.; Werner, op. cit. Brief reviews of Tammany's history can be found in several more recent sources; e.g., Garrett, op. cit., pp. 6–11; and Frederick Shaw, The History of the New York City Legislature (New York, 1954), Chap. I.

return to power with horror. To men like E. L. Godkin, Mugwump editor of *The Nation* and the *New York Evening Post* and one of the city's leading spokesmen for the patricians, the class of people then governing the city was intolerable. New York was governed, Godkin complained,

by three or four men of foreign birth, who are very illiterate, are sprung from the dregs of the foreign population, have never pursued a regular calling, and who now set the criticism of the intelligent and educated classes at defiance.[45]

The anti-Tammany sentiment of New York's civic leaders also had its religious aspect. The Irish Catholic-dominated Tammany Hall (the Irish began to dominate Tammany Hall in the 1870's and elected their first Mayor in the eighties) had "to contend against that dread of Catholicism which," Godkin averred in 1890, "has now become among all classes of Anglo Saxons, . . . an integral part of their mental and moral make-up." [46] The city's public school system was inextricably involved, both as cause and consequence, in every aspect of the anti-Tammany feeling rife in the city in the early 1890's.

A brief description of the structure of the city school system will be appropriate here. Under the State School Law by which the city schools were then governed, the Mayor appointed twenty-one Commissioners of Common Schools. These constituted the Board of Education. The latter in turn appointed the ward trustees (five trustees for each of the twenty-four wards into which the city was divided), the Superintendent of School Buildings, the Superintendent of Schools, and the Assistant Superintendents of Schools. The Mayor also appointed the school inspectors, three for each ward. Local control of the schools was the overarching principle. Under this system, the ward trustees exercised the real power. Laymen, they appointed all teachers and janitors, nominated principals and vice-principals for promotion, furnished school supplies, made contracts for school repairs and alterations, purchased school sites, and erected schoolhouses.[47] Here was a terrific opportunity for graft and patronage; and Tammany, contemptuously dismissed by the reform ele-

[45] E. L. Godkin, "The Problems of Municipal Government," *The Annals*, IV (May, 1894), 858. See also Godkin's "Criminal Politics," *North American Review*, CL (June, 1890), 706–10; "New York City," *Encyclopaedia Britannica* (9th ed.; London, 1875), p. 462. See also Allan Nevins, *The Evening Post: A Century of Journalism* (New York, 1922), Chap. XXII.

[46] Godkin, "Criminal Politics," pp. 709–10.

[47] New York City, Department of Education, *Manual of the Board of Education* (New York, 1894), pp. 13–34; Palmer, *op. cit.*, pp. 163–66; Rose Naomi Cohen, *The Financial Control of Education in the Consolidated City of New York* (New York, 1948), pp. 14–21.

ment as the embodiment of ignorance and criminal politics, had had time since 1888 to become entrenched right in the vitals of the school system.

But Tammany also evoked the spectre of Rome. Protestant–Catholic relations came to a head in New York City in the late eighties and early nineties. One of the chief sources of the crisis, as we have seen, was the continued success of the Irish Catholic in city politics. Another copious source of anti-Catholic sentiment had its locus in the schools. The deep-rooted Protestant belief that Rome was the implacable foe of the public schools, the spectacular growth of the Roman Catholic parochial school system after the Baltimore Plenary Council of 1884, and the more insistent Catholic appeals for state support to parochial schools, coming at a time when the common school was becoming for Protestants more and more a potent symbol of Americanism, provides the background against which New Yorkers, in the closing decades of the nineteenth century, discovered a Papist threat to the city's public school system.[48]

In 1880 the *New York Sun* and the *New York Herald* broke with the Democratic party over the mayoralty candidacy of William R. Grace, the millionaire Catholic, for, among other reasons, fear of the fate of the public schools in a city controlled by Papists.[49] The excommunication in 1887 of Father Edward McGlynn, a conspicuous dissenter from the Baltimore Plenary Council and parochial schools, as well as an outspoken Single-Taxer, again alerted New Yorkers to the school question.[50] At the same time the New Yorkers awoke to the newly arriving Italian. Speaker after speaker at the Christian Conference of 1888, a forum for the leading lay and clerical figures in Protestantism in the city, lashed out at the Italians as breeders of social disorders and as "enemies of the public schools with their living and Christian element."[51] In 1889 an eminently respectable group of

[48] Higham, *op. cit.*, pp. 59–60; E. M. Winston, "The Threatening Conflict with Romanism," *Forum*, XVII (June, 1894), 428; Daniel F. Reilly, *The School Controversy, 1891–1893* (Washington, D.C., 1943); Thomas T. McAvoy, *The Great Crisis in American Catholic History, 1895–1900* (Chicago, 1957), pp. 12–13, 70.

[49] Candace Stone, *Dana of the "Sun"* (New York, 1938), p. 152; Florence E. Gibson, *The Attitudes of the New York Irish toward State and National Affairs, 1848–1892* (New York, 1951), p. 317.

[50] Edward McGlynn, *Public Schools and Their Enemies, An Address Delivered in Cooper Union, N.Y., Feb. 24, 1889* (Oakland, Calif., n.d.); Stephen Bell, *Rebel, Priest and Prophet: A Biography of Dr. Edward McGlynn* (New York, 1937), pp. 13–14, 20ff, 153–54; Gregory Weinstein, *The Ardent Eighties and After* (New York, 1928), p. 105; Rainsford, *The Story of a Varied Life*, p. 369; Gibson, *op. cit.*, p. 397.

[51] *The Religious Condition of New York City* . . ., pp. 3, 49.

New Yorkers formed a propaganda organization called the National League for the Protection of American Institutions, whose chief aim was to protect the public schools from the Catholic menace.[52]

The continued success of Tammany at the polls greatly increased the reformers' concern for the public schools. The knowledge that Tammany, Irish Catholic as well as ignorant and crooked, was in control of the schools heightened their anxiety about city government and helped spur the anti-Tammany uprising of 1894.

IV

"Is New York More Civilized than Kansas?" Thus J. W. Gleed retorted to E. L. Godkin's gibe that we do not want any more states until we can civilize Kansas.[53] Gleed pointed to the extreme of poverty and want in the city, the slums, the overcrowded schools, the children crowded out of schools, the scandals and crimes, and the apathy of its citizenry. As for New York's political history, the Kansan depicted the long record of disrespect for law, of maladministration, and of government by bribery and cunning. "If there is a community in the United States whose history proves it unfit to rule itself, and totally unfit to participate in the federal government that community would seem to be New York City." [54] Mr. Gleed's polemic was well-written, eloquent, and persuasive. And it came at precisely the wrong historical moment. Even as he wrote, a crusade for municipal reform was under way.

The "great political revolution" of November 6, 1894, which ended a reign of corruption unknown since the days of Tweed and which ushered in a whole new era of reform in New York, was due mainly to the religious muckraking of the Rev. Dr. Charles H. Parkhurst and the political activity of the City Club and the Good Government Clubs. Dr. Parkhurst fired off his moral crusade on the morning of February 14, 1892, in a memorable sermon against the "lying, perjured, rum-soaked, and libidinous" city administration.[55] The City Club and the Good Government Clubs directed moral indignation into political channels.

[52] *National League for the Protection of American Institutions, Its Officers, Organizations and Objects—A Condensed Statement of Its Accomplished Work and Future Purposes* (New York, 1896); James M. King, *Facing the Twentieth Century. Our Country: Its Power and Peril* (New York, 1899); Higham, *op. cit.,* p. 60.

[53] *Forum,* XVII (April, 1894), 217–34.

[54] *Ibid.,* p. 232.

[55] Parkhurst, *Our Fight with Tammany* (New York, 1895), p. 10. See also *My Forty Years in New York* (New York, 1893), esp. Chap. VII; *The Triumph of Reform* . . . , pp. 214–15; Steffens, *op. cit.,* pp. 197–98 and Chap. VI.

In the autumn of 1891 Edmond Kelly, a young New York lawyer, returned to New York from Paris eager to meet some "cranks" who might be willing to help him realize a unique plan to rescue the city from Tammany. Kelly's idea was to establish permanent anti-Tammany political clubs in every Assembly District in the city, thereby to compete with Tammany at the grass roots. The exclusive City Club, founded in April 1892 on the initiative of Kelly and some of his young friends in the City Reform Club, was the first fruit of Kelly's inspiration. Although the conservative leaders of the City Club, James C. Carter, William C. Gulliver, August Belmont, and such, were reluctant to organize the tenement districts for reform, they did take steps to organize the great numbers of the solid middle class. To reach this "good element" the City Club sponsored, organized, and helped finance the Good Government Clubs, the "neighborhood City Clubs." Before the end of 1893 Good Government Clubs A, B, D, and E, the last the progenitor of the Public Education Association, had been organized. By early 1894, twenty-four Good Government Clubs with a total membership of six or seven thousand were in existence, and a Council of Confederated Good Government Clubs had been formed to coordinate their activities.[56] To keep up an active interest on the part of the membership and better to harass the city administration, the Council, under the energetic leadership of J. Augustus Johnson, also president of Club E, assigned to each of its affiliated Clubs some department of city government for special supervision and investigation so that every branch of city government was under surveillance.[57] The movement to oust Tammany from City Hall began to pick up momentum.

The reformers were sure of their appeal among the wealthy and the well-educated, and among all those who could be swayed by the good government credo. They could also count on the widespread antipathy towards Irish Catholics among large sections of the Protestant electorate. But for reform to triumph in November it was absolutely necessary that there be defections from Tammany in the downtown

[56] Edmond Kelly, "The City Club" in William Howe Tolman and William I. Hull, *Handbook of Sociological Information with Special Reference to New York* (New York, 1894), pp. 208–10; Edmond Kelly, "Good Government Clubs," *Outlook*, L (December 29, 1894), 1124–26; Richard R. G. Welling, *As the Twig Is Bent* (New York, 1942), pp. 57, 65; James W. Pryor, "The City Club," *The Triumph of Reform . . .*, pp. 256–57; Everett P. Wheeler, *Sixty Years of American Life* (New York, 1917), pp. 338–39; Richard B. Hovey, *John Jay Chapman—An American Mind* (New York, 1959), pp. 64–65; Johnson, *op. cit.*, pp. 149–53; Tolman, *op. cit.*, pp. 91–93; Garrett, *op. cit.*, pp. 23–24.

[57] Johnson, *op. cit.*, p. 151; Tolman, *op. cit.*, p. 91; Kelly, "Good Government Clubs," p. 1125.

section of the city, which normally delivered overwhelmingly Democratic majorities. The reformers seemed suddenly to learn that the city
masses do not usually become excited about police graft or inefficient
government. Accordingly, in late 1893 the City Club and the Good
Government Clubs, joined by most of the daily press, launched an
all-out campaign of investigation and exposure aimed at the complete
discrediting of Tammany Hall. Wide circulation was given to the
police scandals, of course, but Tammany was also arraigned for the
foul tenements, the filthy streets, and the inadequate transportation
facilities. And, for the first time in its history, the city's public school
system became a major political issue.

"Turn on the light of publicity upon the evils of the school system,"
a Good Government Club E circular declared, "and they will soon
disappear." [58] This was a cardinal article of the reformers' faith. No
aspect of the school system escaped the harsh glare of publicity. The
woeful condition of the schools on the East Side, in Tammany's own
backyard, was an especially fruitful source of anti-Tammany ammuni-
tion. The reformers charged that the schools were dark, noxious, unsani-
tary, and overcrowded. Jacob Riis, an enemy of the slum wherever it
was to be found, depicted "herds of rats" foraging about the old
Wooster Street school.[59] The reformers charged not only that the downtown schools were dangerously overcrowded, but that thousands of children, who should have been in school and wanted to be in school, were
turned away because there was no room for them at all. Charles C.
Wehrum, a member of the Board of Education and a friend of reform,
made a timely inspection of all 132 public school buildings in the city
in 1893 and found scarcely one without some glaring defect in light,
sanitation, or safety. The *New York Herald* broadcast the results of
Wehrum's investigation with the banner headline:

Frightful Abuses in City Schools—Shocking Condition of School Buildings
—Many Rooms without Desks—Children Sitting on the Floor Studying by
Gaslight, Breathing Foul Air and Becoming Cripples—Illness among the
Pupils.[60]

[58] Good Government Club E, "Circular Letter to the Delegates to a Conference on the Public Schools of New York," *Public School Buildings in New York
City*, Publication No. 7 (New York, 1895), p. 8.
[59] "Playgrounds for City Schools," pp. 657–64; "The Making of Thieves in
New York," *Century*, XLIX (November, 1894), 109–16; *The Making of an American*, p. 365.
[60] New York City, Board of Education, *The Common Schools of the City of
New York*, prepared by Charles C. Wehrum (New York, 1894); *New York Herald*,
May 7, 1894; *New York Times*, March 29, April 28, 1894.

More schools and decent schools became watchwords of the anti-Tammany crusade.[61]

The issue of city school administration was broached during the campaign. When the apostles of good government applied their principles of efficiency, expertise, concentration of authority and responsibility, and nonpartisanship to the system by which the city's school system was then managed, they were appalled. The reformers denounced the school system as archaic and "unscientific" in the extreme. Among the three groups of school officials, it was charged, authority was divided, responsibility diffused, negligence hidden, and the whole system shot through with incompetency. Through the trustee system, the reformers asserted, Tammany was degrading the public schools to the level of political spoils.[62] In June, 1894, in the pages of the *Educational Review*, of which he was editor, Nicholas Murray Butler urged New York municipal reformers to put school reform on "next winter's program and make sure of the abolition of the trustees and inspectors first of all." [63] School reform was placed on the agenda of reform, but Butler's proposal to abolish the trustees and inspectors was too audacious to be brought up in 1894. Popular control of the schools was a formidable tradition. There was no sense making it an election issue. The turn of the trustees and inspectors would come in 1895-96, and this is properly a subject for the next chapter.

The religious issue simmered just beneath the surface of the campaign. It sometimes rose to the surface, however; the *New York Tribune*, in a campaign editorial, made a blatant appeal to Protestant fears for the public schools. The *Tribune* pointedly observed that of the

[61] A conference of the City Vigilance League, the Good Government Clubs, the University Settlement, and other reform organizations agreed that the goal to be reached was "a seat for every child and every child in its seat." *The City Vigilant*, II (September, 1895), 135.

[62] Stephen H. Olin, "Public School Reform in New York," *Educational Review*, VIII (June, 1894), 1–6; *New York Sun*, April 8, 1894, ed.; *New York Tribune*, March 19, 1894, ed.

[63] *Educational Review*, VIII (June, 1894), 101–02, ed. New York's schools won little praise from outside observers, either: Joseph Mayer Rice, "The Public School System of New York City," *Forum*, XIV (January, 1893), 616–30. This was subsequently reprinted as Chap. I of Rice's *The Public School System of the United States* (New York, 1893). The school awakening in the middle 1890's was nationwide. See Rice, *The Public School System of the United States*; James H. Penniman, "The Criminal Overcrowding of Public Schools," *Forum*, XIX (May, 1895), 289–95; Robert L. McCaul, "Dewey's Chicago," *The School Review*, LXVII (Summer, 1959), 268–73; Charles Hirschfeld, *Baltimore, 1870–1900* (Baltimore, 1941), pp. 85–89, 129–31; Bayrd Still, *Milwaukee: The History of A City* (Madison, Wisc., 1948), p. 416; Blake McKelvey, *Rochester: The Quest for Quality, 1890–1925* (Cambridge, Mass., 1956), pp. 74, 82, 83.

fifteen standing committees of the Board of Education, ten committee
chairmanships were held by "Catholics or Tammany Hall men." [64]
Their religion as well as their politics was anathema to the reformers.
"The one thing before all others some of us strove for in that [1894]
campaign," Rainsford, a staunch friend of the Catholic layman but
not of his priest, recalled, "was better schools."

> New York schools, as all charitable institutions in the city, were in a terrible
> state. . . . The vastly greater proportion of the employees of these institu-
> tions were practically appointees of the house at the corner of Fiftieth Street
> and Madison Avenue, the residence of the Catholic Archbishop of New
> York.[65]

The anti-Tammany movement of 1894 was in many respects an anti-
Catholic crusade, and it left its permanent imprint on city school reform. The reformers' battle cry, "Take the schools out of politics,"
not only meant take the schools out of the hands of Tammany Hall;
it also meant take the schools out of the hands of the Roman Catholic
Church.

The aggressive grass-roots politicking of the Good Government
Clubs and a score of newly organized reform groups which made their
appearance in the city in the early 1890's, the relentless muckraking
of Dr. Parkhurst, and the daily revelations of police corruption by the
Lexow Committee made it a virtual certainty that if the numerous
anti-Tammany groups in the city could unite, victory was theirs. The
smashing reform triumph in Brooklyn in November 1893 was a harbinger of what would happen in Manhattan in November 1894.[66] To
fuse the anti-Tammany forces in the city and direct the election campaign proper, the City Club and the Chamber of Commerce called
the Committee of Seventy into being.[67] The chief task of the Seventy,

[64] *New York Tribune*, March 19, 1894, ed. Although a Protestant, Charles
Knox, was then president of the Board of Education, a post which carried considerable weight, to the *Tribune* this only signified that Tammany deemed it still too
soon for a Catholic to be president of the board, but not for a "Protestant who
would do the bidding of Tammany Hall."

[65] Rainsford, *The Story of a Varied Life*, p. 360. The extent of anti-Irish,
anti-Catholic feeling in the air at the time may be gauged from the sermon
preached by the Rev. Dr. Arthur S. MacArthur of Calvary Baptist Church shortly
after the election. MacArthur excoriated Tammany Hall as "an aggregation of un-
American, unprincipled men." On the head of the Tammany organization, he said,
"is a tiara of the Pope of Rome." He denounced the Irish flag as a "green rag." *New
York Times*, November 30, 1894.

[66] Charles Edward Russell, *Bare Hands and Stone Walls* (New York, 1933),
pp. 116–23; Harold C. Syrett, *The City of Brooklyn, 1865–1898* (New York, 1944),
Chap. XIII.

[67] *New York Times*, Sept. 7, 1894; "The Committee of Seventy," *Harper's
Weekly*, XXXVIII (October 13, 1894), 966; A. C. Bernheim, "The Committee of

composed almost exclusively of the financial, commercial, and professional elite of the city, was to formulate a platform and name a ticket acceptable to all the anti-Tammany forces in the city.

In October 1894 the Seventy's platform was proclaimed. The Seventy denounced the corruption, inefficiency, and extravagance of Tammany Hall and extolled the Good Government litany. But the major part of the Seventy's platform, to borrow the words of Joseph Larocque, the Seventy's president, was composed of "progressive social work planks." These included greater care and thoroughness in the enforcement of the health laws, establishment of public baths and lavatories, establishment of small parks in the congested areas, adoption of a thorough system of street-cleaning, increased rapid transit facilities, and reform of the public schools. This last plank deserves to be quoted in full to emphasize the place of the schools in the reform movement.

> We demand that the quality of the public schools be improved, their capacity enlarged and proper playgrounds provided, so that every child between the ages required by law shall have admission to the schools, the health of the children protected, and that all such modern improvements be introduced as will make our public schools the equal of those in any other city in the world.[68]

It was this unique platform that united the various anti-Tammany groups in the city behind the Fusion candidate, Republican merchant and banker William L. Strong, and upon which Fusion successfully appealed to the people on November 6, 1894.[69]

V

On the morning of November 7, 1894, with Tammany beaten and Dick Croker in retirement in England, the *New York Herald* gave vent

---

Seventy," *The Triumph of Reform* . . . , p. 7; Parkhurst, *Our Fight with Tammany*, Chap. XXI; Tolman, *op. cit.*, p. 85.

[68] *New York Times*, October 5, 1894; Bernheim, *op. cit.*, pp. 11–12; Tolman, *op. cit.*, pp. 86–87. European influences were also at work. As one reformer put it, the Seventy's platform would give the people of New York "those public improvements that the citizens of all great European capitals enjoy." Bernheim, *op. cit.*, p. 11. For European municipal developments, see Albert Shaw, *Municipal Government in Continental Europe* (New York, 1895); Albert Shaw, *Municipal Government in Great Britain* (New York, 1904); Arthur Mann, "British Social Thought and American Reformers of the Progressive Era," *Mississippi Valley Historical Review*, XLII (1955–56), 685–87.

[69] Strong was elected by a majority of 45,187 votes. *New York Times*, November 7, 1894; *The Triumph of Reform* . . . , p. 329; Myers, *op. cit.*, pp. 333–34; Garrett, *op. cit.*, p. 38.

to the quasi-religious feeling of relief and exaltation which surged through the ranks of reform when it declared:

> Now may the people of this city give themselves up to unbounded jubilation and thanksgiving. New York is redeemed and will be regenerated.[70]

Indeed New York would be regenerated. There was no letup in reformist fervor in the post-election period. The Good Government Clubs were intended to be "permanent, persistent, and aggressive." And the Committee of Seventy, surprising many, not only stayed in the field but also appointed subcommittees to ensure that the promises made the people during the campaign were fulfilled.[71] No phase of the city's municipal life, not police, sanitation, or housing, received more attention from the victorious reformers than did the public school system. School law revision was given top priority. The election of William Strong was a long step toward school reform. But to obtain their ends, the reformers deemed it essential not only to gain control of the city government, but also to oust Tammany from its strongholds in the school system and to modernize that system. This necessitated an appeal to Albany for fundamental school law revision. To draw up suitable school legislation was the chief task of the Committee of Seventy's Sub-Committee on Schools, comprising Nicholas Murray Butler, William Ware Locke, Stephen H. Olin, John B. Pine, and Henry L. Sprague. On January 10, 1895, the Seventy's school bill was introduced into the State Assembly. Thus the stage was set for the resumption of the acrimonious political struggle just concluded, but now with Albany as a battlefield also. At this point Good Government Club E, Nicholas Murray Butler, and the Public Education Association of New York City stepped to the forefront of the school reform movement.

Good Government Club E began like many of the other Good Government Clubs. On or about February 10, 1893, the initial steps for its formation were taken by two prominent City Club men, corporation lawyer and ex-diplomat J. Augustus Johnson and banker Charles M. Perry. The club was duly incorporated on January 3, 1894, with Johnson as president. Its officers and trustees constituted a patriciate of

---

[70] *New York Herald*, November 7, 1894; Tolman, *op. cit.*, pp. 31–33; Rainsford, *The Story of a Varied Life*, p. 360; Wheeler, *op. cit.*, p. 342; Ware, *op. cit.*, p. 113.

[71] The Seventy organized committees on street cleaning, civil service, small parks, public baths and lavatories, tenement house reform, garbage disposal, investigation of payrolls, improvement of the waterfront, and public school reform. *New York Times*, November 10, December 12, 1894; Bernheim, *op. cit.*, pp. 19–21; Tolman, *op. cit.*, pp. 89–91.

wealthy Protestant families of old American ancestry: Johnson, Perry, Robert Center, Charles Lee, Charles Barney, Valentine Mott, and such. Its district was the Twelfth A.D.—the district southeast of Fourth Avenue between Twenty-ninth Street and Seventeenth Street. Club E swung promptly into political activity. First, it set up an Employment Committee to help alleviate the distress in its district caused by the terrible depression of that winter. Next, the club inaugurated the customary series of public talks and debates publicizing the penalties of boss rule, police graft, fraudulent elections, and the other evils of mal-administered cities. Then, early in April 1894, the Council of Good Government Clubs, of which Johnson was president, distributed its reform assignments. To E went "Education and the Public Schools." [72] No club worked harder or with more permanent results.

During the election campaign Club E helped the reform movement publicize the evils of the school system, and also successfully agitated for positive school reform. On June 6, 1894, before a large audience, Club E sponsored a forum on "The public school question." The speakers included E. Ellery Anderson, Stephen H. Olin, Jacob Riis, and the Reverend William Ware Locke, chairman of the Club's Public School Committee. They spoke feelingly about the packed schools, the truancy problem, and the plight of the children on the East Side during the hot summer months. At the close of the meeting, a Club E resolution requesting that summer "vacation schools" be established as part of the city's public school system was advanced and carried. The purpose of the resolution was

to test the present system, to advance the cause of practical education, and to show our interest in the welfare of the great mass of the working people, whose families are obliged to remain in the city throughout the summer.[73]

Testimony enough for the variety of motives—educational, political, and philanthropic—which motivated the school reformers.

To meet the expected objections to the expense involved in the proposed experiment, R. Fulton Cutting, president of the Association for Improving the Condition of the Poor, was prevailed upon to notify the Board of Education that his organization would give the sum of $5,000 to subsidize several vacation schools. The Board of Education

---

[72] Good Government Club E, *Annual Report of the Trustees for the Year Ending November 26, 1894;* Good Government Club E, *Report of the Committee on Schools, November 26, 1894,* pp. 3–4; Johnson, *op. cit.,* pp. 150–51; "Good Government Club E," *The Triumph of Reform . . . ,* p. 164.

[73] Good Government Club E, *Report of the Committee on Schools, November 26, 1894,* pp. 3–8.

promptly gave its assent to the project. On July 23, 1894, vacation schools were opened in three East Side public schools, with Club E's William Ware Locke, who had had previous vacation school experience in Boston, in charge.[74]

Good Government Club E took its reform assignment with the utmost seriousness. The club's leaders represented that fairly homogeneous class of New Yorkers who, half a century earlier, through the Public School Society, financed and controlled the education of the poor in New York. But since 1853, when the Society surrendered all of its assets to the new Board of Education, the schools, like all the other branches of city government, had slipped from their grasp. Now Johnson, Perry, Barney, and the rest held themselves to blame for the mess the school system was in and dedicated Club E as the system's voluntary guardian. After Strong's election, the club's Board of Trustees changed hats, became the club's Public School Committee, and joined hands with the Committee of Seventy to overhaul the system.

Shortly after the election, in December 1894, Club E released a spirited manifesto spelling out in somewhat greater detail the school reform program hinted at in the Seventy's platform. Club E proposed to undertake the following measures: to investigate the charges concerning the lack of proper school accommodations, inadequate provision for kindergarten and manual training, and the "complicated political system" affecting the public schools; to recommend improvements in school buildings with regard to ventilation, light, and sanitary conditions; to urge greater appropriations for education; and, finally, to cooperate with the Committee of Seventy in securing new school legislation.[75] It was inevitable, if the Club were to realize such an ambitious program, that it send out a call for help. The manifesto announced that an organization of women was being formed to awaken interest in public education and to furnish "associates and workers" to the Educational Committee of Club E. It concluded with an appeal to the public-spirited women of New York to "associated action" on behalf of the great cause of school reform.[76] The Woman's Association for Improving the Public Schools was born of this call. In April 1895

[74] *New York Times*, July 18, 1894; New York Association for Improving the Condition of the Poor, *Report of Department of Schools and Institutions on Vacation Schools* (New York, 1895); Sadie American, "The Movement for Vacation Schools," *American Journal of Sociology*, IV (November 1898), 315–17.

[75] Good Government Club E, *Education and the Public Schools*; Good Government Club E, *Report of the Committee on Schools, Nov. 26, 1894*; Good Government Club E, *Annual Report of the Trustees for the Year Ending November 26, 1894*.

[76] Good Government Club E, *Education and the Public Schools*, p. 2.

the ladies separated themselves from Club E. In October they took the next bold step and became the Public Education Association of New York City.

J. Augustus Johnson had no intention of creating a permanent reform organization when he called the WAIPS into being. This was the master stroke of someone else, the man who had just assumed the leadership of the school reform movement in New York City, Nicholas Murray Butler.

VI

"A meeting of the Association without Dr. Butler," the president of the Public Education Association stated fondly in 1896, "was like the play 'Hamlet' with Hamlet left out." [77] We may assume, then, that it was on the initiative, advice, and encouragement of the ubiquitous Nicholas Murray Butler that the rapid sequence of steps from WAIPS to PEA were taken. An informed observer with little more to go on than the mere appearance of a new organization on the New York City educational scene in the 1890's might have surmised that Butler would be the dominant figure in its establishment.

Professor Butler has recently been characterized as an "independent thinker, but not a creative one, a man of action, not of contemplation. . . . Never content to contemplate ends, his vast energies were concentrated on means. He fathered organizations, not ideas." [78] It is a perspicacious description. Butler founded and was the first editor of the *Educational Review*. He organized and edited the *Great Educator Series*. He was the man behind the famous Committee of Ten on the Reorganization of Secondary Studies of the National Education Association. He helped launch other important committees concerned with educational reform on the national level. In New York City school reform, Butler was ubiquitous. In 1888 he assumed the presidency of the Industrial Education Association. While president of the Association he conceived the New York College for the Training of Teachers, later to become Teachers College. He was one of the founders of the New York Kindergarten Association.[79] All this is rather well-known.

[77] *New York Tribune*, November 21, 1896.

[78] Richard Whittemore, "Nicholas Murray Butler and the Teaching Profession," *History of Education Quarterly*, I (September, 1961), 22.

[79] *Ibid.*, pp. 22–24; Nicholas Murray Butler, *Across the Busy Years* (New York, 1939–40), Vol. I, Chap. I; Cremin *et al.*, *A History of Teachers College, Columbia University*, pp. 18–27. There is much new material on Butler in Whittemore's "Nicholas Murray Butler and Public Education, 1862–1911" (unpublished Ph.D. thesis, Columbia University, 1962).

What is less well-known is that no sooner had he taken over the leadership of the IEA than he organized a citizens' group with general school reform goals called the Public Education Society: "the forerunner of the present Public Education Association," Butler calls it in his memoirs. The time was apparently not ripe for the organization of the Society, and it was shortly disbanded.[80]

Butler, a Republican, enjoyed the hurly-burly of politics. However, since he had just recently moved into Manhattan from Paterson, New Jersey, he played a negligible role in the 1894 election campaign. But when the Committee of Seventy appointed a Sub-Committee on Public Schools in December, it was quite natural that Butler—already, although only thirty-three years old, one of the most renowned and influential educators in the country—be assigned a place on it. From this position Butler just as naturally assumed the role of leader of the school reform movement.

On March 14, 1895, J. Augustus Johnson urged Butler to accept election as a Club E trustee and to take charge of the club's Public School Committee. If Butler gave his time and direction to the efforts of the Committee, wrote Johnson, "then we feel that we cannot go astray." [81] Butler promptly accepted Johnson's invitation.[82] This was just a few months after the organization of the Woman's Association for Improving the Public Schools. It was inevitable that Butler, already known to some of the ladies socially, would replace Johnson as the ladies' mentor. One month after Butler joined Club E, the ladies formally separated themselves from the club. In October the Woman's Association for Improving the Public Schools became the Public Education Association.

What lay behind this transformation? In the long run Butler probably conceived the PEA as the alter ego of himself, another Industrial Education Association or Teachers College, but with more general objectives. That is, the PEA was to be another, but more permanent, Public Education Society, an organization which would represent the interests of reform independent of the fate of any particular reform movement. There were, however, immediate, tactical reasons behind the change from WAIPS into PEA which require no speculation to eluci-

---

[80] Public Education Society of the City of New York, *Memorial to the Board of Education, February 6, 1889* (New York, 1889), in a volume entitled "Documents 1889–1896" at Teachers College Library, Teachers College, Columbia University; Butler, *op. cit.*, I, 17.

[81] J. Augustus Johnson to Butler, March 14, 1895, Columbiana Collection, Low Memorial Library, Columbia University, New York.

[82] Butler to Johnson, March 16, 1895, Columbiana Collection.

date. Butler and the reform party needed the ladies' help in shaping a school system to meet the needs of the city. While the ladies' Club E name, Woman's Association for Improving the Public Schools, described their objective to perfection, it carried a fatal implication of criticism. Under the bland, ambiguous name, Public Education Association, the ladies could be of more service to the cause of reform.

The milieu of social and political crisis in which the PEA has its roots is now completely sketched. Behind the emergence of the PEA lay at least a decade of increasing school criticism and demands for school reform. Its birth came at a critical moment in the history of the city, a time when the city was undergoing enormous growing pains and profound change. Its birth came at the end of the old era in education in New York City and the beginning of a new era; what the new would be like, no one could yet foretell.

Chapter 2

ESTABLISHMENT AND EARLY TRIUMPHS

1895-1905

On May 3, 1897, by the stroke of a pen, New York City was trebled in size and more than doubled in population. The state legislature had passed and the Governor had signed the "Greater New York" bill enlarging the city to its present boundaries. The "consolidation" placed New York City beyond challenge as the nation's first city and added a new dimension, in scale and quality, to the government and politics of urban America.[1]

Greater New York began its civic life under an out-and-out Tammany administration. The "triumph of reform" for which E. L. Godkin had the pleasure of writing the preface chronicled only a temporary triumph. William L. Strong gave New York City a model government. But not until the La Guardia era of the 1930's would a city reform administration win re-election. On November 7, 1897, to the cheers of "To Hell with Reform," a new Tammany administration headed by Robert Van Wyck was voted into City Hall.[2]

Despite the brevity of his stay in office, Strong's election in 1894 ushered in a whole new era of reform. The Committee of Seventy's campaign promises were largely redeemed, as Jacob Riis's *The Battle with the Slum* (1902) testifies. Nowhere can the awakening of the civic conscience be more clearly traced than in the city schools: greater appropriations, new buildings, a school census, open-air playgrounds, promotion of vacation schools, extension of kindergarten and manual

---

[1] Wallace S. Sayre and Herbert Kaufman, *Governing New York City: Politics in the Metropolis* (New York, 1960), pp. 11–14; Allan Nevins and John A. Krout (eds.), *The Greater City: New York, 1898–1948* (New York, 1948), Chap. I; David M. Ellis *et al., A Short History of New York State* (New York, 1957), p. 379.

[2] Charles Garrett, *The La Guardia Years: Machine and Reform Politics in New York City* (New York, 1960), p. 39; Nevins and Krout, *op. cit.*, p. 61.

training, high schools, medical inspection of school children, and more. In the late nineties the reformers made the intoxicating discovery that the public schools were not for the child's use only, but for the use of the whole neighborhood.[3] "The silly old regime," Riis announced in 1902, "is dead." [4] The advance of progressivism in the city school system can be traced under all city administrations in the decade 1895–1905, Tammany or reform.[5] The critical event was the enactment of the so-called Compromise School Bill of 1896.

The election of Strong as Mayor was a big step in the direction of public school reform, but no real progress was deemed possible until the State School Law under which the city school system was then governed was fundamentally revised. When the reform party ran into unexpectedly stiff opposition in Albany as well as in New York, the result was another acrimonious struggle, a "school war," to use Nicholas Murray Butler's phrase, which, after a temporary setback for reform in April 1895, culminated finally in the real "triumph of reform" in the spring of 1896. The PEA was born in the midst of the school war.

Butler's foresight in calling the PEA into being was to be demonstrated more than once in the course of the decade 1895–1905. During the legislative struggle of 1896 the PEA proved itself an invaluable ally to the cause of reform. Contemporaries gave it much of the credit for the enactment of the Compromise School Bill. Butler's foresight was demonstrated anew a few years later. With the return of Tammany in 1897, Good Government Club E, like the other Good Government Clubs, began to disintegrate; by 1903 they had all disappeared.[6] The PEA, however, was affected neither by the demise of Club E nor by the shifts of political power in the city. Long before 1903 it had become a going concern, quite independent of the fortunes of Club E, although as the heir of Club E's reform assignment, "Education and the Public Schools," still closely tied to the reform movement.

The reformers had their new school law; they still had to shape a school system to meet the needs of the city. After its work on behalf

[3] Jacob A. Riis, *The Battle with the Slum* (New York, 1902), p. 45, Chaps. XIII–XV and *passim*.

[4] *Ibid.*, p. 347.

[5] In 1901 the reformers came back into City Hall with Seth Low. In 1903 Tammany returned with George B. McClellan as Mayor and won again with McClellan in 1905. Garrett, *op. cit.*, pp. 39–41; Nevins and Krout, *op. cit.*, pp. 61–73.

[6] Richard R. G. Welling, *As the Twig is Bent* (New York, 1942), p. 91; Garrett, *op. cit.*, p. 24; Richard B. Hovey, *John Jay Chapman—An American Mind* (New York, 1959), p. 77.

of the good government phase of school reform, the PEA turned to the question of school policy. Now it appended itself to the University Settlement, taking up the settlement demand that the public school become a center of neighborhood life. Once again the PEA proved itself an extraordinarily effective pressure group. When the city's public schools were opened in the late 1890's to serve a wide variety of community needs, the PEA received most of the credit for this portentous development also.

That the PEA would seek direction outside of its own formal leadership is not surprising. Throughout its first decade it was run entirely by volunteers, philanthropy-minded women who sought to give some money and some leisure time to further the reform movement. The ladies had no school program of their own. They had to borrow ideas and to implement or promote the ideas of others. To examine the PEA's activities, then, is to open a window on some of the groups and interests striving to influence the course of public education in New York. Our findings, however, have wider applicability. The PEA's school reform program was in the mainstream of American progressivism. Furthermore, the PEA was typical of an extremely important development at the turn of the century: the surge of organized citizen interest in the public schools. And, as we shall see, this was a movement which the PEA played a considerable role in stimulating.

I

It was generally agreed among American municipal reformers in the 1890's that cities were to be reformed through the activities of local reform groups, churches, and women's organizations. Women were doing effective political work in Philadelphia and Chicago. And they were conspicuous by their presence and activities at the great conference of municipal reformers held in Philadelphia in January 1894 at which the National Municipal League was founded. It was the considered opinion of Herbert Welch, a Philadelphia gentleman, that "women are needed—and if their efforts are guided wisely they may become invaluable allies" in the cause of good city government.[7] It cannot be

[7] Herbert Welch, "A Definite Step Towards Municipal Reform," *Forum*, XVII (March, 1894), 179–85; Mrs. Joseph P. Mumford, "The Relation of Women to Municipal Reform," *Proceedings*, National Conference for Good City Government (Philadelphia, 1894), pp. 134–43; William H. Tolman, *Municipal Reform Movements in the United States: The Textbook of the New Reformation* (New York, 1895), Part IV; Frank Mann Stewart, *A Half Century of Municipal Reform: The National Municipal League* (Berkeley, Calif., 1950), pp. 16–17.

said, however, that this sentiment was the one prevailing among New Yorkers.

In New York City the "new woman" could, with Louisa Lee Schuyler, Josephine Shaw Lowell, Grace Dodge, Maud Nathan, and Jane Robbins, engage in philanthropic and social betterment work of all sorts.[8] But engage in politics? The Reverend Charles Parkhurst's ladies auxiliary, the infant Woman's Municipal League, not withstanding, New York's patrician reformers found the idea vastly amusing; women were barred from membership in the City Club and the Good Government Clubs. Yet the evidence presented at the Philadelphia good government conference could not be laughed away. New York's civic leaders were present in Philadelphia en masse, including a large delegation of Club E men led by J. Augustus Johnson. The germ of the idea for a ladies' auxiliary to Club E was planted on this occasion. When Johnson claimed the school reform assignment for Club E, the idea crystallized. "This was the solution," the patriarchal Johnson observed, "to the problem of cooperation with patriotic women in such departments of club work as are suited to their sympathies and tastes." [9] But the ladies were given to all sorts of enthusiasms; woman suffrage, for instance, and their "sympathies and tastes" would have to be carefully nurtured, especially in a work of such moment as New York City public school reform.

Club E initiated the PEA into the world of New York City politics with a modest program. The PEA's pioneer undertaking was a School Visiting Committee, which kept an eye on sanitary conditions in public schools on the East Side. Library and Lecture Committees came next. The Library Committee helped the Free Circulation and Aguilar Free Libraries circulate books in the downtown public schools. The Lecture Committee organized weekly public lectures. These lectures, which the PEA sponsored through 1895 and 1896, provided a forum for such reform luminaries as Butler, Riis, Adler, Reynolds, and Rainsford.[10] The Lecture Committee also aimed to foster cooperation between

[8] Maud Nathan, *Once Upon a Time and Today* (New York, 1933); Abbie Graham, *Grace H. Dodge: Merchant of Dreams* (New York, 1926); William Rhinelander Stewart, *The Philanthropic Work of Josephine Shaw Lowell* (New York, 1911); Eleanor Flexner, *Century of Struggle: The Woman's Rights Movement in the United States* (Cambridge, Mass., 1959), Chap. XV.

[9] J. Augustus Johnson, "Good Government Clubs," *The Triumph of Reform: A History of the Great Political Revolution, November Sixth, Eighteen Hundred and Ninety-Four* (New York, 1895), p. 135.

[10] *New York Times*, December 24, 1895; *New York Times*, January 12, 1896; PEA, *Annual Report*, 1896, p. 9.

teachers and parents in the downtown section.[11] Thus the PEA was
slowly getting itself established. By early 1896 it had a membership of
about 300. But now everything was pushed aside. The "school war" was
on. Ready or not, Butler needed the ladies' help in getting his school
bill passed.

Victory at the polls in November had left the reformers unappeased.
The city was going to be purged. They did not forget the Police Department nor the streets nor the tenements, but school law revision received
top priority. Beginning in the late 1880's, as we have seen, the city
school system began to come under heavy fire. By 1895 no tinkering
would satisfy the reformers. "The best method of proceeding to reform
the schools," the *Times* advised, "is by reforming the whole system of
their management." [12] Now the victorious reform party intended, in
Butler's words, to "make sure of the abolition of the trustees and
inspectors first of all."

On January 10, 1895, the Committee of Seventy's school bill was
introduced in the State Assembly. The proposed bill legislated out of
existence the old Board of Education and called for the creation of a
new Board of Education of twenty-one, to be appointed by the Mayor,
with full and final control of the school system. The bill also called for
the concentration of pedagogical authority and responsibility in the
Superintendent and Division Superintendents—the "Board of Experts."
A Superintendent of Buildings was to be responsible for the actual care
and custody of the school buildings. The school inspectors were to be
abolished. The ward trustees were retained, but they were to be deprived
of all powers except those of inspection and reporting. The city Board of
Estimate and Apportionment was left in control of the school purse
strings.[13]

The "school war" of 1895–1896 had begun.[14] The "reform party,"

[11] PEA, *Annual Reports*, 1896–1899; *New York Times*, November 25, 1899.
Apparently it accomplished this goal. The historian of the United Parents Associations of New York credits the PEA with launching the parent-teachers association
movement in the city. Margaret Lighty and LeRoy E. Bowman, *Parenthood in a
Democracy* (New York, 1939), pp. 23–25.

[12] January 7, 1895, ed.

[13] *New York Times*, January 11, 1895; Committee of Seventy, *Report of Sub-
Committee on Public School System* (New York, 1894); *Educational Review*, IX
(January, 1895), 102, ed.; A. Emerson Palmer, *The New York Public School* (New
York, 1905), pp. 186–87.

[14] Butler entitled a collection of documents pertaining to the struggle to get
the reform bill passed "The School War." In Columbiana Collection, Low Memorial
Library, Columbia University, New York City. Jacob Riis also uses the term, "school
war," to describe the same event: *The Making of an American* (New York, 1901),
p. 365.

a term Butler frequently employed, greeted the Seventy's bill, or the Pavey bill, with great enthusiasm. It was immediately endorsed by the City Club, the Good Government Clubs, the City Vigilance League, the German-American Reform Union, and virtually the entire daily press. The *Times* spoke for all of them when it asserted that the Committee of Seventy bill proposed to "concentrate power and responsibility, to exclude politics from public trusts, and to apply sound business principles to public affairs, all in a direct line with the general advance in city administration." [15]

Butler and the others had every expectation that their bill would be promptly enacted; a Republican administration headed by New York City socialite Levi P. Morton had been swept into Albany in 1894. But their hopes were to be dashed. Mayor Strong's independence with regard to appointments and removals from office angered Senator Thomas C. Platt, the powerful boss of the upstate Republican machine. In retaliation Platt was determined to kill all bills giving the Mayor additional patronage.

Platt Republicans joined Tammany Democrats, with a timely assist from the city's public school teachers, who demonstrated en masse against it, to kill the reform measure in the 1895 session.[16] The setback greatly intensified the reformers' determination not to let school reform slip away from them. Tammany's comeback in the minor city elections of November 1895, a sharp reminder of the tenuous nature of reform governments in the city, heightened their sense of urgency. Reform of the school system had to be accomplished immediately; by 1897, the

[15] February 17, 1895, ed.; *Harper's Weekly*, XXXIX (March 16, 1895), 243, ed.; *Educational Review*, X (June, 1895), 98–103, ed. Indeed, with the exception of the issue of how School Board members should be selected, a much controverted point among reformers within and without school systems, the Seventy's school bill was the embodiment of contemporary political progressivism: Samuel Train Dutton and David Snedden, *The Administration of Public Education in the United States* (New York, 1908), Chaps. VIII–IX; Truman A. DeWeese, "Better City School Administration," *Educational Review*, XX (June, 1900), 61–71; Frank Rollins, *School Administration in Municipal Government* (New York, 1902); James T. Young, "The Administration of City Schools," *The Annals*, XV (March, 1900), 171–85; Joseph Mayer Rice, *The Public School System of the United States* (New York, 1893), pp. 17–18; Eaton, *op. cit.*, Chap. XV; Lawrence A. Cremin, *The Transformation of the School* (New York, 1961), pp. 5–6; Lawrence A. Cremin, "The Progressive Movement in American Education: A Perspective," *Harvard Educational Review*, XXVII (Fall, 1957), 259–60.

[16] *Educational Review*, X (June, 1895), 98–103, ed.; *Outlook*, LI (May 4, 1895), 722, ed.; DeAlva Stanwood Alexander, *Four Famous New Yorkers, 1882–1905*, Vol. IV of his *The Political History of New York State* (New York, 1923), pp. 230–36; Louis J. Lang (ed.), *The Autobiography of Thomas Collier Platt* (New York, 1910), pp. 268–95.

year of the next mayoralty election, it might be too late. Butler vowed to continue the fight for school reform until "the Platt–Tammany combine and their allies the teachers' 'ring' are beaten." [17]

By 1896 it was obvious to everyone in the city that changes in the school system were coming. In the hope of stealing a march on the reformers, the Board of Education, on which there was still a Tammany majority, introduced a school reform bill into the State Legislature as soon as the latter met for the 1896 legislative session. The Board of Education bill (known as the Strauss bill) included provisions for some increased centralization of power in the Board of Education and in the Superintendent, and also a provision for the establishment of public high schools, an innovation that, so far, the reformers had completely overlooked; there was as yet no public high school in the city. As for the ward trustees, *the* crucial issue, the Strauss bill not only left them with most of their powers intact, but defiantly increased the number of local school boards from twenty-four to forty-five.[18]

Tammany was going to make a fight of it on the issue of local control. Butler picked up the gauntlet. On February 4, 1896, a bill of about 200 words, prepared by Butler and Professor Frank Goodnow of Columbia University, chairman of the City Club's Committee on Legislation, and sponsored by the City Club, was introduced into the legislature.[19] It contained a single provision: abolition of the ward trustee system. The school war was joined again.

Led by Butler, the reform party went to do battle. The *Sun, Herald, Tribune, Evening Post, Times,* and *World* fell into line. The Good Government Clubs swung into action. The Committee of Seventy was missing, having adjourned sine die the previous June, but the indefatigable Butler called into being the Citizens Committee of One Hundred on Public School Reform, composed mainly of the old Seventy, to lobby for the City Club bill.[20] One of Butler's most effective weapons in the

[17] *Educational Review,* X (November, 1895), 102, ed.; *New York Tribune,* May 5, 1895, ed.

[18] *New York Times,* January 30, 1896; New York City, Board of Education, *Journal* (January 15, 1896), pp. 123–27. Reform comment may be sampled in *Educational Review,* XI (March, 1896), 301–02, ed.

[19] James W. Pryor to Butler, December 18, 1895, "The School War"; City Club, *Monthly Bulletin No. 4* (February, 1896), p. 491; *New York Tribune,* February 5, 1896; *New York World,* February 5, 1896, ed.; *Educational Review,* XI (April, 1896), 409–10, ed.

[20] *Educational Review,* XI (March, 1896), 303–04, ed.; *New York Tribune,* February 7, 1896; *New York World,* February 7, 1896; Richard Whittemore, "Nicholas Murray Butler and the Teaching Profession," *History of Education Quarterly,* I (September, 1961), 34. The call for the organization of the Citizens

school war, however, was the PEA. Under his direction the PEA was transformed into an extremely effective pressure group, emerging from the struggle with much of the glory.

The futile fight for school reform in 1895 convinced Butler that something had to be done about the city's public school teachers: "To gain the sympathy of these teachers, to inform them and widen their horizons, is one of the first and most useful steps the reform party can take." [21] This was naturally a job suited for the PEA. In late 1895 the PEA inaugurated a series of Friday afternoon lectures and Saturday afternoon teas. The former were open to the general public as well as to public school teachers, the latter were especially for teachers.[22] Thus the Association hoped to gain one of Butler's objectives: the education of the benighted teachers.

As the school war went into 1896, Butler decided to cast the ladies into the struggle in a more belligerent role. In February the PEA was invited to join Club E, the City Club, and the Citizens Committee on Public School Reform in a joint petition to the Senate on behalf of the City Club bill. The opportunity thus publicly to join the Grand Alliance almost overwhelmed the ladies. Mrs. Edward S. Mead wrote Butler that the PEA's Executive Committee approved his petition unanimously, adding, "You see what entire confidence we have in our Advisory Board." [23] Then Mrs. Mead confessed that, although she was trying very hard to be calm and judicial, she was "really tremendously excited over being allowed to publicly take a hand in this fight."

Committee was sent out in the name of Butler, ex-Mayor Abram S. Hewitt, Elihu Root, Stephen H. Olin, and J. Kennedy Tod. The committee was composed, the *World* said, of "every kind of citizen best qualified to express an intelligent interest in the future of the city's educational system." *New York World*, February 15, 1896, ed. There is much material on the Citizens Committee in a collection of documents entitled "Citizens Committee of One Hundred," at the Teachers College Library, Teachers College, Columbia University.

[21] *Educational Review*, X (June, 1895), 103, ed.

[22] *New York Times*, December 15, 1895; PEA, *Annual Reports*, 1895–1896. The opening lecture of the winter was given in the Assembly Hall of the United Charities Building on December 6. To get the series off to a good start the Civic League and the League for Political Education joined the PEA to help get Dr. G. Stanley Hall, President of Clark University and the child study expert, to speak. Among the other lecturers scheduled by the PEA were Julia Richman, Charles Loring Brace, Jacob Riis, R. Fulton Cutting, Felix Adler, James B. Reynolds, and Samuel T. Dutton.

[23] Susan Abbot Mead to Butler, Tuesday, n.d. [February 7 or 8, 1896], "The School War"; Citizens Committee on Public School Reform, Document No. 2, *Brief Submitted on Behalf of the City Club of New York, the Citizens Committee on Public School Reform, Good Government Club E, and the Public Education Association, February 8, 1896*, "Citizens Committee of One Hundred"; PEA, *Annual Report*, 1896, pp. 7–8.

The PEA did especially effective work in Albany. In 1896, Platt decided to adopt a hands-off attitude towards New York City school reform. Republican legislators were, therefore, free to follow their own inclinations on the issue. This gave Butler an excellent opportunity to exploit the prestige, social status, and, presumably, the disinterestedness of the PEA's leaders. He kept sending delegations of the ladies up to Albany for all the public hearings on the school bills. The *Herald* described one Senate meeting as a contest between "beauty" and the Tammany-Lauterbach machine. Beauty was represented by Mrs. Levi Morton, the Governor's wife, and the glamorous Mrs. Lorillard Spencer, both of the PEA. The reporter described how, at intervals, legislators would be taken over and introduced to the socialites and then lectured on the need for school reform in New York City.[24] The *Times* referred to the PEA's socially prominent women who made the trip to Albany for the legislative sessions on city school reform as a "charming group" who got more attention than the legislators.[25] The PEA's effectiveness as a lobbyist for school reform was not at all lessened by the fact that several of its leaders were by 1896 officials of the city school system.

Among the first school reforms urged by Club E and the Confederation of Good Government Clubs was the appointment of women to posts in city school officialdom. The Good Government Clubs flooded the Mayor and the Board of Education with recommendations.[26] In one of the first fruits of the reform victory, Mayor Strong and the Board of Education acceded to the reformers' demands. Among their first appointees as school inspectors or ward trustees were Mrs. William S. Rainsford, Mrs. Willard Parker, Mrs. Alice Brevoort Bull, Mrs. Gordon Wendell, and Mrs. Schuyler Van Rensselaer, all of the PEA.[27] As knowledgeable, as well as charming, school officials, the ladies were invaluable to Butler at the Albany hearings.

II

The City Club bill was a transparent stratagem. One month after it was introduced, the Stranahan–White school bill was reported out

[24] *New York Herald*, February 18, 1896.

[25] *New York Times*, February 26, 1896; *New York World*, February 26, 1896; *New York Tribune*, February 26, 1896.

[26] Good Government Club E, *Report and Recommendations of the Committee on Public Schools*, Publication No. 6 [1895]; *New York Times*, February 15, 1895.

[27] *New York Times*, February 21, April 25, May 15, 1895; New York City, Board of Education, *Fifty-Fourth Annual Report*, 1895, pp. 51–56. The *Times* described Mrs. Rainsford as a practical student of education, "not radical" but "progressive," and called her appointment just the kind needed.

of the Senate Committee on Cities. Labelled a "compromise" bill, actually it gave the reformers everything they wanted. Public high schools were provided for; the school inspectors were retained; the ward trustee system was abolished.[28] Now the reformers were satisfied. The new school reform bill, the *New York World* declared, concentrated power and responsibility, placed professional schoolmen in charge of pedagogical affairs, and "[took] popular education out of politics." [29]

When Governor Morton in a special message to the Legislature urged passage of the Compromise Bill, the issue was no longer in doubt.[30] The Senate adopted the bill by a vote along strict party lines.[31] "If the school bill passes the Assembly," Butler exulted to Albert Shaw, editor of *World's Work,*" it will be one of the greatest triumphs that municipal reform has yet achieved." [32] With the Assembly overwhelmingly Republican and its Speaker, Hamilton Fish, one of the reform party, the bill's passage was assured.[33] Now Mayor Strong, under powers granted by the State Legislature in 1894, had to sign it. There was no doubt that he would. He could hardly go back on a measure that had the almost solid support of the coalition that had elected him. But the Mayor still had to go through the formal procedure of calling public hearings, and opposition to the bill was growing by leaps and bounds.

Few pieces of legislation in the history of New York State have aroused so much opposition as the Compromise School Bill, and withal were still enacted into law. Writing his memoirs, fifty years after the event, Butler was still able to recall what a hard and bitter fight it was to get the bill through.[34] The reformers had many complaints about the city school system: it was an anachronism; it was inefficient; it was hopelessly unprofessional. No doubt all this was true. But the violently partisan nature of the controversy cannot be understood exclusively in terms of efficiency or scientific school management. The school war

[28] *Educational Review*, XI (April, 1896), 411–13, ed.; Palmer, *op. cit.*, p. 188.
[29] March 7, 1896, ed.
[30] *New York Herald*, March 21, 1896; *New York Times*, March 21, 1896.
[31] *New York Herald*, April 1, 1896.
[32] Butler to Shaw, April 2, 1896, "The School War." And from Mrs. William E. D. Scott of the PEA: "We are jubilant . . . but not forgetful of the hard work that has been done by our leaders." Mrs. Scott to Butler, n.d. [late March 1896], "The School War."
[33] The Compromise Bill passed the Assembly by a vote of 88–43, a straight party vote with the exception of two New York City Republicans. *New York Herald*, April 8, 1896.
[34] *Across the Busy Years* (New York, 1939–40), I, 17.

of 1896 was a power struggle in which the bitter religious and class antagonisms aroused in the municipal election of 1894 were raked up all over again. He that runs may read this in contemporary accounts of the struggle. With Butler leading the way, the reform party made it a crusade of "the forces of good, the intelligence and public spirit" of the city against the forces of evil; "a horde of bandits and barbarians," joined by "scores of incompetent teachers." [35] Opponents of the bill gave as good as they received, and not by any means did this group include only those directly affected by the proposed measure. In the furious controversy which raged, issues were raised of great import to an understanding of the future activities of the PEA, and brief reference will have to be made to them.

The Compromise School Bill was opposed by the majority of New York City's elected representatives in the state legislature, a majority of the city Board of Education, and the vast majority of city school officials, principals, and teachers. Tammany orators let few chances go by to call attention to the dominant class and religious composition of the reform party. They assailed the reformers as "Anglo-Maniacs" who wished to turn the city's public schools into charity schools. [36] Many of the reformers' own oft-stated principles were flung at them. Since the Board of Education was opposed to the Compromise Bill, opponents of the bill were able to appeal to that deeply cherished tenet of progressivism, "home rule." But perhaps the most effective weapon of the opposition was their appeal to the progressive tenet of "popular control." The ward trustees had been a fixture in the city since the 1840's. The reformers' zeal and unseemly haste to have them abolished aroused an enormous amount of suspicion and antagonism. Many highly respected figures in the city, men who were usually found in the ranks of reform —James K. Paulding, the Reverend Henry D. Stimson, and Rabbi F. de Sola Mendes—defected on this issue. The ward trustees, they maintained, kept the people informed about their schools and prevented the Board of Education from neglecting the downtown schools. [37] Finally, the reformers' cry, "Take the schools out of politics," while leaving board appointments in the hands of the Mayor and school finance in

[35] *Educational Review*, X (June, 1895), 99, 102, ed.; *ibid.*, XI (March, 1896), 305ff, ed.; *ibid.*, XI (May, 1896), 512ff, ed.
[36] *New York Herald*, February 19, March 27, April 15, 16, 1896; *New York World*, February 13, March 27, 1896.
[37] *New York Herald*, March 27, 1896; *New York Tribune*, April 16, 1896. Dr. Joseph Mayer Rice also spoke out against the reform school bill because it violated the principle of local control. *New York Tribune*, April 19, 1896.

the hands of the Board of Estimate, also raised eyebrows within as well as without the ranks of municipal reform.[38]

The reformers turned all arguments aside, notably in a series of editorials in the *New York World,* the product of a collaboration between Mrs. Schuyler Van Rensselaer and Butler. It was granted that the public schools were considered by many uptowners as little better than charity schools, shunned by all parents who could afford to shun them. But the fault lay with "the system." The common schools would become truly common schools when they were of high quality, managed as parts of a "coherent, consolidated system, in a way which the public can follow and understand." To the criticism that abolition of the ward trustees would remove the schools from the people, the reformers in-souciantly retorted that what the people want is not local control or to be "in touch" with the schools, but good schools run by experts.[39] As to the criticism that they were in violation of the oft-proclaimed progressive principle which called for the complete separation of the schools from politics, as well as that which called for "home rule," there was little the reformers could say.

The New York school reformers were pragmatists, not ideologists. Politics, not abstractions, dictated their strategy and program.[40] The New Yorkers proclaimed their allegiance to the progressive principle that the schools should be completely divorced from politics but could not go along with the idea, advocated by many progressives, that this could best be accomplished if school board appointments were taken out of the hands of mayors and board members secured through some special

[38] E.g., Dorman B. Eaton, *The Government of Municipalities* (New York, 1899), pp. 405–07.

[39] See the editorials in the *New York World* for January 23, February 16, 18, 20, 1896. See also *New York Tribune,* April 1, 1896, ed.; *Outlook,* LIII (April 4, 1896), 620, ed.; *Educational Review,* XI (April, 1896), 408, ed. The editorials in the *World* were part of a series on the school issue dating back to December, 1895. They were written by Mrs. Van Rensselaer of the PEA, a famous art critic, author, and friend of Joseph Pulitzer, who threw open the editorial pages of the *World* for her. Butler collaborated on their composition; Mrs. Van Rensselaer submitted all her editorials to Butler for his correction and criticism. Mrs. Schuyler Van Rensselaer to Butler, December 4, 1895, January 21, February 8, 1896; and Butler to Mrs. Van Rensselaer, December 13, 1895, January 25, February 3, 1896, all in "The School War." The Van Rensselaer–Butler editorials appeared in the *World* under the following dates: December 8, 9, 13, 14, 27, 1895; January 23, 31, February 3, 5, 16, 18, 20, 1896.

[40] I have been much influenced in this discussion by the Sayre–Kaufman analysis of the strategic uses of the "rules of the game" in the contest of New York City politics. *Op. cit.,* pp. 105–08.

form of general election. Given the Democratic proclivity of the city, school board membership could not be thrown open to election. The reformers preferred to take their chances with a Board of Education appointed by the Mayor. Their cry, "Take the schools out of politics," was the cry of the "outs" wanting to be the "ins" and must be seen as part of the strategic vocabulary employed in the contest to decide who gets what and how much of the prizes the city's educational system has to offer.

The same observations hold good for the New York school reformers and the issue of "home rule," perhaps the most deeply cherished principle of *fin de siècle* progressivism. The New Yorkers followed a small, dissenting group of progressives, ably represented by Professor Goodnow of Columbia University, who advocated a pragmatic approach to the question.[41] Considerations of political advantage based on the makeup of the party in power in City Hall and in Executive Mansion in Albany, and not ideology, dictated their strategy. The reformers appealed to the principle of home rule, violated it, or ignored it, as it suited their purpose. Since New York City usually votes Democratic, while the State Legislature is normally Republican, city school politics would frequently present the anomalous spectacle of Tammany raising the banner of "home rule," and insisting on closer city-school relationships, while the reformers cry "state control" and insist that Albany remain a privileged participant in city school affairs. In short, the issue here, to borrow Carl Becker's famous aphorism, was not "home rule," but who should rule at home. No one understood this better than the framers of the Compromise School Bill of 1896.

Mayor Strong called for hearings on the Compromise Bill on April 15 and 16. As proof of its effective work in Albany, the PEA became for the first time the focus of public controversy. There had been prior indications that its lobbying tactics were effective since Tammany orators in Albany frequently anathematized the measure as the "pink tea bill" and "the bill of the four hundred." [42] But now that the Compromise Bill was back in New York City, the pressure on the PEA was increased. On April 15, 1896, at the crowded public meeting at which foes of the bill were heard, Commissioner Strauss of the Board of Education charged that the Governor's special message followed word by word the brief submitted to him by "that body of 'women

[41] Frank J. Goodnow, *Municipal Government* (New York, 1910), pp. 40–42; Rollins, *op. cit.*, p. 95.
[42] *New York Times*, March 21, 27, 1896; *New York Herald*, April 1, 1896; *New York World*, April 8, 1896.

busybodies' who call themselves the Public Education Society [sic]." [43]
A few days later a teacher spokesman, referring to a PEA circular in
support of the bill, sent to all the public school teachers, and signed by
Mrs. Rainsford, asked ominously, "Does it mean sectarianism?" [44]

Despite a last-minute petition in opposition to the Compromise Bill,
containing 100,000 signatures, Mayor Strong signed the measure on
April 23rd.[45] The leaders of the PEA were delighted. "We can be proud
of our reform Mayor," Mrs. Mead stoutly declared.[46] Mrs. Edward R.
Hewitt expressed deep relief. "Philadelphia," she said, in a statement
to the press, "is the only city of any size which still clings to the trustee
system and we certainly don't want to copy ring-ridden Philadelphia." [47]
"The long fight to free the public school system of New York City from
the control of a clique and of petty political bosses is ended," wrote
Nicholas Murray Butler. "The battle has been won." [48]

Not quite. The millenium was at least a few years away. The
passage into law of the Compromise Bill represented a defeat for
Tammany and a great victory for the reform party, true. But Tammany
would be around for a long time to come, and the "outs" would have
to appeal again and again to the State Legislature to seek advantage
through changes in the rules governing New York's school system.
However, if in politics *the* battle is seldom won, nevertheless battles—
sometimes extremely important battles—are won. The school war of
1896 was such a battle. Passage of the Compromise Bill was calculated
to improve the city school system by providing a simpler machinery of
operation, centralizing that operation, and opening up the way for a fuller
utilization of professionals in the management of the system. Perhaps
more important, the new school law gave the reformers full control
of the city school system.

The president of the PEA remarked in 1897 that Mayor Strong
would be known to a grateful posterity as New York's "Public School

[43] *New York Herald*, April 16, 1896; *New York Tribune*, April 16, 1896; *New
York Times*, April 16, 1896.

[44] *New York Herald*, April 19, 1896. One of the school reformers reported that
a young teacher had begged him to speak up against the Compromise Bill because
she feared that under the new system "all Roman Catholic teachers would have
to go." *New York Tribune*, April 17, 1896.

[45] *New York Herald*, April 24, 1896; *New York World*, April 24, 1896; *New
York Tribune*, April 24, 1896.

[46] *New York Herald*, April 24, 1896.

[47] *Ibid.* For a glimpse of the PEA and the school war with Mrs. Hewitt at the
center of things, see Edward Ringwood Hewitt, *Those Were the Days* (New York,
1943), pp. 195–96.

[48] *Educational Review*, XI (May, 1896), 512–16, ed.

Mayor" and that his Board of Education would likewise be remembered
as the city's "first Public School Board." [49] Here is the key to the real
significance of the reform bill. It abolished the existing Board of Education. Subsequently, Mayor Strong used his appointive power to fashion
a new, reform Board of Education. Charles C. Burlingham, Henry Taft,
Henry H. Rogers, Nathaniel A. Prentice, Otto Bannard, James Speyer,
Ellery Anderson, and John A. Agar were some of his appointees.[50]
The Board of Education, in turn, initiated steps to make New York's
schools "the equal of those in any other city in the world." In March,
1898, to cap two years of unprecedented school advance, William H.
Maxwell, the choice of Butler and the reform party, was chosen to be
the first Superintendent of Schools of the Greater City of New York,
a position he would fill with greatness for the next twenty years.[51] Now
school reforms came pell mell.[52]

Passage of the Compromise Bill, then, opened up a new era in
education in New York City. It paved the way for the conquest of the
city school system by progressive education. The PEA, through circulars,
petitions, delegations, and personal influence, helped considerably to

[49] *New York Times,* November 20, 1897.

[50] New York City, Board of Education, *Fifty-Fifth Annual Report,* 1896,
pp. 304; *New York Tribune,* September 11, 1896, ed.; Riis, *The Battle with the
Slum,* p. 409; Wheeler, *op. cit.,* pp. 344–46; Palmer, *op. cit.,* pp. 189–97; Charles C.
Burlingham, "Reminiscences," Oral History Project, Special Collections, Butler
Library, Columbia University, p. 3.

[51] *Educational Review,* XV (April, 1898), pp. 414–15; Butler to Mrs. Van
Rensselaer, February 18, 1898, Columbiana Collection; Burlingham, *op. cit.,* p. 14;
Everett P. Wheeler, *Sixty Years of American Life* (New York, 1917), p. 347; Sam-
uel P. Abelow, *Dr. William H. Maxwell* (New York, 1934), pp. 62–66; New York
City, Board of Education, *Journal,* March 7, 15, 1898; *New York Times,* March
16, 1898; *New York Sun,* March 16, 1898.

One price the reformers had to pay to get Maxwell and to keep the Strong-
appointed Board of Education was the anomalous and unwieldly Borough School
System embodied in the Greater New York City Charter. In 1902 the city school
law was once again thoroughly revamped. The Borough System was abolished, and
power and authority were concentrated in a central Board of Education composed
of forty-six members and in the City School Superintendent and Board of Superintendents. New York City, Board of Education, *The First Fifty Years, 1898–1948:
Fiftieth Annual Report of the Superintendent of Schools,* pp. 5–6, 23–25; Rose
Naomi Cohen, *The Financial Control of Education in the Consolidated City of
New York* (New York, 1948), pp. 23–43; Palmer, *op. cit.,* Chaps. XXXIII,
XXXV; Abelow, *op. cit.,* pp. 69–72, 85–96.

[52] Riis, *The Battle with the Slum,* Chap. XIII and *passim;* Jacob A. Riis, *A
Ten Years War* (New York, 1902), pp. 208–10, 224ff; Jacob A. Riis, *The Making
of an American* (New York, 1901), pp. 326ff; New York City, Department of Education, City Superintendent of Schools, *Seventh Annual Report,* 1905, pp. 491–502;
Palmer, *op. cit.,* pp. 189ff; "A Tale of Two Cities," *The Dial,* XXIV (February 16,
1898), 101–03, ed.

get the new law enacted. Jacob Riis paid tribute to the effectiveness of the ladies when he wrote: "In the struggle for school reform they struck the telling blows and the credit of the victory is justly theirs." [53]

III

With the enactment of the Compromise School Bill, the first phase of the PEA's career came to an end. During the first few years of its existence the PEA was simply an appendage of Good Government Club E: its leaders actually were Nicholas Murray Butler and J. Augustus Johnson; it was concerned in this period almost exclusively with the good government phase of school reform. But after the enactment of the school bill Club E became absorbed with ordinary politics, and Butler became less interested in both local politics and the PEA. Subsequently, after 1896, the PEA was virtually reborn. This can be seen in its leadership, its strategy and tactics, and its program.

Several important events in the life of the PEA in late 1896 may be remarked upon. In the first place, the PEA moved out of Club E's headquarters into offices of its own, first at 64 Madison Avenue and then at 8 West 40th Street. In the second place, the Association proliferated two branches: a West Side branch and, more important, an East Side Auxiliary. The East Side Auxiliary was composed of a group of ladies active in the Women's Conference of the New York Ethical Culture Society. Headed by Mrs. Miriam Sutro Price, it was in a double sense auxiliary: it reported to the Ethical Culture Society as well as to the PEA.[54] The close relationship thus established between the two reformist groups has been a lasting one. From 1896 down to the present, the Ethical Culture Society has been represented in the inner core leadership of the PEA.

There was an almost complete turnover in PEA membership after the school war. Mrs. Charles Runkle, Mrs. Ben Ali Higgin, and Mrs. Edward R. Hewitt dropped out of the Association to devote their time and energy to the League for Political Education, the City History Club, and the Woman's Municipal League. Their places were taken by Mrs.

[53] Riis, *The Battle with the Slum*, p. 371; see also Riis, *The Making of an American*, pp. 362–63; Riis, *A Ten Years War*, p. 228.
[54] Minutes of the Women's Conference of the New York Society for Ethical Culture, January 27, 1896, in the files of the Ethical Culture Society, 2 West 64th Street, New York City; Women's Conference of the New York Society for Ethical Culture, *65 Years of Study, Service, Friendship: 1893–1958* (New York, 1958), pp. 3–4; Women's Conference of the New York Society for Ethical Culture, *Annual Report*, 1897, pp. 63–64; PEA, *Annual Reports*, 1896–1900.

Price, and Winifred Buck and Helen Moore, both of the University Settlement. Perhaps the most important change in the early life of the PEA occurred in the spring of 1896 when Mrs. Rainsford withdrew from the presidency. She was succeeded by Mrs. Van Rensselaer, the PEA's most widely known member.[55] By the force of her character, her personality, and her interests, Mrs. Van Rensselaer so impressed herself on the Association as to make of it during her tenure as president (1896–1905) merely the lengthened shadow of herself.

Mariana Griswold Van Rensselaer was born in New York City in 1851 to George and Lydia (Alley) Griswold. Her forebears helped settle New England. Her father was one of the famous merchants of the time.[56] Like other young ladies of her privileged station, Miss Griswold was educated by private tutors at home and by travel abroad. She became an expert in archeology, art, and architecture. In 1886 her first book, *American Figure Painters*, appeared. Many other books and articles soon followed from her prolific pen. By the turn of the century she was acknowledged the country's foremost woman art critic, as well as a versatile and gifted writer in the field of *belles lettres*.

In 1873 Miss Griswold married Schuyler Van Rensselaer, who also came of a family with a long history. The Van Rensselaers with their son George, their only child, born in 1877, made their home in New Brunswick, New Jersey. But after the death of her husband in 1884, Mrs. Van Rensselaer returned to New York City. For the remainder of her long and active life she made her home at 9 West 10th Street in lower Manhattan.

By birth and breeding a true aristocrat, Mrs. Van Rensselaer was also a great democrat. Upon the death of her son in 1892, Mrs. Van Rensselaer went down to the University Settlement to work with the young there and forget her bereavement. As a volunteer club leader she shared her cultural riches with a group of young East Side girls. The subjects she chose to read and discuss with the young members of her "Wadsworth Literary Circle" were Egyptian art and archeology and the literary classics of England and America.[57] She poured scorn on up-towners who feared that the immigrant children were being over-

[55] PEA, *Annual Report*, 1896, p. 10.
[56] *New York Herald Tribune*, January 21, 1934, obituary; *New York Times*, January 21, 1934, obituary; Talbot Faulkner Hamlin, "Mariana Griswold Van Rensselaer," *Dictionary of American Biography*, XIX, 207–08.
[57] University Settlement Society, *Report of the Year's Work*, 1894, p. 18; *New York Times*, February 8, 1934, Helen Moore, Letters to the Editor; Mariana Griswold Van Rensselaer, "Places in New York," *Century*, LIII (February, 1897), 511–12.

educated in the settlement classes and in the public schools.[58] Her striking short stories of life on the East Side, based on her experiences at the settlement, reveal an understanding, a compassion, and a respect for the working classes extraordinary for one brought up in her fair world.[59]

Despite her status in the world of art and literature, Mrs. Van Rensselaer was by no means a "new woman." Her opposition to woman suffrage was vigorous and outspoken. Women, she believed, were best fitted by reason of their "peculiar temperament" to keep house and to advance literature, science, art, and philanthropy.[60] Mrs. Van Rensselaer's attitude toward woman suffrage, however, was no barrier to what she considered her duties as a citizen. Her work with the young at the University Settlement stimulated her interest in education, and she eagerly accepted the appointment as school inspector when Mayor Strong offered it to her in 1895.[61] Her indignation aroused by the disgraceful school conditions she saw in her downtown district, and furious at the ward trustee system which she held responsible, she temporarily discarded her repugnance for politics and crusaded for the enactment of the Compromise School Bill. When the struggle was over, Nicholas Murray Butler wrote her that she was entitled to look upon the new law in large measure as a personal triumph.[62] Despite her name, her renown, and her great beauty, Mrs. Van Rensselaer was an extraordinarily diffident individual. It was probably Butler, whom she admired and liked enormously, who persuaded her to take over the presidency of the PEA from Mrs. Rainsford in the spring of 1896.

[58] Mrs. Schuyler Van Rensselaer, "Our Public Schools: A Reply," *North American Review*, CLXIX (July, 1899), 77–89. This was a reply to Rebecca Harding Davis, "The Curse in Education," *North American Review*, CLXVIII (May, 1899), 609–14. See also the letter to the editor of *The Critic*, XXVI (October 31, 1896), 270, by Mrs. Van Rensselaer and Richard W. Gilder.

[59] There is a collection of Mrs. Van Rensselaer's short stories in her *One Man Who Was Content* (New York, 1897). See also the following magazine articles by Mrs. Van Rensselaer: "People in New York," *Century*, XLIX (February, 1895), 534–48; "Places in New York," *ibid.*, LIII (February, 1897), 501–16; "Mid-Summer in New York," *ibid.*, LXII (August, 1901), 483–501.

[60] Mrs. Schuyler Van Rensselaer, "Should We Ask for the Suffrage?" [1895], a pamphlet in a collection of anti-suffrage pamphlets entitled *Why Women Do Not Want the Ballot*, Butler Library, Columbia University, New York City.

[61] *New York World*, May 16, 1895.

[62] Butler to Mrs. Schuyler Van Rensselaer, April 24, 1896, "The School War"; *New York World*, April 24, 1896, ed. Upon being praised, with Butler, in the *World* editorial, Mrs. Van Rensselaer wrote Butler that she was abashed at being bracketed with him when she thought of what his services had meant for so many years, and what hers had meant for just a few months. Mrs. Schuyler Van Rensselaer to Butler, April 25, 1896, "The School War."

Upon taking office as president, Mrs. Van Rensselaer's first steps were to inaugurate a radical shift in PEA strategy and tactics, and to embark the PEA upon a new program. Through 1895 and 1896 the PEA had employed the tactic of public criticism of school officials in order to gain its ends. But after the enactment of the Compromise Bill in May 1896, the PEA disengaged itself from any public identification with anti-Tammany politics and ceased its overt criticism of the school system and its leaders. With steady progress in the schools, allies on a "liberal and progressive" Board of Education, and a friend and ally in City School Superintendent Maxwell, the PEA disengaged itself from ordinary politics and decided "to work with and not against school authorities." [63] But, Mrs. Van Rensselaer stated, the PEA hoped never to forget that its main task was to stimulate the citizens of New York to a deeper and more intelligent interest in the public schools and, next, to show school authorities the public was watching them, ready to criticize or appreciate, as the case might be.[64] In practice, however, the PEA, under Mrs. Van Rensselaer, renounced the use of overt criticism, depending now for its influence in the city school system exclusively upon the prestige and contacts of its leaders. These were sufficient to give the PEA the implicit status of "insider." To what ends it used its privileged access, or influence, is the subject for the next section of this chapter.

IV

After the enactment of the school reform bill the PEA turned its attention to questions of school policy. Its main concern, of course, became the schools on the East Side:

> the schools below 14th Street where the system had been longest at work and where it has had to deal with [a] peculiar environment, an almost foreign population in some localities—and where if the system had not adapted itself to or conquered that environment it was clearly no system for the city at all.[65]

No school reformers in New York City ever forgot the existence of the city's foreign population. The leaders of the PEA, like Jacob Riis and so many others, believed the chief function of the public schools was to Americanize the children of the East Side. In her inaugural

[63] PEA, *Annual Report*, 1897, p. 13; Mariana Griswold Van Rensselaer, "The Public Education Association of New York," *Educational Review*, XVI (October, 1898), 210. In 1900, Jacob Riis, a warm friend and booster of the PEA, noted that the ladies were then working as energetically with school authorities as they before worked against them. A *Ten Years War*, p. 228.

[64] Van Rensselaer, "The Public Education Association of New York," p. 219.

[65] PEA, *Annual Report*, 1896, pp. 8–9.

address on November 20, 1896, Mrs. Van Rensselaer dedicated the PEA to a special effort to aid in sending all children of foreign nationality to the public schools rather than to parochial, national, or charity schools. "Put twenty-eight different nationalities on one bench," the PEA's president confidently asserted, "and each one will turn out a loyal American." [66]

The PEA still needed a program of activities. Library Committee, Legislative Committee, Lecture Committee, and School Visiting Committee assuredly were not sustenance enough for an organization which had made a name for itself in the school war, and which had such powerful and influential allies on the Board of Education as had the Association. Casting about for a program, the PEA quite naturally turned for inspiration and ideas to the social settlement movement. From the beginning the Association had the closest ties with the University Settlement, down on the Lower East Side. James B. Reynolds, the settlement's head worker, was a charter member of the PEA's Advisory Council; Mrs. Van Rensselaer was a volunteer club leader at the settlement; Winifred Buck and Helen Moore, two of the PEA's most active members in the decade 1895–1905, were settlement residents, the former a specialist in club work, the latter the settlement's beloved librarian. Furthermore, in February 1897 when a Woman's Auxiliary of the University Settlement Society was organized, its president was none other than Mrs. Van Rensselaer, and many of its other officers and committee chairmen were PEA activists.[67] In short, after 1896 the PEA became, in effect, an auxiliary to the University Settlement. In the first place, this meant that the PEA would echo the settlement cry that the public schools must become evening play-centers for the young.

"The children ask us daily the great question of the East Side— 'And what shall we do with our nights?' " Thus spoke a harried James B. Reynolds in 1896.[68] At night, on the teeming East Side, the young had no place to study or play. They drifted into gangs and wandered into all kinds of mischief. From their beginnings the social settlements on the East Side tried to meet the social and recreational needs of the young through club and play-center programs. Hundreds of youngsters availed themselves of the evening program at the University Settlement, but hundreds more were shut out for lack of room. In the summer of

---

[66] *New York World*, November 21, 1896; *New York Tribune*, November 21, 1896; Van Rensselaer, "Places in New York," pp. 511–12, 515.

[67] University Settlement Society, *Report for the Year 1897*, pp. 5, 13, 58–60; University Settlement Society, *Report for the Year 1898*, pp. 2, 60, 74–77.

[68] University Settlement Society, *Report for the Year 1896*, p. 21.

1896 Mrs. Van Rensselaer rented the building at 200 Eldridge Street for the use of the settlement, and the building (it soon became known as the Settlement Annex) was soon filled with youngsters.[69] But here was a neighborhood need which all the social settlements in the city combined could never satisfy. The large, expensive, public school buildings, standing deserted afternoons and evenings in the midst of this great need, would have to become more flexible, would have to meet the needs of the neighborhood.

As early as 1892 Jacob Riis had argued that the public schools should be open at night for the use of boys' clubs.[70] In late 1896 the Council of Good Government Clubs, of which Riis was now General Agent, attempted to open some East Side public schools at night, to no avail.[71] Despite the urging of Riis, Good Government clubs, social settlements, and institutional churches, the Board of Education obdurately maintained that it had no right to open the public schools in the afternoon or evening for "other than school purposes." [72] The situation was thus deadlocked between the conservatism of the formalistic and economy-minded Board of Education and the needs of the children when the PEA stepped into the picture.

In April 1897 the PEA appealed to the Committee on Instruction of the Board of Education for permission to conduct some boys' clubs in the evening, as an experiment, in P.S. 7, one of the Tenth Ward schools. The Committee on Instruction, now dominated by the reform element, recommended that the PEA's request be granted. The full Board of Education, whose president was now Charles C. Burlingham, acquiesced. In May 1897 Winifred Buck organized two boys' clubs, "junior Good Government Clubs," in P.S. 7. In September of the same year the PEA was permitted to move its experiment to P.S. 20 on Chrystie Street, where six boys' clubs were soon in operation.[73] These events marked a milestone in the history of public education in

[69] *Ibid.*, pp. 21–23.
[70] Jacob A. Riis, *The Children of the Poor* (New York, 1892), pp. 238–39; Jacob A. Riis, "Playgrounds for City Schools," *Century*, XLVIII (September, 1894), 665.
[71] *New York Times*, January 7, 1897; Riis, *A Ten Years War*, pp. 229–30; Emma Louise Ware, *Jacob A. Riis: Police Reporter, Reformer, Useful Citizen* (New York, 1939), p. 153.
[72] New York City, Board of Education, *Journal*, November 4, 1896, January 13, 1897.
[73] New York City, Board of Education, *Journal*, May 5, October 6, 1897; Winifred Buck, "An Experiment in Citizen Training," *Popular Science Monthly*, LII (November, 1897), 111–16; Winifred Buck, *Boy's Self-Governing Clubs* (New York, 1903), p. 49; Riis, *A Ten Years War*, p. 230; Van Rensselaer, "The Public Education Association of New York," p. 217.

New York. Never before had the city schools been opened for "other than instructional purposes."

The Boys Club Committee of the PEA disbanded on October 30, 1899.[74] By then, another great reform triumph had been secured. In the spring of 1898, the reformers, led by Charles Stover, J. K. Paulding, Winifred Buck, Elizabeth S. Williams, Charles C. Burlingham, and the Outdoor Recreation League, pushed through an amendment to the school section of the City Charter which specifically provided that the public schools of New York City could be used not only for educational purposes but also for "recreation and other public uses." In the fall of 1899 the city Board of Education opened five public schools on the lower East Side in the evenings for the use of the children of the neighborhood. Books, games, and supervisors were provided by the Board.[75] There was no longer any need for the PEA's boys' clubs.

The PEA's experiment was small, the number of children involved insignificant, and the expenses trivial. The tactics, principles, and long-term objectives were crucial. Once again, privately subsidized experiment and political influence had forced innovations in the city school system. Moreover, there was a crucial objective at stake. The PEA's stated purpose in sponsoring the boys' clubs was "to prove the suitability of school buildings for other than instructional purposes."[76] By 1899 this had come to mean something more to the PEA than simply the opening of schools for boys' clubs, or even the opening of schools as play centers for the young of both sexes. The PEA's objective now was to make the public school a neighborhood social center for parents and adults as well as children. Here, too, the PEA borrowed a note from the broader progressive movement.

In the late 1890's the extension of the functions of city government to meet the needs of the city's inhabitants became an important part of reform thinking. The decade 1895–1905 witnessed the beginnings of a vast expansion of municipal activities.[77] The public school was right

[74] PEA, *Annual Report for the Year* 1899–1900, pp. 32–33.

[75] New York City, Board of Education, *Journal*, March 23, June 13, 1898; Joseph Lee, *Constructive and Preventive Philanthropy* (New York, 1902), pp. 192–93; Riis, *The Battle with the Slum*, Chap. XIV, *passim*.

[76] PEA, *Annual Report*, 1899, p. 19; Van Rensselaer, "Our Public Schools: A Reply," p. 881; Buck, *Boys' Self-Governing Clubs*, p. 50; Lee, *op. cit.*, pp. 212–13.

[77] Charles Zueblin, *American Municipal Progress* (New York, 1905), *passim*; Milo Roy Maltbie, "Municipal Functions: A Study of the Development, Scope and Tendency of Municipal Socialism," *Municipal Affairs*, II (December, 1898), 587–799; Charles R. Woodruff, "Expansion of Municipal Activities," *Arena*, XXXIII (January, 1905), 128–34; Frederick C. Howe, *The City, The Hope of Democracy* (New York, 1905), esp. Chap. XIX; Roy Lubove, "The Twentieth Century City: The Progressive as Municipal Reformer," *Mid-America*, XLI (October, 1959), 195–209.

in the center of this movement. The public school, shorn of its formalism, its functions vastly expanded beyond that of instruction of children —"socialized" was the popular term—was one of the reformers' key answers to the problem of urban welfare. New York's East Side and East Sides throughout the nation were to be regenerated through an extended use of school buildings which would take in adults as well as children and, at public expense, provide them with the complete social life they could not affort to purchase for themselves. The spearhead for this reform proposal was the social settlement movement. Philanthropist and social worker James K. Paulding, one of the pioneer University Settlement residents, expounded the new view of the school as early as 1897. For Paulding, the big schoolhouses were to be centers of neighborhood life—artistic, cultural, recreational, and intellectual, for all ages and sexes, and at all times precisely as the social settlements were.[78] In fact, a few years later James B. Reynolds actually proposed to Jacob Riis that they annex a public school and make it "the neighborhood house and soul." To which Riis enthusiastically replied, "Why should they not be used by the people Sunday and weekday and day and night, for whatever will serve their ends . . .?"[79] It was the PEA's fortune to demonstrate the settlement ideal in the public school.

Another bold innovation in the inspired effort to democratize culture

[78] James K. Paulding, "The Public School as a Center of Community Life," *Educational Review*, XIII (February, 1898), 147–54.

[79] Riis, *The Battle with the Slum*, pp. 398–400, 407. The Citizens Union was another important bastion of the new thinking in education in the city; Citizens Union, *More and Better Schools* (New York, 1897); "The New York Campaign: What Reform Has Done for Children," *Outlook*, LXXV (September 26, 1903), 201–02, ed. So was Teachers College, Columbia University. The Speyer School, one of the Teachers College experimental schools, was a combination school and social settlement. Lawrence A. Cremin, David A. Shannon, and Mary Evelyn Townsend, *A History of Teachers College, Columbia University* (New York, 1954), pp. 104–06; Charles Herbert Levermore, *Samuel Train Dutton* (New York, 1922), pp. 63–65. For Chicago, see James Weber Linn, *Jane Addams: A Biography* (New York, 1935), p. 235. There is a thorough discussion of the social center movement in Morris I. Berger, "The Immigrant, the Settlement, and the Public School" (unpublished Ph.D. thesis, Columbia University, 1956).

Characteristically, the reformers looked to Europe as the model for the extended use of school buildings: Robert Archey Woods, *English Social Movements* (New York, 1891), p. 256; Albert Shaw, *Municipal Government in Continental Europe* (New York, 1895), Chaps. I, VI, *passim;* Albert Shaw, *Municipal Government in Great Britain* (New York, 1905), pp. 138–41, 219–21, 308–13; Frederick C. Howe, *The British City: The Beginning of Democracy* (New York, 1907), p. 342. Actually, the community use of the school was in an old American tradition. Schools in colonial Boston were used for a variety of public purposes: Pauline Holmes, *A Tercentenary History of the Boston Public Latin School, 1635–1935* (Cambridge, Mass., 1935), pp. 502–05. And American rural, country, or frontier schools had always been centers of community life.

was attempted by the PEA in 1902. In that year the Board of Education gave the Association permission to hold concerts on Sunday afternoons in P.S. 33, on West 28th Street. The average attendance was over 400. The opposition of some Protestant clergy, however, brought the innovation to an end after its first season.[80] But this was a negligible setback for reform. By 1905 the New York City Board of Education was running a most astonishing variety of activities for young and old, day and night, every day but Sunday, and in the summers too.[81] Many informed contemporaries—Jacob Riis, Lillian Betts, Mary Simkhovitch, Joseph Lee, Robert A. Woods, and Gaylord S. White—considered the opening of New York's schools for a wide variety of public uses as one of the great developments in American educational reform, and all gave the credit for this development to the PEA. The boys' club was the entering wedge.[82]

V

The PEA's program during its first decade was actually extremely modest. Besides play centers, the PEA took up seriously only a few branches of work. On November 21, 1896, in her maiden address as PEA president, Mrs. Van Rensselaer proposed that the Association sponsor a school in the Tombs jail for the boys and young men confined there pending trial. She also proposed that the Association place works of art in every schoolhouse on the East Side and see to it that the barren, ugly schoolrooms were painted in bright and attractive colors.[83] The proposed work in the Tombs had long been urged by Jacob Riis.[84] At that time the Tombs housed a motley crowd of youth, some

[80] *New York Times*, December 11, 1902; Riis, *The Battle with the Slum*, p. 407; Mrs. Vladimir Simkhovitch, "The Enlarged Function of the Public School," *Proceedings*, National Conference of Charities and Corrections (Portland, 1904), p. 479; Winifred Buck, "Work and Play in the Public Schools," *Outlook*, LXXX, (July 22, 1905), 725–26; PEA, *Annual Report for the Year 1902–1903*, pp. 25–26.

[81] New York City, Department of Education, City Superintendent of Schools, *Seventh Annual Report*, 1905, pp. 367–96; "Educational Organization and Progress in American Cities," *The Annals*, XXV (1905), 161; Lillian W. Betts, "The Child Out of School Hours," *Outlook*, LXXV (September 26, 1903), 209–16; Simkhovitch, *op. cit.*, pp. 471–86; Buck, "Work and Play in the Public Schools," pp. 725–32; Riis, *The Battle with the Slum*, Chap. XV; Palmer, *op. cit.*, pp. 287–89.

[82] Paulding, *op. cit.*, p. 152; Woods and Kennedy, *The Settlement Horizon*, p. 292; Betts, *op. cit.*, p. 209; Simkhovitch, *op. cit.*, p. 481; Lee, *op. cit.*, pp. 192–93; Riis, *The Battle with the Slum*, pp. 397–99.

[83] *New York Tribune*, November 21, 1896.

[84] Council of Confederated Good Government Clubs, *Report to the Council of Confederated Good Government Clubs for the Six Months Ending November 1, 1896 by Jacob A. Riis* (New York, 1896).

vicious and depraved, others merely truants from school, many later to be found innocent of any wrongdoing. The PEA promptly won the approval of the Commissioner of Correction, organized a Tombs School Committee, and launched the "Tombs School." The school was supervised by David Willard, a University Settlement resident. It gave the boys a short course in the elements of the three R's, instruction in personal hygiene, and some vocational guidance. Between 1897 and 1905 the number of youths who attended Mr. Willard's school numbered 6,949, at a cost to the PEA of more than $4,000.[85]

The art-in-the-schools movement was a progressive movement of considerable dimension and some importance at the turn of the century. Its roots go back to London of the 1880's and John Ruskin who, in his endeavor to bring culture within the reach of all, organized the Arts for Schools Society. Toynbee Hall in the slums of London had similar interests. American social settlement founders—Stanton Coit of the University Settlement and Jane Addams of Hull House—deeply influenced by the teaching of Ruskin and the example of Toynbee Hall, brought the movement to the United States. It quickly became something of a fad with women's clubs all over the country.[86] It was quite natural, given its close ties with the University Settlement and its president's own absorbing interest in art, that the PEA would take up the public school art movement as one of the most important branches of its work during its first decade.

Late in 1896 the PEA proudly announced that the city Superintendent of School Buildings had agreed to consult with its Art Committee with reference to the colors to be chosen for the walls of the schoolrooms, and that the Board of Education would permit their decoration with pictures and casts purchased by the PEA and approved by the Board.[87] The benefits to accrue from the decorated schools were numerous. Attractive, cheerful schoolrooms would stimulate the little ones in their lessons. Genius and talent would be fostered by the pictures and casts. The moral and ethical motive was ever present; with Plato, the

[85] PEA, *Annual Reports*, 1897–1905; Van Rensselaer, "The Public Education Association of New York," p. 216; Riis, *A Ten Years War*, pp. 231–32; Riis, *The Battle with the Slum*, p. 378.

[86] Woods, *op. cit.*, pp. 204–06; Rho Fisk Zueblin, "Public School Art Societies," *Chautauquan*, XXXVIII (October, 1903), 169–72; James P. Haney, "Decoration of Schools and School-Rooms," *Municipal Affairs*, III (December, 1899), 672–86; Charles Mulford Robinson, "Improvement in City Life," *Atlantic*, LXXXIII (May, 1899), 658.

[87] Mariana Griswold Van Rensselaer, "Pictures for Our Public Schools," *Harper's Weekly*, XLI (December 25, 1897), 1295; PEA, *Annual Report*, 1897, p. 5.

progressives believed firmly in the influence of beautiful forms and sights on right moral development.[88] And, as Winifred Buck pointed out, the decorated schools could serve as local art galleries for the benefit of the neighborhood.[89] In 1901 the Board of Education allowed the PEA to hold two public exhibitions in P.S. 7 on the East Side, completely decorated with reproductions of the masterpieces of Europe and America.[90] By 1905 the ladies had raised and spent over $10,000 in order to decorate the public's schools and had stimulated wide interest in the work.[91]

In the progressive fashion, the PEA was concerned chiefly with the use of the public schools for other than instructional purposes. Yet it did not completely overlook the traditional purpose of the schools. A minor theme in its argument for the introduction of good works of art into the public schools was their value as a stimulant to the children's interest in their lessons. Two branches spawned by the Art Committee— the Portfolio Committee and the Nature Material Committee—were even more positively concerned with aiding teachers to teach and young scholars to learn. Though art and nature study had recently been introduced into the elementary grades of the New York school system, school authorities had not yet provided any visual aids or nature materials, and the school trip was as yet unknown in New York. The Portfolio Committee collected and mounted on cards illustrative materials of all sorts, appropriate for aiding the children's school lessons. By 1903 the PEA had distributed among 188 schools more than 10,000 small, mounted pictures.[92] In that year the Portfolio Committee disbanded. Its work was so successful and clearly so essential (and inexpensive) that after six years of private philanthropic effort the Board of Education took over the job of supplying teachers with suitable pictures for the illustration of school studies.

It was a natural step for the PEA to take to move from supplying teachers and students with images of things to supplying them with the actual objects. The PEA's Nature Committee collected and dis-

[88] Van Rensselaer, "Pictures," p. 1295; Van Rensselaer, "The Public Education Association of New York," p. 214; Winifred Buck, "Pictures in Our Public Schools," *Municipal Affairs*, VI (June, 1902), 189–97.

[89] Buck, "Work and Play in the Public Schools," p. 725.

[90] *New York Tribune*, June 16, 1901; PEA, *Annual Report for the Year 1901–1902*, pp. 23–28.

[91] PEA, *Report of Ten Years Work, 1895–1905*, p. 7. By 1904 the Municipal Art Society of New York was ready to take up the work. Municipal Art Society of New York, *Report of the Committee on Decoration of Public Schools*, Bulletin No. 8, 1904.

[92] PEA, *Annual Reports*, 1896–1905.

tributed among the East Side public schools flowers, fruits, mosses, vegetables, birds' nests, wasps' nests, evergreen sprigs, cones, nuts, shells, cocoons, and many other objects of nature gathered by members or friends who owned country places or who refreshed themselves at Newport during the summer. The good ladies could not conceive how any child cut off from rural life could become physically and morally strong, and they dedicated themselves to continuing their work until something from the sea or the mountains—a talisman—had been given to every child in every public school in the city.[93]

Despite the blatant sentimentality of this Romance of Nature, the results were good. Other agencies were working to alleviate the material evils of the wretched tenements and, as G. Stanley Hall and others were pointing out, the subject matter of the school primers was, after all, largely country life, and few city children knew anything about the country.[94] Furthermore, even here, in nature work, neighborhood needs were not forgotten. In 1900 the PEA, in cooperation with the Educational Alliance and the Association of Normal College Alumnae, organized a flower exhibition at P.S. 1 on Henry Street on the East Side. It was reported that the exhibit was attended by over 4,000 children besides many parents from the neighborhood.[95] Now the school had become a museum of natural history, another example of how the schools could be a center for the life of the neighborhood.

VI

The PEA, then, was making its presence felt in the city in many ways. If the PEA had only a local significance, it would still be an important subject for the light it throws on the how and what and why of public school reform in the nation's greatest city. The PEA assumes an even greater importance, however, as an integral part of a

[93] PEA, *Annual Reports*, 1898–1905.

[94] At least a decade earlier, G. Stanley Hall had pointed out that children in urban public schools had almost no idea of the many things about which they studied. His investigations showed that over half the children entering Boston's primary schools had never seen robins, squirrels, the dew, or a rainbow, did not know the origin of meat or milk, and thought butter grew inside of eggs. G. Stanley Hall, "The Contents of Children's Minds on Entering School," *Pedagogical Seminary*, I (1891), pp. 139–73. The head "Kindergartner" of the College Settlement told a similar story. Rabbits and squirrels, she complained, were unknown to the East Side child, and every bird was a pigeon. College Settlements Association, *Seventh Annual Report*, 1896, pp. 18–19.

[95] PEA, *Annual Report for the Year 1899–1900*, p. 26. The flower show became an annual affair. *New York Tribune*, December 11, 1903.

widespread popular movement for the improvement of the public schools, a movement which, in fact, it helped stimulate.

The nation's public schools were directly caught up in the civic renaissance of the 1890's. Even as the New York City reform movement had its school reform phase, just so the nationwide municipal reform movement was accompanied by a tremendous upsurge of interest in school reform approaching revival dimensions. The innumerable national, state, and local reform organizations with general reformist goals which proliferated in the nineties almost always included public school reform among their interests. For instance, the General Federation of Women's Clubs, with its many state and local affiliates, was a powerful school reform lobby.[96] On the municipal level, the Chicago Woman's Club, the Civic Federation of Chicago, the Civic Club of Philadelphia, and the Arundell Good Government Club of Baltimore were extremely influential in school reform.[97] By the late nineties there were also in existence in some of the larger cities of the country organizations concerned exclusively with public school reform. A few were quite ancient; the Public Education Association of Philadelphia and the Women's Educational Association of Boston dated back, respectively, to 1881 and 1862.[98] Most of them were, however, like the PEA of New York City, offspring of the great municipal awakening of the nineties.

So far the numerous groups with an interest of one kind or another in public school reform knew but little of each other. But the nineties were years of association, confederation, and "nationalization" in municipal reform; witness the National Municipal League and the American Civic Association. It was time for school reformers to get together

[96] At the Louisville biennial conference of the General Federation in 1896 a motion was adopted urging all member clubs to use their influence for the betterment of public education; that is, for the introduction of progressive school reforms. Jennie Cunningham Croly, *The History of the Woman's Club Movement in America* (New York, 1898), pp. 154, 181–83; New York State Federation of Woman's Clubs, *Report of the Education Committee* (Syracuse, 1897); Ellen M. Henrotin, "The Co-Operation of Woman's Clubs in the Public Schools," *Proceedings, National Education Association,* 1897, pp. 73–83.

[97] Albert Shaw, "Our 'Civic Renaissance,'" *Review of Reviews,* XI (April, 1898), 420–22; Charles Hirschfeld, *Baltimore, 1870–1900* (Baltimore, 1941), pp. 111, 118; Albion W. Small, "The Civic Federation of Chicago," *American Journal of Sociology,* I (July, 1895), 82; George S. Counts, *School and Society in Chicago* (New York, 1928), pp. 206–13.

[98] Arthur Mann, *Yankee Reformers in the Urban Age* (Cambridge, Mass., 1954), p. 212; Lewis R. Harley, *A History of the Public Education Association of Philadelphia* (Philadelphia, 1896); Frank Dekker Watson, *The Charity Organization Movement in the United States; A Study in American Philanthropy* (New York, 1922), p. 192.

also. In the spring of 1898 the PEA's Lecture Committee, under the leadership of Mrs. William E. D. Scott, a well-known figure in Eastern society, sent out a call to civic groups in the vicinity of New York, inviting them to send representatives to the city for a two-day get-together as guests of the PEA. Ten organizations responded to the PEA's timely call. School reformers came from Boston, Philadelphia, Brookline, Buffalo, and New Haven. Among the participants were Clinton Rogers Woodruff, secretary of the National Municipal League, representing the Philadelphia PEA; Anne Hallowell of the Philadelphia Civic Club; and Samuel T. Dutton of Boston's famed Twentieth Century Club. The conferees discussed ways and means of advancing such school reforms as the removal of the schools from politics and the introduction of art, music, nature study, free lectures, and sanitary and safety improvements into the schools.[99] The interchange of ideas was stimulating, and arrangements were made to meet in Philadelphia the following year. At the Philadelphia meeting the formation of the Conference of Eastern Public Education Associations, with Mrs. Scott as secretary, was announced.[100]

The Eastern Conference was open to all civic organizations with any kind of interest in improving the public schools. Its main objects were to stimulate interest in public education and to provide a forum from which the most progressive educational thought and practices of the day could be disseminated among laymen. The organizers of the Conference insisted that they "were not educators but promoters striving to know from experts what was worth promoting." [101] Meetings, held annually in different host cities, were devoted each year to some different subject of contemporary interest on which some of the leading progressives of the day could be heard: Charles W. Eliot on "The School as a Center of Neighborhood Life"; Winifred Buck on "Play Centres";

[99] *New York Times*, May 14, 1898; *New York Tribune*, May 14, 1898; Mrs. William E. D. Scott, "The Aims and Work of the Conference of Public Education Associations," *The Annals*, XXV (1905), 372; Marian Johonnot Scott, "Conference of Eastern Public Education Associations," *The School Journal*, LXXIV (April 20, 1907), 396; Van Rensselaer, "The Public Education Association of New York," p. 213; PEA, *Annual Report*, 1898, pp. 8–9.

[100] *New York Tribune*, April 30, 1899; *Educational Review*, XVIII (September, 1899), 201, ed.; Scott, "The Aims and Work of the Conference of Public Education Associations," p. 372; Scott, "Conference of Eastern Public Education Associations," p. 396.

[101] Public Education Association of Philadelphia, *Twenty-Fourth Annual Report*, 1905, p. 22; Scott, "The Aims and Work of the Conference of Public Education Associations," p. 372; Scott, "Conference of Eastern Public Education Associations," p. 397.

Joseph Lee on "Playgrounds"; and so forth.[102] By 1900, thanks largely to the tireless missionary activities of Mrs. Scott, the Eastern Conference had become widely known. In 1902 it was invited to join the League of American Municipalities, the American Park and Outdoor Association, the American League for Civic Improvement, the Architectural League, and the National Municipal League in a new "Alliance of Civic Organizations," the brainchild of Charles Mulford Robinson and Clinton Woodruff.[103] To one English visitor, very much impressed with the Eastern Conference and with the PEA's role in the Conference, its chief importance was in bringing middle-class parents "into the spirit of the 'new education.' " [104]

In 1906 the Eastern Conference returned to New York City. The PEA, assisted by several of its New York City allies—the City History Club, the Round Table, and the Woman's Municipal League—organized four days of lectures, trips, discussions, and dinners. As usual the subject of the meeting was one of contemporary interest: "Education as Related to Social Needs." The PEA arranged visits to the Ethical Culture School, the Manhattan Trade School, the Educational Alliance, Teachers College, the Children's School Farm, and several East Side public schools where the latest in the training of mentally defective children could be observed.[105]

Now there were thirty-four organizations affiliated with the Conference. They came from as far west as Minnesota, as far south as Virginia. Maryland, Connecticut, Massachusetts, New Jersey, Pennsylvania, Rhode Island, and Washington, D.C., were represented. Some of the groups were composed exclusively of women, others only of men, still others of both. Some of the groups were interested exclusively in public school reform, others had general civic improvement aims. They

---

[102] Conference of Eastern Public Education Associations, *Bulletin No. 1*, 1902; Conference of Eastern Public Education Associations, *Bulletin No. 2*, 1904; *Eighth Annual Conference of Eastern Public Education Associations, Under the Auspices of the Richmond Education Association* (Richmond, Va., 1905); PEA, *Annual Reports*, 1899–1905.

[103] Clinton Rogers Woodruff, "The Co-Ordination of Civic Effort," *The Annals*, XXV (April, 1905), 359; *Proceedings*, National Municipal League, 1904, pp. 110–12; Frank M. Stewart, *op. cit.*, p. 137.

[104] H. Thiselton Mark, *Individuality and the Moral Aim in American Education* (London, 1901), pp. 205, 211–12.

[105] *New York Tribune*, April 18, 1906; PEA, *Annual Report for the Year 1905–1906*, p. 6; "Education and Social Needs," *Charities and the Commons*, XVI (May 12, 1906), 223–24. For the program, the speeches, a listing of the entire membership of the Eastern Conference, and a description of the activities of several of the member associations, see *The School Journal*, LXXIV (April 20, 1907).

called themselves Educational Union, Monday Afternoon Club, Village Improvement Society, Twentieth Century Club, Civic Club, and Public Education Association. Whatever their home, composition, or name, they had the same object: to improve the public schools and public education by stimulating public interest, promoting innovations, and prodding educational authorities to keep up with "progressive" education. Surely this citizens' movement, whose influence was remarked upon by so many contemporaries, could, with profit, be more thoroughly investigated.[106]

VII

The 1906 meeting of the Eastern Conference marks the end of the first stage of the PEA's career. A completely reorganized PEA, under a new president, played host at this meeting.

In 1896 Mrs. Van Rensselaer had spoken hopefully of grand plans to start as many committees as possible "as the only way to succeed is to interest all New York" in the subject of public education.[107] The PEA succeeded in stimulating interest in only a small segment of a select public—the upper-class clubwoman. The Association had 300 dues-paying members in 1896; it reached a peak membership of 700 in 1899. After 1899 membership steadily declined; by 1905 it was back to about 300. The PEA did start up many new committees—Truant School, Evening Schools, Kindergarten, Vacation Schools, and others. These provided activity for PEA members for a season or two, but then they were disbanded, made superfluous by advances in the city school system. By 1900 the PEA was no longer vitally involved in the city's political life. Its policy of close cooperation with the Board of Education meant that it could not publicly criticize defects in the school system, or agitate overtly for changes in that system. Its very success with play centers and school decoration eliminated its core program. And, most significant, with the success of the play center movement, Mrs. Van Rensselaer deemed the PEA to have fulfilled its function.

[106] Public Education Association of Philadelphia, *Directory of 156 Education Associations and Committees in the United States*, compiled by Dora Keen (Philadelphia, 1907); Mary Ritter Beard, *Woman's Work in Municipalities* (New York, 1915), pp. 38–43 and *passim*; Elsa Denison, *Helping School Children* (Boston, 1912); Ella Lyman Cabot, *Volunteer Help to the Schools* (Boston, 1914); Howard W. Nudd, "Organized Citizen Effort in Behalf of Public Education," *The Annals*, CV (January, 1923), 58–63; Mark, *op. cit.*, pp. 210–23; Lee, *op. cit.*, pp. 212–13; Robinson, *op. cit.*, pp. 654–58; Zueblin, *American Municipal Progress*, Chap. V and *passim*.

[107] *New York Tribune*, November 21, 1896.

Mrs. Van Rensselaer was actually an old-fashioned kind of person. She thought school social centers were the ultimate objective of school reform, while school reform had just started to pick up momentum. Mrs. Van Rensselaer had great faith in the public school, but she believed that there were limits to what the school should and could do. It should not imitate ancient Sparta, she protested, and supersede church and family. While she believed firmly in a certain measure of manual training for the young, she was utterly opposed to vocational education, the subject by 1900 beginning to agitate the educational world. The function of the school, she asserted, was to train the young for life and not for any special walk of life.[108] The views of the PEA's president placed the Association by the turn of the century outside the main stream of educational progressivism.

The PEA still had preferred access to key officials in the school system, notably to city School Superintendent Maxwell. But after 1900 the PEA became a static organization. In the dynamic world of New York City politics, such organizations are marked for oblivion. The imperialistic Woman's Municipal League was threatening to appropriate the entire sphere of public school activity in the city for itself.[109]

The Greater New York Bill had created a super-school system.[110] It was felt by an important group in the PEA's inner core of leadership that if the PEA were to play an active role in influencing the direction in which this giant would go, changes had to be made. In the spring of 1905, Mrs. Van Rensselaer resigned as president of the PEA. Mrs. Miriam Sutro Price was elected to succeed her, and subsequently the PEA was completely overhauled. Now for the first time men became eligible for membership in the Association, and a full-time executive secretary was employed to supervise an expanded program of activities.

In 1902, at the annual meeting of the Eastern Conference of Public Education Associations, a speaker gave some advise to the assembled guests. Societies that wished to aid the schools, she said, should keep a sharp eye on local needs and not work in accordance with any set theoretical scheme. They should take up new branches of work only after they have commended themselves by careful experimentation, and

[108] Van Rensselaer, "Our Public Schools: A Reply," pp. 80–81.

[109] Scarcely a phase of city life was beyond the scope of the WML. See Woman's Municipal League, *Bulletin*, Vols. I–IV, April, 1902–December, 1905.

[110] For 1898–1899 Greater New York's day school population reached almost 400,000, more than twice that of Chicago—the next largest city in the country. New York City, Department of Education, City Superintendent of Schools, *Seventh Annual Report*, 1905, p. 36; City of Chicago, Board of Education, *Fiftieth Annual Report*, 1904, p. 17.

they should be ready, she continued, to abandon such new branches should they prove unsatisfactory or if any other agency could perform the task equally well. She concluded:

> If lay educational societies should awaken interest in the mind of the public at large, if special branches of work are carefully selected, carefully begun, and pushed with discretion, energy, and Without Undue Haste [*sic*], then the results will be encouraging and the community will be the better for it.[111]

The speaker was Mrs. Schuyler Van Rensselaer. She had simply explicated the principles which she adhered to and which the Association followed while she was its president.

For the first decade of its existence the PEA was run on a shoestring budget by a handful of women volunteers. Altogether, for all of its activities in ten years, its expenditures amounted to but $28,548.[112] Yet, under the guidance of J. Augustus Johnson, Nicholas Murray Butler, James B. Reynolds, Mrs. William S. Rainsford, and Mrs. Van Rensselaer, the PEA had made impressive contributions to the reform movement. Nicholas Murray Butler's homage to the PEA, delivered in 1902, holds up:

> She could say, "All of them I saw and a great part of them I was," with reference to the successive steps in educational progress in the last decade in the city.[113]

[111] Conference of Eastern Public Education Associations, *Bulletin No. 1,* 1902, pp. 3–6; Van Rensselaer, "The Public Education Association of New York," p. 209.
[112] PEA, *Report of Ten Years Work, 1895–1905,* p. 6.
[113] *New York Tribune,* December 5, 1902.

Chapter 3

THE DIE IS CAST

1905-1917

THE PROGRESSIVE MOVEMENT quickened after the turn of the century and retained its momentum until World War I. Whatever it was called, "Reform, the Moral Awakening, the New Idea, the Square Deal, the Uplift, Insurgency," said William Allen White in 1910, the new current in American life was unmistakable.[1] Few fields were so markedly affected by the great surge of reform movements that characterized the Progressive Era as education. In the Progressive Era, the immigrant and the slum, that "peculiar environment," to which the public schools had to adjust or conquer, came under closer scrutiny than ever before. Exposure and public school reform went hand in hand. Muckrakers and social critics heightened the progressives' sense that America was cracking. The more anxious the progressives became, the more intense their concern for children. The more intense their concern for children, the more radical their school reform program. Kindergarten and manual training, playgrounds and play centers receded into a remote halcyon past. Progressive opinion converged more and more upon the public schools as the nation's child welfare agencies par excellence. By World War I this had become the central theme of progressive education.

The most explicit, if not the earliest, formulation of the new progressivism in education was that advanced by muckraker and social reformer Robert Hunter in 1904. *Poverty*, Hunter's impassioned exposé of social conditions in America, is one of the classic muckraking tracts

[1] William Allen White, *The Old Order Changeth: A View of American Democracy* (New York, 1910), p. 30; Harold Underwood Faulkner, *The Quest for Social Justice, 1898–1914* (New York, 1931); Frank Freidel, *America in the Twentieth Century* (New York, 1960), Chaps. II–IV.

63

of the Progressive Era.[2] Since New York City provides the book's chief
locale it takes on special importance for us. The former head-resident
of the University Settlement painted a vivid picture of New York in
extremis, with conditions much worse than those depicted by Jacob
Riis a decade before: the immigrant problem more menacing; poverty
more extensive; crime, vice, and insanity more prevalent and, especially,
the plight of the children more desperate. Immigrant parents, Hunter
asserted, "bring up their children in surroundings which make them in
large numbers vicious and criminally dangerous." [3] Hunter hit hard at
the grim meaning of poverty in terms of stunted and starved bodies of
children. In graphic terms he portrayed the morbid effects of child
labor. His trenchant depiction of the dark side of child life included
the sensational charge: "There must be thousands—very likely sixty or
seventy thousand children—in New York City alone who often arrive
at school hungry and ill-fitted to do well the work required." [4]

Still, Hunter retained an optimistic faith in social reform. To fend
off ultimate catastrophe Hunter called for immigration restriction, a
sweeping program of social legislation of the "welfare state" variety,
and the assumption by the public schools of new and sweeping responsibilities. *Poverty* stands as a seminal work in the history of American
progressive education. The chapter entitled "The Child" is the important one. Hunter argued that due to the Industrial Revolution, social
life in America had undergone radical changes affecting all phases of
child life. The traditional educative agencies of the young had been
gravely and irreparably impaired; fields and neighborhoods of yore replaced by street and street gang; the home destroyed. The child in the
modern city was bereft of every good influence. Some agency, Hunter
warned, would have to take up the slack. All the problems of child life,
he proclaimed, were school problems. The school was obliged to conquer
them.[5] The fateful question Hunter posed in 1904 was this:

Are we to have the school ignore this larger work of education and
remain a sort of dispensary of learning—an inflexible missionary of the
three R's? . . . or is it to take, as its responsibility, the entire problem of
child life and master it? If the school does not assume this responsibility,
how shall the work be done? [6]

[2] Robert Hunter, *Poverty* (New York, 1904); Louis Filler, *Crusaders for American Liberalism* (new ed., Yellow Springs, Ohio, 1950), p. 269; Robert H. Bremner,
From the Depths: The Discovery of Poverty in the United States (New York, 1956),
pp. 149–50.
[3] *Op. cit.*, p. 289.
[4] *Ibid.*, p. 216.
[5] *Ibid.*, p. 209.
[6] *Ibid.* Hunter's vision of the new school encompassed one "whose interests lie
in the whole child, night and day, at work and at play." *Ibid.*, p. 221.

With these words, Hunter struck the keynote of school reform in the Progressive Era. In a mighty chorus progressives answered, "Yes," the school would take as its responsibility the entire problem of child life and master it.[7] In short, the Progressive Era formulated a conception of the public school as a "legatee institution." [8] This was the direction in which the PEA, under Mrs. Van Rensselaer, refused to go. In 1905 Mrs. Miriam Sutro Price succeeded Mrs. Van Rensselaer as president of the PEA. It was Mrs. Price who steered the PEA into the full progressive tide.

I

Miriam Sutro Price was a native New Yorker, born in the city in 1871 to the comfortably situated German Jews, Pauline and Bernard Sutro.[9] She was educated in the public schools of the city, graduating from the Normal College, later to become Hunter College, in 1891. In 1894 she married Joseph M. Price, a prosperous businessman active in the City Club, the East Side Club, and the Outdoor Recreation League. Subsequently Mrs. Price became active in civic affairs, taking a special interest in the Ethical Culture Society and the PEA. As chairman of the PEA's East Side Auxiliary, she was liaison between the two reform groups.

For some time Mrs. Price had chafed at Mrs. Van Rensselaer's cautious leadership of the PEA. Upon assuming the presidency herself, her first steps were to end the PEA's career as strictly a woman's organization and to employ an executive secretary to supervise an expanded program of activities.[10] On the heels of the reorganization, but for Carlotta Lowell, Martha Lincoln Draper, and of course, Mrs. Price, virtually an entire new cast of leaders made their appearance in the PEA. The critical post of executive secretary went to Dr. Jane Robbins, one of the founders of the College Settlement and an activist in a

---

[7] E.g., John Spargo, *The Bitter Cry of the Children* (New York, 1906), Chap. II; Lillian D. Wald, *The House on Henry Street* (New York, 1915), p. 132, *passim*; George B. Mangold, *Child Problems* (New York, 1910), Bk. II, Chaps. I–IV; Delos F. Wilcox, *The American City* (New York, 1904), pp. 98–117; Charles A. Beard, *American City Government* (New York, 1912), pp. 275–79; Ellwood Cubberley, *Changing Conceptions of Education* (New York, 1909), Part II, esp. pp. 62–66; Irving King, *Social Aspects of Education* (New York, 1912); James Phinney Monroe, *New Demands in Education* (New York, 1912), Chap. III.

[8] Lawrence A. Cremin, *The Transformation of the School* (New York, 1961), p. 17.

[9] *New York Times*, March 4, 1957, obituary.

[10] PEA, *Report of Ten Years Work, 1895–1905*, pp. 3–4; PEA, *Annual Report for the Year 1905–1906*, pp. 6–7.

handful of reform agencies in the city including the New York Child
Labor Committee, and the New York Association of Neighborhood
Workers. Among the first men to be recruited for the PEA's Executive
Committee were James K. Paulding, like Miss Robbins a ubiquitous
figure in reform movements in New York; John Martin, an Ethical
Culture Society leader, well-known in civic circles; and Gaylord S. White
of the Union Settlement. A handful of representatives of New York's
elite of wealth and status: society leader Mrs. Edward C. Henderson,
whose philanthropic interests included the Working Girls Society and
the Alliance Employment Bureau; Nathalie Henderson Swan, one of
the founders of New York's Junior League; her husband, banker Joseph
R. Swan; fabulously wealthy Dorothy Whitney, also a Junior Leaguer;
Felix M. Warburg of Kuhn, Loeb and Co.; and lawyer Charles P.
Howland, who would succeed Mrs. Price as PEA president in 1909,
round out the leadership picture of the PEA in the years immediately
following the reorganization of 1905.[11]

The PEA's new leadership possessed several important virtues:
they were a small, cohesive group who placed the PEA in close contact
with powerful reform agencies in the city; they put the PEA in funds;
and, finally, the new leadership was more adept than the old in the
method and practice of New York City government and politics. Men
like Paulding, Swan, and Howland knew the right people: lawyers,
bankers, and big businessmen, who usually showed up in important city
positions no matter who occupied City Hall. It was the men who
smoothed the PEA's way during the Democratic city administrations
of Mayors George B. McClellan (1904–1909) and William J. Gaynor
(1910–1913).[12] Thus, bank director Egerton L. Winthrop, Jr., and Wall
Street lawyer Robert L. Harrison, among McClellan's first appointees

11 PEA, *Annual Reports*, 1905–1911. Although Mr. Warburg was never to
become active in the PEA, the Association could always depend upon him for token
financial contributions and for the exercise of his influence on its behalf. Especially,
he gave the PEA access to the New York Foundation, organized in 1909 by a small
group of New York Jews. New York Foundation, *Forty Year Report, 1909–1949* (New
York, 1950), p. 50.
12 The fact that McClellan and Gaynor were political mavericks who frequently
ignored party lines when making appointments also helped the PEA. Everett P.
Wheeler, *Sixty Years of American Life* (New York, 1917), p. 398; Allan Nevins and
John A. Krout (eds.), *The Greater City: New York, 1898–1948* (New York, 1948),
pp. 69–73; Charles Garrett, *The La Guardia Years: Machine and Reform Politics in
New York City* (New York, 1961), pp. 41–43; Wallace S. Sayre and Herbert
Kaufman, *Governing New York City: Politics in the Metropolis* (New York, 1960),
pp. 695–96.

to the Board of Education, were both accessible to the PEA.[13] And two PEA officials, Martha Lincoln Draper and John Martin, were actually appointed to the Board of Education by crusty, able, Mayor Gaynor.[14]

After the changing of the guard the PEA caught the crusading spirit of the time. Now no matter affecting the child was beyond its ken. It scarcely knew where or how to begin, but sampled everything. From 1905 to 1911 it attempted to propagate the new education through a profusion of committees whose rosters read like a *Who's Who* in the fields of social work, philanthropy, and education. In 1911 this strategy was deemed ineffective and most of the committees were disbanded. From 1911 to 1914 it followed a new policy, one which involved the employment of a staff of professional social workers, the publication of special studies, and the publication of a *PEA Bulletin*.[15] Finally, in 1914, the PEA streamlined its activities even further and joined the newly elected Fusion Mayor John Purroy Mitchel and the city administration in the incredible effort to install the Gary School Plan in New York.

II

Several of the PEA's old committees were continued for various lengths of time after the reorganization of 1905: Tombs, School Visiting, Art, and Nature. But the PEA had not been reorganized simply to perpetuate its old program. It is in the many new committees that the PEA proliferated after 1905, Truancy, Compulsory Education, Special Children, School Lunch, Parents Meeting, Vocational Education, Vocational Guidance Survey, Visiting Teacher, and more, that its commitment to a new conception of the public school emerges. Since the committees were numerous and space is limited, only the work of the most important committees can be touched upon, and then only briefly.

If the public schools were to help solve the problems of immigration and congestion of population, of child labor and child welfare, then all the children must be gotten into the school and kept there as long as possible. This was a cardinal article of the progressive creed. In the

[13] Mrs. Winthrop was a generous financial backer of the Association. PEA, *Report for the Years September 1, 1911 to September 1, 1913*, pp. 39, 41, 44. For Robert L. Harrison and the PEA, see below, p. 72n.

[14] New York City, Department of Education, *Thirteenth Annual Report of the City Superintendent of Schools*, 1911, pp. 9, 10.

[15] The *Bulletin* made its appearance on February 26, 1912. In all thirty-one numbers were issued irregularly to September, 1917, when it ceased publication.

city, the New York Child Labor Committee led the fight for the
tightening and extension of the compulsory education law, the PEA
helping wherever and whenever it could.

The New York Child Labor Committee was hardly a year old when
it manifested itself as a powerful pressure group by pushing the model
Compulsory Education Law of 1903 through Albany.[16] Successful
upstate, the child labor reformers ran into trouble in New York City.
While some of the city's top school professionals supported the child
labor and compulsory education movements, e.g., Superintendent Maxwell and District Superintendent Julia Richman, many schoolmen,
especially the principals, were opposed.[17] The PEA, a bystander in the
1903 legislative struggle, now threw itself into the controversy. Thanks
to the PEA's School Visiting Committee, Helen Marot and other agents
of the Child Labor Committee were able to make firsthand investigations in the city's schools into the administration of the new law. After
it was ascertained that city public school principals were generally
opposed to the law, the PEA assumed the role of mediator between the
child labor reformers and the recalcitrant principals. In 1907 the PEA
organized a large Compulsory Education Committee composed of representatives of the two groups to iron out their differences.[18] Apparently
the stratagem worked. The Compulsory Education Committee was
soon working on new legislation increasing the compulsory school age
limit to include the years seven to sixteen, and extending the period of
enforcement so as to include September and June.[19] The PEA also
joined with child labor reformers and others interested in the child
labor problem in successful agitation to persuade the New York State

[16] The act required that all children between the ages of eight and fourteen
attend school from October to June, that all children between the ages of fourteen
and sixteen be at work or at school, and, notably, required documentary proof as
to age and amount of schooling. Mary Stevenson Callcott, *Child Labor Legislation
in New York* (New York, 1931), p. 7; Fred S. Hall, *Forty Years, 1902–1942: The
Work of the New York Child Labor Committee* (New York, 1942), p. 12; Josephine
Goldmark, *Impatient Crusader: Florence Kelley's Life Story* (Urbana, Ill., 1953), pp.
81ff.

[17] Hall, *op. cit.*, pp. 14, 23–25; Goldmark, *op. cit.*, pp. 86–87. The story was
much the same elsewhere in the country. Merle Curti, *The Social Ideas of American
Educators* (New York, 1935), pp. 234–36.

[18] PEA, *Annual Report for the Year 1906–1907*, pp. 30–32. The Compulsory
Education Committee was composed of representatives of the New York Child Labor
Committee, the Women Principals' Association, the Male Principals' Association,
the Charity Organization Society, and the Association for Improving the Condition
of the Poor.

[19] *The School Journal*, LXXIV (April 20, 1907), 398; PEA, *Annual Report for
the Year 1906–1907*, p. 32.

Legislature to enact the School Census Law of 1908, which led to the first permanent census of children of school age in the state.[20]

The same reform coalition that agitated on the state level for the extension and tighter enforcement of the compulsory education law, agitated on the municipal level to open the school doors to those children still exempt from the operation of such law: the deaf, the blind, the crippled, and the mentally defective. The progressives' "open door" school policy is admirably set forth in the following resolution which the PEA sent to the New York City Board of Education in 1911:

> Resolved: that the Public Education Association begs the Board of Education to adopt as its working policy the principle that all children of whatever condition and capacity are entitled to as much education as they are capable of receiving; and that the Board of Education, accordingly shall include in its plans the children now lacking such provision.[21]

It was clear that the city was sympathetic to the plea that the school take on at least one responsibility traditionally considered outside of its province: the education of physically defective children.[22] But, although a start had been made in the so-called "ungraded classes," public school responsibility for the mentally defective was not so readily acceptable either to professional schoolmen, to economy-minded elements in the city, or to the general public. The PEA's new Committee on Special Children, later to become the Committee on Hygiene of School Children, was created to stimulate public school responsibility for such children.[23] Through special publications, public meetings, and conferences, the committee, greatly influenced by the investigations of

[20] New York City, Board of Education, *The First Fifty Years, 1898–1948: Fiftieth Annual Report of the Superintendent of Schools* (New York, 1948), p. 47; PEA, *Annual Report for the Year 1908–1909*, p. 10.

[21] Minutes of the Special Children Committee of the PEA, April 21, 1911; Minutes of the Executive Council of the PEA, May 4, 1911; in the files of the PEA. All PEA committee minutes cited are on file at PEA headquarters. See also Spargo, *op. cit.*, pp. 101–05; Hall, *op. cit.*, pp. 47–50; Robert A. Woods and Albert J. Kennedy, *The Settlement Horizon* (New York, 1922), pp. 282ff.

[22] New York City, Department of Education, *First Annual Report of the City School Superintendent*, 1899, pp. 112–19.

[23] PEA, *Annual Reports*, 1908–1913. The committee was led by Miss Eleanor Hope Johnson, a salaried social worker. She was assisted by Elisabeth Irwin, in a few years to play a prominent role in the PEA. The committee was composed of representatives of virtually every major social and philanthropic agency in the city concerned with the problem of mentally defective children: Children's Aid Society, Association for Improving the Condition of the Poor, New York Child Labor Committee, Association of Neighborhood Workers, and New York State Charities Aid Association.

Dr. Henry H. Goddard, Director of the famous Vineyard School for the Feeble-Minded and American adapter of the Binet intelligence scale, propagated the view that there were many thousands of "mentally defective" or "feeble-minded" children in the city's public schools, and that it was the schools' responsibility to cope with them.[24]

III

The reformers' concern with social justice and child welfare was also belatedly extended to the Negro child. The PEA, sympathetic to every movement in behalf of child welfare, reminded New Yorkers of the existence of this considerable group of children whose claim to fair play and well-being was almost totally ignored.

In 1912 the PEA, through an anonymous grant of funds to its Committee on Hygiene of School Children, employed Mrs. Frances Blascoer, former secretary of the National Association for the Advancement of Colored People, to investigate and report on the social factors affecting the poor school achievement of Negro children.[25] Three years later Mrs. Blascoer's pioneering study appeared.[26] Mrs. Blascoer found that the social environment of Negro children "clearly was affected by forces in which color or race consciousness played a more or less dominating role."[27] She found principals, teachers, and pupils cool to Negroes, although there was no deliberate policy of discrimination.[28] Still, the public schools, she noted, met more nearly the ideal of equality in the treatment of the races than did industry, organized amusements, or private agencies which dealt with children.[29]

Mrs. Blascoer argued that the solution to the problem of securing a more hopeful future for Negro children than the condition of their

[24] Anne Moore, *The Feeble-Minded in New York: A Report Prepared for the Public Education Association of New York* (New York, 1911); "Work for Mentally Defective Children in New York City," *PEA Bulletin*, No. 8, January 20, 1913; Elisabeth Irwin, "A Study of the Feeble-Minded in a West Side School in New York City," *PEA Bulletin*, No. 21, December 8, 1913; PEA, *Report for the Years September 1, 1911 to September 1, 1913*, pp. 19, 25–26.

[25] Minutes of the Executive Committee of the PEA, December 12, 1912; PEA, *Report for the Years September 1, 1911 to September 1, 1913*, p. 19. About a year earlier there had appeared the first thorough study of the Negro adult in New York. Mary White Ovington, *Half a Man: The Status of the Negro in New York* (New York, 1911). The PEA's study was evidently to complement this one.

[26] Frances Blascoer, *Colored School Children in New York* (New York, 1915).

[27] *Ibid.*, p. 84.

[28] *Ibid.*, pp. 13–22.

[29] *Ibid.*, p. 4.

parents would seem to promise them did not lie in more playgrounds, or more clubs, or even more schoolhouses. "That part of the problem of the Negro school child which exists because he is colored," she concluded prophetically, "does not seem possible of solution so long as public opinion continues to find itself unable to come to a decision on the question of whether the Negro race should or should not be under a separate regime in the social fabric." [30] Neither the PEA, nor any considerable group of progressives, nor the as yet politically impotent NAACP, would be disposed to follow up this fundamental question for another forty years. Then, in the aftermath of the 1954 school desegregation decisions of the United States Supreme Court, the PEA would once again call the attention of New Yorkers to the plight of colored school children in the city, and Mrs. Blascoer's question would take on new pertinency.[31]

IV

One of the progressive movement's greatest triumphs was the success of the compulsory education movement.[32] Progressives forced open the doors of the public school wider than they had ever been before. Through these doors there entered an astonishing number of children, of all kinds and conditions. All right. The children were in school. Now what? True, the school had to change. But the direction of change and the shape the new school would take were not foreordained. This was the historic role of the progressive movement in general and of progressive organizations like the PEA in particular.

> We realize that the school cannot well do the work of the church and the home, but where these fail to live up to their privileges the community falls back on the school and asks that it be helped to do its best.[33]

Thus wrote Mrs. Price in 1908. The PEA had no doubt that church and home had failed to live up to their privileges and that the community had now to fall back on the school. Many of the PEA's activities in the Progressive Era translate this widely shared progressive sentiment into terms of new school responsibilities.

[30] *Ibid.*, p. 130.
[31] PEA, *The Status of the Public School Education of Negro and Puerto Rican Children in New York City* (New York, 1955).
[32] Cremin, *op. cit.*, pp. 127–28.
[33] PEA, *Annual Report for the Year 1908–1909*, p. 6; Jane E. Robbins, "The Settlement and the Public Schools," *Outlook*, XCV (August 6, 1910), 785–87.

In 1909 the PEA took the newly organized New York School Lunch Committee under its wing. For the next three years the Association led the campaign to persuade city authorities that provision of noon meals for school children "at cost" was a proper responsibility of the public schools.[34] Another case in point is provided by the PEA's venture into an even more traditionally sacrosanct preserve of home and family than feeding: sex education. For several years, through a new Parents Committee, the PEA disseminated the propaganda of the American Society for Sanitary and Moral Prophylaxis. Under the sponsorship of the PEA, the American Society was enabled to go ahead with sex hygiene lectures to parents' meetings in the public schools after school hours, and even, in several cases, to groups of school children.[35]

The PEA's activities on behalf of school lunches and sex education, while important, were peripheral. The PEA, and the progressives in general, had more basic concerns; namely, reform of public school curricula and instructional procedures. Of all the demands made by progressives in the pre-World War I period, that for vocational education, beginning at about the turn of the century, was pressed most aggressively.[36] Some officials of the PEA had been interested in trade training from the first; Mrs. Price and Mrs. Henry Ollesheimer were early patrons of the Manhattan Trade School for Girls.[37] But under Mrs. Van Rensselaer the PEA, per se, took no part in the agitation. After the reorganization of 1905, as if to make up for its previous years of neglect, the PEA scrambled frantically to get aboard the bandwagon.

The PEA attempted to promote the new education through a handful of new committees—High School, Technical and Trade School, Vocational Education, Curriculum, and Vocational Guidance Survey. It is worthy of note that none of these committees had as their objective the extension of vocational education at the secondary school level. Thus, High School, Technical and Trade School, and Vocational

[34] "Shall the Schools Serve Lunches?", *PEA Bulletin*, No. 10, February 25, 1913; PEA, *Annual Report for the Year 1909–1910*, pp. 5, 16–17; PEA, *Report for the Years September 1, 1911 to September 1, 1913*, p. 29; Paul Kennaday and Burton J. Hendrick, "Three-Cent Lunches for School Children," *McClure's*, V (October, 1913), 125–32.

[35] *Social Diseases*, III (April, 1912), 3; PEA, *Annual Reports for the Years 1908–1913*. The PEA's contact on the Board of Education in this matter was Robert L. Harrison. Minutes of the Executive Committee of the PEA, April 6, 13, May 18, 1911. Mr. Harrison was a member of the Executive Committee of the Board of Education at this time. New York City, Department of Education, *Fourteenth Annual Report*, 1911, p. 328.

[36] Cremin, *op. cit.*, pp. 34–41, 50–57.

[37] Manhattan Trade School for Girls, *First Annual Report*, 1904, p. 3.

Education Committees aimed to promote the idea of an "intermediate school" which would offer vocational education to children between the ages of twelve and fourteen; that is, at the end of the sixth grade.[38] After a few years of desultory activity, all the aforementioned committees were disbanded, and the PEA ventured into a yet more novel area.

In late 1910 the PEA organized a small Committee on Curriculum, composed of Dr. Ira S. Wile, a specialist in work with atypical children, Elizabeth S. Williams, head worker of the College Settlement, and Amy Schussler and Frederick G. Bonser, both of Teachers College, to explore the possibility of vocational education in the lower grades.[39] While the Curriculum Committee prepared its report, the PEA set up a series of public conferences to open up the subject in the city.[40]

The Curriculum Committee reported in 1912. It called for the establishment of an "intermediate school" of the seventh and eighth grades in which children could elect to study along academic, commercial, or industrial lines. It also recommended that elementary school principals be given wide discretionary powers to choose what subjects should be taught in the particular neighborhoods in which their schools were situated. The PEA did not publish the report but submitted it confidentially to the Board of Education, of which body Wile was, by 1912, a member, and also leaked it to the *New York World*, which proceeded to publish large excerpts from it. Subsequently the PEA became the target of some criticism. (The "intermediate school" idea was already old in 1912. But as for the "neighborhood school" idea, its time had not yet come. Not while Superintendent of Schools Maxwell was still on the scene.) The PEA protested that it was simply setting forth some tentative proposals for discussion.[41]

In the meantime the PEA sought to advance the same end from still another angle: an investigation and report on a question arousing much concern at the time, "What vocational guidance should mean to the public schools of New York." The PEA's vocational guidance survey was released to wide publicity in late 1912. The PEA's investigator, after

[38] PEA, *Annual Report for the Year 1906–1907*, pp. 18–19. See also City Club, *A Suggested Readjustment of the Years of Study of the Public Schools of New York City: A Memorandum Addressed to Those Interested in the Public Schools of New York City* (New York, 1908).

[39] Minutes of the Executive Council of the PEA, November 3, 10, 17, 1910; PEA, *Annual Report for the Year 1909–1910*, p. 10.

[40] PEA *Bulletin*, No. 3, April 5, 1912; Minutes of the Executive Committee of the PEA, February 7, 1912.

[41] *New York Times*, January 31, 1913; PEA, *Report for the Years September 1, 1911 to September 1, 1913*, p. 26; Minutes of the Executive Committee of the PEA, January 29, March 14, 1912, January 23, February 6, 1913.

an "intensive study" of 327 children who left school as soon as they turned fourteen, concluded that poverty was not an important factor in early school leaving, and that "vocational guidance should mean guidance for [vocational] training, not guidance for jobs." [42]

The general history of the vocational education movement has been well told elsewhere [43] and will not be repeated here. But there is one aspect of the movement which deserves to be emphasized. Progressives urged vocational education in the public schools for many reasons: social, economic, and educational. But study of the movement, at least in New York City, leads to the inescapable conclusion that the progressives' school reform program in the pre-World War I decade was coming increasingly to be influenced by a hardening judgment as to the intrinsic mental capacity of the schools' population. A widely shared scepticism about the capacity of the immigrant child to benefit from "book-learning" is a melancholy strain in the vocational education movement. The zeal with which progressives pursued vocational education into the lowest grades of the elementary school can scarcely be understood if this factor is overlooked.

V

Of all the special projects undertaken by the PEA in the Progressive Era, none was more significant or more successful than its "visiting teacher" project. With the visiting teacher, the PEA began a steadily deepening linkage with the social work profession. With the visiting teacher the culmination of the "legatee" concept of the public school is reached.

The visiting teacher was a brainchild of social settlement residents.

[42] "What the children want is vocational training. The kernel of truth in this popular movement for vocational guidance is the need of vocational training for children. Vocational guidance should mean guidance for training, not guidance for jobs. . . . under present conditions the interests of public-school children can best be served, not by the establishment of a vocational bureau, but by the development of vocational training." Alice P. Barrows, "Report of the Vocational Guidance Survey," *PEA Bulletin*, No. 9, 1912; Winthrop D. Lane, "Education and Work: A Twilight Zone," *Survey*, XXIX (November 23, 1912), 225–27; "What Children Who Leave School Really Need," *Survey*, XXX (May 24, 1913), 273–74; U.S. Bureau of Education, *Report of the Commissioner of Education for the Year Ended June 30, 1912* (Washington, D.C., 1913), Vol. I, pp. 24–26; John M. Brewer, *History of Vocational Guidance: Origins and Early Developments* (New York, 1942), pp. 90–91.

[43] See Cremin, *op. cit.*, pp. 34–57.

Like many other innovations in school organization and procedure in New York, the work was originally intended for the benefit of the children of the East Side. In 1906 two settlements—Hartley House and Greenwich House—assigned one resident each to work with some settlement children in several East Side public schools as "home and school visitors." Shortly thereafter the work was placed under the supervision of a Visiting Teacher Committee composed of representatives of the two aforementioned settlements and also the College Settlement and Richmond Hill House. In January 1907 at the behest of Mary Marot, one of the pioneer visitors, and District School Superintendent Julia Richman, in whose district the work began, the PEA adopted the Visiting Teacher Committee as one of its own branches of work, immediately raised funds to pay the salary of one full-time visiting teacher, set about raising funds to employ others, and thenceforth assumed national leadership of a movement whose ramifications were many indeed.[44]

The visiting teacher was "a social worker who worked with difficult children" in the schools.[45] Herein lies the tale. The PEA joined forces with professional social workers at a time when the latter were being stirred by a technique then in its infancy: social case work, or the "individualization" of social work.[46] The emphasis in case work is on individual deficiencies in character and personality; its goal is the right adjustment of the individual. Thus the PEA emerges as the promoter of one of the most important developments in American public education in the twentieth century. As Mary Richmond notes in her classic *What Is Social Case Work?*, the PEA's visiting teachers were the first

[44] Julius John Oppenheimer, *The Visiting Teacher Movement* (New York, 1924), pp. 1–2; PEA, *The Visiting Teacher in the United States: A Survey by the National Association of Visiting Teachers and Home and School Visitors* (2d ed.; New York, 1923), pp. 12–13; Harriet M. Johnson, *The Visiting Teacher in New York City* (New York, 1916), p. vii; "PEA Conference," *Charities and the Commons*, XVII (1907), 1057; Julia Richman, "A Social Need of the Public School," *Forum*, XLIII (February, 1910), 163; Woods and Kennedy, *The Settlement Horizon*, pp. 280–81; PEA, *Annual Report for the Year 1905–1906*, pp. 9–10; PEA, *Annual Report for the Year 1906–1907*, pp. 12–14.

[45] Richman, *op. cit.*, p. 163.

[46] Mary C. Richmond, *Social Diagnosis* (New York, 1917); Mary C. Richmond, *What Is Social Case Work?* (New York, 1922); Virginia C. Robinson, *A Changing Psychology in Social Case Work* (Chapel Hill, N.C., 1930), pp. 8ff; Nathan Edward Cohen, *Social Work in the American Tradition* (New York, 1958), pp. 130–32; Frank J. Bruno, *Trends in Social Work, 1874–1956: A History Based on the Proceedings of the National Conference of Social Work* (New York, 1957), pp. 183–87.

extension of case work to the public schools.[47] Ultimately, the visiting teacher helped pave the way for the adoption by the schools of the mental hygiene point of view. This development, however, is properly the subject for the next chapter. In the years before World War I, case work was still in the experimental stage. So was the visiting teacher.

The visiting teacher worked with children who were normal in all respects, but who were failing or suffering difficulty in school. The visiting teacher, the inquirer is told, "individualizes" the child. She gets to know "the child whole," and then "adjusts home and school environment" to "smooth out the rough places in life" in order to keep the child from joining the ranks of the truant, the child laborer, or the delinquent.[48] Despite the high-flown rhetoric, most of the adjustments secured involved rule-of-thumb changes in the child's home regimen, or in some other phase of the child's out-of-school environment. But the visiting teacher and her sponsors knew that the practitioner's real opportunity lay not with the few children whom she could help individually, but in the education of the regular public school teaching staff to a more flexible conception of their responsibilities. Some day, Julia Richman prayed, in the course of an appeal on behalf of the PEA's visiting teachers, the regular school teacher would be trained to look after the child "socially," as she was already trained to look after him mentally and physically; trained to detect the child's social needs and to remove his social disabilities. "When that time comes," Miss Richman exclaimed, "then we will be able to rescue all the children." [49] The PEA's visiting teachers tried hard to hasten the reluctant schoolmarms to Utopia. At one staff meeting in 1911 someone complained that teachers were still mainly concerned with getting "results" from children. But

[47] Richmond, *What Is Social Case Work?*, pp. 196–201; Cohen, *op. cit.*, p. 116. Actually the visiting teacher movement started simultaneously, albeit independently, in New York, Boston, and Hartford. In each case the impulse came from outside the school systems: in Boston from the Women's Educational Association, in Hartford from the Psychological Clinic. Oppenheimer, *op. cit.*, pp. 3–4. At the same time that settlement residents were discovering the need to "individualize" children, industry was beginning to address itself to employee welfare, and hospitals to the individual needs of patients. William H. Tolman, *Social Engineering* (New York, 1909), Chap. II; Ida M. Cannon, *Social Work in Hospitals: A Contribution to Progressive Medicine* (New York, 1913).

[48] Mary Flexner, "The Visiting Teacher in Action," *Survey*, XXX (May 3, 1913), 179–82; Mary Flexner, "Report of the Visiting Teachers of the PEA," *PEA Bulletin*, No. 15, April 5, 1913; PEA, *The Visiting Teacher in the United States*, pp. 11–12; PEA, *Annual Reports for the Years 1906–1913*.

[49] Richman, "A Social Need of the Public School," p. 168; Eleanor Hope Johnson, "Social Service and the Public Schools," *Survey*, XXX (May 3, 1913), 173–78.

another rose to the defense. Teachers were getting "the social point of view," she said.[50]

The PEA promoted the visiting teacher project with the utmost vigor. A strong committee led by Mrs. Nathalie Henderson Swan raised funds and supervised a vigorous campaign of demonstration, publicity, and personal pressure. Financed by generous subsidies from Dorothy Whitney, the Junior League, and two newly organized foundations—the New York Foundation and the Russell Sage Foundation, to mention only the largest contributors, the visiting teacher thrived. By 1913 the PEA had ten visiting teachers in the city's public schools.[51] In the meantime, the campaign to persuade the city to take up the work went on apace.

In 1913 there was success at last. The city finally granted the Board of Education a small sum of money for the work. The board subsequently appointed two visiting teachers to begin work in September with mentally defective children in Elizabeth Farrell's Department of Ungraded Classes.[52] Here was a breakthrough progressives had been waiting for. The *Survey*, the social workers' organ, called it one of the most important steps yet taken in the socializing of the public schools.[53] A *Times* feature writer, probably copying from a PEA handout, predicted that from this cautious beginning schooling would eventually become a matter of the all-day "social training" of children.[54]

By 1916, the Board of Education's visiting teacher staff numbered seven. But the PEA, reluctant to drop the visiting teacher project since its usefulness to the schools or to itself had not yet been fully exploited, not only stayed in the field but intensified its promotional efforts. In 1916 the PEA sent out a call for a nationwide conference of visiting teachers. The conference met in New York from July 5 to July 7 in conjunction with the annual meeting of the National Education Association. Now leaders of public school systems from all over the nation

[50] Minutes of the Committee on Visiting Teachers of the PEA, January 19, 1911.

[51] Howard Nudd, "The Origin and Significance of the Visiting Teacher Experiment," in Johnson, *op. cit.*, p. viii; PEA, *Report for the Years September 1, 1911 to September 1, 1913*, pp. 23–24, 34–53, *passim*; Flexner, "Report of the Visiting Teachers of the PEA"; Oppenheimer, *op. cit.*, p. 2.

[52] New York City, Board of Education, *The First Fifty Years*, p. 70; Oppenheimer, *op. cit.*, p. 6.

[53] "Visiting Teachers for Ungraded Classes," *Survey*, XXXI (October 18, 1913), 67.

[54] *New York Times*, January 4, 1914. At about the same time Boards of Education in other cities were adopting the work. E.g., Rochester, Kansas City, Philadelphia, and Minneapolis. Oppenheimer, *op. cit.*, pp. 6–7.

could be introduced to "The Changing Conception of Public Education." [55]

In connection with the meeting, the PEA published a popular booklet entitled *The Visiting Teacher in New York City*.[56] The work contains a thorough description of its subject, but it has a far greater significance. In the course of her prefatory remarks, Harriet Johnson, chief of the PEA's visiting staff, wrote as follows:

> The work of the visiting teacher is not radically new, but rather a very natural extension of the public schools as a child welfare agency, adapted to meet the social needs of children in a large municipal organization.[57]

Thus, explicitly if inadvertently, Miss Johnson revealed the basic core of PEA educational doctrine. Here was the culmination of trends which began with the forcing open of the schools for purposes other than the academic instruction of children. And here was the signpost for the future. The die was cast. The PEA's program would never be a static one. But henceforth all of its changes in program, so far as they concerned public school practices and procedures, would be in the nature of strategy and tactics. The long-range goal would be constant: the transformation of the public schools into child welfare agencies.

VI

The PEA was furiously active in the years 1906–1911. But in most of its activities the PEA seemed to be a tail tied to a kite flown by other organizations: the Child Labor Committee, the Association of Neighborhood Workers, the Society for the Promotion of Industrial Education, and the city's leading charity organizations. The PEA was without shape or form. It was rudimentary in organization, unsystematic in activities, limited in resources, vague as to goals. By 1915 all this had changed; its character had been completely altered. By 1915 the PEA had evolved from an impecunious clearinghouse for educational reform into a monied, authoritative, political pressure group in posses-

[55] Hazel Frederickson, *The Child and His Welfare* (San Francisco, 1948), p. 72; "Program of the First National Conference of Visiting Teachers and Home and School Visitors, July 5th to 7th, 1916, New York City," in the files of the PEA. The organization of the National Association of Home and School Visitors was another product of the conference. In 1919 the group was reorganized as the American Association of Visiting Teachers.

[56] Johnson, *The Visiting Teacher in New York City*.

[57] *Ibid.*, p. 1.

sion of its own set of ultimate school reform objectives.[58] It had evolved
from the status of an auxiliary to the school reform movement in the
city to a position of dominance in the movement. The decisive experience was a crisis that shook the PEA during the period 1911–1914, a
crisis intimately linked to developments in the broader reform movement during this same period.

"The school systems of our cities present one of the most inspiring
aspects of our municipal advance," wrote Charles A. Beard in 1912.[59]
Undoubtedly, school systems were the phase of municipal life most
affected by the triumphal advance of urban progressivism. Yet all was
not well. Progressive education was expensive. As municipal budgets
soared and the millennium seemed no closer than before, a substantial
element in the progressive movement, the leaders and backers of good
government crusades, those who hated high taxes as well as corruption
and mismanagement, became alarmed at the steady rise of school
budgets and began to wonder how a program of socialized education
was to be financed. More and more in the pre-World War I decade
school reform became the focus of a wracking tension within progressivism.

The school crisis was felt most acutely in New York. It began in
the first decade of the new century. The organization in 1907 of the
New York Bureau of Municipal Research, financed largely by R. Fulton
Cutting, John D. Rockefeller, Andrew Carnegie, and Mrs. Edward H.
Harriman, is a prime example of the progressives' heightening concern
with efficiency and economy in city government.[60] Led from 1907 to
1914 by a triumvirate of efficiency experts among whom William H.
Allen was most conspicuous, the bureau insisted that cost accounting

[58] To borrow the terminology of sociologists, in retrospect the period 1895–1911
may be considered the "incipient phase" of the PEA's career. By 1914 the PEA had
clearly entered the "organizational phase" of its career. C. Wendell King, *Social
Movements in the United States* (New York, 1956), pp. 41–46.

[59] Beard, *American City Government*, pp. 312–13, 263, 275–79, and Chap.
XII; Charles Zueblin, *American Municipal Progress* (new and revised ed., New
York, 1916), Chaps. X–XII and *passim*. For the expansion of city functions in gen-
eral, William Bennet Munro's authoritative 416-page *Bibliography of Municipal
Government in the United States* (Cambridge, Mass., 1915), is illuminating.

[60] William H. Allen, "Reminiscences," Oral History Project, Columbia Univer-
sity, I, 92–93; Henry W. Bruere, "Reminiscences," Oral History Project, Columbia
University, I, 18ff, 36–45, 61ff; Bureau of Municipal Research, *Purposes and
Methods of the Bureau of Municipal Research* (New York, 1907); Lent D.
Upson, "Contributions of Citizen Research to Effective Government," *The Annals*,
CXCIX (September, 1938), 171–72; Norman N. Gill, *Municipal Research Bureaus:
A Study of the Nation's Leading Citizen-Supported Agencies* (Washington, D. C.,
1944), pp. 13–19, 166; Garrett, *op. cit.*, pp. 25–26.

principles be enforced in all municipal departments. From the very first, the city's Department of Education, dealing with measurable and, as School Superintendent Maxwell insisted, non-measurable units, was the favorite target of Allen's zeal.[61] The dedicated Allen also applied efficiency procedures to prominent civic groups in the city which championed expensive school programs, as we shall see.

The famous survey of the city schools undertaken by the Committee on School Inquiry of the Fusion-controlled Board of Estimate in 1911, largely on the instigation of Allen and the Bureau of Municipal Research, was another sign of the times. The School Inquiry, or Hanus Survey, came about as a result of the inability or unwillingness of the Board of Education and Superintendent Maxwell to furnish the Board of Estimate with a satisfactory explanation for certain items included in the school budget request for fiscal 1911; namely, school sites and buildings, vocational and trade schools, school gardens, and visiting teachers.[62] At this point the PEA was drawn into the deepening school crisis.

In 1912, in connection with the Hanus Survey, Allen submitted a report on "outside cooperation" with the public schools of New York to the Fusion School Committee.[63] The report contains an indiscriminate listing and description of 124 organizations or agencies in the city with an interest of one kind or another in the public schools. What gives the document its chief significance is this: it was a scarcely veiled attack on the Public Education Association. Of all the organizations in the city offering cooperation to the schools, Allen singled out the PEA for special censure. "The one central agency, the Public Education

[61] William H. Allen, *Efficient Democracy* (New York, 1907), p. 128. There is a sharp portrait of Allen in Bruere, *loc. cit.*, pp. 38–41. Allen particularly enjoyed goading Maxwell. With obvious relish he recalls that Maxwell once "told the president of the PEA [Charles P. Howland], 'So help me God, I'll never do anything that man Allen wants.'" Allen, "Reminiscences," I, 77–82.

[62] Allen, "Reminiscences," II, 218–25; "A Catechism for School Officials," *Survey*, XXVI (September 30, 1911), 900–01; Rose Naomi Cohen, *The Financial Control of Education in the Consolidated City of New York* (New York, 1948), pp. 78–79; New York City, Board of Education, *The First Fifty Years*, pp. 54–55; Paul H. Hanus, *Adventuring in Education* (Cambridge, Mass., 1937), pp. 172, 180, 183–86. The Board of Estimate's Committee on School Inquiry comprised John Purroy Mitchel, President, Board of Aldermen; William A. Prendergast, Comptroller; and Cyrus C. Miller, President, Borough of the Bronx. In the spring of 1913, after many vicissitudes, a report in three bulky volumes totalling 2500 pages was finally issued. New York City, Board of Estimate and Apportionment, *Report of Committee on School Inquiry* (New York, 1911–1913), 3 vols.

[63] Bureau of Municipal Research, *Outside Cooperation with the Public Schools of Greater New York* (New York, 1912).

Association," Allen charged, was inefficient and ineffective, hampered by lack of facts, lack of funds, lack of continuity, lack of comprehensive, definite, all-borough program, and lack of central direction.[64] Allen pointedly challenged the value of the PEA's key project: the visiting teacher.[65] Finally, Allen took another poke at the PEA in his conclusions, where he recommended that a strong, well-financed central agency be created to organize, coordinate, and clear all outside cooperation with the public schools.[66]

It was perhaps inevitable, given Allen's obsession with school economy, that he take on the PEA. The PEA was, as he pointed out, the one civic group in New York City with an exclusive interest in the public schools. Furthermore, the school program the PEA advocated required that large sums be added to what Allen and many others in the city considered a swollen educational budget. Finally, the PEA was Superintendent Maxwell's most constant and dependable ally among the city's civic groups in his annual fight with the Board of Estimate for school appropriations. Still, Allen displayed remarkable boldness, or egregiously bad judgment, or perhaps both, in attacking the PEA.

After all, the PEA was flesh and blood of the reform movement. More crucial, the PEA was a fellow traveler of the interlocking directorate of wealth that financed and controlled the Bureau of Municipal Research. Unwittingly, by attacking the PEA, Allen triggered a crisis in the highest echelons of policy-making in the New York City reform movement, with far-reaching ramifications for all concerned. The reorganization of the PEA was one fruit. The removal of the Bureau from an active role in New York City politics was a second. The Gary School War was a third.

VII

Miriam Sutro Price's reign as president of the PEA was brief. She assumed the presidency in order to preside over its reorganization. But while she would be active in the PEA until her death in 1957, her first love was the Ethical Culture Society. In any event Mrs. Price believed the Association could be more effective if it were led by a man. In 1909 she stepped down. She was succeeded by Charles P. Howland, who stayed on as PEA president until 1925. It was during Mr. Howland's

[64] *Ibid.*, pp. 31, 72–78.
[65] *Ibid.*, pp. 36, 47.
[66] *Ibid.*, p. 42.

tenure that the PEA's core program was set, its character determined, and its dominance in New York City public education established.

Charles P. Howland epitomizes the patrician New Yorker. He was a descendant of John Howland of the Mayflower Company.[67] His father, Judge Henry E. Howland, was one of the most respected lawyers of his day, a prominent municipal reformer and a philanthropist of note. Young Charles followed in his father's footsteps. From 1900 to 1921 he was successively a member of the firms of Howland and Murray; Howland, Murray, and Prentice; and Murray, Prentice, and Howland. His associates were George Welwood Murray, John D. Rockefeller's attorney, and E. Parmelee Prentice, Rockefeller's son-in-law. Howland sat for a time, in the early 1900's, on the New York Board of Aldermen, and also served as a civil service examiner. In the world of philanthropy he ranked high, becoming a trustee of the General Education Board in 1918, and later a trustee of the Rockefeller Foundation.[68] The PEA was another outlet for the expression of Howland's broad humanitarian concerns.

Howland was no mere figurehead. He took his duties as PEA president with the utmost seriousness, presiding regularly over executive committee and board meetings. Howland kept in close touch with the developments which led to the Board of Estimate's school inquiry and watched with increasing impatience the interference of Allen and the Bureau of Municipal Research in matters of school policy in the city as well as their unwonted interest in the PEA. Finally, with the aid of a new power in the Association, Abraham Flexner, he moved to put an end to the harassment.

Howland was much impressed with Abraham Flexner's first book, *The American College* (1908), and requested a meeting with the author.[69] A strong friendship subsequently developed between the two. Howland and Joseph R. Swan did much to smooth Flexner's way in

[67] *Who's Who in New York*, 1928; *Who's Who in America*, XIV (Chicago, 1926–1927); *Who Was Who in America*, I (Chicago, 1942); *New York Times*, November 13, 1932, obituary; Yale University, *Obituary Record of Graduates of Yale University*, Number 92 (New Haven, Conn., 1933), pp. 74–76.

[68] Mr. Howland was also one of the founders of the Foreign Policy Association. In 1925 he left the PEA to head the League of Nations' Greek Refugee Settlement Commission. At the time of his death in 1932 he was a member of the faculty of Yale University as an expert in international relations. In a eulogy of Mr. Howland, the *New York Times* paid him this extraordinary tribute: "The death of Charles P. Howland has left America without his like." "Charles P. Howland," November 14, 1932, ed.

[69] Abraham Flexner, *I Remember* (New York, 1940), p. 110.

New York.[70] In return, Flexner did much for the PEA. In early 1911, Howland persuaded the brilliant critic to become active in the PEA.[71] Dr. Flexner was brought into the PEA's inner circle of leadership just as the Allen affair was beginning to run its course. Howland and Flexner set the machinery in motion to consolidate the PEA's position in the city and remove the Bureau of Municipal Research as a militant force in local politics.

Allen's criticisms of the PEA struck home. Between 1911 and 1914, the PEA set itself the task of eradicating any impression that it was simply a many-tentacled nuisance run by some settlement do-gooders on a penny-ante budget. First, in 1911 Jane Robbins was replaced by Arthur W. Dunn, secretary of the City Club of Philadelphia and chairman of the Committee on Civic Education of the National Municipal League.[72] In 1914 Dunn was replaced by Howard Nudd. Mr. Nudd, trained in social work as well as education, was the man the Association was looking for.[73] He would be its director until 1940.

The leadership structure of the PEA which emerges after 1911 is extremely significant. It was obviously put together with a great deal of care. Only the rich and the powerful, bankers and corporation lawyers, possessors of private fortunes, or those who had access to fortunes, private or public, were sought out. Flexner has already been referred to. In the winter of 1912 that perturbed soul in search of a cause, Willard D. Straight, married a few months earlier to Dorothy Whitney, himself became a PEA activist.[74] Leonard P. Ayres, director of educational research for the Russell Sage Foundation, and Clyde Furst, of the Carnegie Foundation, soon appeared on the PEA's small

[70] *Ibid.*, pp. 110, 132. Upon the publication of his epoch-making study of American medical colleges for the Carnegie Foundation for the Advancement of Teaching ("the Carnegie expert" became his sobriquet), Flexner became the brightest star in the new world of foundation philanthropy. He remained with the Carnegie Foundation until 1913, when he received the coveted appointment as assistant secretary of the Rockefeller-financed General Education Board, becoming secretary in 1917. *Ibid.; Who's Who in New York,* 1928; *New York Times,* September 22, 1959, obituary.

[71] Minutes of the Executive Council of the PEA, January 5, 1911; PEA *Report for the Years September 1, 1911 to September 1, 1913,* pp. 3, 4. Flexner had his fingers in many educational pies. For his role in the founding of the Lincoln School of Teachers College, Columbia University, see Cremin, *op. cit.,* pp. 280–81, 282.

[72] James K. Paulding, "Arthur W. Dunn," *Survey,* XXVII (February 24, 1912), 1811–12.

[73] *Leaders in Education,* I (New York, 1932).

[74] PEA, *Report for the Years September 1, 1911 to September 1, 1913,* p. 3; Minutes of the Executive Committee of the PEA, October 31, 1912.

Executive Committee.[75] George D. Strayer, professor of administration at Teachers College, Columbia University, gave the PEA the representative from the world of education Mr. Howland felt it needed.[76]

In 1912, in order to forestall the report of the Bureau of Municipal Research, the Association disbanded most of its committees, employed a large staff of professional social workers, began a program of research publications, and began the publication of a *PEA Bulletin*.[77] The PEA's new look required a vastly increased budget. Its expenditures for the period for which figures are available rose from about $10,000 in 1910 to more than $42,000 for the year ending June 30, 1913. While there was a 75 per cent increase in membership in this period—membership climbed from 444 at the end of 1912 to 756 at the end of 1913—their contribution to income was negligible. In 1912 only $1,878 was raised from membership dues; in 1913, only $2,421.[78] The Association's search for funds to support the new program led it to the same sources that sat, or whose representatives sat, on its governing boards: a handful of foundations and wealthy individuals.

Among the dozen or so individuals who subsidized the Association in the period 1911–1914, Mrs. Willard Straight is pre-eminent.[79] Among the foundations, the Russell Sage Foundation and the New York Foundation contributed generously to the PEA's visiting teacher project.[80] On

[75] Minutes of the Executive Committee of the PEA, February 25, 1915; *PEA Bulletin*, No. 30, March 22, 1917.

[76] PEA, *Report for the Years September 1, 1911 to September 1, 1913*, pp. 2–4; Minutes of the Executive Council of the PEA, January 5, 1911. The PEA was sponsored in the years 1912–1917 by a new Board of Trustees which included such prominent New Yorkers as Chester Aldrich, Charles C. Burlingham, John Agar, Robert C. F. Brown, Mrs. George McAneny, Ogden L. Mills, Mrs. Arthur M. Dodge, and Percy Straus.

[77] PEA, *Report for the Years September 1, 1911 to September 1, 1913*, pp. 7–9; *PEA Bulletin*, No. 1, February 26, 1912.

[78] PEA, *Report for the Years September 1, 1911 to September 1, 1913*, pp. 34–50.

[79] The following "angels" were also generous contributors to the PEA: Misses Irene and Alice Lewisohn, Mrs. Egerton L. Winthrop, Felix Warburg, V. Everit Macy, Mrs. George W. Jenkins, Mrs. Edward H. Harriman, Mrs. Arthur M. Dodge, Carlotta Lowell, and Mrs. Edward C. Henderson, and also the Junior League. PEA, *Report for the Years September 1, 1911 to September 1, 1913*, pp. 38–50. The PEA secured something of a reputation as quite the fashionable organization to be active in. Thus when Lucy Sprague Mitchell, wife of economist Wesley Clair Mitchell and heiress to the Sprague dry goods fortune, came to New York in 1913 she was immediately taken in by "the rich, philanthropic set," and, since she was enormously interested in public school reform, directed to the Association. Lucy Sprague Mitchell, *Two Lives: The Story of Wesley Clair Mitchell and Myself* (New York, 1953), pp. 226, 250.

[80] PEA, *Report for the Years September 1, 1911 to September 1, 1913*, pp. 34, 39, 44.

May 12, 1914, the Rockefeller Foundation made its first grant to the PEA, $2500 to be used for general purposes.[81] This was followed by grants of $5000 in each of the next three years.[82] The relationship between the foundations and the PEA was mutually beneficial. For the new foundations, with millions to spend for social work and child welfare, the Association presented a wonderful opportunity for the strategic investment of small amounts of "seed money" or "venture capital." [83] For the Association, the foundations provided a relatively permanent and dependable source of income, thus enabling it to maintain its elite character.

By 1914 the Allen affair had run its course. The PEA was reborn. And the PEA's chief opponent and chief competitor had been eliminated. Allen was out as the director of the Bureau of Municipal Research; after 1914 the Bureau's program veered distinctly into research and general problems of government and away from any specific contact with the New York City situation.[84] Inadvertently, Allen had done the PEA a good turn. By his criticism, he had forced the PEA to take stock, to take a long, hard look at what it was and what it wanted to be. By 1914 the die was cast. The PEA had evolved from an amorphous channel organization, from a center of cooperation for many social and philanthropic agencies in the city, from a clearinghouse for educational

[81] Rockefeller Foundation, *Annual Report*, 1914, pp. 146, 203.

[82] Rockefeller Foundation, *Annual Reports*, 1915–1917.

[83] There is an illuminating discussion of the principles of foundation philanthropy in New York Foundation, *Forty Year Report*, 1909–1949 (New York, 1950), pp. 1–2, 6.

[84] The reasons why the Bureau veered away from local politics after 1914 are still obscure. In an intriguing document, Allen laid the blame for its troubles on Abraham Flexner, who, according to Allen, came between Rockefeller, the Bureau's largest benefactor, and himself. Apparently, some time before May of 1914, Rockefeller offered the Bureau a grant of $100,000 annually for a five-year period if the Bureau would meet certain conditions, including the cessation of its activities in charities, in public health, and in the public school field in New York. Allen stated that Rockefeller was especially influenced by Flexner's disparagement of the Bureau's activities in the public school field in the city. But Allen disputed this, stating that the Bureau had worked "over and over again with the Public Education Association," worked "to strengthen the Public Education Association's hold on this city and to broaden its program." Finally, Allen characterized Rockefeller's offer as an attempt to prevent the Bureau from playing a role in the "school fight" in New York City and urged the Bureau to turn it down. William H. Allen, *Reasons Why Mr. Allen Believes that Mr. Rockefeller's Conditional Offer of Support to the New York Bureau of Municipal Research Should Not Be Accepted. Prepared May 11, 1914 by William H. Allen. . . . Presented Orally at a Trustees Meeting, May 13, 1914* [1914], pp. 4, 15–16, 19. This privately printed pamphlet is at the New York Public Library, New York City. See also Allen, "Reminiscences," II, 227, 244–50. And also Upson, *op. cit.*, p. 175; and Gill, *op. cit.*, p. 19.

reform with little initiating or directing influence, into a unique pressure group controlled and directed by a handful of rich and influential men and women, representatives of New York's financial and business elite, who knew what they wanted. Now the PEA was ready to take charge of the disatisfaction with the schools rife in the city, and direct it into the proper channels.

VIII

In 1913 anti-Tammany elements in New York coalesced and in November elected John Purroy Mitchel, an independent Democrat, as Mayor on a Fusion ticket calling for economy, efficiency, and home rule.[85] The youthful Mayor knew well that the school problem was his number one headache.

New York's public school system could be described only in superlatives. Between 1898–99 and 1914–15 average day school register climbed from about 398,000 to a staggering 776,000, the latter figure greater than the combined public day school populations of Chicago, Philadelphia, St. Louis, Boston, and Cleveland, the next five largest cities in the country. Between 1899 and 1914 the city's public school teaching and supervisory staff had doubled from about 10,000 to more than 20,000. By 1914 the Board of Education was running the most varied and extensive program of socialized activities of any public school system in the country.[86]

The New York City school system was one of the marvels of the world of education. Yet no one was happy. Social workers and philanthropists, the leaders and backers of child welfare movements, were unhappy. The perennial problem of school overcrowding and part-time attendance grew ever worse.[87] Furthermore, reformers were becoming

[85] Nevins and Krout, *op. cit.*, p. 84; Richard B. Morris, "John Purroy Mitchel," *Dictionary of American Biography*, XIII, 1934, pp. 37–38; Garrett, *op. cit.*, p. 43; Louis H. Pink, "Reminiscences," Oral History Project, Columbia University, p. 22; Charles C. Burlingham, "Reminiscences," Oral History Project, Columbia University, pp. 5–6; Edwin R. Lewinson, "John Purroy Mitchel, Symbol of Reform" (unpublished Ph.D. thesis, Columbia University, 1961).

[86] William H. Maxwell, "Improvements in the Public Schools of New York, 1898–1911," Report of Committee on School Inquiry, *op. cit.*, I, 69–97; John Martin, "Social Work of New York Schools," *Survey*, XXVIII (May 18, 1912), 295–96; New York City, Board of Education, *The First Fifty Years*, pp. 33–36; New York City, Board of Education, *Annual Financial and Statistical Report*, 1914, pp. xxviii–xxix; New York City, Department of Education, *Annual Reports of the City Superintendent of Schools*, 1899–1915.

[87] New York City, Board of Education, *The First Fifty Years*, p. 60; New York City, Department of Education, *Fifteenth Annual Report of the City Superintendent of Schools*, 1913, pp. 48–50.

increasingly impatient with cautious and piecemeal introduction of school reforms they deemed necessary if the schools were to meet the needs of the city. For instance, in 1914, despite a decade of insistent agitation, there were only three vocational high schools in the city and not even a start had been made on a reform by then deemed even more imperative: vocational education in the grades.

Key elements in the good government wing of reform, bankers, merchants, lawyers, and newspapers like the *New York Times*, all those whose watchword was "economy," were unhappy. Between 1899 and 1914 city school appropriations mounted from about $15,300,000 to more than $44,600,000, the latter figure more than 20 per cent of the 1914 city budget of about $192,000,000. An additional $105,000,000 in special appropriations was expended in this period for school sites and buildings.[88] The outbreak of war in Europe plunged the city into a brief but intensive financial panic. It was essential to economize, yet there was the swollen city budget, and there were the insatiable social workers with their demands for more socialized education and "a seat for every child." The reform movement which backed Mitchel was being drawn in two different directions at once and was being racked in consequence.

The criticisms that New Yorkers had of the city's public schools: their weak holding power, their meager provision for vocational education, their inflexibility, and their expensiveness, were hardly unique. These were typical of a nationwide spirit of dissatisfaction which was leading progressives of every stripe in a desperate search for some panacea to the problems of urban education. At the Second National Conference on Vocational Guidance in New York City in 1912, some were saying that the solution had been found by William A. Wirt, Superintendent of Schools in Gary, Indiana.[89] Little-known in that year, the "Gary Plan" (or "Platoon School," or "Work-Study-Play School"; it had several names) would soon capture the imagination of Progressive America.[90] Immediately after his inauguration, Mayor Mitchel moved to solve the New York school dilemma by importing the Gary Plan into the city.[91]

On October 31, 1914, Wirt arrived in New York City as newly ap-

[88] William A. Prendergast, "Why New York City Needs a New School Plan," *American Review of Reviews*, LII (November, 1915), 584; William A. Prendergast, "Reminiscences," Oral History Project, Columbia University, V, 696, 703, 721–22, 745–47; Henry Bruere, "New York's Municipal Problems," *American Review of Reviews*, XLVIII (October, 1913), 468; "The School Situation in New York," *New Republic*, VI (February 5, 1916), 7; New York City, Board of Education, *Annual Financial and Statistical Report*, 1921, p. xvi.

[89] Lane, *op. cit.*, p. 228.

[90] Cremin, *op. cit.*, pp. 154–58.

[91] *New York Times*, May 16, 30, 1914.

pointed educational consultant for vocational and prevocational work in the city's elementary schools. In his pocket he had a one-year contract made with the Mayor and Comptroller, and approved by the Board of Education, calling for a $10,000 salary for one week's work in each month.[92] Wirt had already, a month before, given satisfactory demonstration of his "platoon school" plan in P.S. 45 in the Bronx. In November he took up the task of relieving congestion in P.S. 89 in Brooklyn.[93] Now the stage was almost set for the eruption of the Gary School War.

It was rather peculiar for the economy-minded Mayor and Comptroller to go a thousand miles west to bring a little-known educational consultant to New York at $10,000 a year for twelve weeks' work when the School Superintendent of New York was William H. Maxwell. By 1914, however, progressivism had bypassed Maxwell.[94] Therefore, it was necessary to bring Wirt to the city. But so far, so good. The Gary reorganization had been introduced into only two schools, in boroughs to which the daily press paid little attention. Neither the Gary Plan nor Wirt was news yet. In the spring of 1915 the Board of Education agreed to extend the Gary Plan to twelve more overcrowded Bronx schools in lieu of asking for funds for new schools.[95]

Then in the fall, as time drew near for consideration of the 1916 City Budget, the city administration launched the main thrust. Comptroller William Prendergast came out against any increase in the Board of Education budget over that of 1915, urging that the Gary Plan be extended immediately to all the congested areas of the city. Prendergast pointed out that the Gary Plan would not only provide vocational education in the grades, but would also eliminate part-time schooling, over-crowding, the necessity of constructing new schools except in newly populated areas of the city, and 10 per cent of the

[92] *New York Times,* October 29, November 1, 1914.

[93] "Two Schools in One Building," *New York Times,* September 19, 1914, ed.; William Wirt, "The Reorganization of Public School 89, Brooklyn, New York: Report Made January 19, 1915, to Thomas W. Churchill, Board of Education, New York City," in PEA, *Official Wirt Reports to the Board of Education of New York City* (New York, 1916).

[94] Maxwell, a disciple of William Torrey Harris, was committed to the idea that the grades were for liberal education. He scored the "trumpet of arrogance" with which the calls for vocational education in the grades were being sounded. And he insisted on the older progressive notion of a seat for every child. William H. Maxwell, "On a Certain Arrogance in Educational Theorists," *Educational Review,* XLVII (February, 1914), 175–76; New York City, Department of Education, *Sixteenth Annual Report of the City Superintendent of Schools,* 1915, pp. 71, 118–44, 165–69; Samuel P. Abelow, *Dr. William H. Maxwell* (New York, 1934), pp. 171–73.

[95] *New York Times,* April 25, July 2, 1915.

school teaching staff.[96] When Superintendent Maxwell, a large element of the Board of Superintendents, and many on the Board of Education, including its president, Thomas Churchill, defied the administration, the storm broke. Now the PEA stepped forward as the city's foremost champion of the Gary cause.

We do not know all we would like to know about the PEA for the period 1914-1917. It issued no annual reports for these years. No Minutes of its Executive Committee or Board of Trustees are to be found. Much work remains to be done on the history of the Mitchel administration.[97] There is strong reason to believe, however, that the PEA occupied the position of educational advisor to the Mitchel administration. For example, the PEA's leadership—Howland, Swan, Straight, Flexner, and such—were the class of people with whom Mitchel liked to hobnob. Joseph M. Price, husband of the PEA's Miriam Sutro Price, was chairman of the Fusion Committee of 107 which nominated Mitchel in 1913 and directed the mayoralty campaign. Willard Straight and Charles C. Burlingham played important roles in securing Mitchel's nomination.[98]

Also, the PEA shared in the patronage of the Mitchel regime. Among the new Mayor's first official acts on the day he assumed office, January 1, 1914, were the appointment of Abraham Flexner to the Board of Education and the reappointment of Martha Lincoln Draper, John Martin, and Ira S. Wile to the board.[99] Furthermore, in late January 1914, a few weeks after Mitchel's installation as Mayor, the PEA kicked off a campaign to abolish the then Board of Education and replace it with a new, small board to be appointed by the Mayor.[100] Finally, even before Mitchel left for the west, the PEA had taken the preliminary steps to open up the subject of the Gary Plan in New York. In March 1914 it sent Harriet Johnson and Mrs. Wesley Clair Mitchell to Gary to study and report on the "Gary Idea." The reporters brought back a highly enthusiastic description of the work at Gary which pro-

[96] *New York Times*, September 17, 1915; Prendergast, "Why New York City Needs a New School Plan," pp. 584-87; Prendergast, "Reminiscences," pp. 696, 745-47; *School and Society*, II (October 9, 1915), 528-29; "New York School Budget," *Elementary School Journal*, XVI (November, 1915), 108, ed.; Lewinson, *op. cit.*, pp. 222, 234, 229-30.

[97] The aforementioned doctoral study by Edwin Lewinson is helpful but not definitive.

[98] Gregory Weinstein, *The Ardent Eighties and After* (New York, 1928), p. 135; Pink, *op. cit.*, I, 22; Burlingham, *op. cit.*, pp. 5-6; Garrett, *op. cit.*, pp. 43, 61.

[99] New York City, Department of Education, *Sixteenth Annual Report of the City Superintendent of Schools*, 1914, p. 8.

[100] See below, pp. 94-95.

vided the substance for a number of civic conferences arranged by the PEA in the spring of 1914 and which was subsequently issued as a *Bulletin* in June of that same year.[101] After the fall of 1915 circumstantial evidence is no longer required to substantiate the PEA's leading role in the Gary affair.

Relying chiefly on the tactic of letters to the editor of the *Times* by Howard Nudd, and on its own *Bulletin*, the PEA waged a frenetic campaign to educate lay opinion leaders, professional schoolmen, and Board of Education officials to the merits of the Gary Plan, and to refute all critics of the new education.[102] It was Nudd's contention that the merits of the Gary Plan were primarily pedagogical, although the plan also had interesting financial bearings. The unique feature of the Gary Plan, which, according to Nudd, had already been successfully adapted to New York, was that it would enrich the children's school life, seat thousands, and save millions. Nudd reminded the readers of the *Times* that such remarkable effects could be duplicated in "such crowded districts as the lower and upper East Side." The Gary Plan should be extended at once. "There should be," Nudd reiterated, "no delay." [103] The public was assailed by similar perfervid pleas from the *Times*, the *New Republic*, *Survey*, the Woman's Municipal League, the Association of Neighborhood Workers, and the Bureau of Educational Experiments.[104] It was as if the progressives feared that such an opportunity would never recur.

---

[101] Harriet M. Johnson, "The Schools of Gary," PEA *Bulletin*, No. 23, June 5, 1914.

[102] The *New York Times* published an extraordinary number of the PEA's letters during the 1915 push: one in June, four in September, one in October, and two in November. They may be found in its "Letters to the Editor" section under the following dates: June 17, September 13, 14, 17, and 23, October 13, and November 7 and 24, 1915. The letters were subsequently reprinted in Howard W. Nudd, "What the Gary Plan Means for the New York City Schools," PEA *Bulletin*, No. 26, December 16, 1915.

[103] All of Nudd's letters to the editor of the *New York Times* bear essentially the same message.

[104] *New York Times*, March 17, 1915, ed., June 17, 1915, ed.; Winthrop D. Lane, "From Gary to New York City: A Demonstration in Better and Cheaper Schools," *Survey*, XXXIII (March 6, 1915), 628–30, 637–38; Woman's Municipal League, Report of the Education Committee, *Modern Schools for New York* (New York, 1916). See also the following articles by Randolph Bourne: "Schools in Gary," "Communities for Children," "Really Public Schools," "Apprentices to the Schools," and "The Natural School," which appeared in the *New Republic* for March 27, April 3, 10, 24, and May 1, 1915. They were later reprinted in Bourne's *The Gary Schools* (Boston, 1916). See also his *Education and Living* (New York, 1917), esp. Chaps. XIV–XVIII, XXII–XXIV. See also John Dewey and Evelyn Dewey, *Schools of Tomorrow* (New York, 1915), Chap. XII and pp. 251–68.

During the critical public debate, William Maxwell, the 63-year-old giant of American public education, fell ill.[105] William E. Grady, Principal of P.S. 64, in a few years to become as District School Superintendent one of the PEA's chief contacts in the school system, entered the arena to challenge Nudd. The eulogies of Wirt, wrote Grady, reminded him of the eulogies of Joseph Lancaster, who once also promised more education for less money. Grady congratulated Nudd for the latter's "undaunted courage" in praising the Gary schools and in urging haste in the extension of a revolutionary scheme that had not even proved its value in P.S. 45 or P.S. 89.[106]

Indeed it had been only nine months since the first school, P.S. 45, had been reorganized and that, on the testimony of Wirt himself, not satisfactorily. In late September 1915, under public questioning before a group of School Superintendents, Wirt admitted that of the twelve Bronx schools authorized to be reorganized the previous June not one was ready and not one would be ready before 1916. He was not in favor, he testified, of extending the Gary system until the demonstration in the twelve Bronx schools had been evaluated, which would not be for several years.[107] But Wirt had been brought to New York as an ornament. Two days after his testimony before school officials, Mayor Mitchel urged that the Gary Plan be extended at once to all the public schools of the city.[108]

The Gary School War was an extremely complex and confusing affair. What exactly was going on in the Gary-ized schools of the city is impossible to ascertain. But the intent of the reformers emerges rather clearly in the writings of their spokesmen. Prendergast spoke for the City Administration and the devotees of good government: economy was their goal. The PEA spoke for social workers and philanthropists, progressive intellectuals and avant-garde educators. Although the PEA never ignored the school economy argument, the financial bearings of the Gary Plan were of slight importance to it. To the PEA, the city school system was the most important branch of city government; money was no object. The emphasis on economy was a short-range tactic to place it in line with the Mitchel administration. But neither was the Gary Plan's pedagogical bearing of any great import to the

[105] Abelow, *op. cit.*, p. 148.
[106] *New York Times,* July 19, September 17, 1915, Letters to the Editor.
[107] *New York Times,* September 24, 25, 1915; Joseph S. Taylor, "A Report on the Gary Experiment in New York City," *Educational Review,* LI (January, 1916), 27–28.
[108] *New York Times,* September 28, November 1, 1915.

92	The Die is Cast

PEA. The argument that the Gary Plan meant the enrichment of the school life of children was a sales slogan. There were public schools in the city which were already equipped with playgrounds, auditoriums, shops and such; Maxwell was a champion of these progressive innovations.

It was something other than economy, or the promise of a richer education, or even the Gary Plan *per se* which moved the PEA to ardently espouse the Gary cause. At stake was nothing less than the complete reorganization of the traditional system of public elementary education. By 1914, progressives, at least those in New York City, knew what they wanted from the public schools: preventive social work or social hygiene. This could not be stated right out for general consumption, but this is what Howard Nudd admitted in 1916 before a meeting of the National Conference of Charities and Correction:

> It is in the . . . preventive rather than mere corrective work in the field of social economy that I believe the school can contribute most toward the solution of the problem of social maladjustment.

The Gary Plan, Nudd granted, was no panacea for all of America's social ills; it was simply the best plan available.[109] If the Gary Plan could be installed, good. The important thing was to overthrow the traditional in education.

By 1916 although the Gary reorganization had been extended to some fifty schools in overcrowded sections of the Bronx, Manhattan, and Brooklyn, it was in serious trouble. The opportunity the Gary Plan offered for children to be excused during school hours for purposes of religious instruction raised a storm.[110] The Gary Plan was now also up against a stone wall of opposition in all levels of school officialdom; Maxwell and the Board of Superintendents were becoming more and more outspoken in their revolt against the city administration.[111] And even with its new "progressive majority," as the *New Republic* put it, the Board of Education was out of control. It insisted on larger school

109 Howard W. Nudd, "The Gary Plan and Its Social Bearing," *Proceedings*, National Conference of Charities and Correction (Indianapolis, 1916), p. 559. A similar sentiment was expressed, of course, but in slightly different terminology, by the PEA's Harriet Johnson in connection with the visiting teacher project. See above, p. 78.
110 *New York Times*, September 25, 27, 1915, and the *Times* for the months of October, November, and December 1915.
111 Abelow, *op. cit.*, p. 173; New York City, Department of Education, *Seventeenth Annual Report of the City Superintendent of Schools*, 1915, pp. 118–44, 165–69; New York City, Board of Education, *The First Fifty Years*, p. 62.

appropriations, procrastinated about extending the Gary Plan, and even gave indications that it would deny re-election to Dr. Joseph S. Taylor, the Superintendent of the Bronx district in which the Gary Plan had first been introduced.[112]

The PEA took it upon itself to counter all criticism and to admonish all opponents of the Gary Plan. Those who worried about the religious issue were assured that the time taken out for religious instruction would not be taken from the regular school work, that it was time which children in the "traditional" school would have spent in the street, and since the instruction would be given off school premises, it was no concern of the school.[113] The Superintendents were dismissed as "unobjective" and censured for "spreading falsehoods." [114] As for the Board of Education, Howard Nudd advised it to reconsider its failure to re-elect Superintendent Taylor. "The public," Nudd earnestly protested, "is extremely sensitive to any action which has any appearance of undue infringement upon legitimate professional functions." [115]

The religious issue could be eliminated. The Superintendents could be overridden or swayed. The Board of Education was the intolerable stumbling block in the way of action.

IX

The school provisions of the Revised City Charter of 1901 left New York with an extraordinarily large Board of Education of forty-six; even at this early date the trend in municipal reform was to small boards or commissions and the concentration of responsibility in all departments of city government.[116] Not until the Mitchel regime, however, was the

---

[112] *New York Times*, October 5, 26, 1915; "Politics Against the Schools," *New Republic*, VI (February 12, 1916), 32. By late 1915 Mitchel could count on the following members of the Board of Education, among others: Flexner, Martin, Wile, Draper, Harrison, Raymond Fosdick, Mary E. Dreier, Louis Pink, Franklin Giddings, John Whalen, Leo Arnstein, and William G. Willcox.

[113] *New York Times*, October 13, 1915, Letters to the Editor.

[114] Howard W. Nudd, " 'Evaluating' the Gary Schools in New York City. A Critical Analysis of the Report of Dr. Burdette R. Buckingham," *PEA Bulletin*, No. 29, April 20, 1916; Howard W. Nudd, "The Buckingham Tests of the Gary Schools in New York City," *School and Society*, III (April 8, 1916), 529-32.

[115] *New York Times*, February 3, 1916, Letters to the Editor. Nudd jumped the gun here. Taylor was re-elected.

[116] James T. Young, "The Administration of City Schools," *The Annals*, XV (March, 1900), 172; Truman A. DeWeese, "Better City School Administration," *Educational Review*, XX (June, 1900), 65; Samuel Train Dutton and David Snedden, *The Administration of Public Education in the United States* (New York, 1908), pp. 139-40; Frank J. Goodnow, *Municipal Government* (New York, 1910),

PEA, the City Club, the Citizens' Union, or, indeed, any reform organization in the city interested in one or another aspect of the school system, to be unduly perturbed by the board's size. Their interests were well represented on the Board of Education during the McClellan and Gaynor administrations; their school reform program made considerable headway. Nevertheless, when prompt action was called for, or action that might embroil it in controversy, the board became an uncertain element, even a hindrance to progress.

From the very first days of the Mitchel administration, varied efforts were made to give the city a reform Board of Education. Mayor Mitchel appointed many well-known progressives to the board. And when the Mayor finally gained control of the board in late 1915, he publicly hand-picked its new president, William L. Willcox.[117] Mitchel also used the power of the purse to make the board more amenable to progressive school reforms.[118] City School Law revision was another means of exerting pressure on the board or, perhaps, reconstituting it at one stroke.

The PEA started the ball rolling for school law reform three weeks after Mitchel's inauguration as Mayor. On January 21, 1914, at a well-publicized meeting on "Efficiency in Public School Administration" held under the PEA's auspices, Charles W. Eliot and Frederick C. Howe came out for a drastic reduction in the size of the board.[119] The PEA let the idea set for almost a year. Then in early 1915 it sponsored legislation at Albany calling for the abolition of the then Board of Education and its replacement by a small, unpaid board to be composed of nine members, appointments to be left in the hands of the Mayor.[120] "Democracy consists not in number and noise," the PEA stated, in

---

pp. 84, 270–71; Frank J. Goodnow and Frederick C. Howe, "The Organization, Status, and Procedures of the Department of Education, City of New York," in Report of Committee on School Inquiry, *op. cit.*, III, 197; New York City, Board of Education, *The First Fifty Years*, p. 56.

[117] *New York Times*, October 27, December 29, 1915.

[118] When Thomas Churchill, Willcox's predecessor as Board president, complained about the city school budget, Mitchel angrily retorted that the question of financing the schools was a business question, and if Churchill couldn't run the schools on what the city gave him he should resign. *New York Times*, October 26, 1915.

[119] *New York Times*, January 19, 22, 1914; *New York Times*, January 22, 1914, ed.; "The Board of Education and the Professional Staff," *PEA Bulletin*, No. 22, February 2, 1914.

[120] *New York Times*, February 23, 1915; Howard W. Nudd, "A Small Board of Education for New York," *PEA Bulletin*, No. 24, December 22, 1914; Howard W. Nudd, "An Unpaid Board of Nine for the New York City Schools," *PEA Bulletin*, No. 25, February 24, 1915.

anticipation of the objection that a small board would be unrepresentative and, therefore, undemocratic, "but in accountability to the community." [121] A small board, the PEA explained, could be held responsible for its acts more easily than could a large one.

The PEA's bill received the endorsement of New York's entire progressive community. The Mitchel administration endorsed the bill.[122] So did the City Club and the Citizens Union. Charles C. Burlingham, Seth Low, Nicholas Murray Butler, and Henry W. Taft came out for the bill.[123] So did the *New Republic*.[124] The *Times* threw its weight behind "the measure supported by that admirable organization, the Public Education Association." [125] Abraham Flexner tried to swing the Board of Education itself behind the measure but failed.[126] The bill was finally killed by the legislature. A similar bill suffered the same fate in 1916.

Finally, in the spring of 1917, legislation was passed and signed into law by the newly elected Governor, Republican Charles S. Whitman, amending those sections of the Education Law of 1901 applicable to New York City.[127] The new law increased the mandated minimum city school appropriations from 4 to 4.9 mills, increased somewhat the power of the City School Superintendent, and reduced the size of the Board of Education from forty-six to seven. And, as of December 31, 1917, the old board was to be abolished, and on January 1, 1918, a new board was to be chosen by the Mayor. Now all that the municipal reformers and the social workers, civic leaders and philanthropists, intellectuals and publicists, the pro-Mitchel, pro-Gary reformers had to do was win the impending mayoralty election.

X

As the year 1916 drew to a close the *Times* articulated the sentiments of most progressives in the city when it queried: "Has New York ever had as conscientious, intelligent and businesslike conduct of its

[121] Nudd, "A Small Board of Education for New York," p. 3.

[122] Prendergast, "Why New York City Needs a New School Plan," p. 588; Prendergast, "Reminiscences," V, 747.

[123] *New York Times*, February 23, 1915; Nudd, "A Small Board of Education for New York," p. 3, contains a list of endorsements from leading progressives.

[124] "The School Situation in New York," *New Republic*, p. 7.

[125] "Cut Down the Board," *New York Times*, December 23, 1914, ed.

[126] *Ibid.*, Lewinson, *op. cit.*, p. 217.

[127] *New York Times*, June 10, 1917; Cohen, *Financial Control* . . . , pp. 43–44; New York City, Board of Education, *The First Fifty Years*, pp. 76–78.

affairs as under this administration?" [128] Echo answered on November 6, 1917.

The anti-Tammany coalition which backed Mitchel in 1913 split apart in 1917. Mitchel, the incumbent, received the Fusion nomination for mayor but lost the support of the city's Republican party. William M. Bennett received the Republican nomination. Morris Hillquit was the Socialists' choice. John F. Hylan, an obscure, Hearst-picked, Brooklyn judge, ran on the Democratic line.

The election campaign was one of the most turbulent in the history of the Greater City. Tammany's general campaign strategy was to identify Mitchel with "the Rockefeller interests." The Gary School Plan was thus a heaven-sent gift. "We will banish the imported Gary system, which aims to make our public schools an annex to the mill and factory," the Democratic platform proclaimed.[129] From San Simeon, California, Col. W. R. Hearst denounced Mitchel for putting children on "half rations of education." [130] Hylan, pointing to Abraham Flexner and Raymond Fosdick, two of Mitchel's school board appointees, repeatedly accused the Mayor of delivering the city's public schools into the hands of the Rockefeller Foundation.[131] Allies of the Mitchel regime and partisans of the Gary Plan did not escape unscathed. A Hearst publicist charged that Rockefeller was out to get control of the city school system through the "Public Education Association, of which Mr. Rockefeller's attorney, Charles P. Howland, is President," and which "[is] supported largely by Rockefeller, who aims to dominate public school affairs." [132] Organized labor in New York State and New

[128] *New York Times*, December 13, 1916, ed.
[129] *New York Times*, August 8, 1917.
[130] *New York Evening Journal*, September 1, 1917; *New York Times*, September 1, 1917.
[131] *New York Times* and *New York Evening Journal* for September and October 1917; "The Gary Plan as a Campaign Issue," *Survey*, XXXVIII (September 29, 1917), 577; Joseph D. McGoldrick, "John Francis Hylan," *Dictionary of American Biography*, XXII, Supplement Two, 1958, pp. 330–31. William M. Bennett, the designee of the Republican party for the Mayoralty, and Frank D. Wilsey, Republican designee as President of the Board of Aldermen, made similar charges. *New York Evening Journal*, September 1, 11, 13, 1917; *New York Times*, September 1, 1917. Flexner resigned from the Board of Education on May 17, 1917. Fosdick had resigned some months previous. *New York Times*, May 18, 1917.
[132] From "The Money Power Behind Mayor Mitchel and 'Reform Fusion'," a leaflet published in 1917, and "Rockefeller in the Public Schools," extracts of a speech delivered at P.S. 37, Bronx, on February 9, 1917, in Henry H. Klein, *Politics, Government, and the Public Utilities* (New York, 1933), Kilroe Collection, Butler Library, Columbia University, New York.

York City was also up in arms against Rockefeller, the General Education Board, and the PEA.[133]

Fusion and its supporters were no less determined than Tammany to go to the people with the Gary Plan. Again and again Mitchel affirmed that the introduction of the Gary Plan into New York meant the "democratization" of the city school system.[134] The *Times* maintained that through the Gary Plan the public's children would get the same education as the children at Groton, Exeter, and Andover.[135] A newly organized Fusion Committee on Education, headed by Michael Friedsam of Altman's and including John Dewey among more than a score of civic and educational leaders in the city, also met attacks on the Gary Plan and espoused its merits.[136]

The PEA played as inconspicuous a role as possible during the campaign. It did not overtly press the Gary issue, or undertake to publicly dispute or challenge Tammany or Hearst or organized labor, or come out openly in support of Mitchel. But it created a front organization—the Gary School League—to keep up the agitation for the Gary Plan;[137] Howard Nudd continued his educational work among the city's leading civic groups;[138] and the PEA was represented on the special Education Committee formed by the Mitchel board of strategy to answer the attacks on the Gary system.[139]

By the fall of 1917 groups old and new, opposed to the Gary Plan for political or educational reasons, or both, began to exert themselves. The New York State Federation of Labor and the Central Federated

[133] As early as 1915 the New York State Federation of Labor called for "a full investigation of the Rockefeller Foundation, Rockefeller General Education Board, and Rockefeller Public Education Association. . . ." *Proceedings*, New York State Federation of Labor, 1916, p. 159, as quoted in Philip R. V. Curoe, *Educational Attitudes and Policies of Organized Labor in the United States* (New York, 1926), p. 154. See also Jack Cohn, "Attitudes and Policies of Organized Labor Toward Public Education in New York State" (unpublished Ed. D. project, Teachers College, Columbia University, 1952), pp. 132ff, 213.

[134] *New York Times*, September, October, 1917.

[135] "Study, Work, Play," *New York Times*, October 5, 1917, ed.; "The Rockefeller Foundation Myth," *New York Times*, September 13, 1917, ed.

[136] *New York Times*, September 15, 1917.

[137] *New York Times*, April 4, May 2, 1916; *Survey*, XXXVII (March 24, 1917), 731, ed.

[138] Women's City Club of New York, *Bulletin*, I (January, 1917), 4; Woman's Municipal League, *Report of the Work Done by the Woman's Municipal League of the City of New York for the Twelve Months Ending March 31st, 1917*, 1917, p. 14.

[139] E.g., Percy Straus and Mrs. Sidney Borg.

Union of New York City condemned the Gary Plan.[140] Public School
Neighborhood Associations, Parents Associations, and Parents School
Betterment Leagues were organized to fight Mitchel and the Gary Plan.
Hastily formed Anti-Gary Leagues made their appearance.[141] At a meet-
ing of one of these groups early in September 1917, Dr. Ira S. Wile of
the Board of Education was refused permission to speak, and Howard
Nudd was bodily thrown out for decrying the lack of fair play.[142]

Inflamed emotions, exacerbated by America's entry into the War
and the bitter electioneering over peace and patriotism, erupted finally
in school riots in the Bronx, Brooklyn, and Manhattan. For a week,
from October 17 to October 23, children and parents marched, picketed,
fought police, stoned schools, and smashed school windows. The *Times*
reported that Brownsville was in a "state of war." The news from P.S.
72 was "rioting"; from P.S. 110 "Big Riots"; and from P.S. 125 "Rioting
outside the building, only twelve students inside." [143] The story was
the same from Manhattan's lower East Side, and from the East Bronx.

The election ended in a debacle for reform. What many progressives
believed was the best administration the city had ever known was
decisively repudiated. Tammany came back to power with the greatest
plurality for any mayoralty candidate in the city's history up to that time.
Hylan carried every borough and almost doubled Mitchel's vote. Even
the Socialist candidate, Morris Hillquit, received only a shade fewer
votes than Mitchel.[144]

The causes of the Fusion disaster were complex: the controversy
over city subsidies to private charities, the charges that Mitchel was
"too much Fifth Avenue, too little First Avenue," Mitchel's super-
patriotism and his alienation of German and Irish voters, all contributed
to bring his administration to an end.[145] But Mitchel's extreme effort

[140] *New York Times*, October 27, 1917; Curoe, *op. cit.*, pp. 156–57; and Cohn,
op. cit., p. 133.
[141] *New York Times*, July 10, 15, October 21, 1917; *New York Evening Journal*,
September 17, 1917; "The Gary Plan as a Campaign Issue," *Survey*, p. 576; Margaret
Lighty and LeRoy E. Bowman, *Parenthood in a Democracy* (New York, 1939),
pp. 31–33; Lewinson, *op. cit.*, pp. 232–34. The main charges brought forward against
the Gary Plan were: it was an expedient to avoid the construction of new school
buildings; it was being forced on the city; it gave too little attention to the academic
subjects; and it opened the door of the schools to religious proselytizing.
[142] "The Gary Plan as a Campaign Issue," *Survey*, p. 576.
[143] *New York Times*, October 17–23, 1917; *New York Evening Journal*,
October 17, 18, 19, 1917; Mary Graham Bonner, "School Riots and the Gary
System," *Outlook*, CXVII (October 31, 1917), 117.
[144] *New York Times*, November 7, 1917.
[145] Eda Amberg and William H. Allen, *Civic Lessons from Mayor Mitchel's
Defeat* (New York, 1921); Emanie M. Sacks, "Being Human: A Great Mayor and

to force the Gary system down the throats of New Yorkers must also be given a prominent place in any explanation for his failure to win re-election. As John Dewey pointed out, after the election to be sure, even the friends of the Gary Plan were aware that its success was "fundamentally compromised if not doomed by the autocratic way in which it was formulated and imposed from above." [146] Likewise, the autocratic way the Gary Plan was formulated and imposed from above helped sink the Mitchel administration.

The election over, the Gary system ceased to be an object of excitement in New York City. It disappeared from public discussion as suddenly as it arose. The city's Board of Education gave orders to dismantle the shops and "de-Garyize" the schools, and the board went back, under Tammany, to the erstwhile progressive notion of "a seat for every child." [147] The appearance ten months after the election of Abraham Flexner's stringent critique of the Gary public schools, undertaken in 1916 for the General Education Board, helped bury the Gary Plan and Wirt, as such, for good so far as New York was concerned.[148]

The PEA took Mitchel's defeat in stride. And why not? The PEA had won by 1917 the allegiance of many of the rich and powerful in the city; it was a strong and confident group; there was no longer any question of its dominance in the field of public education. True, educational progressivism had just suffered its worst defeat in the city's history. But many of the other school reforms for which the PEA had worked

What Happened to Him," *Century*, CXI (February, 1926), 390–403; Garrett, *op. cit.*, pp. 44–45; Nevins and Krout, *op. cit.*, p. 88; McGoldrick, *op. cit.*, pp. 37–38; Sayre and Kaufman, *op. cit.*, p. 694; Morris, *op. cit.*, p. 38.

[146] John Dewey, "Public Education on Trial," *New Republic*, XIII (December 29, 1917), 246.

[147] *New York Times*, November 8, 1917; *Elementary School Journal*, XVIII (December, 1917), 249, ed.; New York City, Board of Education, *The First Fifty Years*, p. 62.

[148] Flexner, *I Remember*, pp. 253–56; Abraham Flexner and Frank P. Bachman, *The Gary Schools: A General Account* (New York, 1918), pp. 46–47, 77, 90–105, 107, 120–21, 132, 177, 195, and "Conclusions," pp. 196–206. Perhaps a last note is in order on this extraordinary affair. On September 12, 1917, the Republican candidate for President of the Board of Aldermen, Frank D. Wilsey, charged that the General Education Board's report on the Gary schools was completed but was being suppressed until after the election because it severely condemned the Gary system. *New York Evening Journal*, September 13, 1917. Another author, a few years later, made the same charge. Amberg and Allen, *op. cit.*, p. 19. Examination of the annual reports of the General Education Board indicates that the Gary report was indeed ready before the fall of 1917. The investigation of the Gary schools began in February 1916, and closed in June 1916. The General Education Board promised the report to the public within the course of the year (1916); the report was not issued until the fall of 1918. General Education Board, *Annual Reports of the Secretary*, 1915–1918.

so hard in the past decade—compulsory education, vocational education, special classes for the mentally and physically defective, and visiting teachers—were now part of the municipal scene and were not going to be erased.

As for the future, the PEA had its work cut out for it. On the political side, now that Hylan controlled the Board of Education, the PEA had its assignment to protect the schools from this unregenerate Tammanyite. And on the educational side, the PEA had its long-range objective of transforming the public schools of New York into effective centers of social work. While the Gary Plan, a long step in this direction, had been decisively rejected at the polls, there were many ways to skin a cat. The PEA still had its visiting teacher project. And, as things settled down, something might be done with a small experiment in the use of the new intelligence tests which it had been granted permission to undertake in an East Side public school in 1914 before the Gary excitement began.

Chapter 4

HEY-DAY

1917-1931

IT IS A WIDELY SHARED VIEW among American historians that the post-World War I decade constitutes a bleak interregnum in the history of American progressivism; a period in which progressivism, if not actually dead, was disillusioned, tired, and impotent. This view has recently been challenged by Arthur Link.[1] In a provocative re-interpretation of the twenties, Link suggests that while on the national level the progressive movement may have been in decline, on the state and municipal levels reform energies were very much alive. The career of the PEA lends impressive support to Link's thesis.

In the 1920's the PEA displayed more vigor and enterprise in its promotional and political activities than at any other time in its entire history. Through its visiting teacher project the PEA became a partner in one of the largest privately sponsored demonstrations of social work ever attempted in the United States: the Commonwealth Funds' Program for the Prevention of Juvenile Delinquency. By virtue of an all-out public relations campaign, it created a nationally famous experiment in progressive education: the Little Red School House. And finally, by virtue of its constant, extensive, and aggressive intervention in New York City politics, it made itself the city's leading civic group. In short, in a decade when progressivism is frequently supposed to have been dead, the PEA was in its prime.

That the PEA flourished in the twenties was due to a combination of circumstances involving its leadership and the times of which it was

[1] "What Happened to the Progressive Movement in the 1920's?" *American Historical Review*, LXIV (July, 1959), 838–50. See also Henry F. May, "Shifting Perspectives on the 1920's," *Mississippi Valley Historical Review*, XLIII (December, 1956), 405–27.

a part. Charles P. Howland stayed on as PEA president until 1925, when he accepted a League of Nations appointment as Special Envoy to Greece. He was succeeded by Joseph P. Cotton of the blue-ribbon law firm of Cotton and Franklin, who served until 1930 when he joined the Hoover Administration as an Under Secretary of State. So far as the PEA was concerned, however, Cotton was strictly window dressing. Among the men, besides Howland, the activists were Henry W. Taft, brother of ex-president and Chief Justice William Howard Taft, and a senior partner of Cadwallader, Wickersham and Taft, and William M. Chadbourne of Chadbourne, Hunt, Jaeckel and Brown. As lawyers are wont to do, they dabbled in politics. Howland and Chadbourne were veterans of many a Fusion campaign; Taft, a pillar of the Republican party. Attracted by the magnificent opportunity the PEA presented to make contacts and to start on a career of public service and politics, several young lawyers soon appeared in the Association's policy-making councils. Alfred Jaretzki, Jr., just starting out with Sullivan and Cromwell, and Kenneth M. Simpson, whose flair for politics would lead him to become a powerhouse in Republican politics in city and state in the thirties, were most active in this group. The legal monopoly of the PEA's leadership was broken by Percy Straus of Macy's and William B. Nichols, a young stockbroker and protégé of Mrs. Henderson, who would go on to become the PEA's sixth president in 1935. As a group the men shared a deep-rooted antipathy toward Tammany Hall and an inclination to perceive the role of the PEA in broad and inclusive terms. Here Mr. Howland *et al.* would receive no argument from their feminine counterparts in the PEA.

In the early twenties, Mrs. Miriam Sutro Price, Mrs. Edward C. Henderson, and Mrs. Joseph R. Swan were joined in the inner circle of PEA leadership by a small coterie of young socialites who infused the PEA with new money and new energy. Most conspicuous in this group were Mrs. Thomas K. Schmuck, Mrs. J. Culbert Palmer, Mrs. Walker E. Swift, Mrs. Louis S. Levy, and, notably, Mrs. Samuel A. Lewisohn. Female suffrage had finally come to New York State in 1917 and the ladies of the PEA, no less than the men, were eager to push the PEA into the city's political and social life in a more energetic manner than before.

Given the PEA's leadership and its fundamental school objectives, the times were exceedingly propitious for it to broaden its sphere of operations. The 1920's saw fast-breaking developments in the fields of progressive social thought and local politics upon which the PEA was fully willing and able to capitalize. When the prevention of social ills, that much-bruited topic among social workers in the pre-World War I decade, seemed in the 1920's, thanks to the new psychology, finally to be capable of realization, the PEA was ready with its staff of visiting teachers, ably led by Howard Nudd and Jane Culbert, to help social workers push into the schools. Developments in progressive education proper were equally favorable to the PEA, and the PEA fully exploited them. When the Progressive Education Association launched its drive to transform the country's public schools, the PEA was ready with its contacts in the progressive education movement and in the New York City public school system, and with its own Elisabeth Irwin, to establish a progressive beachhead in the city schools. Finally, in the turbulent reconstruction years there was opportunity aplenty in New York for any aspiring civic organization with a special interest in the public schools to show its mettle. The city school system was seething, caught up in questions of academic freedom, inflation, and politics. The PEA lost no time in mourning the humiliating Fusion defeat of 1917, but commenced the publication of a weekly newsletter, *The Public and the Schools*, and took the plunge into New York's political life as a major power.[2]

I

During the period of the "Red Scare" of the early 1920's, thanks to the activities of Attorney General Palmer, the Overman Committee of the United States Senate, and the Lusk Committee of the New York state legislature, New York City was spotlighted as the center of American Bolshevism.[3] Stimulated by the antics of the super-patriots, city school officials redoubled their efforts to scour the school system of Communists, Socialists, and all other forms of unorthodoxy, especially that heresy embodied in the New York Teachers Union.[4] The New

[2] *The Public and the Schools*, a printed newsletter or bulletin, was sent to all members of the PEA, to influential individuals and to every major civic group in the city, to all school officials and to every public school in the city, to the daily press, and to several periodicals featuring school news, *viz.*, *The School Review* and *School and Society*.

[3] Robert K. Murray, *Red Scare: A Study in National Hysteria, 1919–1920* (Minneapolis, Minn., 1955), pp. 98–102, 197, 235–38, 243–44; Harold M. Hyman, *To Try Men's Souls: Loyalty Tests in American History* (Berkeley, Calif., 1959), pp. 317–20; Zachariah Chafee, Jr., *Freedom of Speech* (New York, 1920), pp. 302–10, 332ff.

[4] Robert W. Iversen, *The Communists and the Schools* (New York, 1959), pp. 12–13; Bessie Louise Pierce, *Public Opinion and the Teaching of History in the United States* (New York, 1926), pp. 112–27; Howard K. Beale, *Are American Teachers Free?* (New York, 1936), pp. 23, 25, 28–37, 68, 586–87.

York legislature was no less concerned than the New York City Board of Education with enforcing a rigid orthodoxy upon the city's teachers, their concern resulting finally in 1920 in the notorious Lusk Laws, the quintessential legislative expression of the Red Scare.[5] During this time of hysteria New York's public school teachers had few friends. But some groups refused to be swayed by the turgid climate of opinion. The PEA threw its weight to the side of that small band led by the American Civil Liberties Union and the New York Bar Association in the fight for sanity, civil liberties, and academic freedom.

The PEA did not consider the times propitious for educating city school leaders in the principle of *Lehrfreiheit*, nor was the PEA sure itself what meaning this principle had for the public schools. But for the PEA freedom for public school teachers was at least something to debate. On April 26, 1919, the PEA threw open its annual public meeting to a debate on the topic: "Freedom and Initiative in the Schools." [6] For its annual meeting the following year, the PEA chose as the topic for debate the equally timely and contentious: "Should Teachers Affiliate with Organized Labor?" [7] Thus the PEA tried to create an environment in which the question of the bounds of teacher freedom would at least be a debatable one, a question about which reasonable men could differ, and not a question to be decided by summary administrative action on the part of city school officials.

The PEA was much more vehement in its opposition to the Lusk

[5] Lawrence H. Chamberlain, *Loyalty and Legislative Action: A Survey of Activity by the New York State Legislature, 1919–1949* (New York, 1951), Chap. I, esp. pp. 40–48; Iversen, *op. cit.*, p. 13; Murray, *op. cit.*, p. 238; Chafee, *op. cit.*, p. 361; Beale, *op. cit.*, pp. 61–63; Pierce, *op. cit.*, p. 112.

[6] Henry Linville, president of the New York Teachers Union, joined Professor Zachariah Chafee, Jr., on the "pro" side of the debate. Dr. George D. Strayer, President of the National Education Association and professor of educational administration at Teachers College, Columbia University, joined Associate School Superintendent John L. Tildsley in the "con" position. *New York Times*, April 27, 1919. All the addresses were subsequently reprinted in *The Public and the Schools*; see No. 23, May 3, 1919; No. 25, May 17, 1919; and No. 26, May 24, 1919. Professor Chafee reprinted his address, a ringing defense of the social value of the unfettered pursuit of truth, as the concluding chapter of his *Freedom of Speech*, Chap. VII.

[7] The speakers "pro" were Dr. Henry A. Overstreet of the College of the City of New York, a member of the Teachers Union, and Mr. Joseph Jablonower, an instructor at the Ethical Culture School, and also a member of the Teacher's Union. David S. Snedden, professor of educational sociology at Teachers College, Columbia University, and Miss Olive M. Jones, President of the New York Principals Association, took the "con" position. *New York Times*, February 15, 1920. For the complete text of the addresses, see *The Public and the Schools*, No. 56, February 28, 1920; No. 57, March 6, 1920; No. 58, March 13, 1920; and No. 60, March 27, 1920.

Laws. No threat to freedom of thought has ever come under such strong criticism from the PEA. For years, through *The Public and the Schools,* the Association aimed a steady stream of invective at the laws. "Misguided patriotism gone mad," *The Public and the Schools,* in a characteristically pungent phrase, called them.[8] In 1922 the PEA organized a "Citizens Committee to Repeal the Lusk Laws" comprising four score of the city's civic, education, and religious leaders, to back up newly elected Democratic Governor Al Smith in the struggle, ultimately successful later that year, to have the laws repealed.[9]

With its fight against the Lusk Laws the PEA began a long and consistent record of hostility against all the "flag-flaunting patriotism bills" constantly introduced over the years into the New York state legislature. Similarly, the PEA, in the reconstruction period, began a long history of efforts to restrain city school officials from the abuse of their administrative powers and to educate them to a somewhat greater understanding of the meaning of academic freedom.

II

Rocked by the activities of the radical hunters, the city's public school system was further demoralized by the financial inflation which plagued the nation during and after the War. By 1920 the cost of living had risen 112 per cent over prewar levels. Teacher salaries were simply left far behind.[10] The result was not only an aggravation of teacher unrest (some attributed teacher radicalism to low salaries), but also an acute teacher shortage. With all teacher and school supervisory groups in the city in full cry for Albany in pursuit of pay raises, the PEA moved quickly to back up their demands and to establish itself

[8] *The Public and the Schools,* No. 62, April 10, 1920; No. 69, May 29, 1920; No. 98, April 16, 1921; No. 102, May 14, 1921; No. 139, May 27, 1922; No. 156, January 30, 1923.

[9] *School and Society,* XVI (December 9, 1922), 658–59; *The Public and the Schools,* No. 153, January 6, 1923; No. 156, January 30, 1923. The activities of the PEA point to the need of revising Professor Chamberlain's plaint about "the almost complete absence of protest except from the American Civil Liberties Union and a few left-wing labor groups" against the Lusk Laws. *Op. cit.,* p. 45.

[10] By 1920 real wages of teachers in the United States had dropped to 19 per cent below prewar levels. Between 1914 and 1920 teachers suffered a more severe loss from the lag in their salaries behind living costs than did manual workers in any classification in the country. Paul H. Douglas, *Real Wages in the United States, 1890–1926* (Boston, 1930), Chap. XXI, esp. pp. 381–85, 581; William E. Leuchtenburg, *The Perils of Prosperity, 1914–1932* (Chicago, 1958), p. 70.

as the civic leader of their cause. Through 1919, article after article in
The Public and the Schools played up "The Teaching Crisis." [11] In
1920, after New York City school personnel introduced two bills calling
for radical salary increases into the state legislature, the PEA organized
a "Citizens Committee of One Hundred to Save the Schools," which
included such dignitaries as Charles Evans Hughes, Felix Warburg,
Rabbi Stephen S. Wise, and Archbishop Patrick J. Hayes, to lobby for
their passage.[12] The PEA kept up this aggressive advocacy of school
spending throughout the 1920's, sharply and insistently prodding the
city administration for increased appropriations for school services and
capital outlay, as well as for teacher salaries. At the same time it agitated
to secure a greater amount of state monies for the city schools.[13]

The PEA's militancy in the matter of school finance was dictated
for several reasons. Fundamentally, the educational ideal to which by
then it was firmly wedded, of the public school as a center for social
work with children, required large expenditures of money. Progressive
education was expensive. The PEA was reconciled to this. Nevertheless,
when the PEA stepped forward in the twenties as the Board of Education's best friend, it had more immediate tactical ends in view. In
the first place, support of the demands of school officialdom and school
teachers for the scarce dollars available through the city budget was
seen as good public relations.[14] And in the second place, and most
compellingly, there was the PEA's eagerness to embarrass the administration of Democratic Mayor John Francis Hylan: if school appropriations

[11] *The Public and the Schools*, No. 7, January 11, 1919; No. 15, March 8, 1919;
No. 16, March 15, 1919; No. 22, April 26, 1919; No. 24, May 10, 1919.

[12] *New York Times*, March 14, 1920, Sec. II; *The Public and the Schools*, No.
59, March 20, 1920; No. 60, March 27, 1920. Bills were finally passed in the 1920
legislative session granting teachers and school officials a 20 per cent across-the-
board salary increase. Rose Naomi Cohen, *The Financial Control of Education in
the Consolidated City of New York* (New York, 1948), p. 102; New York City,
Board of Education, *The First Fifty Years, 1898–1948: Fiftieth Annual Report of
the Superintendent of Schools* (New York, 1948), p. 74.

[13] The PEA was represented by Martha Lincoln Draper and Mrs. Edward C.
Henderson on Governor Smith's Friedsam Commission, which recommended legislation drastically revising the state aid to education formula, proposals which, with
the hearty support of the Governor, were enacted into law in 1926. Cohen, *op. cit.*,
pp. 169–73; New York City, Board of Education, *The First Fifty Years*, pp. 109–10;
David M. Ellis, *et al.*, *A Short History of New York State* (New York, 1957), p.
403.

[14] By the mid-twenties organized labor had ceased its attacks on the PEA. Jack
Cohn, "Attitudes and Policies of Organized Labor Toward Public Education in
New York State" (unpublished Ed.D. project, Teachers College, Columbia Uni-
versity, 1952), pp. 185, 209, 214.

were forced up, the Hylan administration might be compelled to resort to the unpopular expedient of raising the city's property tax rate or imposing some new tax or taxes on the city; if the city administration turned a deaf ear to the PEA's pleas, it could be accused before the electorate of being an enemy of the public schools. The latter is exactly what happened in 1920 when Hylan refused to grant funds to cover the teacher salary increases voted by the state legislature.[15] In fact, much of the PEA's history in the twenties must be described in terms of a highly partisan, anti-Tammany civic organization deeply involved in the contest of city politics.

III

Democratic hegemony over all branches of New York City government was virtually complete during the long period beginning with the investiture of Mayor Hylan on January 1, 1919, and ending with the resignation under fire of Mayor James J. Walker on September 1, 1932.[16] When the machine was thus at the zenith of its power, the PEA engaged in the most extensive, the most continuous, and the most aggressive anti-Tammany acts of its entire history, even exceeding the City Club and the Citizens Union in the degree and vigor of its partisanship.

Since the PEA was led by such anti-Tammany stalwarts as Charles Howland, William Chadbourne, and Henry Taft, and since the schools had proved their value as a political weapon in the 1917 Mayoralty election, one would have expected the PEA to take the lead in turning that weapon against Tammany. And this is exactly what happened. One might also have predicted that a machine regular like Hylan, unlike the last Democratic Mayor before him, William J. Gaynor, would utterly ignore the PEA or its allies in the making of school appointments and thereby intensify the PEA's belligerence. And this, too, is exactly

[15] Cohen, *op. cit.*, p. 102. Hylan claimed the city could not afford the pay increases at that time. The New York state legislature was forced to superimpose a special tax upon the city to provide the necessary funds.

[16] Charles Garrett, *The La Guardia Years: Machine and Reform Politics in New York City* (New York, 1961), Chap. III, "An Age of Tammany"; Wallace S. Sayre and Herbert Kaufman, *Governing New York City: Politics in the Metropolis* (New York, 1960), p. 175; Frederick Shaw, *The History of the New York City Legislature* (New York, 1954), p. 28. General exceptions to Tammany's supremacy in the twenties were East Harlem's Twentieth Congressional district, the domain of that singular Republican, Fiorello H. La Guardia, and the two Manhattan "silk-stocking" Assembly districts. Arthur Mann, *La Guardia: A Fighter Against His Times, 1882–1933* (Philadelphia, 1959).

what happened. Hylan gave notice immediately upon taking office, on January 1, 1918, that the PEA's years of easy access to school officialdom were numbered when he filled the new, seven-man Board of Education with loyal Braves, personal friends, or, to the progressives anyway, otherwise undistinguished choices.[17] Because of the political inclinations of its leadership then, because the schools had proved to be an effective political weapon in 1917, and because its vital stake in school appointments was threatened, the PEA launched a frontal assault to oust Hylan from City Hall, and thereby embarked on a stormy, decade-long venture in partisan politics.

In 1893, when the reformers launched their successful drive to oust Tammany from City Hall, they exploited the deplorable condition of the public schools as an extremely fertile source of anti-Tammany propaganda. The PEA turned to this strategy in preparation for the mayoralty election of 1921. Beginning as early as 1919 the Association launched an all-out campaign of school muckraking aimed at discrediting the Hylan administration. In this campaign the *Times* played the megaphone for *The Public and the Schools.* Hylan was assailed for the existence of school "pest holes" and "firetraps," for school congestion, for part-time, and for economizing in the city budget at the expense of children. *The Public and the Schools* demanded increased school appropriations "even if this will embarrass certain aspirants for office in the next municipal election." [18] The politically motivated nature of the PEA's interest in the schools was readily identifiable. The headline in *The School Review,* over its summary of one of the PEA's exposés, read: "Republican View of the Democratic Administration of the New York City Schools." [19]

[17] "In what secret recesses of personal or Tammany acquaintance," the *New York Times* wanted to know, "did Mayor Hylan find his seven appointees to the new Board of Education? They are almost entirely unknown to the public, their names suggest nothing, there is no record by which their promises can be judged." January 2, 1918, ed. The Mayor's appointees were: Joseph Yeska and Mrs. Emma L. Murray, Manhattan; Mrs. Isaac Franklin Russell and Arthur S. Somers, Brooklyn; Frank D. Welsey, Bronx; Anning S. Prall, Richmond; and George J. Ryan, Queens. *New York Times,* January 2, 1918.
[18] *The Public and the Schools,* No. 10, February 1, 1919; No. 19, April 5, 1919; No. 20, April 12, 1919; No. 22, April 26, 1919; No. 24, May 10, 1919; No. 28, June 7, 1919; No. 33, September 13, 1919; No. 34, September 20, 1919; No. 35, September 27, 1919; No. 51, January 24, 1920; No. 77, November 6, 1920; No. 79, November 20, 1920; No. 87, January 29, 1921; No. 106, June 11, 1921; No. 107, October 1, 1921. And see the *New York Times,* February 1, 1919; February 3, 1919, ed.; April 4, 1919; April 5, 1919, ed.; April 26, 1919; September 20, 1919; January 25, 1920, Sec. II; October 10, 1920, Sec. VIII; June 4, 1921; June 12, 1921, Sec. VI; June 21, 1921; July 3, 1921.
[19] XIV (October 22, 1921), 342.

Anti-Tammany forces in the city in 1921 were directed by a Coalition Campaign Committee headed by Republicans Henry W. Taft and Ogden L. Mills. Republican Henry H. Curran was their mayoral candidate. The Fusion campaign centered around attacks on Tammany for the high cost of living, and appeals to the electorate to "save the schools from Tammany." [20] But all resemblance to the campaign of 1894 ends here. On November 8, 1921 the Democratic party, led by incumbent Hylan, won an unprecedented victory. The organization swept every A.D. in the city; Hylan doubled Curran's vote in every borough.[21]

In the aftermath of their second consecutive humiliation, a lethargy settled over the city's good government forces. The City Club, the Citizens Union, and the city's Republican party went into virtual retirement for the remainder of the decade. But the PEA, which had worked strenuously for the ouster of the "Blunder Bund," as *The Public and the Schools* was wont to call the Hylan administration, was still full of fight. In early 1922, at the first post-election meeting of the Board of Trustees, President Howland boasted of the PEA's school muckraking activities during the preceding year. And Henry W. Taft stated to his fellow members of the board: "Now the Association has become a real factor and influence in the community." [22] No doubt in the eyes of New York's civic community, no less than in its own eyes, Taft's appraisal was absolutely correct. The difficulty, however, was that Mayor Hylan obstinately, infuriatingly, refused to accept this verdict.

The next four years were marked by constant and bitter warfare between the PEA and Mayor Hylan. The Mayor, flushed with his second mandate from the people, brazenly attempted to exploit school appointments as a horn of plenty for his closest friend and political ally, Brooklyn Democratic boss John H. McCooey, while the PEA tried frantically to thwart the Mayor's designs and to exert its own influence on school appointments. A few examples will suffice of the battles which waged furiously during Hylan's second term over school appointments.

In 1922, to the accompaniment of the PEA's anguished cries of "pull" and "politics," the Board of Education appointed Miss Margaret

[20] *New York Times*, October 12, 15, 21, 22, November 1, 2, 4, 6, 1921. Hylan, the heavy-handed but honest proselyte of publisher William Randolph Hearst and Brooklyn Democratic boss John H. McCooey, ran on a ticket calling for the retention of the five-cent fare, home rule, and "a seat for every child." Hylan flayed his school critics as "Gary propagandists" and promised a vast school building program if re-elected. *New York Times*, June 12, 21, 22, July 12, October 7, 8, 15, 21, and 28, 1921. See also Henry H. Curran, *Pillar to Post* (New York, 1941).
[21] *New York Times*, November 9, 1921.
[22] Minutes of the Board of Trustees of the PEA, March 28, 1922.

McCooey, a teacher-in-charge of a small Brooklyn school, and the sister of the Brooklyn boss, as an Associate Superintendent of Schools.[23] In 1923 Miss Lucile Nicol, another minor Brooklyn school official, was appointed to a District Superintendency. "Politics Wins Again," *The Public and the Schools* fumed.[24] One year later, Hylan inflicted the sharpest blow yet on the school reformers when he blocked the re-appointment of City School Superintendent William L. Ettinger, the PEA's most important ally inside the school system (as the PEA was Ettinger's most important ally outside).[25] When Ettinger failed of reappointment, he became the first City School Superintendent in the history of the Greater City of New York, and to this date the last, to fail thus. The Board of Education chose Associate Superintendent William J. O'Shea, a man acceptable to Hylan, to succeed Ettinger. The outcome stirred an angry protest in the reform press. The *Times* declared that "Mayor Hylan has descended to the lowest level in personal politics by virtually dismissing Dr. Ettinger." [26] The PEA cried, "Hylan reigns with his strong right hand intact." [27] O'Shea, who began his career in the city school system in 1888 as an evening elementary school teacher, would make the PEA rue these words.

Although the PEA was unable to thwart Hylan's designs in the Board of Education, it was able to deter the Mayor's bold moves to capture or make more receptive to his claims the Board of Examiners, the reformers' sanctum sanctorum. When a bill designed to bring the Board of Examiners closer to City Hall was introduced in the State Legislature in 1923, the PEA raised a loud hue and cry against the

[23] *New York Times*, December 18, 1922; *The Public and the Schools*, No. 152, December 16, 1922.

[24] When the PEA learned that Miss Nicol did not meet the minimum educational requirements of the post, it announced, to the huzzahs of the reform press, that it would take her to court, and that "Mr. Henry Taft would argue the case before the highest courts if necessary." *New York Times*, November 26, 28, December 10, 1923. And see the excerpts from editorials in the *New York Evening Post*, *New York Times*, *New York Tribune*, *New York World*, and *New York Evening Mail* in *The Public and the Schools*, No. 186, December 11, 1923. The Hylan administration was also prepared to make a fight of it. The "Nicol Case" dragged through 1924 and 1925. In 1926, by which time her educational deficiency had been repaired and even the PEA was tired of the whole affair, the State Commissioner of Education ruled Miss Nicol's appointment legal.

[25] *New York Times*, October 5, 26, November 9, 16, 1919. For a general review of the squabbles between Ettinger and the Mayor and the Board of Education, see Cohen, *op cit.*, pp. 107–14.

[26] "The Lowest Level," *New York Times*, April 25, 1924, ed.

[27] *New York Times*, April 25, 1924; *The Public and the Schools*, No. 204, April 25, 1924.

measure as "spoils legislation." [28] The *Times* and other newspapers in
the city joined the fight against the "School Spoils Bill," and the resulting widespread protest killed it. [29]

Repulsed in Albany, Hylan turned to the investigative tactic. In
late 1923, George J. Ryan, president of the Board of Education,
launched a one-man investigation into alleged mispractices in the Board
of Examiners. The PEA raised the cry of "politics," rallied the press
behind the Board, and formed a distinguished committee comprising
Charles Howland, Charles C. Burlingham, A. Leo Everett, and Albert
DeRoode to furnish it with legal advice and assistance. Thanks to the
PEA's legal aid committee, which pressed for State adjudication, the
Examiners were ultimately cleared. [30]

After it rebuffed Hylan's bid to annex the Board of Examiners to
City Hall, the PEA went on the offensive. On January 15, 1924, the
PEA, the Men's City Club, the Women's City Club, the Civil Service
Reform Association, the New York League of Women Voters, and some
eighty distinguished New Yorkers, inspired and led by the PEA, petitioned State Commissioner of Education Frank P. Graves to investigate
"politics" in the New York City school system. [31] But these were Democratic years in Albany, too, and the petition was ignored.

The PEA's action moved the ponderous Hylan to an outburst of
letter-writing, the Mayor's favorite medium of expression. After the
demagoguery is discounted, there is an important element of truth in
Hylan's furious riposte that the proposed inquiry was "an attempt to
blackjack the Board of Education . . . into filling vacancies in the
school system with sympathizers of the Rockefeller–Gary educational
interests." [32] During the Hylan regime, all municipal reformers (deroga-
torily labelled "goo-goos"), eggheads, and civic leaders, all "high-brow
politicians" as Hylan labeled them, were scrupulously ignored in the
making of school appointments. William B. Nichols emphatically recalls
that so far as the PEA was concerned, "Hylan and the School Super-

[28] *The Public and the Schools*, No. 158, February 13, 1923; No. 161, March 6,
1923; No. 164, March 27, 1923; No. 165, April 3, 1923.
[29] *New York Times*, March 3, 1923, ed.; *New York Tribune*, April 10, 1923,
ed.; New York City, Board of Education, *The First Fifty Years*, p. 108.
[30] *New York Times*, October 29, 1923; Minutes of the Board of Trustees of
the PEA, May 29, 1923; *The Public and the Schools*, No. 191, January 29, 1924;
No. 219, December 16, 1924; No. 223, January 27, 1925; No. 251, February 9, 1926.
[31] *New York Times*, January 16, 1924; *The Public and the Schools*, No. 190,
January 22, 1924.
[32] *New York Times*, January 12, 17, 24, February 17, 1924. Excerpts from some
of Hylan's letters may be found in *The Public and the Schools*, No. 190, January 22,
1924.

intendent [William J. O'Shea] were absolutely inaccessible." [33] The PEA's appeals to Albany, its watchdog tactics, its muckraking, its appeals to the electorate, all were tactics through which it hoped to force its way into the school appointment process, and protect its lines of communication to top school officials upon whom it was so dependent for its influence in the school system.

Hylan ignored the PEA and the others with impunity. The reformers could exert no effective pressure against him. He was invulnerable to the PEA's appeals to Albany; he was invulnerable to the PEA's appeals to public opinion at home. Hylan's school appointments may have been undistinguished, but the PEA never found any corruption in the school system while he was Mayor. Equally important, under Hylan's aegis, and perhaps spurred by the criticism of the PEA itself, city school expenditures were vastly increased and the greatest school construction program in the city's history to that time was launched.[34] By 1924 even the *Times* was ready to acknowledge that a Tammany Mayor had done a good piece of work for the city. The *Times* praised Hylan for carrying forward a great school construction program and informed him that it was time he stopped belaboring the "interests." [35] But Hylan and the "interests" remained irreconcilable to the end.

For a brief spell in the mid-twenties it seemed as if there might be a rapprochement between the PEA and City Hall. In 1925 Hylan was dumped by the "New Tammany" of Governor Al Smith in favor of Smith's own protégé, the dapper songwriter and State Senator from Manhattan, James J. Walker.[36] The political career of "Beau James" would end in 1932 with his ignominious retirement while under fire from the Seabury investigation. But this ugly denouement was some years off.

---

[33] William B. Nichols, Interview, September 29, 1959, New York City.

[34] It was during Hylan's second term that the city saw its first $100,000,000 school budget. From just short of $44,000,000 in 1917, the figure rocketed to more than $100,600,000 in 1925, exclusive of capital outlay. The latter sum for the whole period 1920–1930 totalled $284,000,000, most of which was appropriated during 1921–1925. With the average daily school attendance rising from 694,829 in 1918 to 898,256 in 1925, Hylan apparently attempted to make good his campaign pledge to provide "a seat for every child." New York City, Board of Education, *Annual Financial Reports*, 1917–1925; New York City, Board of Education, *The First Fifty Years*, p. 86.

[35] Quoted in *School and Society*, XX (September 13, 1924), 345. For further acknowledgement of Hylan's school program, see Gregory Weinstein, *The Ardent Eighties and After* (New York, 1928), p. 138; Joseph D. McGoldrick, "John Francis Hylan," *Dictionary of American Biography*, XXII, Supplement Two, 1958, p. 331.

[36] Gustavus Myers, "The New Tammany," *Century*, CXII (August, 1926), 394; Garrett, *op. cit.*, pp. 53–54.

In 1925 Walker came out against graft, promised to make non-partisan appointments, and won over civic organizations with his spirit of cooperation.[37] *The Public and the Schools* noted "a welcome change in the official atmosphere." [38]

It was a short-lived Era of Good Feelings. Walker was no more accessible to the PEA than Hylan. *The Public and the Schools* was soon attacking "politics" in school appointments, "badly overcrowded" schools, and the inadequate school budget.[39] There were urgent appeals to the Mayor, the Governor, and the state legislature for an investigation of the city schools.[40] But who was listening? In 1929 when Walker ran for re-election, despite insistent prodding from *The Public and the Schools* and the *Times*, he snubbed the school questionnaire sent out by the PEA to the mayoralty candidates.[41] A public thoroughly entertained by the antics of its flashy Mayor sent him back to City Hall with an even larger plurality than he received in 1925.

Thus the PEA intervened in New York City politics in the twenties in a manner scarcely distinguishable from that of a political party. But the picture of the PEA in politics is still incomplete. As the authors of *Governing New York City: Politics in the Metropolis* point out, there is a tripartite formula for the successful participation of Republicans, independents, and reformers in New York City politics: Fusion in the municipal election, the state legislative investigation, and charter revision from Albany.[42] The PEA tried all three. Throughout the twenties, while it entreated the electorate in New York City, and while it petitioned the state legislature for an investigation, it sued for charter revision as still another means of asserting its claim to be a consultant in school appointments in the city.

[37] In October 1925, Walker dutifully answered the school questionnaire sent out by the PEA to all the Mayoralty candidates, and pledged, if elected, to keep the schools free from politics. After his smashing victory in November, the Mayor-elect consented to speak at the PEA's annual public luncheon. *New York Times*, October 26, November 30, December 28, 1925.

[38] *The Public and the Schools*, No. 248, December 29, 1925.

[39] *The Public and the Schools*, No. 254, March 23, 1926; No. 281, December 13, 1927; No. 302, October 8, 1929.

[40] *New York Times*, January 16, September 25, November 4, ed., 1930; *The Public and the Schools*, No. 281, December 13, 1927; No. 319, October 9, 1930; No. 321, November 4, 1930.

[41] *New York Times*, October 15, 22, November 14, 1929. Representative Fiorello H. La Guardia and Norman Thomas, respectively the candidates of Republican-Fusion and the Socialist parties, promised to keep all forms of politics out of the schools.

[42] Sayre and Kaufman, *op. cit.*, p. 16.

IV

It had been a long time since the PEA had appealed to the state legislature to "take the schools out of politics"; not, in fact, since 1896. Through the years the PEA had been quite satisfied with the City School Law, with its basic pattern of overlapping corporate, administrative, and financial relationships between the city government and the Board of Education. With the PEA's encouragement and support, it will be recalled, as well as with that of other reform elements in the city, Mayor Mitchel had fully exploited the possibilities for political maneuvering which the schools' financial dependence on the city administration, as well as his appointive power over the Board of Education, gave him. And the PEA and the Mitchel administration fought hard for the new City School Law of 1917, which perpetuated these possibilities.[43] But under Mayor Hylan enormous defects in city-school relationships began to reveal themselves to the PEA. With Hylan's re-election in 1921 the PEA was ready for drastic measures.

On November 12, 1921 the PEA declared that the lesson of the past four years was that "the schools must be taken out of sordid politics." The key to the solution of the "school crisis," the PEA continued, was to change the school law.[44] Three months later it came out with a radical four-point blueprint for school reform. The PEA's program called for the following: financial independence for the Board of Education; removal of the Mayor's sole power of appointment over the Board of Education and the lodging of that power in an Educational Commission comprising the Mayor and the members of the State Board of Regents residing in the city; concentration of executive responsibility for school affairs in the City School Superintendent; and, finally, extension of the merit system to all school appointments below the rank of Associate School Superintendent. The aim of this sweeping school reform program was to "eliminate politics as far as possible from the New York City school system." [45]

On February 16, 1922 the Meyer–Ullman bill incorporating the school law reforms outlined by *The Public and the Schools* was intro-

[43] The new State School Law of 1917, which superseded the educational chapters of the 1901 Charter, reduced the size of New York's Board of Education from forty-six to seven, but altered nothing affecting the close relations between the Board of Education and the municipal government. *Laws of New York*, 1917, Chap. 786; Cohen, *op. cit.*, pp. 43–49.

[44] *The Public and the Schools*, No. 113, November 12, 1921.

[45] *The Public and the Schools*, No. 124, February 11, 1922.

duced into the state legislature.[46] The PEA tried hard to work up
support for the omnibus measure: articles in *The Public and the Schools*;
a public forum at Town Hall; appeals to the citizenry of New York to
"Go to Albany"; but the bill died in committee.[47] Even if Executive
Mansion in Albany had been occupied by a Republican rather than by
Al Smith, it would have been impossible to line up any wide support
for a legislative program such as that advocated by the PEA. In the
context of progressive theory of school administration the PEA's reform
program was a crazyquilt pattern which had, inherently, the capacity
to alienate many more potential supporters than it could possibly win.

The recommendations regarding the concentration of responsibility
in the City School Superintendent, and the extension of the merit
system in school appointments were the least controversial. On these
two issues, the consensus on school administration which existed in the
1890's between educationists and specialists in political science and
public administration—between, for instance, Nicholas Murray Butler
and Frank J. Goodnow, or Samuel T. Dutton and James T. Young—
still held up. But on the broader question of city-school relations there
was a sharp split. By the early twenties most professional school administrators were of the opinion that city public schools should be an independent governmental agency operating under state supervision,[48] while
political scientists held that the most effective administration could best
be obtained by close co-ordination of the schools and municipal government.[49] So, by its advocacy of "fiscal independence" for the city's Board
of Education, the PEA aligned itself with the theory of school administration held by professional schoolmen and drifted away from some
of its early sources of support, as well as of ideas: university experts in
the field of government and organized good government groups in the
city. On this count, the PEA lost the support of the City Club and the
Citizens Union with whom it usually made common cause, as these
organizations continued to hold to the theory of city-school relations
advanced by political scientists.

[46] *New York Times*, February 17, 1922; Cohen, *op. cit.*, pp. 119–20.
[47] *The Public and the Schools*, No. 126, February 25, 1922; No. 127, March 4,
1922; No. 130, March 25, 1922; *New York Times*, March 1, 1922; Cohen, *op cit.*,
p. 120.
[48] Ellwood P. Cubberley, *Public School Administration* (Rev. ed., Boston,
1929), pp. 188, 189.
[49] William Anderson, *American City Government* (New York, 1925), pp. 90–
96; Thomas Harrison Reed, *Municipal Government in the United States* (New
York, 1926), pp. 296–98; Nelson B. Henry and Jerome G. Kerwin, *Schools and City
Government* (Chicago, 1938); Cohen, *op. cit.*, pp. 82–92.

Headed for difficulty through its advocacy of what amounted to a sovereign school system for the city, the PEA proceeded to compound its predicament. In progressive theory any serious attempt to separate the public schools from politics via "fiscal independence" started with an elected school board. But, "while this may be ideally desirable," as *The Public and the Schools* put it, "the peculiar political situation of New York City renders this method of choice impracticable at this time for the welfare of the schools." [50] Because of the Democratic proclivity of the electorate in the city, an elected school board had always been anathema to the PEA. With its attempt to remove from the Mayor his sole appointive power over the Board of Education via the proposed Education Commission, the PEA again departed radically from good government theory. This proposal egregiously defied one of the progressives' most deeply held tenets—simplicity and direct responsibility in political machinery. It is a symptom of how desperate the PEA saw the school situation to be in New York in 1922. Principles or not, considerations of strategy dictated that the "School Board [Be] Taken From Hylan Control." [51]

With the failure of the Meyer–Ullman bill the PEA dropped its plea for fundamental changes in city-school relations and began its long advocacy of the extension of the merit system in school appointments and the concentration of responsibility in the City School Superintendent, the two least radical planks in its 1922 school reform program. A PEA-sponsored "Merit Bill," as well as a "Superintendent's Bill," were brought forward in every session of the State Legislature from 1923 to 1930. But despite the fact that the PEA secured for them the backing of almost a score of the city's civic groups, and despite the fact that it pulled out all stops in its use of behind the scenes lobbying tactics, the record was one of complete frustration.[52]

[50] *The Public and the Schools*, No. 124, February 11, 1922; Minutes of the Executive Committee of the PEA, January 13, 1922.
[51] The headline over the *New York Times* story of the Meyer-Ullman bill, February 17, 1922.
[52] *The Public and the Schools*, No. 189, January 15, 1924; No. 225, February 10, 1925; No. 281, December 13, 1927. In 1929, at a joint meeting of the PEA and the groups "most interested in merit"—the Civil Service Reform Association, the Men's City Club, and the Women's City Club—it was decided to employ a professional lobbyist. Mrs. Henry Morgenthau, Jr., the wife of the close friend of Governor Franklin Delano Roosevelt, volunteered to ask one of the Governor's top aides, Judge Samuel I. Rosenman, to recommend a good one. Mrs. Samuel A. Lewisohn had already, but vainly, requested Mrs. Roosevelt to suggest to the Governor that he get the State Commissioner of Education to introduce the merit bill. Minutes of the Executive Committee of the PEA, January 22, 1929.

Frustration in Albany. Frustration in New York City. Despite its most strenuous, its most enterprising, its most resolute efforts, neither the PEA nor any of its allies could break into the politics of school appointments in the city in the twenties. In 1931 the PEA momentarily dropped the strategic vocabulary in which it usually advocated school reform and revealed the basic reason for its decade-long warfare with the city administration. Mayors Gaynor and Mitchel, *The Public and the Schools* explained, had a policy of consulting the Merchants Association, the Chamber of Commerce, the City Club, "and other nonpartisan bodies," when making appointments to the Board of Education. But, the newsletter sadly noted, Mayor Hylan had discontinued the practice and Mayor Walker never revived it.[53]

The PEA was thus extensively, energetically, and continuously involved in political activities during the twenties. It became so involved in "skinning the tiger" that it almost, but never quite, lost sight of its main objective; namely, to influence the content and practice of public education. Indeed, this was the major reason for its intense concern with school appointments; direct access to top school officials was a major channel through which school policy could be influenced. But the PEA had traditionally employed the less direct techniques of the mass media and special demonstrations toward the same end. It continued to do so in the twenties and, as in everything it did in this decade, on a larger scale and more intensively than ever before.

V

Two major themes run through the PEA's school reform program. In the first place, the PEA never lost sight of the major objective with which it was charged by the founders: to shape a public school system to meet the needs of the city. The second major theme, and one following from the first, is a conception of the public school whose functions are vastly expanded beyond mere formal instruction to encompass responsibilities formerly left to other social agencies; a conception of the public school as a "legatee" institution. Between 1895 and 1917 the belief that the school must broaden its functions to meet the needs of the city had led the PEA from recreation, manual training, and hygiene to a position in which the public school was conceived as "a child welfare agency adapted to meet the social needs of children in a large municipal organization." In the 1920's this sentiment found

[53] *The Public and the Schools,* No. 327, February 10, 1931.

ultimate, if fantastic, expression in the form of a demand that the school assume the responsibility for the complete socialization of personality; for the deliberate training of "the whole child." The PEA's school reform program had always reflected, while it forwarded, the pedagogical thrust of social work: before the reorganization of 1911–1914 that of the social settlement movement, after 1914 increasingly that of the emerging profession of social work. In the 1920's the PEA's program breathed the spirit of social case work and the mental hygiene movement.

"Childhood," in the notable words of William Alanson White, was "the golden period for mental hygiene." [54] It was inevitable that leaders in the mental hygiene movement, as well as social workers steeped in mental hygiene principles, would formulate a comprehensive school reform program incorporating those principles. In the writings of White, Adolf Meyer, William H. Burnham, and Jessie Taft, the pattern for such a school program can be found.[55] In this pattern the following are key strands: the emotional life of the individual is the key to behavior; the emotions can be molded or controlled if the right environment is supplied in childhood; the public school is the strategic agency for training the emotions; and, finally, the school's essential task is the adjustment of the child or, to quote Dr. Burnham, "the integration of personality that makes right adjustment possible." [56]

With the emergence of the public school as an agency responsible for the deliberate adjustment of personality, progressive school reformers were finally satiated. So far as expanding its functions, they could ask the school to do no more. Now they had to implement their vision in the classroom. The PEA, through its two major school demonstrations in the 1920's—a nationwide visiting teacher project, and a new experiment in public school curricula and teaching methods—and through the propaganda activities of its professional staff, took its place, as usual, in the vanguard of the progressive movement.[57]

[54] William A. White, "Childhood: The Golden Period for Mental Hygiene," *The Annals*, XCVIII (November, 1921), 54–67.

[55] *Ibid.*; William A. White, *The Mental Hygiene of Childhood* (New York, 1919); William H. Burnham, *The Normal Mind* (New York, 1924); Jessie Taft, "The Relation of the School to the Mental Health of the Average Child," *Mental Hygiene*, VII (October, 1923), 673–87; Jonathan Clark, "The Educational Ideas of Adolf Meyer" (unpublished Master's thesis, Teachers College, Columbia University, 1960).

[56] Burnham, *op. cit.*, pp. 18–19.

[57] The PEA had several other new projects in the schools in the 1920's which warrant mention. Children with heart trouble were the last to receive special attention in New York's schools. The PEA's Committee on Cardiac Cases, organized in

VI

Between 1906, when it began, and 1921, when it entered upon its period of greatest expansion, the visiting teacher movement cannot be said to have made much progress. In New York City in 1921, despite energetic promotion by the PEA, the Board of Education had only nine visiting teachers in its employ. Elsewhere in the nation, despite the efforts of the National Association of Visiting Teachers, progress was equally slow.[58] Undaunted by their slow progress and goaded by their new awareness of the role of the emotions in behavior, school social workers were becoming more and more imperialistic and grandiose in their aspirations. In 1921, Jane Culbert, supervisor of the PEA's visiting teacher staff and president of the National Association of Visiting Teachers, gave notable expression to these aspirations when she exhorted her follow social workers "to push into the schools" and eliminate the need for social work at the source.[59] Miss Culbert's cry was not to go unheeded in a decade whose keynote was prevention.

In November, 1921, the Commonwealth Fund launched a far-reaching "Program for the Prevention of Juvenile Delinquency," the first and one of the best financed efforts of its kind ever attempted in the United States. The Program's objectives, as stated by the Fund,

1918 by Mrs. Louis Levy (wife of the director of the Commercial Bank and Trust Company, Schenley Distillers Corp., and Thompson–Starrett Co.), first demonstrated the need, the type of education, and the techniques of caring for children so afflicted. The Committee, employing leading medical specialists, supervised special classes in the schools, established a boarding house in the country and organized a special subcommittee for the vocational guidance of cardiac children. *The Public and the Schools*, No. 5, December 21, 1918; No. 140, June 3, 1922; New York City, Board of Education, *The First Fifty Years*, p. 69. The PEA's Continuation School Committee, the special interest of Percy Straus, fought throughout the decade to preserve the always threatened continuation schools, and demonstrated a model health and vocational guidance program for youth in such schools. *The Public and the Schools*, No. 87, January 29, 1921; No. 231, March 24, 1925; No. 258, May 18, 1926; No. 275, May 31, 1927; No. 300, May 14, 1929; No. 313, March 25, 1930.

58 PEA, *The Visiting Teacher in the United States: A Survey of the National Association of Visiting Teachers and Home and School Visitors* (2d ed., New York, 1923), pp. 47–48; Julius John Oppenheimer, *The Visiting Teacher Movement* (New York, 1924), pp. 4–9.

59 Jane F. Culbert, "The Public School as a Factor in the Training of the Socially Handicapped Child," *Proceedings*, National Conference of Social Work (Milwaukee, 1921), pp. 95–98; Jane F. Culbert, "The Visiting Teacher," *The Annals*, XCVIII (November, 1921), 82; M. Edith Campbell, "The Strategic Position of the School in Programs of Social Work, From the Point of View of the Social Worker," *Proceedings*, National Conference of Social Work (Washington, D.C., 1923), p. 362.

were: the promotion of the psychiatric study and treatment of children showing behavior problems; the development of opportunities for the training of psychiatric social workers; and the nationwide promotion of the visiting teacher. Responsibility for carrying out the program was entrusted to the PEA, the National Committee for Mental Hygiene, the New York School of Social Work, and the Joint Committee on Methods of Preventing Delinquency. The PEA was assigned the task of carrying out the largest phase of the program: the national visiting teacher demonstration. A specially organized National Committee on Visiting Teachers was established under its auspices, placed under the direct supervision of Howard Nudd and Jane Culbert, and assigned the task of placing thirty visiting teachers in thirty different communities around the country, for 3-year demonstration periods.[60]

Why the emphasis on the visiting teacher in a program for the prevention of juvenile delinquency? Barry C. Smith, the Fund's director, raised this query himself, before setting about to answer it. "The public school," Smith explained, "coming into close contact with the lives of over twenty million young boys, girls, and adolescents, is—or should be— our greatest social welfare agency." [61] The public school teachers of the nation, Smith continued, "if they can be socialized can accomplish more to prevent delinquency than all the social workers together." [62] But he disclaimed any intention on the Fund's part of adding to their burden. This was where the visiting teacher came in.[63]

Regardless of the Fund's stated objectives, and despite its specific disclaimer, the key strategic objective of the Fund's program from its inception, as insiders knew, was "to socialize eventually the teaching force." [64] In line with this objective, in 1925 the Fund deemed the time ripe to launch a special program of promotion and publicity work among public school teachers and teachers-in-training. It sponsored and published a number of textbooks and pamphlets designed to give school

[60] Commonwealth Fund, *Fourth Annual Report*, 1922, pp. 8–25; Barry C. Smith, "The Commonwealth Fund Program for the Prevention of Delinquency," *Proceedings*, National Conference of Social Work (Chicago, 1922), pp. 168–74; *New York Times*, June 18, 1922, Sec. VI; Frank J. Bruno, *Trends in Social Work, 1874–1956: A History Based on the Proceedings of the National Conference of Social Work* (New York, 1957), Chap. XXX; Oppenheimer, *op. cit.*, pp. 9–12; *The Public and the Schools*, No. 134, April 22, 1922.
[61] Commonwealth Fund, *Fourth Annual Report*, p. 21.
[62] *Ibid.*, pp. 21–23.
[63] *Ibid.*, p. 23.
[64] Minutes of the Executive Committee of the PEA, October 4, 1921.

personnel the "behavior point of view." [65] More significantly, the Fund strove to educate the teaching force directly in mental hygiene principles through lectures and courses at teacher-training institutions. During the summer of 1927 the staff of the PEA's National Committee on Visiting Teachers gave the pioneer courses on the behavior problems of children to teachers and teachers-in-training at Harvard, George Peabody College for Teachers, the University of Washington, the University of Kansas, the University of North Carolina, Western Reserve University, and Michigan State Normal School.[66]

In the meantime throughout the decade the PEA was helping to forward the new view of the public school through the media of articles in *The Public and the Schools* by Howard Nudd, and Nudd articles and speeches aimed at fellow social workers. Nudd's writings, needless to say, also reveal much about the mind of the PEA.

The mental health influence is ubiquitous in Nudd's writing. It received one of its most complete expressions in Nudd's description of the nature of visiting teacher work, which, in a pamphlet, was widely disseminated by the Commonwealth Fund.[67] The basic theme running through the pamphlet is that "useful citizenship and right living" are the true ends of education, and that these ends are an outgrowth of sound training in childhood. Here was the educator's problem and his opportunity. School dissatisfaction and failure, which could lead to retardation, truancy, delinquency, and other problems of social mal-adjustment would have to be forestalled; wholesome experiences pro-vided. Nudd averred that the preceding decade had witnessed many

[65] E.g. Howard W. Nudd, *The Purpose and Scope of Visiting Teacher Work* (New York, 1928); Jane F. Culbert, *The Visiting Teacher at Work* (New York, 1929); Mary B. Sayles, *The Problem Child in School* (New York, 1925); Mary B. Sayles (ed.), *Three Problem Children: Narratives from a Child Guidance Clinic* (New York, 1926); E. K. Wickman, *Children's Behavior and Teacher's Attitudes* (New York, 1928).

[66] William I. Thomas and Dorothy S. Thomas, *The Child in America: Behavior Problems and Programs* (New York, 1928), pp. 254–55; W. Carson Ryan, Jr., "The Preparation of Teachers for Dealing with Behavior Problem Children," *School and Society*, XXVIII (August 18, 1928), 208–15; Commonwealth Fund, *Annual Reports*, 1925–1928; *The Public and the Schools*, No. 271, April 5, 1927; No. 275, May 31, 1927.

[67] *The Purpose and Scope of Visiting Teacher Work*. Originally this work appeared as an introduction to Sayles, *The Problem Child in School*. The Joint Committee of the Commonwealth Fund thought it covered the broader aspects of the visiting teacher movement so well that its wider distribution seemed desirable. It was reprinted in pamphlet form in 1925; by 1928 it had gone through three printings.

advances in education, in differentiated courses of study, flexible programs of grading, and the like, but he noted that these were all developments in the intellectual field, in manual training, and in the improvement of physical well-being, while the emotional life of the child was being neglected. "By itself alone," Nudd cautioned, "the intellectual appeal is inadequate in the training of personality. Feelings and habits of behavior must be constantly nurtured or corrected, as the case may be, in the entire daily life of the child." [68] However, Nudd went on, the growing acceptance of the visiting teacher by "progressive educators" was a hopeful sign that the schools were beginning to achieve a wider influence upon the "whole life" of the child.

Infrequently a voice from the academy was raised to protest that the public schools were moving in the wrong direction. In 1925 President Nicholas Murray Butler, in his annual report to the trustees of Columbia University, placed the major responsibility for the prevalence of crime and lawlessness on the "lack of right education"; i.e., neglect of subject matter and the academic disciplines in the grades. Howard Nudd answered this Founding Father for the PEA. Nudd agreed that "right education" was the solution to the problem of juvenile delinquency— an education which facilitated the discovery of unwholesome trends in the behavior and personality formation of children. [69]

Throughout the decade, in addresses before the National Conference of Social Work, before which he appeared frequently, and in *The Public and the Schools*, Nudd reiterated and elaborated these themes. In 1927 Nudd warned of the danger that efforts to improve school practices were based on the traditional concept of the school as an agency to impart facts and certain elementary skills. This was true, Nudd admitted, but "now education requires the development of the emotional life of the individual." [70] A few years later he could report more hopefully that "schools no longer seek to impart standardized information but have begun to assume responsibility for the whole child —physically, mentally, socially, and emotionally." [71]

The Commonwealth Fund terminated its juvenile delinquency

[68] Nudd, *The Purpose and Scope of Visiting Teacher Work*, pp. 10–12, 22–25.

[69] Columbia University, *Annual Report of the President and Treasurer to the Trustees for the Year Ending June 30, 1925*, 1925, pp. 18–20; *The Public and the Schools*, No. 247, December 15, 1925.

[70] Howard W. Nudd, "The School and Social Work," *Proceedings*, National Conference of Social Work (Des Moines, 1927), p. 42; "Social Work Enters the Schools," *Survey Graphic*, LIV (April, 1925), 30–34.

[71] *The Public and the Schools*, No. 301, June 11, 1929; No. 310, February 11, 1930.

prevention program in 1930. The visiting teacher phase of the program, as such, had succeeded but not in any spectacular fashion.[72] The real success of the program lay elsewhere, in the forwarding of the goal to have the schools take on further responsibilities. By 1930 the tendency, given impetus by the work of the Fund and the PEA's visiting teacher staff, was to involve public school teachers in the behavior problems of children at the very beginning of their careers, in teacher-training courses.[73] By 1930 the visiting teacher had become superfluous; the PEA dropped her also.

Social work was pushing into the public schools: the visiting teacher brought social case work directly into the schools; the regular teaching staff was being socialized. But the school reform program of avant-garde progressives in the twenties was nothing short of revolutionary. It aimed not at reforming the old school order but at its overthrow and replacement by a completely new order. By the twenties, progressives had come around to the view that all of America's social ills were to be conquered or prevented in the public schools. They were now equally convinced that this denouement could come about only if a completely hygienic or therapeutic school environment were created. And the schools, they knew, were far from this. Accordingly, the PEA and other avant-garde school reformers sought, along with the basic objective of socializing the regular public school personnel, the equally basic objective of transforming public school curricula and procedures according to the principles and precepts of mental hygiene.

VII

In the winter of 1922 the PEA inaugurated a small curriculum experiment in the newly created annex of P.S. 61, the top floor of the old Children's Aid Society building on East 16th Street and Avenue B in Manhattan. In charge of the experiment was Elisabeth Irwin of the PEA staff. Only 100 first-graders, in four classes, were involved, but the

[72] Commonwealth Fund, *Annual Report*, 1930, p. 61; William S. Deffenbaugh, "Significant Movements in City School Systems," *Biennial Survey of Education*, 1926–1928, United States Office of Education Bulletin No. 16, 1930, pp. 101–02; Thomas and Thomas, *op. cit.*, pp. 255–57; Bruno, *op. cit.*, p. 296; Nudd, *The Purpose and Scope of Visiting Teacher Work*, pp. 28–29; Walter C. Reckless and Mapheus Smith, *Juvenile Delinquency* (New York, 1932), p. 180.

[73] Thomas and Thomas, *op. cit.*, p. 223; Lawrence K. Frank, "Childhood and Youth," *Recent Social Trends in the United States*, Report of the President's Research Committee on Social Trends (New York, 1933), II, 775, 784; Lois Meredith, "Education and Social Work," *Social Work Year Book*, 1933, p. 139; Reckless and Smith, *op. cit.*, p. 182.

PEA promptly christened the experiment the "Little Red School House." [74] The experiment was to have a ten-year existence in the city school system: from 1922 to 1924 in the P.S. 61 annex; from 1924 to 1929 in P.S. 61 proper; and from 1929 to 1932 in P.S. 41, all in lower Manhattan. At its peak size, in 1931, the experiment would involve only 267 children in a school with a population of more than 2,500 children, but the "Little Red School House" it remained, while it went on to win fame as one of the country's foremost examples of a progressive public school.

With the inception of the Little Red School House the PEA joined forces with the latest and most powerful permutation of educational progressivism: child-centered progressive education.[75] New York City was the nation's chief center of educational experimentation. The PEA fit nicely into the circle of progressive education revolving around the Bureau of Educational Experiments, which, under the aegis of Lucy Sprague Mitchell, subsidized Caroline Pratt's City and Country School and the Nursery School directed by Harriet Johnson, and in general served as a clearing house and research center for progressive education in the city. The fortunes of the PEA and the leading figures of the Bureau had long intertwined. Harriet Johnson and Caroline Pratt became charter members of the Bureau. And when Mrs. Mitchell decided to organize the Bureau she also sought out Elisabeth Irwin.[76]

Caroline Pratt has written that "a background of experience in social work seemed to produce the best kind of teachers." [77] If this is correct, and Miss Pratt writes with great authority on matters pertaining to progressive education, then the PEA could scarcely have found a more qualified individual than Elisabeth Antoinette Irwin to head the Little Red School House. She earned an A.B. from Smith College in 1903, a time when Smith was one of the main fonts of social work in the country. A Smith graduate in those years followed Vida D. Scudder, Jean Fine, and Jane Robbins into the social settlements. So, upon graduation, the young Brooklynite, armed with a few courses in eco-

[74] Elisabeth Irwin, "The Little Red School House," *The Public and the Schools*, No. 174, June 5, 1923; Elisabeth Irwin and Louis Marks, *Fitting the School to the Child* (New York, 1924), pp. 1–2; Agnes De Lima *et al.*, *The Little Red School House* (New York, 1944), pp. 1–2; "News of the Schools," *Progressive Education*, I (July–September, 1924), 192–93.

[75] For the streams of "scientism," Freudianism, and Expressionism which converged in the child-centered pedagogy of the twenties, see Lawrence A. Cremin, *The Transformation of the School* (New York, 1961), Chap. VI, esp. pp. 185–215.

[76] Caroline Pratt, *I Learn from Children* (New York, 1948), p. 55; Lucy Sprague Mitchell, *Two Lives: The Story of Wesley Clair Mitchell and Myself* (New York, 1953), pp. 252, 408–14, 466–67; Cremin, *op. cit.*, p. 204n.

[77] Pratt, *op. cit.*, p. 64.

nomics and sociology and the spirit of social service, the chief equipment of a social worker in those halcyon days, became a resident at the College Settlement, on New York's lower East Side.[78] In 1910 or 1911 Miss Irwin joined the PEA's Committee on Special Children as a combination visiting teacher-psychologist.[79]

The PEA offered Miss Irwin a varied career. From 1911 to 1916 she worked closely with the Board of Education's Department of Ungraded Classes, administering Binet Tests and studying mentally defective children in and out of school.[80] In 1916, after she helped Elizabeth Farrell reorganize the Department of Ungraded Classes, Miss Irwin began an experiment in P.S. 64, Manhattan, in the identification and education of "superior children"—those with I.Q. of 120 or higher— which attracted a great deal of attention.[81] This interlude of interest in "superior children," interest in "the hope of democracy," was short-lived. The problem of public education is, after all, the problem of mass education. By 1921 the experiment had blossomed under the sympathetic ministry of William E. Grady, principal of the school when the experiment began, and then under Louis Marks when Grady became a District School Superintendent, into a demonstration in classifying all the children of a large city public school into homogeneous classes on the basis of the new group mental tests.[82] The next step was inevitable:

[78] *New York Times*, October 17, 1942, obituary; *Who Was Who in America*, II, 1950; *American Women, 1939–1940*, III, 1939.

[79] PEA, *Report for the Years September 1, 1911 to September 1, 1913*, p. 18.

[80] *Ibid.*, pp. 18–19; Elisabeth A. Irwin, "A Study of the Feeble-Minded in a West Side School in New York City," *PEA Bulletin*, No. 21, December 8, 1913; Elisabeth A. Irwin, *Truancy: A Study of the Mental, Physical and Social Factors of the Problem of Non-Attendance at School* (New York, 1915); Mary Ritter Beard, *Woman's Work in Municipalities* (New York, 1915), pp. 19–20. Miss Irwin kept abreast of the latest developments in her field via courses at the New York School of Philanthropy, later renamed the New York School of Social Work, earning an M.A. in 1923. The new world opened up by the American adaptation of the work of the Frenchman Binet especially fascinated her, and she became one of the country's pioneer experts in the field of mental testing.

[81] Louise F. Specht, "Terman Class in Public School No. 64, Manhattan: An Experiment in Selecting, Grouping and Training a Number of Children of Very Superior Intelligence," *School and Society*, IX (March 29, 1919), 393; "Experiments in Education," *World's Work*, XLIII (February, 1922), 353; *The Public and the Schools*, No. 14, March 1, 1919; No. 105, June 4, 1921; Irwin and Marks, *op. cit.*, pp. 8–12, 72–73, 221, and *passim*.

[82] Under Dr. Marks P.S. 64 became truly "an experimental school." There was a class for "neurotic children." Miss Marietta Johnson gave a demonstration of her "organic education" here. The Bureau of Educational Experiments conducted a nutrition experiment and an experiment in sex education here. Irwin and Marks, *op. cit.*, pp. v–ix, 1–2, 87, 115–16, 286–87, and *passim*; *The Public and the Schools*, No. 69, May 29, 1920; No. 105, June 4, 1921; No. 136, May 6, 1922; Mitchell, *op. cit.*, pp. 457, 575n; "Experiments in Education," *World's Work*, pp. 353–54; De Lima, *The Little Red School House*, p. 2.

"the adaptation of the curriculum to the various types of children." [83]
This was the objective of Miss Irwin and the Little Red School House.[84]

Descriptions of the Little Red School House at various stages of
its career may be found in the *Nation*, the *New Republic*, *Progressive
Education*, and in Agnes De Lima's full-length progressive tract, *Our
Enemy the Child*.[85] The best accounts of the work, however, are those
carried in *The Public and the Schools* toward the end of the twenties
when the experiment reached its mature form. Children in the Little
Red School House were grouped in classes according to mental measure-
ment. But all were exposed to the same curriculum and teaching
methods. No academic work was undertaken until the 2B grade, and
then only informally. Instead, the children were given many opportunities to learn "from direct experience." Trips into the neighborhood were
much employed. Activities, of course, were all-important: "Here some
two hundred small workers don overalls and go about their occupations,"
building, hammering, painting, modeling, singing, dancing, and "constantly creating and solving problems." There was "no retardation problem in Miss Irwin's classes, since no child is ever left behind." Classroom
discipline was maintained by "popular agreement." The aim of the
program was to "interest the children, and make their social relations
easy and happy." [86] Here was a demonstration under actual working

[83] *The Public and the Schools*, No. 174, June 5, 1923; Minutes of the Board
of Trustees of the PEA, March 28, November 14, 1922.

[84] The substance of Miss Irwin's pedagogical convictions may be found in
Fitting the School to the Child, the volume which she co-authored with Louis
Marks, a classic of its type, and a handful of articles which appeared in the
twenties in some of the nation's leading liberal journals of opinion: "Personal Education," *New Republic*, XL (November 12, 1924), 7–9; "The Youngest Intellectuals,"
ibid., XLVIII (November 10, 1926), 339–41; "We Watch Them Grow," *Survey*,
LX (June 1, 1928), 273–76; "The Teacher Steps Out," *ibid.*, LXIII (December 15,
1929), 340.

[85] Agnes De Lima, "A Public School Experiment," *New Republic*, XXXVIII
(April 9, 1924), 174–75; Agnes De Lima, "The New Education in the Public
Schools," *Nation*, CXVIII (June 18, 1924), 702; "News of the Schools," *Progressive
Education*, I (July–September, 1924), 192–93; Stanwood Cobb, "Contributions
from the Field," *Progressive Education*, III (July–September, 1926), 231–32; Agnes
De Lima, *Our Enemy the Child* (New York, 1926), pp. 32–42. And see the follow-
ing articles, all by Miss Irwin: "Personal Education," "The Youngest Intellectuals,"
"We Watch Them Grow," "The Teacher Steps Out."

[86] *The Public and the Schools*, No. 274, May 17, 1927; No. 317, May 30, 1930.
There is also a splendid account of the Little Red School House in Mitchell, *Two
Lives*, pp. 415ff. Mrs. Mitchell taught at P.S. 41 for a time. Since she needed a New
York City teaching license, she "took some written examinations and an oral examination with Dr. Louis Marks, received a teaching certificate and became the kindergarten teacher." *Ibid.*, p. 414. Dr. Marks had won an appointment to the Board
of Examiners in 1921.

conditions, *The Public and the Schools* declared, of "the practicability of modern progressive school methods for public schools generally." [87]

This sentiment strikes at the real significance of the Little Red School House experiment. It may have involved only a handful of children, but the PEA had ecumenical aspirations for it. Here the PEA made common cause with the Progressive Education Association, which aimed at nothing short of transforming the entire public school system of America.[88] The publicity value inherent in the establishment of a progressive beachhead in New York City was fully exploited. The Public Education Association launched the first public relations campaign in American education to promote the idea that progressive education was attractive and feasible under public school conditions. Throughout the twenties the Association kept a steady stream of photographs and copy on the Little Red School House flowing out to newspapers and periodicals all over the nation.[89] The publicity barrage was remarkably effective. Progressive education made inroads in many public schools in the nation in the twenties, but few could approach the Little Red School House in fame. In 1926 *The New Era*, the official organ of the New Education Fellowship, the European wing of the progressive movement, carried a description of Miss Irwin's classes as part of an issue devoted to "Ideas from the Progressive Schools of the U.S.A." [90]

It is hardly surprising that William Heard Kilpatrick, the doyen of American progressive education, would say: "Elisabeth Irwin was the first to introduce progressive education into a public school." [91]

The PEA helped further the progressive movement in still other ways, which, in turn, redounded to its prestige in the movement. Its annual meetings provided a public forum for the leading ideologists of the movement, and *The Public and the Schools* provided another medium for the dissemination of the propaganda of the movement.[92]

[87] *The Public and the Schools*, No. 317, May 30, 1930; No. 274, May 17, 1927; De Lima, *The Little Red School House*, p. 2.

[88] Cremin, *op. cit.*, pp. 240–42.

[89] There is a magnificent collection of photographs: "Happy Kids in the Overall School," "A Graceful Class of Four-Year-Olds," "Children Decorating School Walls with Scenes of Manhattan," and so forth in the folders "Photographs P.S. 61" and "Photographs P.S. 41" at the Little Red School House, 196 Bleecker Street, New York City. A collection of newspaper clippings is at Elisabeth Irwin High School, 40 Charlton Street, New York City.

[90] *The New Era*, VII (July, 1926), 100.

[91] William Heard Kilpatrick, Interview, New York City, June 29, 1959.

[92] In 1925 the PEA's annual public meeting was addressed by Professor Kilpatrick, Dr. Ira S. Wile, and Dr. Eugene Randolph Smith, headmaster of the Beaver Country Day School in Brookline, Massachusetts, and president of the

In 1928, when the Progressive Education Association met in New York City, the PEA helped publicize the event, provided a Hospitality Committee, and quite accurately pointed up its own place in "the liberal movement." [93] For, through a broad range of propaganda activities, the PEA was in alliance with the Progressive Education Association in the task of building up that broad base of support among the middle classes without which fundamental and large-scale public school reforms are impossible. It was an alliance that would last almost until the demise of the Progressive Education Association in 1955, for the PEA stayed on the bandwagon longer than most. But when the Progressive Education Association finally expired, it was quite alone.

VIII

The Little Red School House had a ten-year existence as a PEA-sponsored unit in the city's public school system. Although it may have enjoyed an international reputation, at scarcely any time in its historic career did it know a moment's peace or security. Around it there raged an almost constant, frequently bitter, behind-the-scenes struggle which pitted the PEA against political leaders, school officials, regular classroom teachers, and parents. But again and again the PEA pulled the necessary strings to keep the experiment going still another year in the public school system.

The happiest years of the school were those it spent in the Children's Aid Society building at East 16th Street, the specially created annex of P.S. 61. Mayor Hylan, however, was not one to let the PEA live in peace, especially when it was one of his chief tormentors. In 1924 the Children's Aid Society building was condemned by city building inspectors as unsafe for public school classes, and the removal of such classes was demanded forthwith.[94]

Progressive Education Association. In 1926 a leader of the European phase of the movement, Miss Beatrice Ensor, headmistress of Heights School, Chutney, England, chairman of the Executive Committee of the New Education Fellowship, and editor of *The New Era*, spoke to the PEA on the new education in Europe. The speeches were all reprinted in *The Public and the Schools:* No. 227, February 24, 1925; No. 228, March 3, 1925; No. 239, May 19, 1925; No. 241, June 2, 1925; and No. 255, April 6, 1926.

[93] *The Public and the Schools*, No. 282, January 10, 1928; No. 285; February 21, 1928.

[94] Minutes of the Executive Committee of the PEA, May 6, 20, 27, October 7, 1924. Agnes De Lima later recalled that the PEA was not "too popular" with Tammany Hall then and that Hylan got the Building Department to condemn the Children's Aid Society building as a fire hazard, "which," she adds, "of

Although the PEA was forced to vacate the building, it was able, in late 1924, to move Miss Irwin's classes into the main building of P.S. 61. The years at P.S. 61 were black ones for Miss Irwin. She complained constantly to the PEA's Executive Committee about the school, the teachers, and the principal.[95] The failure of School Superintendent Ettinger, who had personally approved of the Little Red School House, to win reappointment in 1924, and the PEA's inability to get any response from his successor, William J. O'Shea, when it sent out feelers to him via Louis Marks, placed a pall of insecurity over the whole enterprise.[96] There was also an impending financial crisis. The Commonwealth Fund, which had been contributing about $10,000 a year to the support of Miss Irwin's experiment as part of its Program for the Prevention of Juvenile Delinquency, would no longer do so after June 30, 1927, the date it had set for closing all of its visiting teacher demonstrations.[97]

In 1926 a thoroughly exasperated Elisabeth Irwin threatened to quit the PEA.[98] The threat shook the Association, and it took prompt steps to mollify Miss Irwin. First, Mrs. Samuel A. Lewisohn prevailed upon Felix Warburg to "secure assurances" from M. Samuel Stern, one of the two Manhattan members of the Board of Education, that the Little Red School House would not be forced out of the city school system.[99] Second, the PEA took steps to shake the dust of P.S. 61. In late 1928, thanks to the intercession of Stern with O'Shea's office and the intercession of Marks with a lower West Side district school super-

course, it wasn't." She also tells the story, which is probably apocryphal, of the time when Mayor Hylan and three policeman drove up to move the furniture of the school out on the sidewalk because he was not going to have any fooling around in his school system, but got the wrong address and landed in a school on West 13th Street, where he was unable to locate anything queer. De Lima, *The Little Red School House*, p. 1.

[95] Minutes of the Executive Committee of the PEA, October 28, November 18, December 9, 1924. Occasionally the difficulties experienced by the Little Red School House reached the public. One journalist complained that Miss Irwin's experiment in progressive education was running into the opposition of certain of the school supervisory staff who "do not believe in the physical and emotional development of children." De Lima, *Our Enemy the Child*, p. 42. However, the PEA, Elisabeth Irwin, and the Little Red School House had the support of the New York Teachers Union and its appendage, the Teachers Union Auxilliary, a group composed of lay people sympathetic to the organization of teachers and to progressive education. Cohn, *op. cit.*, pp. 202ff, 207, 282ff, 293, 294.

[96] Minutes of the Executive Committee of the PEA, November 18, December 9, 1924. Dr. Marks was now a member of the Board of Examiners.

[97] Minutes of the Executive Committee of the PEA, October 5, 1926.

[98] Minutes of the Executive Committee of the PEA, March 2, 1926.

[99] Minutes of the Executive Committee of the PEA, March 30, April 13, 1926.

intendent, the school received a third lease on life, now in P.S. 41, in Greenwich Village.[100] But in its resolution permitting the PEA to move its experiment to P.S. 41, the Board of Superintendents required that a special, joint evaluation committee be set up to appraise the experiment when it reached its third year.[101] This marked the first time in the history of PEA–School Board transactions that such a condition was imposed on the PEA. Conditions or no, the PEA snapped at the chance to leave P.S. 61. Furthermore, Mrs. Lewisohn was prevailed upon to take charge of the Little Red School House Committee, the body responsible for financing the experiment. At the same time, the PEA organized a new Advisory Committee, composed of prominent laymen and public school officials, to build up and widen the experiment's base of support.[102] This committee too was headed by Mrs. Lewisohn, who was now emerging as the leader of the cause.

If wealth or the prestige of some of the greatest Jewish names in America could deliver the Little Red School House, then the PEA could have found no one better to lead the cause than Mrs. Samuel A. Lewisohn, née Margaret Valentine Seligman.[103] She was the daughter of Isaac N. and Gerta (Loeb) Seligman. Her father was a noted banker; her mother, the granddaughter of Solomon Loeb, one of the founders of the great banking house of Kuhn, Loeb and Company. She married financier Samuel A. Lewisohn, a childhood friend. Mrs. Lewisohn not only gave generously of her own fortune to causes she believed in but, in consequence of the dynastic character of the relationships among the highest strata of New York Jewry, she was related through ties of family or close friendship to the Warburgs, Schiffs, Lehmans, Sulzbergers, Guggenheims, Heinsheimers, and Hofheimers of the city, and enjoyed preferred access to the New York Foundation and the Hofheimer Foundation. Mrs. Lewisohn's active interest in an organization then, assured it of funds and contacts; in turn, Mrs. Lewisohn was assured of a leader-

[100] Minutes of the Executive Committee of the PEA, February 7, March 27, 1928.

[101] De Lima, *The Little Red School House,* pp. 2–4; Mitchell, *Two Lives,* p. 414; *The Public and the Schools,* No. 293, October 16, 1928. When the children in the first grade reached the 3A grade, they were to be compared with the children of a control school in terms of achievement in the three R's as well as in manual training, art, character, and personality development.

[102] *The Public and the Schools,* No. 293, October 16, 1928; No. 294, November 13, 1928; Minutes of the Executive Committee of the PEA, March 5, 1929.

[103] *Who's Who in American Jewry,* III, 1939; *American Women,* III, 1940; *Musical America,* LXXIV (July, 1954), 28; *New York Times,* June 15, 1954, obituary.

ship position in any organization in which she was active. That she was gay and lovely and cultured helped, of course. From the moment Mrs. Lewisohn became involved in the Little Red School House until her death in 1954, she was to be the dominant figure in the PEA's history.

Mrs. Lewisohn was born in New York City on February 14, 1895. She was educated in private schools in the city; then came the study of piano abroad, and finally a degree from the Institute of Musical Art (now the Juilliard School of Music) in 1914. After graduating from the Institute, Mrs. Lewisohn did "post-graduate" work teaching music at the Hudson Guild Settlement and in some ungraded classes in one of the city's public schools. While at the latter she met Elisabeth Irwin, who brought her, in 1921, into the PEA.[104]

The times were propitious for the paths of Mrs. Lewisohn and the PEA to cross. Mrs. Lewisohn had the leisure and, encouraged by her husband, a habitué of Mabel Dodge's famous Greenwich Village salon, the inclination to pursue avidly the new ideas brewing in the twenties in modern art, psychiatry, and child-raising. From her parents she inherited an interest in the Ethical Culture Schools. Mrs. Lewisohn's interests coalesced in progressive education. She would send her four children, all girls, to the progressive Lincoln School. She would become a trustee of Vassar and one of the founders of Bennington. At a time when Mrs. Lewisohn's varied interests were leading her to progressive education, the PEA, too, had begun to focus on the same subject. With its Little Red School House the PEA gave Mrs. Lewisohn an opportunity to further a cause in which she believed deeply, and she rushed into the breach. She would do the same in the early 1940's, as full-time director of the PEA, when progressive education was once more threatened.

In February 1929, with higher hopes than ever, the Little Red School House began the new term in P.S. 41. But difficulties continued to dog it. The term had barely started when Howard Nudd reported "serious trouble" with the principal. Her replacement was also "cold." [105] But potentially more serious inconveniences were brewing at P.S. 41 than the hostility of principal and teachers. Miss Irwin's classes became the focus of a clash between two worlds which lived an uneasy co-existence in Greenwich Village: the world of the "Villagers," and the

[104] Mrs. Samuel A. Lewisohn, Interview by Nancy Craig, Radio Station WJZ, April 17, 1945; transcript in the files of the PEA.
[105] Minutes of the Executive Committee of the PEA, December 16, 1930; Mitchell, *op. cit.*, pp. 437, 439–40.

world of the "Local People." [106] One of the few places these two worlds made contact was in Miss Irwin's classes at P.S. 41. The contact was anything but friendly. The villagers were staunch champions of the school. In Miss Irwin's classes, explained Dr. Regina Stix, one of the leaders of the villager faction in P.S. 41, "the children not only profit from their work but also get a happy education." [107] On the other hand, the local parents, with their orthodox values, had no use for Miss Irwin's experiment. They resented the postponement of reading, and the shift in emphasis from the traditional three R's to a curriculum based on neighborhood trips and manual activities left them cold. The marked emphasis on group activity in Miss Irwin's classes and on a healthy emotional development likewise had little appeal to them. As viewed by the local people, progressive education was single-interest education. It was an education suited for children of the villagers. But what was good for children of the villagers was not necessarily good for their children.[108]

Parent opposition to her school experiments was no new phenomenon to Miss Irwin. She had run into it at P.S. 64 and at P.S. 61.[109] But at P.S. 41 it was more widespread than at the other two schools, more bitter, and slightly better organized. In March 1929, Howard Nudd informed the PEA's Executive Committee that a parents' meeting had been called to organize a protest against Miss Irwin's classes, that Miss Irwin was told not to come, and that "her parents" were not invited.[110] But this threat to the existence of the Little Red School House came to nothing. In November 1931 when the new principal of P.S. 41, Mrs. Mary G. Chisholm, was asked by the Board of Superintendents–PEA Evaluating Committee how the parents were reacting to Miss Irwin's classes, she replied coldly: "After awhile they become quiescent." [111]

[106] I am greatly indebted for the following discussion to Caroline Ware, *Greenwich Village, 1920–1930: A Comment on American Civilization in the Post-War Years* (Boston, 1935).

[107] *New York Times*, May 1, 1932, Sec. III; Ware, *op. cit.*, p. 342.

[108] Ware, *op. cit.*, p. 343.

[109] At P.S. 64 attempts to introduce manual activities ran into the opposition of what the authors of *Fitting the School to the Child* called the "prejudices" of parents who "interfered with the true education of their children by exaggerating and emphasizing the value of formal academic display." At P.S. 61 Miss Irwin had to introduce formal instruction in reading and arithmetic, in spite of her inclinations, "since the gifted children demand these subjects—largely because of pressure on the part of their parents." Irwin and Marks, *op. cit.*, p. 233; De Lima, *Our Enemy the Child*, pp. 38–39.

[110] Minutes of the Executive Committee of the PEA, March 19, 1929.

[111] "Minutes of the Evaluating Committee, Nov. 5, 1931," in the files of the Little Red School House.

The end of the Little Red School House came finally on the heels of the first report of the aforementioned Evaluating Committee, which was duly appointed in January 1930.[112] On September 15, 1931, the committee submitted its confidential report.[113] In the light of the suspicions and fears of the local population, as well as the paucity of research on experiments in progressive education, the report takes on more than parochial significance. In arithmetic, vocabulary, and language usage, the evaluation was markedly unfavorable to Miss Irwin's classes. In reading there was a "definite superiority" for the pupils in P.S. 173, the control school. Especially among pupils with I.Q. below 120, the report noted, the differences were very great. As for the postponement of reading to the 2B grade, the committee reported that the children in Miss Irwin's classes wanted to read early and that a number of them learned to do so at home. But, they went on to say: "This is a job that the school must do if it expects the normal and dull normal pupils to reach any degree of facility."

While the work in art at P.S. 41, the report continued, might bring out the abilities of pupils who possessed some natural talent, there was doubt as to whether this work gave training to pupils lacking such talent. As to Miss Irwin's claims concerning "more unified personality" and "better adjustment," it was asserted: "How to determine objectively whether these statements are borne out by practice the committee does not at this time know." The Evaluating Committee submitted the following recommendations to the Board of Superintendents:

> Your committee earnestly recommends that the experimental program of P.S. 41 be continued for another year, and that such further evaluations be made as may be necessary for more conclusive findings. . . . It is the conviction of your Committee that the children in P.S. 41 be taught to read as early as possible, certainly in earlier grades than at present. . . . A similar recommendation applies to some of the other tool subjects especially spelling

[112] It will be recalled that the Board of Superintendents, as part of its resolution permitting the establishment of Miss Irwin's experiment in P.S. 41, required that an Evaluating Committee be appointed to appraise the results of her work. It was composed of Dr. William Jansen, representing the Board of Superintendents; Mrs. Thomas K. Schmuck, representing the PEA; and Dean Paul Klapper of the CCNY School of Education, appointed jointly by the Board and the PEA. As per the Board's resolution, children who had been in Miss Irwin's classes for two and one-half years and who were in the 3B grade were to be compared with a control group of children from P. S. 173 in the three R's, art, manual activities, and character and personality. *The Public and the Schools*, No. 310, February 11, 1930.
[113] "Report of Evaluation Committee on Experimental Classes in P.S. 41, Manhattan. Submitted to the Board of Superintendents, Sept. 15, 1931," in the files of the Little Red School House; Ware, *op. cit.*, pp. 343-44.

and number work. In our judgment a little more effort directed toward these formal studies need not interfere in any significant way with the activities developed in P.S. 41. On the contrary they may even be furthered.[114]

The recommendations of the Evaluating Committee were the last straw. In February 1932, with the Little Red School House under fire from school officials, teachers, and parents, and now faced with the choice of radically altering everything that was progressive about the experiment if it were to meet the Board of Superintendents' approval, the PEA decided to withdraw its support from the experimental classes. On March 24, Superintendent O'Shea was informed that "because of lack of funds" the PEA would be unable to continue its experimental work beyond June 1932.[115] But the end was not yet. The Little Red School House was not to bow out in obscurity. After such a long, prominent, and stormy career, how could it?

On April 9, 1932, amidst wide publicity in the daily press, a small group of P.S. 41 villagers, encouraged by the PEA, launched a financial drive to keep the experimental classes in P.S. 41.[116] If they raised $10,-000, Mrs. Lewisohn promised to raise a matching sum "from foundations." [117] Two weeks later, the sum of $8,000 having been raised, the villagers petitioned the Board of Superintendents to reopen Miss Irwin's classes in the fall. This provided the occasion for Superintendent O'Shea to inform the public, briefly, that an appraisal of the work of the children in the experimental classes in the three R's had been made, and that the

[114] "Report of Evaluation Committee. . . ."

[115] New York Times, March 26, 1932; De Lima, The Little Red School House, p. 4; Minutes of the Executive Committee of the PEA, February 2, March 15, 1932. Enough funds to cover the expenses of the Little Red School House for the entire year 1932, except for $2,000 which Mrs. Lewisohn had promised to secure, had already been raised. Minutes of the Executive Committee of the PEA, October 20, 1931.

The Little Red School House was rather expensive. There was a staff of five to be paid, and there were expenses for material and publicity. From September 1, 1927, to August 31, 1932, the PEA had to raise about $75,000 for its support. The breakdown of donors and their donations follows: John D. Rockefeller, Jr., $27,500; Hofheimer Foundation, $20,000; New York Foundation, $20,000; Mrs. Samuel A. Lewisohn, $3,300; Mrs. Edward C. Henderson, $2,000; Junior League, $1,089.45; Guggenheim Foundation, $1,000; and Miscellaneous, $464.20. "Receipts Experimental Classes from September 1, 1927, to August 31, 1932," in the files of the Little Red School House.

[116] New York Times, April 10, 13, 15, 1932; Ware, op. cit., p. 344; De Lima, The Little Red School House, pp. 4, 210, 211; Minutes of the Executive Committee of the PEA, April 5, 1932; "Minutes, April 5, 1932, Informal Meeting of Parents of Experimental Classes of P.S. 41, Manhattan, Held at 355 Sixth Avenue, New York City," in the files of the Little Red School House.

[117] Minutes of the Executive Committee of the PEA, April 19, 1932; New York Times, April 19, 1932.

results did not justify continuing the program even if enough funds were raised; the PEA countered that "in questions of personality" the children in the experimental group were "statistically superior" to those in the control group and were also "superior in manual and artistic achievement." [118] In the end the Board of Superintendents refused to reconsider its decision to halt the classes as of June 1932. Whereupon, in the darkening shadows of breadlines and apple stands, a group of PEA officials and villagers decided to keep the Little Red School House going, but now as an independent, private progressive elementary school. In the fall of 1932 the Little Red School House opened up in its own quarters at 196 Bleecker Street, still in Greenwich Village, to begin another famous career.[119]

Thus the PEA's demonstration of the feasibility of progressive education for the public schools came to an end. That the Little Red School House was able to cling to its position in the public school system in the face of constant opposition from political leaders, school officials, teachers, and parents is eloquent and unimpeachable testimony to the influence of the PEA in the twenties. It is also striking proof of the compelling importance which the PEA attached to the experiment. The highest stakes were involved in the PEA's aggressive promotion and stubborn defense of the Little Red School House. For the PEA, it represented the ultimate embodiment of its conception of public education; namely, that the school was society's social welfare agency par excellence; or, in sum, that public education was only a continuation of social work by other means. Miss Irwin's classes, asserted *The Public and the Schools* in 1927, were "the natural corollary of visiting teacher work." [120] That the Little Red School House was the obverse of the visiting teacher coin explains the Commonwealth Fund's subsidizing of the experiment from 1922 to 1927, no less than the interest of the Hofheimer Foundation and the New York Foundation in the experiment.[121]

But the Little Red School House was a demonstration in progres-

[118] *New York Times*, April 30, May 7, 9, 1932.
[119] *New York Times*, May 12, 13, 1932, eds.; De Lima, *The Little Red School House*, p. 211. And see the latter volume for the post-P.S. 41 career of the Little Red School House.
[120] *The Public and the Schools*, No. 275, May 31, 1927.
[121] In the words of the Commonwealth Fund, "physical and emotional adjustment were thoroughly stressed" in Miss Irwin's classes. The program there "was being developed in the recognition that health, happiness and general adjustment to life are more important than conventional school standards." Commonwealth Fund, *Sixth Annual Report*, 1924, pp. 34–35; Commonwealth Fund, *Seventh Annual Report*, 1925, p. 43; New York Foundation, *Forty Year Report*, 1909–1949 (New York, 1950), p. 44.

sive education, not, ostensibly, in social work. Here lay its chief importance. Social work, *qua* social work, could not be pushed into the public
schools, not in any fundamental way at any rate. The aroma of charity
still clung too heavily to it. For instance, for forty years the school social
worker was called visiting teacher, home and school visitor, or school
counselor—anything but a social worker.[122] The suspicion had to be
avoided that the schools were being turned into social welfare agencies.
At this point the PEA found its school ideal perfectly embodied in
child-centered pedagogy. Progressive Education provided the PEA with
the superb legitimation of its social work ethos. After the PEA embraced
the cause of progressive education, it released its hold on social work.
It completely severed its relations with the visiting teacher movement,
and Howard Nudd appeared no more at meetings of the National Conference of Social Work. Now the PEA could stand forth as the champion of an education that was offered by the best private schools, the
champion of an education that the wisest and best parents desired for
their own children.

IX

What a remarkable decade it had been for the Association. Almost
everything it did seemed to be more exciting, more noteworthy, on a
grander scale than ever before: the constant, energetic, and well-publicized feuding with Mayors Hylan and Walker; the nationwide visiting
teacher demonstration; and the spectacular experiment in progressive
education. Public Education Association had become a name that meant
something to an extensive circle of opinion leaders throughout the
country. The PEA had earned the reputation as the premier civic group
in New York City. But by the end of the decade a peculiar pattern had
begun to emerge: while the PEA's long-range goals were steadily advancing, its specific programs were failing, and its vigor was declining.

Even while the PEA was at the apogee of its career, its strength
was being sapped because of its inability to maintain a viable political

---

[122] It wasn't until the 1940's that "visiting teacher" was superseded by the
more accurate term, "school social worker"; in 1942 the National Association of
Visiting Teachers changed its name to the American Association of School Social
Workers. Hazel Fredericksen, *The Child and His Welfare* (San Francisco, 1948),
p. 72; Bruno, *op. cit.*, p. 296. And see LeRoy E. Bowman, "What the Press
Thinks of Social Work," *Proceedings*, National Conference of Social Work (Washington, D.C., 1923), pp. 477–83; Lucia Johnson Bing, "What the Public Thinks
of Social Work," *ibid.*, pp. 483–87; Nathan Edward Cohen, *Social Work in the
American Tradition* (New York, 1958), pp. 142, 339.

existence. The PEA never made any reconciliation with the long Tammany reign of 1917–1932. It paid dearly for its insurgency. Ignored in the making of school appointments, opposing those which were made, its influence as a pressure group progressively deteriorated. By the end of the twenties there were many high officials in the school system who not only felt no obligation to the PEA, but were hostile towards it because it had questioned their appointments or supported other candidates for their positions. In the meantime, civic groups with a special interest in public education had arisen that did not have the handicap of an open identification with anti-Tammany politics to contend with, and were beginning to rival the PEA in influence. The United Parents Associations of New York City, at whose birth the PEA was midwife, is a case in point.[123]

But because its essential demand to be consulted in the making of school appointments was ignored, the PEA retaliated with an unremitting watch on the public schools. The outcome of its decade-long vigil was that the influence of political leaders and elected officials in the making of school appointments was gradually reduced, the principle of merit appointments served, and its objective of removing the schools from "politics" that much nearer accomplishment. Furthermore, the schools were kept free of scandal. The school system was untainted by the corruption rampant in the city government during Walker's second term.[124]

The same paradox of failure and success emerges at the end of the decade in that part of the PEA's program concerned with school principles and practices. Its visiting teacher demonstration was closed in

[123] At one point apprehension was expressed that the president of the UPA's, Robert E. Simon, was "too ambitious" and might take on work "properly within the province of the Association." Minutes of the Executive Committee of the PEA, January 19, 1926. Overlapping memberships eased such threats: Mrs. J. Culbert Palmer was chairman of the Committee on Education of the Junior League; Mrs. Lewisohn was a member of the Advisory Board of the United Parents Associations; Martha Lincoln Draper was president of the Women's City Club; Howard Nudd sat on the Committee on Education of the Men's City Club.

For the United Parents Associations in the twenties, see Margaret Lighty and LeRoy Bowman, *Parenthood in a Democracy* (New York, 1939), Part I, Chaps. II–V; and Maria Lambin Rogers, *A Contribution to the Theory and Practise of Parents Associations* (New York, 1931).

[124] Contemporary muckrakers did rake over the schools, but they turned up only what might be considered venial sins. E.g., the schools were shot through with "all kinds of politics"; there was waste in the condemnation of school sites; the Board of Education refused to restrict the size of high schools to 2,000 pupils. Norman Thomas and Paul Blanshard, *What's the Matter with New York?* (New York, 1932), pp. 234–38, 323, 324.

1930 without any notable increase in the number of school social workers in the country, and in 1931 the Little Red School House had only a
most tenuous hold in the city's school system. But by 1931, it was no
longer so essential to demonstrate progressive practices or to promote
progressive ideas in the public schools as it had been a few years before.
Thanks to the educational experiments carried on in the country in the
twenties, of which the visiting teacher project and the Little Red School
House were notable examples, there was a change occurring in society's
conception of public education. "Social case workers who once used
the public schools merely as sources of information," wrote a leading
social worker in 1933, "have come to use them increasingly as cooperative agencies for treatment." [125] And school officials in New York were
increasingly taking the mental hygiene point of view.[126] "With increasing hopefulness," *The Public and the Schools* pointed out in 1930,
"those who are concerned with the problem of crime and delinquency
or who are seeking to ameliorate the personal and social ills which result from a lack of adjustment to life are turning to the public schools
as centers through which preventive measures may be mobilized." [127]

The PEA's fundamental objectives may have been advancing, but
the PEA itself was becoming tired and disheartened. As its leaders surveyed the scene in 1930, all was failure and gloom. The PEA was ignored,
except to be mocked, by Walker and O'Shea; [128] its decade-long legislative efforts were a failure; its visiting teacher demonstration was terminated; the experimental classes in P.S. 41 were existing only from day
to day.[129] There were financial woes also. The PEA's general program
had benefited to the extent of about $10,000 annually from the Com-
monwealth Fund's juvenile delinquency prevention program. It was
increasingly difficult to raise this kind of money as the effects of the

[125] Meredith, *op. cit.*, p. 140; Frank, *op. cit.*, pp. 751–800, *passim*; Thomas
and Thomas, *op. cit.*, Chap. V.
[126] *The Public and the Schools*, No. 310, February 11, 1930; No. 318, June 3,
1930; No. 329, March 10, 1931; No. 331, April 7, 1931; No. 333, May 5, 1931.
[127] *The Public and the Schools*, No. 310, February 11, 1930.
[128] Superintendent O'Shea made the Association a butt of ridicule. "I want
the schools entirely free from politics," he stated as he banned an issue of the Junior
Red Cross News from circulating in the schools because it carried a quotation from
a Hoover speech. *The Public and the Schools*, No. 293, October 9, 1928.
[129] Other phases of its program had slipped away. The work of the Cardiac
Committee was now carried on by the Cardiac Vocational Guidance Service of the
New York Tuberculosis and Health Association and by Irvington House, the Tombs
School work by the Welfare League Association. *The Public and the Schools*, No.
300, May 14, 1929; "A Program of Problems for the Consideration of the Executive Committee of the Public Education Association. Respectfully Submitted by the
Staff, Oct. 1, 1930," mimeographed, in the files of the PEA.

stockmarket crash began to dry up foundations as a source of support. Internal struggles for power between old and new generations racked the PEA throughout the 1920's and contributed to its declining vigor. Gradually the Old Guard faded away: in 1924 Mrs. Joseph R. Swan resigned from the Executive Committee; in 1928, Mrs. Miriam Sutro Price; in 1931, Mrs. Edward C. Henderson.[130] They stayed on as trustees but were no longer active except for a querulous supervision of the younger generation. Leadership in the PEA passed to Mrs. Samuel A. Lewisohn, Mrs. Thomas K. Schmuck, Mrs. Louis S. Levy, and Mrs. J. Culbert Palmer, Jr. The election of Martha Lincoln Draper to succeed Joseph P. Cotton as president in April 1930 indicated that the PEA was losing the interest and support of the men, and more and more becoming a woman's club, in which the "social lobby" might become the predominant strategy and sociability the only aim.[131]

On November 4, 1930, when the PEA was celebrating its 35th birthday, the *Times,* in an editorial, reminded New York's citizens and taxpayers to visit the public schools during "Open School Week." "The public should be glad," the *Times* asserted, "that there is an association of men and women who take an interest in the schools year in and year out—to whom every week is an 'Open School Week'—the Public Education Association." Thus the *Times* tried to give an old friend a helping hand.

In late 1930, because of grave schisms in its inner circle, the PEA was giving serious consideration to the question of whether it should bow out of existence. After some discussion of the matter, a "Reorganization Committee" was formed to consider the Association's future.[132] The committee worked from December 1930 through March 1931, profiting from consultation with some of the PEA's old leaders: Nicholas Murray Butler, Abraham Flexner, and Charles P. Howland. Finally, on March 31, 1931, at a joint meeting of the Board of Trustees and the Executive Committee, it was unanimously decided that the PEA should

---

[130] Minutes of the Executive Committee of the PEA, October 14, 1924; December 15, 1928; January 13, 1931.

[131] This is not to imply that Miss Draper was not widely respected. The PEA's new president was one of the "Grand Dames" of New York. As a "friendly visitor" of the Charity Organization Society in the 1890's, as a member of the city's Board of Education from 1910 to 1917, as a member of the New York State Friedsam Committee, and through a service as a field official of the American Red Cross in the Spanish-American War and World War I, Miss Draper had served her city, her state, and her nation well.

[132] Minutes of the Executive Committee of the PEA, October 21, December 2, 1930, January 13, 1931.

continue, that every effort should be made to recruit more men into the active leadership, and that a reorganization increasing the influence of the Board of Trustees should be effected immediately.[133] With this internal accommodation worked out, a new spirit pervaded the PEA headquarters at 8 West 40th Street. Miss Draper loaned the PEA $1,500. Mrs. William H. Childs gave it $5,000 outright as a gift. Mrs. Lewisohn arranged an art benefit. The entire staff was given a vacation with pay.[134] The PEA would carry on. The first program decided upon for 1932 was a series of five educational conferences under the title "Quo Vadis?" [135]

[133] Minutes of a joint meeting of the Board of Trustees and the Executive Committee of the PEA, March 31, 1931.
[134] Minutes of the Executive Committee of the PEA, June 15, October 6, 1931.
[135] *The Public and the Schools*, No. 338, December 15, 1931.

Chapter 5

THE PERILS OF PROSPERITY

1932-1940

IT IS PARADOXICAL BUT TRUE: the PEA thrived best on adversity. In the twenties, confronted with a hostile city administration and an unfriendly Board of Education, when every inch of ground it coveted in the city school system had to be fought for tooth and nail, the PEA thrived. In the thirties everything was reversed. Confronted with a cordial city administration and a friendly Board of Education, with all its major school objectives triumphant, the PEA stagnated and declined. Success imperiled its very existence.

I

In 1932, as it entered its fourth decade, the PEA was suffused with a new spirit. The crisis through which it had lately passed had served to bring everyone; Board of Trustees and Executive Committee, old and new generations, closer together. And the crisis had elicited from that outstanding group of men—Henry Taft, Kenneth Simpson, William Chadbourne, Alfred Jaretzki, Jr., and William B. Nichols, whose connections with the PEA had become, by the end of the twenties, extremely tenuous—reaffirmations of active interest in its affairs. Furthermore, in line with the reorganization proposals of March 31, 1931, a handful of distinguished men had been recruited into the PEA's inner circle of leadership, including lawyers Harrison K. Tweed, Abbott Ingalls, Mason H. Bigelow, Morris Brownell, Jr., Frank E. Karelsen, Jr., and merchant and civic leader Leo B. Arnstein. Long-awaited political changes in the city in the early years of the thirties were even more persuasive auguries that the PEA's fourth decade would be a fruitful one.

The Mayoralty election of November 7, 1933, brought victory to the

Fusion ticket headed by the extraordinary Republican insurgent, Fiorello
H. La Guardia. The Democratic monopoly of the city government had
finally been broken. Now, thanks to La Guardia's political acumen, and
to schisms within the Democratic party organization, Tammany would
be the "out" group for a long time to come. Victory in 1933 was the
beginning of an unprecedented twelve-year reign for the ebullient Little
Flower.[1] For the PEA, November 7, 1933 was a great day. The Association had been waiting and working for this day for sixteen long years,
since November 6, 1917. At last the inaccessibles were out of City Hall.
At last officials and friends of the PEA such as Charles C. Burlingham,
William Chadbourne, Richard S. Childs, and allies such as the City
Club, the Merchants Association, and the Citizens Union, all "the old
watchdogs of civic conscience," as Charles Belous called them, would get
a hearing at City Hall.[2] Furthermore, during the election campaign
La Guardia had pledged to seek legislation making the Superintendent
of Schools the responsible executive officer of the school system and
extending merit procedures through the school system.[3] These were
reforms the PEA had been urging for more than a decade. It all added
up to a profound change in the PEA's environment, and called forth
an equally profound change in the PEA's strategy and tactics.

After La Guardia's triumph, the PEA's hue and cry and watchdog
tactics changed to those of sympathetic guidance and unconditional
support. There would be no need now to publicly scrutinize school appointments. Again to quote Belous, "instead of the old system of political
appointment to these boards [the Board of Education and the Board
of Higher Education], the Mayor selects his appointees on the basis
of their particular abilities." [4] In 1934, to ensure that the Mayor would

[1] We shall have to await the second and concluding volume of Arthur Mann's
biography of La Guardia for a truly satisfactory account of the election of 1933 and
La Guardia's subsequent career as Mayor. In the meantime, Charles Garrett, *The
La Guardia Years: Machine and Reform Politics in New York City* (New York,
1961), is most useful. See also Charles Belous, *Faith in Fusion* (New York, 1951);
Newbold Morris, *Let the Chips Fall: My Battles Against Corruption* (New York,
1955); Warren Moscow, *Politics in the Empire State* (New York, 1948). There is
an excellent summing-up of La Guardia as Mayor in Wallace S. Sayre and Herbert
Kaufman, *Governing New York City: Politics in the Metropolis* (New York, 1960),
pp. 690–92.
[2] Belous, *op. cit.*, p. 25, *passim.*
[3] *School and Society*, XXXVIII (November 18, 1933), 668; *The Public and
the Schools*, No. 353, November 28, 1933; *The Fusion Handbook*, Fusion Campaign
Committee, Periodical Publications No. 1 (New York, 1933), pp. 94–95; Garrett,
op. cit., p. 108.
[4] Belous, *op. cit.*, pp. 38–39; Garrett, *op. cit.*, p. 200. La Guardia's School
Board congratulates itself in Rebecca B. Rankin, ed., *New York Advancing, World's*

be able, as quickly as possible to begin to exercise a wholesome influence
on the school system, the PEA, after years of opposing similar measures,
supported legislation in Albany increasing the membership of New
York's Board of Education from seven to eleven.[5] Although this species
of ripper legislation failed to impress the state legislature, the sought-for
goal was soon accomplished. In October 1935, the *Times* pointed out
that the Mayor now controlled the School Board by four Fusion men
to three hold-over Democrats.[6] The PEA was particularly pleased with
La Guardia's appointment of James Marshall, distinguished Republican
lawyer, philanthropist, and Jewish community leader, to the Board.[7]
The PEA did not laud all of La Guardia's school appointments as it did
his appointment of Marshall, but, on the other hand, it criticized none
of them. The PEA's policy regarding the board had shifted from one
of carping opposition to one of acceptance and accommodation. It had
already made an auspicious start in mending its fences with another
center of power in the city school system, the Board of Superintendents.

By the end of 1931 the PEA was ready for a fundamental shift in
its approach to the professional hierarchy of New York's school system.
Its decade-long firing at school officials had become a debilitating habit.
Superintendent O'Shea, its old foe, was close to retirement. It was time
to patch up old quarrels with members of the Board of Superintendents.
When Mrs. Levy proposed to a meeting of the PEA's Executive Committee on December 1, 1931, that the PEA inaugurate a series of small
meetings at private homes at which top school leaders could meet officials and friends of the PEA, the committee readily accepted.[8] Accordingly, in 1932 the series of meetings, "Quo Vadis," was carried forward.
Deputy School Superintendent Harold G. Campbell, Associate Super-

---

*Fair Edition, The Result of Five Years of Progressive Administration in the City
of New York, F. H. La Guardia, Mayor* (New York, 1939), pp. 137–43; and Rebecca B. Rankin, ed., *New York Advancing: A Scientific Approach to Municipal
Government . . . 1934–1935* (New York, 1936), Chap. V.

[5] *The Public and the Schools*, No. 354, December 26, 1933; Minutes of the
Executive Committee of the PEA, December 5, 1933.

[6] *New York Times*, October 27, 1935.

[7] *The Public and the Schools*, No. 366, April 16, 1935. By 1937 the city had
a completely La Guardia-appointed Board of Education. The seven members were
James Marshall, President, and Miss Johanna Lindlof, Daniel P. Higgins, Dr. Albert
C. Bonaschi, Ellsworth P. Buck, Walter J. Carlin, and Henry C. Turner. In 1937,
the mayoralty election year, the PEA bitterly opposed legislation which would have
replaced the then present Board of Education with a new and larger board to be
selected by the next city administration. *The Public and the Schools*, No. 382, April
27, 1937. This measure passed the Senate but was killed in the Assembly.

[8] Minutes of the Executive Committee of the PEA, December 1, 1931.

intendents William E. Grady and Joseph Sheehan, District Superintendent John Loftus, and other school officials came to the fashionable residences of Adolph Lewisohn, Mrs. Felix Warburg, Mrs. Richard Aldrich, Mrs. Richard S. Childs, and Mrs. Joseph R. Swan to discuss school activities, and stayed to become acquainted with the PEA.[9]

For the PEA, then, the political climate in the early thirties was more auspicious than at any time since 1917. On the other hand, the PEA was at a loss for a program. For the first time since 1896 it found itself without a school project, without something exciting or dramatic with which to occupy members or entice prospective members; without fund-raising appeal. Furthermore, its new policy of cultivating political leaders and school officials meant that another one of its traditional activities, school muckraking, was out. The PEA's Board of Trustees, meeting in February 1932 to discuss policies and programs for the coming year, were at a loss for ideas.[10] And casting its bleak shadow over everything was the Great Depression. In 1932 it hit with full impact on the city. The depression threatened to snuff out the PEA's life, since it cut sharply into the PEA's main sources of income—foundation grants, and large subsidies from individual benefactors—but it eased another crisis by thrusting a program into the PEA's hands.

II

It was not immediately apparent that the stock market collapse of October 1929 was the beginning of the longest and most severe depression in the nation's history. For instance, for several years after the crash New York City's budget continued to mount—from $539,000,000 in 1929 to $631,000,000 in 1932. By the spring of 1932, however, there were 800,000 unemployed in New York and the full calamitous nature of Black Thursday had struck home. The city would have to dig deep into its pockets if it were to finance a halfway adequate system of unemployment relief. But at the same time tax revenues were sharply off, and bankers, businessmen, and real estate owners, with the newly organized Citizens Budget Commission in the forefront, were on an

[9] *The Public and the Schools*, No. 388, December 15, 1931; Howard Nudd, "The Public Education Association at Work: A Resume of the Work of the Association for the Fiscal Year 1931–1932," mimeographed, in the files of the PEA. The PEA issued no annual reports for the years 1913–1931. From 1932 to 1940, a mimeographed annual resume was prepared by Mr. Nudd for the Board of Trustees. The PEA began to publish annual reports again in 1943.

[10] Minutes of the Board of Trustees of the PEA, February 16, 1932.

economy rampage, imperiously demanding a $100,000,000 cutback in the city budget.[11]

The appropriation for the city's school system was the largest item in the city's operating budget, excluding the sacrosanct debt service, school appropriations amounting to almost $141,500,000 in 1932. For economy-minded groups in the city then, one of the most promising forms of economy was to slash away at the appropriations for education. And this is what such groups, led by the Citizens Budget Commission, did.[12] Here was one threat to the city school program. But, in the early thirties, the schools faced attack on two fronts.

Public education in New York State is financed by both state and local authorities. Under the gubernatorial administrations of Al Smith and Franklin D. Roosevelt, state aid to education had skyrocketed from $44,000,000 in 1924 to more than $100,000,000 in 1931.[13] But in 1932 Governor Roosevelt, under duress of providing monies to finance a state program of unemployment relief and under extreme pressure from an economy bloc led by Merwin K. Hart and the New York State Economic Council, reduced the state subvention for education, the largest item in the state's operating budget, a flat 10 per cent. The blow fell heavily on New York. The cut meant that although the state sub-vention to the city would still be more than $46,000,000, the city would get $5,000,000 less than in the preceding year.[14] And the pressure was mounting on Albany for more drastic economies in 1933.[15]

The school crisis galvanized the PEA. It had to act or abdicate its claim to leadership in the public school field in the city. The situation, however, was not uncomplicated. The leaders of the PEA, corporation

[11] William F. Whyte, *Financing New York City* (New York, 1935), pp. 22–23, 29–34; Joseph D. McGoldrick, "Storm Warnings in New York City's Finances," *National Municipal Review*, XXI (February, 1932), 168–75; Garrett, *op. cit.*, pp. 80–81.

[12] *New York Times*, September–December, 1932; William Wattenberg, *On the Educational Front* (New York, 1936), pp. 21–29; Whyte, *op. cit.*, pp. 7–8.

[13] Paul E. Malone, *The Fiscal Aspect of State and Local Relationships in New York*, State of New York, Special Report of the State Tax Commission No. 13 (Albany, 1937), p. 185; Rose Naomi Cohen, *The Financial Control of Education in the Consolidated City of New York* (New York, 1948), p. 181; Wattenberg, *op. cit.*, p. 29; Whyte, *op. cit.*, p. 8.

[14] Cohen, *op. cit.*, pp. 183–85; Wattenberg, *op. cit.*, pp. 29–32. For the depression in New York State and Governor Roosevelt's pioneer efforts to cope with the disaster, see Bernard Bellush, *Franklin Delano Roosevelt as Governor of New York* (New York, 1955), Chap. VII; Arthur M. Schlesinger, Jr., *The Crisis of the Old Order, 1931–1933* (Boston, 1957), pp. 391–93; David M. Ellis, *et al.*, *A Short History of New York State* (New York, 1957), pp. 416ff.

[15] Allan Nevins, *Herbert H. Lehman and His Era* (New York, 1963), p. 133.

and trust lawyers, bankers, and merchants, were committed to the orthodox economic philosophy of liquidation, deflation, and balanced budgets. They never questioned the city's need for retrenchment and economy. On the other hand, the PEA's basic commitment to the ideal of the public school as a social agency had to be served. As *The Public and the Schools* pointed out in the fall of 1932, now more than ever, in the confusion and social demoralization apt to follow in the wake of a crisis such as a worldwide depression, was the time to turn to the schools.[16] This posed a dilemma for the PEA. How could it adhere to classical economic theory and yet not violate its equally fundamental commitment to progressive education? The Association solved the problem by employing a double strategy. In the first place the PEA would accept retrenchment in city school appropriations as inevitable, but it would be a retrenchment in the appropriation for teacher salaries, and not, if the PEA could help it, in the appropriation for school services. (Since teacher salaries constituted about 85 per cent of the school budget, this position had some logic.) In the second place, the PEA would make an all-out fight to keep state aid to the city schools at the highest levels.

In New York City there was little the PEA could do except fight a delaying action against budget cuts affecting city school services. In May 1932, "in an effort to preserve the program of public education in the City, and at the same time suggest possible methods for reducing the budget," the PEA called twenty-five of the city's leading civic organizations to an emergency meeting. At the conclusion of the meeting, the Association had received assurances from most of the groups in attendance that if large cuts had to be made in city school appropriations, school services would be the last to be curtailed, and that this step would not be taken until "the possibility of a temporary reduction in the salaries of the school staff can be thoroughly canvassed." [17] In

16 *The Public and the Schools*, No. 345, November 22, 1932.

17 *New York Times*, May 23, 1932; *The Public and the Schools*, No. 343, May 24, 1932; No. 344, October 11, 1932. In December, the state legislature, in emergency session, enacted legislation giving the city's Board of Estimate power to reduce all state-mandated salaries, excepting those of employees of the Board of Education. The lawmakers enacted a separate bill which reduced teacher salaries according to fixed schedules. The teachers' salary cuts ranged from 6 to 33.9 per cent. The total savings on city employee salaries amounted to almost $19,000,000, of which the city's teachers and school officials contributed $8,800,000. A bond issue was subsequently floated by New York bankers enabling the city to meet its current expenditures. *New York Times*, December 15, 1932; *The Public and the Schools*, No. 346, December 21, 1932; Cohen, *op. cit.*, p. 115; Whyte, *op. cit.*, pp. 34–35; Garrett, *op. cit.*, pp. 104, 142; Wattenberg, *op. cit.*, p. 23.

the spring of 1933, at another large public meeting called by the PEA, this one on "How Can We Be Fair Both to the Child and the Tax-payer," a similar position was aired.[18] In the meantime the PEA's voice was one of the few in the city raised in opposition to the school budget economies of interim Mayors McKee and O'Brien.[19]

In early 1934 the PEA was confronted with a new challenge, this one coming from no less than the newly-elected Fusion administration. Mayor La Guardia, as soon as he was installed in City Hall, like Mayors O'Brien and McKee before him went energetically to work to balance the city budget and to find some way to escape the thraldom in which bankers held the city. Later in 1934, La Guardia would, in his despera-tion, successfully propose the imposition of a 2 per cent city sales tax, but first, like his predecessors, he turned to the question of the salaries of city employees. In January 1934 the Mayor sponsored a sweeping "Economy Bill" in Albany. Among other provisions it gave City au-thorities power over all municipal expenditures for salaries, including those of the Department of Education. The bill was backed by the City Fusion Party, the City Club, the Citizens Union, and many other good government groups in the city.[20]

The PEA was stunned by this development. Here was La Guardia asking the state to relax its control over education, and he was being spurred on by organizations that, in the eyes of the PEA, should have known better. But the PEA had for forty years been educating the oc-cupant of City Hall in the doctrine that education was and must be a state function; it would educate La Guardia too. "The established principle of state control of education must not be destroyed," *The Public and the Schools* declared.[21] The newsletter went on to concede the importance also of balancing the budget and of teacher sacrifices. Now what was to be done? (The legislature refused to take the onus for cutting city salaries again.) The PEA suggested that the Mayor in-troduce a separate bill empowering the city's Board of Education, as the local agent of the state, to make such adjustments in the compensa-tion of school employees as it might deem necessary upon being advised

[18] *New York Times*, April 28, 1933; *The Public and the Schools*, No. 350, April 25, 1933.

[19] *New York Times*, October 12, 1932, ed., October 14, December 12, 21, 1932, February 8, October 1, 11, 1933.

[20] Margaret I. Tanzer, "The Situation in New York City," *National Municipal Review*, XXIII (March, 1934), 190; Nevins, *Herbert H. Lehman And His Era*, pp. 146ff; Garrett, *op. cit.*, pp. 143–44; Whyte, *op. cit.*, p. 41; Cohen, *op. cit.*, pp. 123–24.

[21] *The Public and the Schools*, No. 357, March 27, 1934.

by the Board of Estimate of the total amount that would have to be cut from school appropriations in order to balance the city budget.[22]

La Guardia's Economy Bill was finally revised along lines similar to those recommended by the PEA. In April 1934, the Albany solons passed legislation granting New York's Board of Estimate authority to impose compulsory "furloughs" without pay for all employees of the city government covered by state mandatory salary laws, with the exclusion of the city's teachers. They were covered in a separate bill which required the Board of Education to prescribe for the teachers the same furloughs imposed by the Board of Estimate for other city employees.[23] The PEA was satisfied:

> Now the legitimate demands of the city's economy program have been adequately met. . . . The principle of state control of education has also been fully recognized.[24]

On the state level, it was a different story. If, in New York City, the PEA asserted itself like the general who first saw in which direction the army was headed, and then placed himself in front of it, on the state level the PEA seized the initiative and masterminded a shrewd campaign on behalf of school support.

On January 17, 1933, the PEA's Board of Trustees decided to take a stand against any reduction in state aid to education.[25] The board's decision couldn't have come at a more timely moment. Two days later the storm burst around newly-elected Governor Herbert H. Lehman's head. On January 19, demands for a 20 per cent cut in state aid to education were voiced in Albany by a score or more speakers marshalled by the New York State Economic Council. The New York State Chamber of Commerce, local merchants associations, and Republican legislators jumped on the school economy bandwagon. There were demands that the state suspend all laws prescribing minimum educational standards in its local school districts.[26] "The big item," Governor Lehman said, "is State aid, and I have wrestled with this thing prayerfully for weeks and months." Then the Governor told Merwin K. Hart and the others that he was willing to cut back and economize everywhere along

[22] *Ibid.*
[23] Margaret I. Tanzer, "New York City's Economy Bill," *National Municipal Review*, XXIII (May, 1934), 287–88; *School and Society*, XXXIX (May 26, 1934), 667; Garrett, *op. cit.*, p. 144; Whyte, *op. cit.*, p. 41; Wattenberg, *op. cit.*, p. 28.
[24] *The Public and the Schools*, No. 358, April 30, 1934.
[25] Minutes of the Board of Trustees of the PEA, January 17, 1933.
[26] *New York Times*, January 20, 1933.

the line, but he would do nothing to impair public education in the state.[27]

Developments in Albany confronted public education in New York State with a peril of the first magnitude. Could and would local school boards absorb the burden of further cuts in state aid, or would they reduce teaching staff, eliminate school services, or close down entirely? Governor Lehman, a "Henry Streeter," as Lillian Wald affectionately called him, could be counted upon. But the economy panic was in full swing, and it was questionable how long Lehman could hold out. He had to be backed up by the public. It was at this point that the PEA entered the fight.

The PEA mapped and coordinated battle strategy for a coalition which included the City Club, the United Parents Associations, and two state-wide organizations—the League of Women Voters and the New York State branch of the National Council of Jewish Women.[28] The PEA moved along a broad front to protect state educational standards: news releases, public meetings, and personal influence were all used. But the PEA's most successful tactic was perhaps the most hackneyed political formula of all—the call for an investigation and report. On February 7, 1933, with Governor Lehman under relentless pressure to drastically cut state aid and to suspend state control over minimum educational standards, the PEA called upon the Governor to appoint a commission to investigate and report on the whole question of state–local relations in education.[29] The PEA's resolution concluded with the following paragraph:

Pending the completion of such a study, the Association recommends that State protective laws be maintained without material modification and that State aid be continued at not less than the 1932 level.

[27] *Ibid.*; and see the editorial in the same issue. The Democratic sweep in 1932 which brought Roosevelt to the White House brought Herbert H. Lehman and the "Little New Deal" to Albany. Governor Lehman, scion of a New York City banking family, and humanitarian, was the kind of a man with whom leaders of the PEA, of whatever political convictions, had an affinity. Nevins, *Herbert H. Lehman and His Era*; Moscow, *op. cit.*, pp. 19–23; Ellis, *op. cit.*, Chap. XXXII.

[28] *The Public and the Schools*, No. 347, January 31, 1933; No. 348, February 28, 1933; No. 349, March 28, 1933; Minutes of a Joint Meeting of the Executive and Legislative Committees of the PEA, March 7, 1933; Margaret Lighty and LeRoy Bowman, *Parenthood in a Democracy* (New York, 1939), p. 82. The city's teachers were also active in the fight against school economy on both city and state levels. For the powerful teachers' lobby see Belle Zeller, *Politics in New York: A Study of Group Representation Before the Legislature* (New York, 1937), pp. 167–73; Wattenberg, *op. cit.*, Chaps. IX, XI; and Moscow, *op. cit.*, p. 201.

[29] *New York Times*, February 8, 1933; Minutes of the Executive Committee of the PEA, February 7, 1933.

President Draper of the PEA reported that the Governor had greeted the PEA's resolution with relief and was anxious to appoint such a commission, but that it would have to be financed by private funds. Accordingly, the PEA voted that Miss Draper and Mrs. Swan should consult with foundations in order to raise the necessary money.[30]

In July 1933, funds having been secured from the New York Foundation, the Altman Foundation, and the General Education Board (Miss Draper and Mrs. Swan were effective fund-raisers), Lehman appointed the Governor's Commission on the Costs of Public Education in New York State.[31] In the meantime the Governor was able to grant as much state aid for 1933 as had been granted in 1932, and all efforts to get the state to relax its protective machinery over public education had been stalled.

The Governor's Commission reported in late 1933. Two reports were filed. The majority report recommended the full statutory provision for state aid for 1934, some $116,000,000. The minority report agreed in principle with the majority, but stated that, because of financial conditions, an increase in state aid was unwarranted at the time, and recommended continuation of state aid at 1933 levels, about $102,000,-000. Both reports were adamantly against any relaxation of state standards.[32] Although Governor Lehman followed the politically more feasible recommendations of the minority, Merwin K. Hart and his supporters had been finessed, and the crusaders for state aid, led by the PEA, had won a great victory.

In August 1934, Mayor La Guardia, the Board of Estimate, the Board of Education, and the city's civic groups mounted an intensive assault on Albany for supplementary legislation to implement the full statutory amount of state aid. On the 19th of August such legislation was passed.[33] The crusade for state aid was over. By 1935, although the state subvention for education was again cut 10 per cent, the state was beginning to feel a measure of recovery, and federal relief appropriations had begun to ease the pressure for draconic acts of retrenchment. In

[30] Minutes of the Executive Committee of the PEA, February 21, May 9, 1933.

[31] *New York Times*, July 24, 1933; New York City, Board of Education, *The First Fifty Years, 1898–1948: Fiftieth Annual Report of the Superintendent of Schools* (New York, 1948), p. 116; Cohen, *op. cit.*, p. 184. Charles C. Burlingham was appointed chairman; George D. Strayer, in charge of research. Both were members of the board of the PEA. Also in the group of forty financiers, educators, businessmen, and civic leaders whom the Governor appointed to the Commission were Miss Draper, Mrs. Swan, Leo Arnstein, Henry W. Taft, and Mrs. Nathan Straus, Jr., all of the PEA.

[32] Cohen, *op. cit.*, pp. 184–85; *The Public and the Schools*, No. 354, December 26, 1933; No. 355, January 30, 1934.

[33] *New York Times* for June, July, and August, 1934; Wattenberg, *op. cit.*, p. 30.

1936 Lehman's budget provided for full state aid at the statutory level. Thanks to a courageous Governor, and to a vigorous counterattack led by the PEA, efforts which, if successful, might have seriously undermined the state system of public education were decisively repudiated.

To summarize, the PEA's program and strategy during the darkest days of the depression was clearly, so far as Albany was concerned, a success. In New York City proper, however, concerning protecting the schools from taxpayer groups, no such positive statement can be made, one way or another. From 1932 to 1934, appropriations for school operating expenses and capital outlay declined $26,000,000, from $152,000,- 000 to $125,790,000, while average daily attendance in the day schools for the same period climbed from 997,000 to 1,014,000.[34] In the wake of the economy drive new school construction was halted, class size increased, the four municipal teacher-training colleges abolished, summer schools and school gardens eliminated, and heavy curtailments made in allowances for school playgrounds, community and recreation centers, baths, pools, and evening schools.[35] But, on the other hand, schools had been kept in regular session, public high schools were still free, and kindergartens and medical services had been retained.[36] What can be said is that the PEA's efforts to protect school services in the city should be deemed, on the whole, successful. The city school system came through the worst years of the Great Depression relatively unscathed.[37]

III

In 1937 the New York State Legislature repealed the New York City teachers' salary cut law of 1932.[38] Thanks to the New Deal—more

[34] New York City, Board of Education, *Annual Financial and Statistical Reports*, 1932–1934; Cohen, *op. cit.*, p. 181.

[35] New York City, Board of Education, *The First Fifty Years*, pp. 115–16; Wattenberg, *op, cit.*, p. 28; *The Public and the Schools*, No. 345, November 22, 1932; No. 347, January 31, 1933.

[36] The school systems of some of the nation's largest cities, Chicago, Cleveland, and Detroit, fared much worse. See Eunice Langdon, "The Teacher and the Depression," *Nation*, CXXXVII (August 16, 1933), 182–85; Avis D. Carlson, "Deflating the Schools," *Harpers*, CLXVII (November, 1933), 705–13; Wayne W. Parrish, "The Plight of Our School System," *Literary Digest*, CXVI (September 23, 1933), 32.

[37] Although the teaching and supervisory staff suffered the brunt of the city's economy drive, on closer examination they had little cause for complaint. As any adult New Yorker who has been a student or teacher in the city public school system knows, the city's teachers, though they execrate La Guardia, look back to the 1930's as their Golden Age.

[38] New York City, Board of Education, *The First Fifty Years*, p. 115; *The Public and the Schools*, No. 383, May 25, 1937.

specifically, thanks to the Public Works Administration and the Works
Progress Administration—the crisis in the city over the maintenance of
a satisfactory educational program had passed several years earlier. They
were a real boon to the city's public schools. Between the fall of 1934,
when, thanks to La Guardia's budget-balancing measures, the city became eligible for PWA assistance, and January 1936, the city school
system was aided by PWA funds for school construction and equipment
amounting to $34,500,000.[39] So far as WPA is concerned, its full impact
has yet to be calculated. For example, in the period August 1, 1935, to
June 30, 1937, WPA expenditures on programs under the joint sponsorship of the Board of Education and WPA amounted to more than
$44,000,000. By June 1938 there were 14,500 WPA personnel employed
on such joint programs. With the aid of WPA funds and personnel, old
educational services such as adult education and school lunch programs
were extended, and numerous new and exciting services were launched:
correction of speech defects, arts and crafts programs, instruction for
home-bound children, lip-reading, and remedial reading and remedial
arithmetic.[40] Describing the ferment in the public schools to the Board
of Trustees of the PEA, Associate Superintendent William Grady said:
"With the aid of relief funds, the schools are enjoying a depression
prosperity which was beyond our wildest dreams of realization during
the good times and easy budgets of the 20's [sic]." [41]

The Board of Trustees of the PEA was dubious. It was not impressed with the school officials' eulogy of the WPA. Nor was it moved
by the representative of WPA who, one year before, had requested the
PEA's interest and cooperation in the federal program.[42] A PEA "study
group" examined the operation of the WPA's remedial reading and
remedial arithmetic projects.[43] A few numbers of *The Public and the*

[39] *New York Times*, January 26, 1936, Sec. II; January 17, 1937, Sec. II; New
York City, Board of Education, *The First Fifty Years*, p. 117; Garrett, *op. cit.*, p.
200.

[40] John D. Millett, *The Works Progress Administration in New York City*
(Chicago, 1938), pp. 110–13; Alexander Leopold Radomski, *Work Relief in New
York State, 1931–1935* (New York, 1947), pp. 246–99; New York City, Board of
Education, *The First Fifty Years*, pp. 118–20.

[41] Minutes of the Board of Trustees of the PEA, May 26, 1936. Also, beginning in 1935 total city school appropriations began to approach and then to pass
the school budgets of the 1920's. Total disbursements for education rose from
approximately $139,300,000 in 1935 to $182,285,000 in 1938. New York City,
Board of Education, *Annual Financial and Statistical Report*, 1938, p. 9. Meanwhile,
beginning also in 1935, school registers began to drop.

[42] Minutes of the Board of Trustees of the PEA, March 5, 1935.

[43] Minutes of the Executive Committee of the PEA, November 18, 1935.

Schools, spread three years apart, referred to the WPA program.[44] Otherwise, the Association was vastly indifferent to the WPA's existence.

It was an indifference born of ambivalence. On the one hand, WPA succored and extended school services, and that was good. But on the other hand WPA was a "relief project," and to the leaders of the PEA anything smacking of relief was looked upon as contaminated. And when *The Public and the Schools* in an article critical of the National Youth Administration said: "Many fear federal aid may eventually mean control and nullification of the whole American philosophy of education as a state function, administered locally under state-set standards," it was undoubtedly expressing PEA reservations about WPA, no less than NYA.[45] And, if one reads between the lines, there is more at stake here than adherence to principle. That is, WPA entry into the public school field in the city posed a threat to the web of established relations built up over the years between the PEA and the Board of Education. Finally, the realization that the WPA had deprived it of a major phase of its school program may also have contributed to the Association's apathy toward the WPA.

IV

The year 1934 marked a watershed: the PEA was suddenly deprived of virtually its entire program. In 1934 the PEA witnessed the installation of a Fusion administration with its promise that good government in school administration could now be taken for granted. In 1934 its program of preserving educational services was ended, terminated by the New Deal. And, finally, in 1934, in the ultimate triumph, the PEA saw its conception of progressivism in school principles and procedures capture New York City school officialdom.

In June 1932, the PEA's experiment in progressive education, the Little Red School House, was virtually evicted from the public school system while being branded as substandard education. In June 1934, the Superintendent of Schools of New York City initiated steps to make every elementary school in the city a Little Red School House. In the

[44] *The Public and the Schools,* No. 361, November 27, 1934; No. 386, December 21, 1937.
[45] *The Public and the Schools,* No. 368, October 22, 1935. For more on New Deal programs in education, and the estrangement of large groups of progressive educators from them, see Lawrence A. Cremin, *The Transformation of the School* (New York, 1961) pp. 318–24; and Harry Zeitlin, "Federal Relations in American Education, 1933–1944: A Study of New Deal Efforts and Innovations" (unpublished Ph.D. thesis, Columbia University, 1958).

perspective of just two years' time, the loss of Miss Irwin's experiment in P.S. 41 became only the loss of a minor battlefield, not the loss of a war; it became a blow inflicted on the PEA by the Board of Superintendents for the sin of arrogance, not a defeat for the fundamental school objectives for which the PEA stood. The triumph of progressivism, at least two decades in the making, came finally with unforeseen swiftness. Two milestones in the early thirties stand out as being of crucial importance on the road to victory: the first, the survey of the New York City school system conducted by the New York State Department of Education in 1933; the second, the election of Harold G. Campbell as City School Superintendent in 1934.

Throughout Mayor Walker's second term in office, the PEA had kept up a barrage of fire against "politics" in the city schools and had persistently, though vainly, appealed to Albany for an investigation. Then in May 1931, the City Affairs Committee of the National Republican Club took up the PEA's charges. In a slashing critique the committee denounced Mayor Walker for playing "politics" with the school system.[46] But it was Superintendent O'Shea, the bête noire of the PEA, who came in for the most mordant criticism. The Republicans described O'Shea as "a product of Tammany politics," a man of "mediocre intellectual equipment, educationally unprogressive, who never contributed an important idea to educational progress and who resents even friendly and constructive criticism of the schools." [47] No New York City school official, not even John Jasper in the mid-1890's, when another group of Republicans and anti-Tammany city reformers also sought to make political capital out of the city's school system, had ever been subjected to such public abuse. The Republicans went on to charge "that 'in half the elementary schools the pupils cannot properly read, spell or do arithmetic. . . . The trouble is not with the teachers but with the leadership of the system.' " The *Times* immediately called upon State Commissioner of Education Frank Pierrepont Graves to investigate the charges.[48] A day later, George J. Ryan, president of the Board of Education, stung by the Republicans' criticism, made a formal request for the Commissioner to do the same.[49]

Here was a development which the PEA and its allies had long sought. Graves, classicist, historian, and former university president, had, since his appointment in 1924, worked most cooperatively with the city's civic leaders. Furthermore, the State Education Department was

[46] *New York Times*, May 6, 1931.
[47] *Ibid.*
[48] *New York Times*, May 7, 1931, ed.
[49] *New York Times*, May 8, 1931.

pedagogically far in advance of its downstate counterpart. In 1931, a group of state school officials under the leadership of J. Cayce Morrison had drawn up a list of "Cardinal Principles of Elementary Education," which broke sharply with the traditional specific, subject-matter oriented goals of education, and was vigorously urging their adoption by local school systems in the State.[50] New York City's educational reformers perceived that an anti-Tammany fishing expedition in the city schools was of slight importance (it was, as a matter of fact, impossible; Governor Roosevelt would never allow his Commissioner of Education to be party to such a manoeuvre) compared to an inquiry into school practices which would lend the voice and authority of State educational officials to reform demands for the transformation of the city's school system.

Commissioner Graves was authorized by the State Board of Regents to make the survey. He was instructed to eschew politics and to concentrate on the "pedagogical efficiency" of the city schools. The Board of Regents advanced the Commissioner $2,500 out of its own funds to start the investigation, while it urged a $50,000 grant from the legislature to subsidize the entire venture.[51] When the legislature declined to grant appropriations for the proposed inquiry, Graves, prodded by the PEA, used regular State Education Department funds to go ahead with the survey anyway, but narrowed its scope to an evaluation of the administrative machinery of the city system and the efficiency of its elementary school division only.[52]

The Graves Report came out in late 1933.[53] It was a sweeping endorsement of the PEA's program of school reform. And why not? Graves virtually allowed the PEA and its allies to write the report. As if to make this point unmistakably clear, Graves wrote:

From the beginning it was apparent that any changes to be effected in the New York City school system must be made through the leadership of

[50] New York State, University of the State of New York, State Education Department, *Twenty-Fifth Annual Report for the School Year Ending July 31, 1928* (Albany, 1929), pp. 11–14; New York State, University of the State of New York, *Cardinal Objectives in Elementary Education: A Second Report Prepared by the Committee of Elementary Education of the New York Council of Superintendents,* October 1, 1929 (Albany, 1929); J. Wayne Wrightstone, *Appraisal of Newer Elementary School Practices* (New York, 1938), p. 29.

[51] *New York Times,* May 22, December 8, 1931.

[52] *New York Times,* February 15, 1932; *The Public and the Schools,* March 16, 1932; Minutes of the Board of Trustees of the PEA, February 16, April 19, 1932.

[53] New York State University, Department of Education, *Report of a Study of New York City Schools, Part I: The Administrative-Supervisory Organization; Part II: Evaluation of Achievement,* by Frank Pierrepont Graves (Albany, 1933).

men and women now in the system with the support of the organized groups in the city. . . . The Commissioner . . . sought interviews with representatives of these groups in order to obtain a fuller understanding of the problems involved and especially of the attitude of the people of the city toward their school system.[54]

Graves held frequent meetings and discussions with the members of a specially appointed Advisory Commission composed of educators and civic leaders, with Howard Nudd of the PEA, and with representatives of other leading civic groups in the city. Graves discussed with them the procedures and the conduct of his survey and secured their advance approval for his findings and recommendations.[55] The Graves Report is therefore in effect the embodiment of the educational views and philosophy of the civic conscience of New York City. As such, even if it had no impact on city education, it would still be a noteworthy document.

Graves' findings and recommendations were published in two parts: the first dealing with the managerial aspects of the city's school system; the second, with principles and practices in its elementary schools. The major recommendations of Part I were all aimed at tightening the authority and responsibility of the Superintendent and streamlining the efficiency of the Board of Education and Board of Superintendents.[56] Here, Graves simply included the proposals that the PEA had repeatedly urged and that were incorporated in the "Superintendent's Bill" which the Association had sponsored for the past decade in the state legislature. The PEA's board, discussing the Commissioner's recommendations six months in advance of publication, were unanimously of the opinion that they "were in every way sound and far-seeing." [57]

Part II of the Graves Report, the "Evaluation of Achievement," is the crucial one. Given its unique sponsorship, it is one of the most

[54] *Ibid.*, Part I, p. 12.

[55] *Ibid.*, pp. 10, 11–13, 15; Minutes of the Executive Committee of the PEA, May 3, 1932; Minutes of the Board of Trustees of the PEA, April 18, 1933. The special Advisory Commission included the following: William F. Russell, Dean, Teachers College, Columbia University; Herbert S. Weet, Superintendent of Schools, Rochester; John W. Withers, Dean, School of Education, New York University; Judge Victor J. Dowling of the New York State Supreme Court; Henry W. Taft, lawyer, and trustee of the PEA; and Robert E. Simon, vice-president of the United Parents Associations of New York City.

[56] New York State University, Department of Education, *op. cit.*, Part I, pp. 6–7; *New York Times*, November 23, 1933; New York City, Board of Education, *The First Fifty Years*, pp. 121–22.

[57] Minutes of the Executive Committee of the PEA, May 9, 1933; *The Public and the Schools*, November 28, 1933.

provocative documents in the history of New York City education. The findings and recommendations of Part II must be seen in the context of the School Commissioner's prefatory remarks to the whole report. In his introduction, Graves pointed out that any evaluation of the New York City school system had to bear in mind "the complexity of the school problem" in the city. Then follows a summary of the 1930 census: 33 per cent of the city's total population was foreign-born; from 1920 to 1927 the city's share of illiterate immigrants was almost 38,000 annually; whereas before 1910 the foreign-born residents of New York were predominantly from Northern and Western Europe, in 1930 the large majority were from Eastern and Southern Europe, and so on.[58] One would have thought that the "immigrant problem" would have slipped quite out of consciousness by 1924 when Congress finally shut the door to immigration, leaving only the narrow crack of the quota system through which a thin trickle of aliens might squeeze. But to the established classes of New York City, Yankee Protestants and German Jews, the well-to-do, cultured, professional classes, the "alien in our midst" was still a pressing problem. What was the nature of the problem? The anonymous writer of "The Melting Pot" in the notable July 1939 issue of *Fortune* described it thus:

Those peasants and proletarians have stopped coming, but they are still here. And all of the basic questions asked in 1900 and in 1920 about their assimilation into a democratic system can still be asked with point today.[59]

Nor was the presence of the foreign-born and their children all that entered into the calculations of the New York City school reformers. The 1930 census pointed to another troublesome statistic. "While foreign immigration has been restricted somewhat since 1921, another exceedingly difficult problem has arisen through the rapidly accelerated migration of Negroes from the Southern States, Porto Rico [*sic*] and the West Indies." The Negro population of the city, Graves noted, had more than doubled in the decade 1920–1930, from 152,467 to 327,706.[60]

"In one sense," Commissioner Graves concluded, "New York is

[58] New York State University, State Department of Education, *op. cit.*, Part I, pp. 32–35.
[59] "The Melting Pot," *Fortune*, XX (July, 1939), 74. The entire July issue was on New York City.
[60] New York State University, Department of Education, *op. cit.*, Part I, p. 35. The writer in *Fortune* went on to quote John R. Commons' 1907 assertion that the question of the Negro was "the most nearly insoluble of all our problems." "The Melting Pot," pp. 74–75. As for the problem of the Jew, that had "changed only in becoming more distressingly urgent." *Ibid.*, pp. 75, 177.

already a Southeastern European city. The Russian-born population pre-
dominates." "What," he thoughtfully inquired, "does this factor signify
in the teaching of American ideals of government and citizenship? In
the recruitment of teachers? In the development of curriculum? In
guiding the out-of-school experiences of children and youth? . . . Here
is a rapidly growing Negro population. . . ." [61] This is the context in
which the public elementary schools of New York City were evaluated.

Commissioner Graves acclaimed the scores of 10,000 children tested
in the three R's. He found their average achievement considerably above
children of the same age in other schools throughout the country.[62] The
amenities to New York City school officials over, the Commissioner,
albeit slipping into the oblique and euphemistic terminology of progressivism, got down to cases. "The point of approach throughout the
survey has been," he asserted, "with what success are the varying needs
of pupils being adequately cared for, not with what success are the
elementary schools preparing for high school?" [63] Here the elementary
schools were falling down. The Commissioner's major criticism was that
"with one of the most heterogeneous school populations in the world,
the New York schools have scarcely touched the problem of adapting
curriculum programs to the individual needs of the children." [64]

Graves' criticism was mitigated, however, by a report of some progress. There were, Graves observed, wide variations in average achievement in different city schools. This indicated that "the attempt to reduce the percentage of overageness has resulted in a low level of achievement in the less favored communities and a high level in the more
favored." This was good. Here was a feather in the cap of city school
officials. "Such a policy" Graves continued, "has much to commend it.
This is far better for children than for them to suffer discouragement
from frequent failure and repetition of work, or to be held to a low
level of achievement when they are capable of more. . . . To expect all
elementary schools to succeed in getting all their children to attain a
certain standard level of achievement would be futile and detrimental
to the needs of the majority of students." [65]

The major recommendations of *Evaluation of Achievement* were
few and brief: "each local school should make further adaptation to
meet the needs of its pupils"; "teaching ability . . . should be evaluated
not in academic terms but in growth in personality, character, social

[61] New York State University, Department of Education, *op. cit.*, Part I, p. 37.
[62] *Ibid.*, Part II, pp. 1–5.
[63] *Ibid.*, pp. 43–44.
[64] *Ibid.*, p. 6.
[65] *Ibid.*, p. 39.

responsibility and those other characteristics which are essential to the desirable citizen"; a program of educational guidance should be organized to begin at least as low as the sixth grade.[66]

The PEA greeted the Graves recommendations enthusiastically. It was obvious to *The Public and the Schools,* from what the Commissioner said,

> that certain activities in the school system often referred to as "fads" and "frills" cannot be casually dismissed, but must be considered in the light of a comprehensive and long-view program for training a vast army of children with widely different capacities and interests.[67]

In December 1933, then, the New Yorkers finally had the state stamp of approval for their school reforms. Now the scene of action shifted to the city, where an election was in the offing to decide on a successor to Superintendent William J. O'Shea, who was to retire on February 1, 1934.

V

It was apparent weeks before January 10, 1934, the date set by the Board of Education for the election of a new school chief, that there were only two candidates in the running: Harold G. Campbell and William E. Grady, with the former the heavy favorite.[68] The PEA called both men acceptable, but indicated a preference for Grady by asking for the election of the "most dynamic personality." But whoever the next superintendent might be, the PEA advised:

> The fundamental changes that are occurring in our social order demand a thorough reorganization, not only of the administrative machinery of the school system, but of the processes of instruction from top to bottom.[69]

The election of Campbell as Superintendent of Schools was another key landmark in the triumph of progressivism.[70] There was little to suggest the educational radical in Campbell's thirty-two year career in the city school system previous to his elevation to the superintendency. In a thumbnail portrait, *School and Society* characterized the Superin-

---

[66] *Ibid.,* pp. 42–45. *The New York Times* carried a summary of Part II of the Graves Report on January 27, 1934. See also New York City, Board of Education, *The First Fifty Years,* pp. 122–23.

[67] *The Public and the Schools,* No. 356, February 27, 1934.

[68] *New York Times,* January 10, 1934.

[69] *New York Times,* October 23, 1933; *The Public and the Schools,* No. 352, October 24, 1933.

[70] *New York Times,* January 11, 1934.

tendent-elect as "a Republican, a Presbyterian, and regarded as a conservative in education." [71] During his tenure in office, Campbell did nothing to mar this portrait. He earned a reputation for his hostility to any form of unorthodox teacher or student activity. Campbell stood for "old-time Americanism," The *Times* wrote.[72] Campbell was conservative to the core. That he directed a pedagogical revolution is indicative of how profoundly conservative the objectives of this revolution were.

Campbell had been a witness to the decade of bitter animosity between his predecessor and the city's civic leaders. He had been a witness to the abuse and contempt which had been heaped upon O'Shea's head. It was not going to happen to him. No Republicans, none of the city's respectables, would call Superintendent Campbell mediocre, unprogressive, or inaccessible. Unlike O'Shea, he would be progressive and accessible. A few months after his installation as Superintendent, Campbell was the guest of honor at a meeting of the PEA's Board of Trustees.[73]

Superintendent Campbell had barely taken office when he seized firm control of the labyrinthic city school system and, using the just-published Graves Report as a lever, sent it hurtling along the road long mapped out for it by the PEA. True the times were propitious for radical innovations: the distractions of the Depression; the excitment generated by the mayoralty election; and the inauguration of a new city administration. Still, Campbell was to demonstrate statemanship of the highest calibre. The Superintendent and the Board of Superintendents wooed the elementary school principals and other supervisory heads of instruction through conferences, meetings, special committees, and appeals to *amour-propre*. The rank and file were given orientation via study groups composed of principals and teachers formed for the purpose of exegesis of the Graves Report. The Board of Education was engaged via a Joint Committee on Maladjustment and Delinquency.[74]

[71] *School and Society*, XXXIX (January 30, 1934), 80–81, ed.; *Who Was Who in America*, II, 1950; *New York Times*, June 17, 1942, obituary.

[72] *New York Times*, June 17, 1942, obituary.

[73] Minutes of the Board of Trustees of the PEA, May 22, 1934. If at times it looked as if Campbell were not only accessible to the city's civic groups, but their servant, this was because in serving them he was also serving the ends of school officialdom. City school administrators had long been concerned with the inefficiency of the school system. They were receptive to any scheme which would, at a stroke, eliminate the problems of retardation, non-promotion, overageness, and overcrowding, and thus restore the vaunted efficiency of the system. And the possibility that city school leaders shared the social attitudes and prejudices of the class to which they aspired to belong should not be ignored.

[74] New York State, University of the State of New York, State Education

In the meantime, the city's civic watchdogs were not merely waiting upon the schoolmen. In February 1934, thanks to the efforts of the PEA and Charles C. Burlingham, Mayor La Guardia, just inaugurated, was prevailed upon to organize, in cooperation with the Board of Education, a joint committee of civic leaders and educators to survey the effects of the city's economy measures on the public schools.[75] The School Survey Committee, as it was called, interpreted its function as that of prodding school officials to extirpate school retardation and failure and to implement the Graves Report.[76]

Finally, in early May 1934, Superintendent Campbell, carrying wood into the forest, sent out a call for a conference "to focus the best thinking of schools, institutions, social agencies and citizens" on the "pressing problems of maladjustment, retardation, truancy, and delinquency." [77] On May 20, 1935, representatives of a large number of the city's major civic groups and social agencies, as well as important city and school officials, gathered in the auditorium of the Board of Education. The subjects for discussion were "maladjustment" and "retardation." Campbell spoke first, and outlined the agenda for the conference. The following excerpts are a fair sample of Campbell's address:

In the past a child was considered retarded when he failed of promotion, if he was over-age for his grade. He was maladjusted if he was unable to master the curriculum. . . . School success was possible only for an aristocracy of the intellect.

Department, *The Activity Program. The Report of a Survey of the Curriculum Experiment with the Activity Program in the Elementary Schools of the City of New York*, under the direction of J. Cayce Morrison (Albany, 1941), pp. 11, 15; *School and Society*, XLII (October 5, 1935), 455–56, ed.; *ibid.*, XLIV (August 1, 1936), 143–44; *New York Times*, May 13, June 27, 1934, February 15, 17, September 16, 1935; New York City, Board of Education, *Reports of the District Superintendents in the Field, Submitted with the Thirty-Sixth Annual Report of the Superintendent of Schools, 1933–1934*, 1934, pp. 237–38; New York City, Board of Education, *The First Fifty Years*, pp. 123–24, 126–27, 140–42.

75 *New York Times*, February 2, 9, 19, March 22, 1934. And Minutes of the Executive Committee of the PEA, December 5, 1933, January 9, 1934; Minutes of the Board of Trustees of the PEA, January 23, 1934. The Survey Committee comprised Dean Russell of Teachers College, Dean Withers of New York University, State Supreme Court Justice James E. Cropsey, Prof. A. A. Berle, Sr., of Columbia University, Fred O. Chambers of the Board of Education, Robert E. Simon, and Mrs. Nathan Straus, Jr.

76 The committee contended that "the curriculum can be so adapted to pupil needs, and the school so organized and administered that there are no failure pupils and consequently no retardation." *New York Times*, March 31, 1935, Sec. XI, April 7, 1935, Sec. II.

77 *New York Times*, May 7, 1935; *School and Society*, XLI (May 18, 1935), 668–69.

In the newer conception a child is retarded if he fails to make progress in accordance with his individual interests, aptitudes and mental capacity. . . .

Instead of considering a child "maladjusted" if he is unable to master the curriculum, particularly the fundamental knowledges and skills, he is to be considered maladjusted now if he is unable to get along happily in his surroundings; with persons as well as with books, and if he falls short in social sensitiveness and social responsiveness.[78]

Howard Nudd was one of the panel of speakers at the conference. *The Public and the Schools* subsequently pointed to the significance of Campbell's agenda in these words: it "really summarized the specific objectives which its creators had in mind." [79] The PEA had waited a long time to hear such objectives coming from the lips of a New York City Superintendent of Schools. "If they can be realized, and we hope they can," *The Public and the Schools* exclaimed, "New York City will, indeed, have a school system for which it long has yearned. . . . Here, indeed, is a vision of school development which all may approve." "It was in keeping," *The Public and the Schools* continued, "with the best modern thought in education, and in line with the practice employed in the best progressive schools." It embraced the objectives, the newsletter went on, which the PEA sought for so many years to attain through the Little Red School House. "Hats off, we say, to the school leaders who have embarked on this enterprise, and may their fondest hopes be realized in the not too distant future." [80]

In September 1935, an "activity program" was introduced into approximately 64 elementary schools, involving 671 teachers and about 25,000 pupils. The new program was introduced as an "experiment," to be evaluated at the end of six years by the New York State Department of Education. By 1937 the activity program involved some 70 schools, 2250 teachers, and 75,000 children. It would be redundant to describe the program, which was virtually identical with the practices and procedures demonstrated in the PEA's Little Red School House experiment.[81]

[78] *New York Times*, May 12, 1935, Sec. II; *New York Times*, May 21, 1935; *The Public and the Schools*, No. 367, May 28, 1935.
[79] *The Public and the Schools*, No. 367, May 28, 1935.
[80] *Ibid.*
[81] *The Activity Program*, pp. 15–18; Wrightstone, *Appraisal of Newer Elementary School Practices*, pp. 24–25; New York City, Board of Education, *All the Children, Thirty-Seventh Annual Report of the Superintendent of Schools, 1934–35*, pp. 7–22; New York City, Board of Education, *All the Children, Thirty-Eighth Annual Report of the Superintendent of Schools, 1935–36*, pp. 23–29; Harold G. Campbell, "Grade System Changed," article in *New York Times*, June 30, 1935, Sec.

And so a great issue of public policy, perhaps the greatest in the history of the Greater City, was decided. As Assistant Superintendent of Schools John Loftus, in answer to a query as to how parents in the city were receiving the activity program, said, with not a little boastfulness, there was no trouble. The new program, he explained, was introduced with a minimum of fanfare of publicity, no blowing of trumpets.[82] So far as curriculum policies and procedures were concerned, in New York City the public schools were no longer in "politics."

New York's program of progressive education would, beginning in the 1940's, come under increasingly severe attack for its neglect of the fundamental skills and subjects of study. In 1955 the Board of Education would begin to liquidate some of the practices of the activity program.[83] And in 1961 the Superintendent, during the course of a plea for increased funds with which to establish an effective remedial reading program, would deliver the following ultimatum to the Board of Estimate:

> Either you give us the money we need or we will go back to 100 per cent promotion and say, "To hell with education, we don't need it." [84]

This would happen in 1961. But in the mid-thirties progressive education was at its peak. The secretary of the Progressive Education Association pointed to 1936 as the turning point in its history: it was finally solvent; it was the recipient of large research grants from foundations; and it saw activity programs of the type it sponsored introduced in public schools all over the country, notably in California and New York City.[85] In the city itself the activity, or activities, program won much acclaim. The *Times* sang the praises of "individuation," asserting

---

X; John J. Loftus, "New York City's Large Scale Experimentation With an Activity Program," *Progressive Education*, XVII (February, 1940), 116–24; John J. Loftus, "Learning Comes to Life," *Progressive Education*, XXI (April, 1944), 186–89; New York City, Board of Education, *The First Fifty Years*, pp. 126–27.

[82] *New York Times*, March 31, 1937, Sec. II, article by Benjamin Fine; Loftus, "Learning Comes to Life," p. 186. A great deal of credit must go to the United Parents Associations, which did the essential work of parent education at the grass roots. Lighty and Bowman, *op. cit.*, Part II, *passim*; Loftus, *loc. cit.* Organized labor in New York State and in New York City also supported the activity program. Jack Cohn, "Attitudes and Policies of Organized Labor Toward Public Education in New York State" (unpublished Ed.D. project, Teachers College, Columbia University, 1952), pp. 294–96.

[83] *New York Times*, May 11, June 30, 1955.

[84] *New York Times*, April 15, 1961.

[85] *New York Times*, March 7, 1937, Sec. II; "Progressives Progress," *Time*, XXXII (October 31, 1938), 31–35.

that the activities program meant "more teacher satisfaction, less retardation, less truancy, and in the long run a repayment many times over in the vastly increased contribution to the common welfare." [86] The Board of Education favored the new program, James Marshall, its vice-president asserted, because pupils would no longer have the sense of failure that came when they failed to meet the requirements of the "old rigid curriculum." [87] The PEA triumphantly asserted, "The School System Is Definitely On the March." [88]

VI

The activity program was indeed a great victory for the PEA. And so was the election of La Guardia, and so was the state aid crusade. But now what about a program? The PEA was in trouble. In 1935 Mrs. Levy pointed out that the PEA was losing its public appeal and that it needed to undertake something "spectacular" to maintain public interest in its work.[89]

Some of the slack in the PEA's activities was taken up by the organization of three big public luncheon conferences during 1936–37. The conferences, which the PEA induced forty-five civic, religious, and philanthropic organizations in the city to co-sponsor, were devoted to the following subjects: "The School Child and His Health," "The School Child and Crime Prevention," and "The School Child and His Education for Peace." [90] The meetings meant a great deal to the PEA. They meant much-needed publicity, opportunity to renew old contacts and make new ones, and additional forums from which to continue the education of the city's opinion leaders. Of the three meetings the PEA was most enthusiastic about the one on "The School Child and Crime Prevention," starting the drums rolling for it some months before the subject was to be aired.[91]

The *Times* hailed the PEA for launching a civic movement against juvenile delinquency.[92] Examination of the *Times Index* for 1936 as well as for several years prior to the launching of the movement fails

[86] *New York Times*, June 28, 1934, ed., January 5, 1935, ed., January 21, 1936, ed.

[87] *New York Times*, December 13, 1936, Sec. II; Rankin, ed., *New York Advancing: World's Fair Edition* . . . , p. 138.

[88] *The Public and the Schools*, No. 372, February 25, 1936.

[89] Minutes of the Executive Committee of the PEA, September 24, 1935.

[90] *The Public and the Schools*, No. 376, October 27, 1936; No. 377, November 17, 1936; No. 378, December 21, 1936.

[91] *The Public and the Schools*, No. 378, December 21, 1936.

[92] *New York Times*, January 10, Sec. VI, January 11, 1937.

to reveal any news of a "crime wave" or dramatic outbreak of juvenile delinquency.[93] But the thirties were not normal times and the civic community of New York was jumpy. Why wait for trouble? Prevention was better than cure. To stimulate and guide the speakers at the conference, the PEA urged that they give "frank discussion" to the following proposal:

that the school system should develop an activity program which will discover and meet from day to day the child's individual needs and which will provide a continuous flow of wholesome experiences that will develop sound social habits and attitudes.[94]

"The School Child and Crime Prevention" proved to be an irresistible topic. On January 15, 1937, one thousand guests gathered in the banquet hall of the Hotel Commodore to hear the talks by George Z. Medalie, president of the Jewish Board of Guardians; Dr. William E. Grady, Associate Superintendent of Schools; and Austin H. Mac-Cormick, City Commissioner of Correction.[95] Dr. William Mather Lewis, president of Lafayette College, presided. Lewis and Medalie spoke first. Both saw the school's chief role in crime prevention through early training of children in respect for law and custom. Then Associate Superintendent Grady took the rostrum. A well-administered school, he asserted, was the best agency to combat juvenile delinquency. Grady apprised the leaders of the City Club, the Citizens Union, the United Parents Associations, the League of Women Voters, and the other worried chatelaines of the city that "school failure at any level gives rise to emotional maladjustment, frustration and inferiority complexes that are often the bases of much juvenile delinquency." But, he assured his audience, school officials were well aware of the problem and were making progress in "adjusting the curriculum to the child." Among forthcoming advances in the school's contribution to the fight against juvenile delinquency, Grady predicted "more active occupational experience and subordination of the textbook to realistic experience at all levels." [96]

So far as the PEA was concerned, Grady's speech was to have been the *pièce de résistance* of the luncheon meeting. But it was capped, and the affair almost turned into a fiasco, by the unscheduled appearance

[93] However, in 1935 Harlem had its first major race riot. *New York Times,* March 20, 21, 1935.
[94] *The Public and the Schools,* No. 376, October 27, 1936.
[95] *New York Times,* January 17, 1937, Sec. II.
[96] *Ibid.*

# # #

and remarks of the city's unpredictable Mayor. The bluff La Guardia derided the mental hygiene approach to juvenile delinquency and chided the speakers for not paying more attention to the economic causes of crime. Modern, low-rent public housing, La Guardia said, was better than continually poring over crime statistics. A "T-bone steak and German fried potatoes are among the very best preventives of crime," he asserted. The Mayor advised the large audience at the Hotel Commodore to get busy and attack the housing problem, and to speak up for social legislation and to do so publicly and vigorously.[97]

The PEA was disconcerted by La Guardia's remarks and deemed a reply necessary. The Mayor, *The Public and the Schools* explained, "was simply having a good time."[98] No doubt, the newsletter admitted, there were multiple causes of juvenile delinquency, and no single panacea. But, it continued, the Mayor's recommendations for the elimination of slums and poverty would "only partially meet the situation," and if followed would defer a solution of the problem until better conditions obtained. "The inevitable conclusion" drawn by *The Public and the Schools* was that "the most practical immediate step is to give closer attention to the problems of individual children."[99] The bulletin then went on to report at length on Grady's "fine analysis" of the school's role in juvenile delinquency prevention.

VII

A few months after the luncheon meeting on "The School Child and Crime Prevention," the PEA was handed a golden opportunity to demonstrate the proper remedy for juvenile delinquency. On May 12, 1937, Mrs. Moses Blitzer and Miss Leila V. Stott, director and secretary, respectively, of the Extension Service of the City and Country School, proposed to the PEA that it assume the sponsorship of a project which was being developed in one of the public schools by the Extension Service.[100] The project was already some eighteen months old.

Early in 1936 a group of afternoon recreation centers were opened in the city under joint WPA–Board of Education sponsorship. Through the efforts of Mrs. Blitzer, the City and Country School Extension

[97] *Ibid.*
[98] *The Public and the Schools*, No. 379, January 26, 1937.
[99] *Ibid.*
[100] Leila V. Stott to Director [Howard Nudd] [May 12, 1937], mimeographed, appended to Minutes of the Board of Trustees of the PEA, May 13, 1937.

Service was granted permission to assume direction of one of the centers on the condition that a regular City and Country School teacher be placed in immediate supervision of the work. Caroline Pratt, who had lost none of her sense of dedication "to the cause of rescuing children from the dead hand of traditional education," promptly released Miss Adele Franklin, one of her experienced teachers, to take charge of the play center "with the ultimate aim of making a vital connection between the afternoon activities and the regular classroom work." [101] In the spring of 1936, Miss Franklin was again granted permission to supervise a recreation center, but now in a public school of her own choice. Miss Franklin chose P.S. 33, at 418 West 28th Street, in the run-down Chelsea section of Manhattan. P.S. 33's principal was Miss Ruth Gillette Hardy, whose "cooperative attitude and understanding of fundamental educational objectives seemed to offer the best opportunity for developing the desired contact between the afternoon recreation and the rest of the school work." [102] The appeal to the PEA came one year later, in the spring of 1937.

Now, Miss Stott explained, the time was ripe for the development of the desired contact. Miss Hardy and Miss Franklin were ready, if they could secure the permission of the Board of Superintendents, and if they could secure full-time recreation workers, to develop "an all-day work study play program" at P.S. 33. But the City and Country School couldn't do it. "We feel," Miss Stott concluded:

. . . that we need the backing of an organization that has the confidence of the public in order to make an effectual appeal for public support. We turn to you in the Public Education Association, because we trust your educational point of view and we believe this kind of undertaking is in line with your whole tradition of work.[103]

In the discussion of Miss Stott's letter amongst the PEA's Board of Trustees, Frank Karelsen pointed out that the objectives of the proposed demonstration were indeed in line with the educational theories long advocated by the PEA and demonstrated by it in the Little Red School

[101] *Ibid.*; Caroline Pratt, *I Learn from Children* (New York, 1948), p. 181.

[102] Stott to Nudd. Miss Hardy had earned some repute as a progressive. See her article "The Freeing of the Teacher," *Mental Hygiene*, XIII (January, 1929), pp. 33–44. Miss Hardy was also a veteran of many a Teachers Union battle as a Linville (Right-Wing Socialist) stalwart. Robert W. Iversen, *The Communists and the Schools* (New York, 1959), p. 23; Howard K. Beale, *Are American Teachers Free?* (New York, 1936), pp. 361, 365; Wattenberg, *op. cit.*, 214.

[103] Stott to Nudd.

House. But it was moved that more information be sought before any action would be voted upon.[104]

A few weeks later the board was the recipient of two follow-up letters: one from Mrs. Blitzer and Miss Franklin, the other from Miss Hardy. The letter from Miss Hardy promised her complete cooperation in the enterprise.[105] The letter from the City and Country Extension people is the important one.[106] If it does not reveal much about the mind of those who initiated the proposed school experiment, it does reveal much about the mind of the audience to which their appeal is addressed. Mrs. Blitzer and Miss Franklin pointed out that the afternoon recreation center had already proved its value. Delinquency was high in the Chelsea neighborhood, but the recreation center had "not only helped certain delinquents but has also had theraputic value for many tense high-strung children." The results obtained with children in the afternoon work, the memorandum continued, with impeccable logic, "would serve to show the advantages of a work study play program for the entire school." The memorandum ended with the plea:

> The full day work study play program has been talked of by progressive educators for many years. It would appear that the beginning has been made and that opportunity should be grasped for promoting the idea.[107]

Indeed an all-day school program had long had a certain fascination for the PEA, and for many progressives. After all, the child, the progressives believed, was largely, if not wholly, a product of his environment. Why leave that environment, with all its possibilities for implanting the seeds of later social maladjustment, to chance? It will be recalled that Robert Hunter, in 1904, called for the all-day (and night) school supervision of children, and that progressives, a few years later, saw the chief significance of the visiting teacher as a harbinger of the all-day school supervision of children. And one of the selling points of William A. Wirt's Gary School Plan was the promise of a nine-to-five school day. The tendency in progressive education increasingly was to appropriate not only the functions which out-of-school agencies traditionally performed for children, but also the *time* traditionally belonging to

[104] Minutes of the Board of Trustees of the PEA, May 13, 1937.

[105] Ruth Hardy to Nudd, May 21, 1937, mimeographed, appended to Minutes of the Board of Trustees of the PEA, May 27, 1937.

[106] "Proposed Plan for City and Country School Extension Service in P.S. 33. A Memorandum Submitted to the Director [Nudd] by Mrs. Moses Blitzer and Miss Adele Franklin, May 21, 1937," mimeographed, appended to Minutes of the Board of Trustees of the PEA, May 22, 1937.

[107] *Ibid.*

those agencies, or traditionally left unsupervised. This tendency, however, was still largely in the realm of speculation. The City and Country people, therefore, were offering the PEA a unique opportunity. The board voted to accept the sponsorship of the proposed experiment if three conditions were met: if the "school situation were favorable," if "as expeditiously as possible" the project became a training and observation center for teachers-in-training, and if Mrs. Blitzer and other City and Country School people would interest themselves in the PEA.[108]

On January 22, 1938, *The Public and the Schools* announced that the PEA had accepted the sponsorship of the "Chelsea School Project." The aim of the project in P.S. 33, Manhattan, was to "demonstrate an all-day educational and recreational program based on children's activities which have been proved to contribute to the whole child." "A plan of work and play," *The Public and the Schools* continued, "utilizing rhythms, art, music, construction and all the tools of the activity school is being extended from the after-school program into the regular work of the classrooms." [109] After more than five years' absence, the PEA once more had a project in the public schools.

The Public and the Schools went on to note that neighborhood contacts were being built up and that relations with P.S. 33 parents were being fostered.[110] Strong committees had already been set up to finance and sponsor the project. The Chelsea School Project Committee had on it, besides several officials of the PEA, Mrs. Blitzer, Caroline Pratt, Elisabeth Irwin, and the Honorable Justine Wise Polier. A distinguished board of sponsors for the project included Franklin P. Adams, Lewis Gannett, Max Lerner, Mark Van Doren, and Lewis Mumford, among others, as well as William E. Grady and James Marshall, then president of the Board of Education.[111] There would be no repetition of the P.S. 41 fiasco in Chelsea.

The PEA was content to move slowly on the Chelsea School Project. The city was in the midst of a vast educational experiment. The financial condition of the city was not propitious for an aggressive campaign. A program such as that being worked out at P.S. 33 was very expensive; it not only involved a lengthened school day but also required

---

[108] Minutes of the Board of Trustees of the PEA, May 27, November 16, 1937.

[109] *The Public and the Schools*, No. 388, January 22, 1938; New York City, Board of Education, *Extended School Services Through the All-Day Neighborhood Schools*, Curriculum Bulletin, 1947–1948 Series, Number 3 (New York, 1948), pp. 1–2; New York City, Board of Education, *The First Fifty Years*, pp. 130–31.

[110] *The Public and the Schools*, No. 388, January 22, 1938.

[111] *Ibid.*

social case workers, community workers, and personnel trained in recreational work to supplement the regular teaching staff.[112] Not once in the thirties did the PEA ask to have the experimental program extended to other schools in the city.

Slowly but surely the Chelsea experiment moved forward. The curriculum at P.S. 33 was becoming more progressive. At first, the curriculum was organized around field trips and play activities. Then in the fall of 1938, Miss Franklin, Caroline Pratt's alter ego, reorganized the course of study around "school services": the sale of milk; the school post office; the visual instruction schedules and materials; the school carpentry service; the school library; and the school supply service.[113] More and more the regular teachers at the school were getting into the swing of things and adopting progressive techniques. And the endeavor to train public school teachers generally also moved ahead: New York University and Hunter College students did practice teaching at P.S. 33; members of the PEA's Chelsea staff lectured to different teacher organizations in the city. Toward the end of the project's third year, Miss Franklin pronounced it a success: "The children feel free; they are happy." [114] The time was approaching to request the Board of Education to adopt the project and extend it to other schools in the city.

VIII

Academic freedom was an issue that occupied the PEA much in the latter part of the 1930's, as novel and startling developments in the classrooms of New York City led to greatly intensified anti-radical activity on the part of city school officials and state legislators.

[112] The PEA had little difficulty in financing the Chelsea Project. The WPA personnel were paid from relief funds; the PEA paid the salaries of Miss Franklin and the others on the special Chelsea staff. In 1938 contributions to the project totalled about $3,400; in 1939, when the WPA began to withdraw from the city schools, this figure rose to $7,900. Funds were raised via art and theatre benefits, foundation grants, and individual patrons. "Annual Financial Reports of the PEA for the Years Ending October 31, 1938, and October 31, 1939," in the files of the PEA.

[113] Ruth Gillette Hardy "School Services," *Progressive Education,* XVII (October, 1940), 418; *New York Times,* October 9, 1938, Sec. II; *The Public and the Schools,* No. 392, October 25, 1938. Miss Pratt called her curriculum innovations "job-centered." Pratt, *op. cit.,* Chaps. VII–IX.

[114] Adele Franklin, "The Chelsea School Project. Third Annual Report, September 1939," mimeographed, in "All-Day Neighborhood Schools" folder, in the files of the PEA.

In 1935, after years of internecine warfare, the Communist Party gained ascendancy in the New York Teachers Union over the Linville–Lefkowitz (Right-Wing Socialist) administration. Subsequently the union threw open its gates to a mass membership and stepped up its political activity, notably as an affiliate of Communist front organizations.[115] Of equal or greater moment was the fact that New York had become, by mid-decade, the center of a militant student movement. The chief avenue of expression for student radicalism was the "peace" crusade, a crusade stimulated and exploited by the Communist-dominated National Student League to be sure, but by no means merely a Communist-inspired phenomenon. Annually from 1934 to 1939, college students in New York and elsewhere (but mostly in New York, and most conspicuously at City College and at Brooklyn College, two of the city's municipal colleges) paraded for peace and took the Oxford Oath. High school students in the city also became embroiled in political activity. By 1936 radical political clubs were in existence in some high schools, and high school students were joining their big brothers in the annual peace strikes or simply lending their voices to the pacifist agitation.[116]

New York City school officials responded to the turmoil in the public schools by redoubling their efforts to stamp out both teacher and student radicalism and unorthodoxy. The Board of Examiners undertook to determine the loyalty and patriotism of applicants for positions in the city school system by inquiring into their private beliefs and convictions.[117] Superintendent Campbell warned that students and teachers "who spread subversive doctrines or bring communistic principles" into the schools would not be tolerated, and banned students from joining the peace demonstrations on pain of drastic reprisal.[118] The

[115] By 1938 Communist control of the union was clamped tight. Iversen, *op. cit.*, pp. 55–58, 59, 99, 100–101, 103–4, 107–8, 111.

[116] Iversen, *op. cit.*, pp. 72–73, 123–24; Celeste Strack, "The Student Movement in the United States," *The Communist*, XVI (February, 1937), 142–60; *New York Times*, April 22, 23, 1936, April 23, 1937, April 28, 1938; Arthur M. Schlesinger, Jr., *The Politics of Upheaval*, Vol. III of the author's *The Age of Roosevelt* (Boston, 1960), p. 199; Dixon Wecter, *The Age of the Great Depression, 1929–1941* (New York, 1948), pp. 194–95. For the peace movement in general see Merle Curti, *Peace or War: The American Struggle, 1636–1936* (New York, 1936), Chap. IX, and George Philip Rawick, "The New Deal and Youth: The Civilian Conservation Corps, the National Youth Administration, and the American Youth Congress" (unpublished Ph.D. thesis, University of Wisconsin, 1957).

[117] *The Public and the Schools*, No. 360, October 30, 1934.

[118] *New York Times*, May 30, 1934, April 8, 1935.

Times detected some "infection" in the schools, but was confident Campbell could handle it.[119]

The PEA refused to panic. To the Board of Examiners it said:

> The bounds of freedom should be set by deeds, we believe, and should be determined only by lawful judicial procedure in respect to specific acts— not by the mere dislike of another's political philosophy.[120]

The PEA lectured the Board of Education on how to deal with the anti-war and other political activities of high school students. The PEA urged school authorities to handle the situation in a spirit of liberalism and tolerance. It urged them not to stifle the student's flair for self-expression and leadership, and thereby to drive it underground. It recommended that students be encouraged to interest themselves, even if sometimes injudiciously, in contemporary problems of vital concern; that school officials recognize the importance of allowing students to express opinions and join organizations; that school officials observe strict impartiality by refusing to let students leave class during school hours for any demonstration, whether called by the American Student Union, or the American Legion, or the Daughters of the American Revolution; and that "in no instance" should a student's participation in such a demonstration be looked upon as a permanent black mark on his record.[121]

With the colleges and schools of the city in unprecedented political ferment, it was inevitable that the state legislature should have increased the tempo and intensity of its school anti-radical activities. The 1936 legislative session was a banner one. In this one session alone bills were introduced, among others, requiring students to take a loyalty oath before admittance to any high school or college in the state supported wholly or in part by public funds; requiring the American flag to be displayed in every classroom in every public school in the state; and requiring that every public school bus in the state be painted red, white, and blue.[122] The PEA condemned all of the proposed bills as "just as un-American as the doctrine they seek to suppress." [123] Through

---

[119] *New York Times*, May 30, 1934, ed.

[120] *The Public and the Schools*, No. 360, October 30, 1934.

[121] *The Public and the Schools*, No. 374, April 28, 1938; No. 380, February 23, 1937.

[122] Lawrence H. Chamberlain, *Loyalty and Legislative Action: A Survey of Activity by the New York State Legislature, 1919–1949* (New York, 1951), pp. 54–55, and Chap. II, *passim*; Iversen, *op. cit.*, pp. 186–87; *The Public and the Schools*, No. 373, March 31, 1936.

[123] *The Public and the Schools*, No. 373, March 31, 1936.

the remainder of the tumultuous decade, with the same outspokenness, the PEA denounced all the anti-Red measures introduced annually into the state legislature, and patiently, and sometimes impatiently, explained to the Albany solons what could and what could not be legislated upon in a democracy.[124]

IX

There are peaks and slumps in the history of any organization. The PEA reached its peak in the 1920's. The thirties saw it stagnate and decline, its participation in city affairs sporadic and weak, its program listless.

The chief reason for the PEA's slump lay in its very triumphs. In the thirties the PEA saw its major objectives realized, its program liquidated. One of the major objectives of the PEA, from the beginning, had been to persuade slow-moving and conservative school officials to adopt the principles and practices of progressive education. For more than forty years, through private conferences, public meetings, press and periodicals, and special demonstrations, the PEA had been educating them in progressive education. After 1935, school officials no longer needed to be educated—they were now *plus royaliste que le roi*. The PEA's other long-term objective—to divorce the schools from politics—had also gained much ground. That is, the PEA was satisfied both with La Guardia's school appointments and with its own role and position in the school field. In any event, because of its emotional ties to the La Guardia administration, as well as its new policy of working with school officials, the PEA was inhibited from muckraking school appointments or school building conditions, traditionally two of its most effective channels for vigorous participation in city politics and for bringing attention to itself. WPA and PWA made the issue of school finance, for the time being anyway, academic.

The PEA couldn't cope with success. Without a program, it had no fund-raising appeal. For 1935 its total expenditures were less than $13,000.[125] The *Times* tried to give it a boost. On January 30, 1935, in a lengthy editorial commemorating the PEA's 40th anniversary, the *Times* stated: "It is not too much to say that the best and most constant friend the public schools have had through the last forty years has been

---

[124] *The Public and the Schools*, No. 389, March 29, 1938; No. 397, March 28, 1939.
[125] Minutes of the Executive Committee of the PEA, November 18, 1935.

the Public Education Association   he *Times* pointed out that the
PEA had always been an active   in efforts to improve the
instruction of the children, to incre   tendance and care for
their health; that the PEA had taken   providing visiting
teachers; that it had carried on experiments   ctions, notably
in adapting the school program to fit the needs   al children;
that it had had an active part in the initiation, exten   mprove-
ment of new types of schools, including kindergartens, va   ools,
vocational education, and special classes for the handicapp   t
had been a leader in the effort to extend the merit system.
all, it is ever watchful in the child's interest." The Public Educa
Association, the *Times* concluded, "deserves the continued support o.
the public." Thus the PEA was eulogized. But everything the *Times*
said belonged to history. The PEA seemed unable to accommodate
itself to its new conditions. Perhaps the leadership was worn out.

In September 1935 opportunity for changes came when Miss Draper,
then seventy-one years old, tendered her resignation as president. She
was succeeded by William B. Nichols.[127] Although only forty, Mr.
Nichols was one of the senior members of the PEA. He had been drafted
by Mrs. Edward C. Henderson back in 1921 to be the PEA's treasurer
and had held that post competently and unobtrusively ever since. The
tall, distinguished-looking financier and businessman was the perfect
choice for the presidency. Possessed of the charm and courtly manner
needed to reconcile and conciliate the strong and rival personalities
among the ladies in the inner core leadership of the PEA, Mr. Nichols
has succinctly and accurately described himself as a "harmonizer." [128]
But while the PEA needed cohesiveness if it were to be an effective
pressure group, it also needed strong leadership.

In 1937 there was another change in the PEA's inner circle. Mrs.
Samuel A. Lewisohn, after a few years of inactivity, consented to become
chairman of the Executive Committee.[129] In the sixteen years prior to
1937 during which she had been a member of that committee, Mrs.
Lewisohn had helped the PEA more with her name and money than
with her time and thought. Now she was ready to give of almost her
whole self to the Association. By the late 1930's her children no longer
needed her close supervision and she could take her civic responsibilities

---

[126] *New York Times*, January 30, 1935, ed.; *New York Times*, May 27, 1936,
ed.
[127] Minutes of the Board of Trustees of the PEA, October 8, 1935.
[128] William B. Nichols, Interview, September 29, 1959, New York City.
[129] Minutes of the Executive Committee of the PEA, July 26, 1937.

more seriously. Mrs. Lewisohn was an interlocking directorate of civic, cultural, philanthropic, and educational organizations all by herself.[130] But even someone so zestful as Mrs. Lewisohn could spread herself thin and not obtain any real sense of fulfillment or satisfaction from so many activities. When she took office as the chairman of the PEA's Executive Committee, Mrs. Lewisohn caught a glimpse of a vocation.

Soon Mrs. Lewisohn's good friend, Mrs. Irene Pascal, president of the United Parents Associations, was elected to the PEA's Executive Committee.[131] She joined a small group headed by Mrs. Lewisohn and including Mrs. Thomas K. Schmuck, Mrs. J. Culbert Palmer, Mrs. Douglas M. Moffat, Mrs. Edwin H. Koehler, Mrs. Horace G. Reed, and Miss C. Reinold Noyes, who formed the nucleus of a new inner circle of activists in the PEA. In 1938 Mrs. Moses Blitzer, upon bringing the Chelsea School Project to the PEA, joined this august group. The event is worth remarking upon because it marked the joining of a new element to the coalition of Yankee Protestants and German Jews that had, ever since 1895, monopolized the inner circle of the PEA. Mrs. Blitzer, of a middle-class *nouveau riche* Jewish family, was the first representative of the new immigration to become prominently active in the PEA.

The potential for a vital civic group was there. Yet the PEA's drift into political oblivion continued. The women were active but not in the civic sphere. They became totally involved in Mrs. Lewisohn's benefits. More and more the annual art benefit and cocktail preview, at which the season's debutantes as well as master works of art were displayed, was becoming the be-all and end-all of the PEA's activities. In 1936 it was a Gauguin benefit; in 1937 it was Degas; in 1938, "Great Portraits from Impressionism to Modernism." In 1939 Mrs. Lewisohn capped

[130] In the latter part of the 1930's Mrs. Lewisohn was active in the Federation of Jewish Philanthropies, the Museum of Modern Art, and the Woman's Auxiliary of the Philharmonic Society. She was a member of the Advisory Committee of the Child Study Association, a member of the Executive Committee of the Mayor's Municipal Art Commission, vice-president of the Women's City Club and chairman of its Education Committee, vice-president of the United Parents Associations, chairman of the Board of Trustees of the Little Red School House, and president of the Lincoln School Parent-Teachers Association, all the while being on the Executive Committee of the PEA. *Who's Who in American Jewry*, III (1938–39); *American Women*, III (1939–40); *New York Times*, June 15, 1954, obituary.

[131] Minutes of the Executive Committee of the PEA, October 26, 1937. Although the United Parents Associations was in precarious financial health in the late 1930's, it was quite busy. In the year 1936–37, it had committees on community centers, health of school children, junior high schools, legislation, motion pictures, overcrowding, peace education, personality adjustment of school children, relief, safety, and sex education. United Parents Associations of New York City, *Sixteenth Annual Report, 1936–1937*; Lighty and Bowman, *op. cit.*, pp. 195–97.

all previous efforts with the spectacular art benefit "The Stage," at which the leading lights of the contemporary theater made personal appearances.[132] The PEA was making the society and the art pages of the *Times*, but no longer its education or city news pages. The PEA was becoming defunct as a civic group. There was no will in the Executive Committee to keep it active in the city's civic life, and the finger of blame pointed to Howard Nudd.

By the late thirties the presence of the astute, efficient, and forceful Mr. Nudd had become demoralizing to the PEA. Mr. Nudd had been director of the PEA since 1913. He knew New York's school system and New York's interest-group politics intimately. He used his wide knowledge and seniority to intervene in Executive Committee decision-making. He wrote *The Public and the Schools* and the press releases, and managed the office. He did everything and left nothing for anyone else to do. All were sorry to lose Mr. Nudd, Nichols observed later, but he had begun to think of the PEA as the alter ego of himself, and action was necessary.[133]

This is undoubtedly true as far as it goes. But Nudd had also become a victim of educational progress. Just as the social settlement element in the PEA became superfluous with the adoption of the settlement program by the city's schools, so the social work element in the PEA became superfluous with the success of the activity program. Nudd's expertise in social work was no longer needed. And with someone like Mrs. Lewisohn devoting herself to the PEA, his knowledge of the city's interest-group politics was also superfluous.

On October 18, 1939, the Executive Committee met in the City Midday Club for its first meeting of the new season.[134] Everyone was there, except Mr. Nudd. Mrs. Lewisohn had a prepared statement ready which she proceeded to read. She informed the committee that earlier that month a "small group" of those who had been most active in the PEA had met to discuss the "critical" financial situation of the PEA. The group decided, she continued, that drastic cuts would have to be made in the budget and that under the circumstances it would be best

132 *New York Times*, April 14, 22, 1936; March 1, 1938, April 5, 9, 1939; *The Public and the Schools*, No. 380, February 23, 1937; No. 388, February 22, 1938; No. 379, March 28, 1939. The annual art benefits contributed more to PEA coffers than did annual dues from the membership. For example, that of 1938 produced a net income of $3800, while the total income from membership dues for this year was $2420 (received from 440 members). "Annual Financial Report of the PEA for the Year Ending October 31, 1938," in the files of the PEA.
133 William B. Nichols, Interview, New York City, September 29, 1959.
134 Minutes of the Executive Committee of the PEA, October 18, 1939.

for Mr. Nudd, who was drawing, at $6,000 annually, about 40 per cent of the PEA's annual budget, to seek another position in which he could use his abilities and experience to greater advantage. In the meantime, Mrs. Lewisohn continued, the PEA should ponder what steps to take next. President Nichols then took the floor. The usually affable Nichols rebuked the Committee for devoting more time to art benefits than to public education. Then Nichols went on to say that he, too, believed the time had come for a change. In the discussion that followed it was agreed that the director should seek a new situation. When Nudd, then in his twenty-seventh year with the PEA, joined the meeting, he was so informed.[135]

At a meeting of the board on April 25, 1940, the basis on which the PEA was to continue in existence unfolded. Mrs. Lewisohn took the floor.[136] The PEA, she said, could die in a blaze of glory, reciting past achievements: its school experiments taken over and embodied in the present school system; its fight to keep the schools free from politics less necessary because appointments to higher positions in the school system and to the Board of Education were now mostly non-political; its success in training many groups in the city who could carry on the Association's legislative program. The other solution, suggested repeatedly from outside sources, particularly foundation heads, Mrs. Lewisohn continued, was that the PEA focus attention less on reaching groups and people already interested in the public schools, and more on reaching the larger lay public.

Mrs. Lewisohn said that she was willing to try and proposed that she and Mrs. Pascal, without salary, be permitted to take over the day-to-day direction of the PEA. If the board accepted, Mrs. Lewisohn went on, the PEA would emphasize "a more lay interpretation of expert problems." "Today," she concluded, "we are going to try to make the great New York City public the interested public." The board voted to accept Mrs. Lewisohn's proposals unanimously. The dual kingship of Mrs. Lewisohn and Mrs. Pascal, however, was more apparent than real. It was Mrs. Lewisohn's show. From this moment in April 1940 until her death in June 1954, Mrs. Lewisohn, in the eyes of many New Yorkers, was the PEA.

[135] In the supreme irony, Nudd secured a position, thanks to Mrs. Lewisohn, as confidential secretary to James H. McDonald, a newly appointed member of the Board of Education. This post was frequently scored in *The Public and the Schools* as the epitome of "politics" in the school system.

[136] Minutes of the Board of Trustees of the PEA, April 25, 1940.

Chapter 6

DEFENDER OF PROGRESSIVISM

1940-1954

As THE PEA ENTERED its second half-century it had in the view of its leadership fulfilled itself as an institution. The educational precepts and goals which it had long advocated had finally been accepted by school officials in the city as good education; it enjoyed privileged access to these school officials. Like any organized political interest group, the PEA had labored to secure public policy favorable to its interests. Having secured the enactment of such policy, again like any interest group successful in promoting something, the PEA now dedicated itself to preventing any change in the status quo. During Mrs. Lewisohn's reign, a period lasting from 1940 until her untimely death in the spring of 1954, the greatest part of PEA activities had as its goal the protection or furtherance of progressive education and the preservation or enhancement of the "insider" status of the PEA. Born in protest, by 1954 the PEA had become virtually a lay auxiliary of the Board of Education.

This is not to say that the PEA moved in a straight line toward becoming the voice of school professionals. Under Mrs. Lewisohn's aegis the Association greatly increased the size of its Board of Trustees, doubled its membership, and broadened somewhat its base of support. The expansion brought with it, besides increased influence and increased affluence, a severe threat of disunity. There were constant internecine struggles over questions of tactics, strategy, and policy. Much PEA thought and energy, consequently, was expended in the necessary task of achieving cohesion. It is a measure of Mrs. Lewisohn's skill as a leader that the dissident faction in the PEA was appeased and cohesion achieved without any major departure from fundamental PEA objectives.

I

In the winter of 1941, a New York State Education Department study, directed by J. Cayce Morrison, Assistant Commissioner of Education in Charge of Elementary Schools, approved New York City's activity program and recommended its extension throughout the city school system.[1] *Newsweek*, in characteristically flamboyant language, called the event the "greatest victory" in the history of progressive education.[2] The report caused little stir in New York City, however. As we have seen, the great victory was won several years earlier. It was inconceivable that a six-year experiment which involved some 75,000 children, which embodied the State Education Department's "Cardinal Objectives of Elementary Education," and which was evaluated by the chief promulgator of these objectives, would be deemed other than a success. The Board of Superintendents took steps immediately to implement the state's recommendations.[3]

Even while progressivism was thus on the march, criticism of the new education, hitherto muffled, began to increase in volume and attract attention. The *Times* quoted a city school teacher as saying that many of her fellow teachers were suspicious of the activity program because it neglected the fundamentals.[4] Nicholas Murray Butler assailed progressive education as the "rabbit system of education" in which children were turned loose in the school to develop such tastes as might momentarily attract them.[5] There were also malcontents who made progressive education the target of their diffuse and violent dislike of the New Deal and all its works. In 1938 Milo F. McDonald, principal

[1] New York State University, State Education Department, *The Activity Program: The Report of a Survey of the Curriculum Experiment with the Activity Program in the Elementary Schools of the City of New York, under the direction of J. Cayce Morrison* (Albany, 1941); *New York Times*, October 30, 1941; New York City, Board of Education, *The First Fifty Years, 1898–1948: Fiftieth Annual Report of the Superintendent of Schools* (New York, 1948), p. 129.

[2] "Victory for Progressivism," *Newsweek*, XVIII (November 3, 1941), 50–52.

[3] New York City, Board of Education, *All the Children: Forty-Third Annual Report of the Superintendent of Schools, 1940–41*, pp. 61–62; New York City, Board of Education, Curriculum Bulletin No. 1, *Changing Concepts and Practices in Elementary Education*, 1942–3; John J. Loftus, "Learning Comes to Life," *Progressive Education*, XXI (April, 1944), 186–89; New York City, Board of Education, *The First Fifty Years*, pp. 155–57.

[4] *New York Times*, May 8, 1938.

[5] *New York Times*, January 25, 1943; Columbia University, *Report of the President of Columbia University for 1942* (New York, 1943), p. 39.

of Brooklyn's Bushwick High School, helped form the American Education Association in order to oppose the atheistic and subversive influence alleged to be embodied in New York's activity program.[6]

Criticism of progressive education was not unique to New York City. It was, rather, a widespread phenomenon which began in the late 1930's at the flood tide of the movement, reached one peak in the early years of World War II, abated somewhat in the post-war period, and then reached another climax during the period of the Korean War, 1950–1953.[7] Faced with what it considered a serious threat to its basic policy, the retention of the loyalty of school officials and lay opinion leaders in the city to progressive education became, in the period 1940–1954, one of the PEA's major objectives. In this decision, and in much of its strategy and tactics during the Lewisohn era, the PEA was profoundly influenced by the Progressive Education Association.

During the 1930's the PEA and the Progressive Education Association had drifted apart. Then, in 1942, when progressive education began to come under criticism, Mrs. Lewisohn quickly accepted the suggestion of Frederick L. Redefer, director of the Progressive Education Association, that there be greater cooperation between their organizations.[8] From that moment on, the closest links were established. This can be traced in the PEA's Board of Trustees, enlarged in the early forties, in a new Advisory Council, and in a new Co-Ordinating Committee, both called into being in the early forties.

The composition of the PEA's new Board of Trustees indicates a deliberate effort to embody the united front policy of the Progressive Education Association. By 1945, along with the small, stable, inner core of leadership comprising Mrs. Lewisohn, Nichols, Karelsen, Jaretzki, and Mrs. Blitzer, the following newcomers were prominent in the PEA:

---

[6] *New York Times*, May 4, 1938; *The Public and the Schools*, No. 416, November 25, 1941; Milo F. McDonald, *American Education: The Old, the Modern, and the "New"* (New York, 1952).

[7] Lawrence A. Cremin, *The Transformation of the School* (New York, 1961), pp. 267–70, 324–28, and Chap. IX, esp. pp. 338–47. For the disquieting background in domestic and international affairs from which the educational crisis emerged see Eric F. Goldman, *The Crucial Decade: America, 1945–1955* (New York, 1956).

[8] Minutes of the Board of Trustees of the PEA, May 7, 1942. In 1944, after prolonged debate, the Progressive Education Association decided to meet the sharpening challenge to progressive education with the strategy of the united front. It was able to enlist virtually the whole phalanx of professional school groups behind the movement but was notably lacking in skill in rallying a wider base of support. The firm alliance it was able to cement with the PEA is one of the most notable exceptions to this egregious ineptitude. The story is told in Cremin, *loc. cit.*

Eduard C. Lindeman and Lawrence K. Frank of the New York School of Social Work, Vivian T. Thayer of the Ethical Culture Schools, George Strayer and Paul Mort of Teachers College, Mrs. Charles Riegelman of the Joint Committee on Education, Mrs. Henry Goddard Leach of the New York League of Women Voters, Mrs. Richard O. Loengard of the American Association of University Women, and Miss Ruth DuPont of the Junior League. The bar was represented by Francis A. Truslow, Robert M. Benjamin, and Bethuel M. Webster. Marshall Field, philanthropist and publisher of the liberal newspaper *PM*, was also active in the PEA in the early 1940's.[9]

Later in the decade other individuals who could be useful to the PEA because of their group membership or personal influence were recruited as trustees. In 1945, Mrs. Emily Smith Warner, the daughter of Al Smith, was elected to the board. In 1948, Winthrop Rockefeller, Mrs. Richard Rodgers, Mrs. Samuel I. Rosenman, Dean Ernest O. Melby of New York University's School of Education, and Mrs. Shirley C. Fisk, the daughter of Averell Harriman, became PEA activists. Also in 1948, Dr. Channing H. Tobias, nationally known Negro leader, was elected to the board. Finally, when major new civic groups made their appearance in the city, the PEA moved quickly to co-opt their leaders. In the late 1940's, Mrs. Joseph P. Lash and Mrs. Morris Shapiro of the Citizens Committee on Children (organized in 1945) were brought into the PEA. Thus the PEA sought to use recruitment policy to unify the forces of reform in the city behind progressive education, and to enhance its own prestige and influence. A new Advisory Council helped to decrease considerably any danger of disloyalty to basic PEA policy inherent in the board's enlarged representation.

One of Mrs. Lewisohn's first innovations on assuming full-time direction of the PEA was the formation of the Advisory Council to help PEA plan work and policy. It was composed of specialists in education, health, social work, and mental hygiene.[10] The council enjoyed a fifteen-year existence—from 1940 to 1955. Through the years its membership

[9] PEA, *Annual Reports*, 1943–1954. After a long hiatus PEA resumed the publication of annual reports in 1943.

[10] The membership of the committee in 1943 is typical. Among others there were Redefer and Caroline Zachry of the Progressive Education Association, Lindeman of the New York School of Social Work, Mrs. Sidonie Gruenberg of the Child Study Association, Leonard Mayo of the Welfare Council, Professor Esther Lloyd-Jones of Teachers College, Dr. George S. Stevenson of the National Committee for Mental Hygiene, and two representatives of New York's school officialdom— Associate Superintendent Regina C. M. Burke and Assistant Superintendent William Jansen. PEA, *Annual Report*, 1943, p. 5.

varied only slightly; the agencies and interests represented on it, not at all. The council met monthly with members of the PEA's staff and Board of Trustees. In addition to advising PEA on policy matters, council members brought the problems of their own agencies as they touched the schools and children to the meetings. Given the council's narrow range of interest and perspective, and its ex officio status on the board, it provided an important source of influence upon, and continuity in, PEA policy and strategy.

Another key Lewisohn innovation in which the hand of the Progressive Education Association is apparent was the organization in 1943 of the Co-Ordinating Committee, an informal coalition of fourteen non-governmental groups.[11] By 1948, twenty civic, education, labor, civil liberties, and philanthropic organizations were represented on the committee. By 1954 this number had grown to thirty-one.[12] The purpose of the Co-Ordinating Committee, Mrs. Lewisohn explained, was to give organized citizen groups in the city a larger perspective of the field of public education, to pool experience and information, and to prevent duplication of effort.[13] It is quite clear, however, that as originally conceived by Mrs. Lewisohn and her advisors the Co-Ordinating Committee had also at least three other objectives: the defense of progressive education; the continued education of the city's organizational

[11] *The Public and the Schools*, No. 431, October 26, 1943; PEA, *Annual Report*, 1943, p. 3. The committee's charter members were: Public Education Association, Progressive Education Association, Child Study Association, Play Schools Association, Teachers Guild Associates, United Parents Associations, Vocational Service for Juniors, Community Service Society, Women's City Club, Citizens Union, New York Council of Adult Education, American Association of University Women, New York League of Women Voters, and the Junior League.

[12] The complete list of member organizations includes: American Association of University Women, Americans for Democratic Action, American Jewish Committee, American Jewish Congress, Anti-Defamation League, Association of Local School Board Chairmen of the Borough of Manhattan, Child Study Association, Citizens Budget Commission, Citizens Committee on Children of New York City, Citizens Union, City Wide Citizens Committee for All-Day Neighborhood Schools, Community Service Society, Greater New York Council of Parent Teacher Associations, Junior League of New York City, League for Industrial Democracy, National Association for the Advancement of Colored People, National Conference of Christians and Jews, New York Adult Education Council, New York City CIO Council, New York City League of Women Voters, Parents League of New York, Play Schools Association, Public Education Association, Teachers Guild Associates, United Neighborhood Houses, United Parents Associations of New York City, Urban League of Greater New York, Vocational Advisory Service, Welfare and Health Council of New York City, Women's City Club of New York, Women's Trade Union League. In PEA, *Up-Hill Journey*, 1953–1954, p. 36. Of the city's major civic organizations, only the City Club is missing from this list. The Citizens Budget Commission joined in 1953.

[13] PEA, *Annual Report*, 1943, p. 5.

leaders by the PEA; and the protection of the PEA's status. In short, the PEA's goal was to create a public school bloc.

The PEA, then, by a variety of leadership techniques, attempted to establish a united front in defense of progressive education. Its more explicit activities in defense of progressive education further document the close ties between it and the Progressive Education Association. Mrs. Lewisohn considered it her personal function and responsibility to lobby, through speeches and articles, on behalf of progressive education. In her strident insistence that progressive education was the one permissible manner of teaching, in her identification of progressive education with the democratic way of life, and in her dismissal of all criticism of progressive education, even from the most respectable sources, as a threat to that way of life, Mrs. Lewisohn reproduces with photographic likeness the line of the Progressive Education Association. When the American Education Association charged that New York's activity program was imported from Russia, Mrs. Lewisohn replied that the activity program was "thoroughly American procedure. . . . The PEA, believing this to be the logical type of education for Americans, wishes to see that program expanded." [14] The same polemical style was used not only to reply in kind to lunatic fringe critics, but with all critics. To President Butler's criticism, Mrs. Lewisohn retorted that progressive education "is ideally suited to our democratic state," and then went on to say:

> These are critical times. Our schools like our other democratic institutions are seriously threatened. It is little less than tragic for the president of a great University to align himself now with the forces of reaction.[15]

The PEA and one of its Founding Fathers no longer spoke the same language; indeed, they had not for at least two decades.

Virtually all of Mrs. Lewisohn's articles or speeches in defense of progressive education were aimed at a very limited public: at members of the PEA, the Junior League, the Lincoln School Parents Association, and the Parents League of New York, an organization of private school parents.[16] Mrs. Lewisohn's one major effort addressed to a larger public

[14] *Nation,* CLVI (March 13, 1943), 393, Letters to the Editor; *The Public and the Schools,* No. 426, January 26, 1943.

[15] *New York Times,* March 3, 1943; *The Public and the Schools,* No. 427, February 23, 1943.

[16] E.g., Margaret S. Lewisohn, "Lincoln School Meets a New Challenge," *The Link,* XI (December, 1940), 6–7; "What's the Public Education Association?" *ibid.,* XIII (December, 1942), 20–23; *New York Times,* November 29, 1944, May 17, 1946.

was an article significantly titled "The Battle for Modern Education" which appeared in 1944 in *Progressive Education*.[17] It is notable for being the earliest and most complete expression of an argument in defense of progressive education which would not reach its vogue until the early 1950's; the argument of the isolated and embattled democratic minority against the omnipresent "enemies of modern education." [18]

Between 1944 and 1951 there was a hiatus in overt PEA actions in defense of progressive education. Then, in the train of the Korean War, as criticism of progressive education from intellectual circles, from a growing segment of the well-educated and informed citizenry, and from ultrarightist groups gained momentum, the PEA took to the field once again. And once again it followed the progressive line:

> The schools of Port Washington, Englewood, Scarsdale and White Plains, as well as those of Pasadena and other communities across the nation, were being turned into battlegrounds! Was the next frontal assault to be launched against the New York City system? The question could not be ignored.[19]

On March 1, 1951, the Board of Trustees, acting upon Mrs. Lewisohn's proposal, agreed that the PEA should "take the leadership in the defense of modern education which was under attack." [20] It was decided that the PEA should launch a campaign to rally the citizens of the city to support of their schools, and to inform the public of the techniques and goals of modern progressive education.[21] In pursuance of this goal the PEA devoted an issue of *The Public and the Schools* to a report on right-wing groups sponsoring the attacks on modern education,[22] published a booklet advertising modern educational meth-

[17] Margaret S. Lewisohn, "The Battle for Modern Education," *Progressive Education*, XXI (January, 1944), 29–31.

[18] The article grew out of a meeting of educational progressives at the Second Conference on the Scientific Spirit and Democratic Faith, held in New York City in 1944. Jerome Nathanson of the Ethical Culture Society wrote of the Conference: "It was in the belief that certain organized movements in education constituted a threat to the scientific spirit and democratic faith that its attention was concentrated on the educational issue." Quoted in Cremin, *op. cit.*, p. 341.

[19] PEA, *Annual Report*, 1951, p. 5. The challenge to progressive education in the early 1950's and the progressives' response is covered in Cremin, *op. cit.*, pp. 338–47.

[20] Minutes of the Board of Trustees of the PEA, March 1, 1951.

[21] PEA, *Annual Report*, 1951, p. 5.

[22] *New York Times*, May 9, 1951; *The Public and the Schools*, No. 473, May, 1951. The "front organizations," identified by the PEA, were the National Council for American Education, the Conference of American Small Business Organizations, Friends of the Public Schools of America, Sons of the American Revolution, and the American Education Association.

ods in the city schools,[23] and reprinted and circulated in large quantity an article by Mrs. Lewisohn, originally appearing in *Junior League Magazine*, which warned New Yorkers to beware the "propaganda of well-organized groups" who wished to turn American schools to the educational methods of the totalitarian countries.[24] The climax of the PEA's campaign to save the schools of New York City from dark forces was reached on May 8, 1951 when, at a PEA-sponsored dinner, 800 persons crowded into the Starlight Roof of the Waldorf-Astoria to hear novelist Edna Ferber, Dean Millicent McIntosh of Barnard College, and Roy Larsen, President of the National Citizens Commission for the Public Schools, charge them to defend democracy and modern education.[25] The "battle for modern education" in New York City was over; the enemy routed.

In the very superficial nature of the PEA's defense of progressive education in New York City lies its true significance. It reflects the depth and seriousness of the "attacks" on progressive education in the city. No greater efforts were necessary. There were no serious attacks on the city's educational program from any of the ultra-rightist groups which flourished in the nation during the McCarthy era. Nor was there any serious criticism of the school's program from any of the city's influential civic or taxpayer groups, or, for that matter, from any of its

[23] PEA, Childhood Education Committee, *Look at Your School* (New York, 1951); *New York Times*, April 30, 1951.
[24] Margaret S. Lewisohn, "Look to Your Schools," an article reprinted from the *Junior League Magazine* (November, 1951), and distributed by the PEA. In the "Margaret S. Lewisohn" file at the PEA.
[25] *New York Times*, May 9, 1951; PEA, *Annual Report*, 1951, p. 6. The National Citizens Commission was launched in 1949 by the Educational Policies Commission of the National Education Association and a group of prominent citizens headed by Roy E. Larsen, president of Time, Inc. Mrs. Lewisohn was a charter member of this group. The Commission was formed to stimulate action by local groups in the educational field and to be a clearinghouse for such groups. Thanks largely to its inspiration and support one of the novel developments on the educational front in the early 1950's was the nationwide mushroom growth of organized citizen participation in public schools. Any resemblance between this citizen movement and that of fifty years earlier, in which the PEA and the Eastern Conference of Public Education Associations played such a significant part, is at best superficial. The crucial distinction is that the citizen movement of the 1890's arose to protest existing educational policies and practices; that of the 1950's arose to defend the educational status quo. The earlier movement was also a more genuine grass-roots movement than the latter. For an introduction to the large literature of and about the citizens movement of the 1950's see National Society for the Study of Education, Fifty-Third Yearbook, Part I, *Citizen Co-operation for Better Schools*, Nelson B. Henry, ed. (Chicago, 1954); Herbert M. Hamlin, "Organized Citizen Interest in the Public Schools," *Review of Educational Research*, XXIII (October, 1953), 346–52.

religious groups.[26] In New York City, the united front policy of liberal organizations in defense of progressive education was a huge success.

II

As the keystone of its publicized arguments in defense of progressive education, the PEA stressed the inseparability of public education and democracy. Yet its leaders would not think of sending their children to the public schools. None of the PEA's trustees, Mrs. Lewisohn admitted in 1945, had children in the public schools of New York City. "This is evidence," she ingenuously explained, "of the character of the Association . . . the spirit which has guided all it has undertaken. It is comprised of citizens who have no axe to grind . . . no vested interest. Therefore, it can be much more objective." [27] This is the quintessential expression of the PEA's self-image: altruistic, disinterested, a public service organization. Its class character and its special interests seemed obscured even from some of its leaders. It would seem reasonable to suggest, however, that one of the chief reasons why the PEA's leaders did not send their children to the public schools is that they considered the public schools part of the city's philanthropic and correctional system. The PEA publicly invoked "democracy" in support of progressive education. But never far behind this lofty rhetoric lay its mundane conception of the public school as an agency for molding children into efficient, well-adjusted members of society. The prevention of social maladjustment remained the major concern of the PEA. The passing of the years brought no deviation from this long-time objective, but rather the opposite. True, the old immigration for which the PEA had so long labored to shape the public schools was over, but the flood of newcomers into the city had not ceased; only its source had changed.

After World War I a rapidly growing Negro and Puerto Rican population became domiciled in the city. Between 1940 and 1950 the Negro population rose from 458,000 to 748,000. The same decade also witnessed a sharp rise in the city's Puerto Rican population. By 1950 they numbered about 250,000 people. The influx of Negroes and Puerto

---

[26] True, there were occasional potshots taken at progressive education from Fordham University, but it is improbable that an educational program seriously opposed by the Roman Catholic Church could have been installed in the city school system.

[27] Mrs. Samuel A. Lewisohn, Interview by Nancy Craig, Radio Station WJZ, April 17, 1945; transcript in the files of the PEA.

Ricans into the city continued unabated in the early years of the fifties.[28] The experience of these newest immigrants approached closely the pattern set earlier by the Jewish and Italian Europeans.[29] Their presence, and the increasingly difficult problems they posed to the city as their numbers swelled, helped keep alive the PEA conception of the public school as a legatee institution and a strategic agency for the prevention or treatment of social maladjustment.

"The only possible solution of the [juvenile delinquency] problem," Mrs. Lewisohn asserted in 1942 at a time when the usual youthful unrest in the city was heightened by the war and the rising in-migration to the city of Negroes and Puerto Ricans, "is prevention and the logical center of prevention is the public school, in which we taxpayers already have so large an investment." [30] At a hearing before the City Council she urged municipal authorities to coordinate the work of all public and private agencies and to use the public schools as the center of all juvenile delinquency prevention efforts.[31] What is not explicit in speeches, or magazine articles, or press releases, is implicit in the substance of policy.

While city school authorities extended the activity program, the PEA continued to promote its own experiment in P.S. 33, the Chelsea School Project, as a demonstration in the adaptation of a public school to its neighborhood. At the Chelsea school the effort to place "school services" and recreation at the center of the curriculum moved straight ahead. The experiment kept abreast of the latest tack in progressive school thought. "We are confident," Ruth Hardy, the P.S. 33 principal, earnestly declared, "we have found the way to answer the totalitarian challenge to democracy. We feel we have a pattern of a school which can furnish group mental hygiene and habits of participation in a free society." [32]

[28] Oscar Handlin, *The Newcomers: Negroes and Puerto Ricans in a Changing Metropolis* (Cambridge, Mass., 1959), pp. 48–49, 51, 142; *New York Times*, November 6, November 12, 1947; Charles Garrett, *The La Guardia Years: Machine and Reform Politics in New York City* (New York, 1961), p. 333.

[29] Handlin, *op. cit.*, Chap. IV., esp. pp. 80–83, 93–104.

[30] *New York Times*, November 1, 1942, Sec. IV.

[31] *New York Times*, November 20, December 14, 1942; *The Public and the Schools*, No. 425, December 29, 1942.

[32] "Chelsea School Project: Fifth Annual Report, November, 1941," mimeographed, in "ADNS" folder, PEA Files. In 1944 the PEA's Adele Franklin, director of the project, received the Edward L. Bernays Award of the Progressive Education Association for "outstanding contribution to democratic education." *Progressive Education*, XXI (March, 1944), 122; *The Public and the Schools*, No. 435, February 29, 1944.

In 1942 the Chelsea project was passed by the Greater New York Fund as a "welfare agency," thus becoming eligible for the Fund's support.[33] Aided chiefly by foundation grants, the PEA had little difficulty raising money to promote the experiment.[34] In September 1942 the Board of Education formally incorporated the P.S. 33 project into the school system, renamed it the "All-Day Neighborhood School" project, and extended it to P.S. 194, an all-Negro school in Harlem. The PEA continued its connection with the project as joint sponsor.[35] The Harlem outbreaks of August 1943 provided fertile ground for the PEA to press for the extension of All-Day Neighborhood Schools to all "difficult areas" in the city. "We feel," said Mrs. Blitzer, "that a constructive and practical pattern for difficult area schools has been developed. We are confident that this pattern is the logical approach to the solution of many of our problems and hope that it will be adopted and extended by the school authorities." [36] In the fall of 1945 the Board of Education assumed full responsibility for the All-Day Neighborhood School project and extended it to two schools in the Morrisania section of the Bronx, a section with a rapidly growing Negro and Puerto Rican population.[37]

Although four All-Day Neighborhood Schools after a decade's work might seem like small accomplishment, the PEA was satisfied. From long experience it knew that educational politics, like any kind of politics, is a slow, artful, and unending process. The goal of getting the Board of Education to accept and carry on the Chelsea Project had been

[33] Minutes of the Executive Committee of the PEA, May 7, 1942.

[34] In 1944 the PEA raised $16,500 for the project, $2,500 more than its budget for general expenses. "Annual Financial Report, October 31, 1944," in the files of the PEA. The chief contributors to the project were the Field Foundation, the Greater New York Fund, the New York Community Trust, and the New York Foundation.

[35] New York City, Board of Education, *All the Children. Forty-Fourth Annual Report of the Superintendent of Schools.* 1942–43, pp. 25–28; New York City, Board of Education, *Extended Services Through the All-Day Neighborhood Schools* (1948), pp. 1–2; New York City, Board of Education, *The First Fifty Years*, p. 157; *The Public and the Schools*, No. 420, March 31, 1942.

[36] PEA, *Annual Report*, 1944, p. 11; *New York Times*, December 5, 1943, January 23, May 12, 1944, January 21, January 28, 1945; Adele Franklin, "Is Delinquency the School's Business?" *Progressive Education*, XX (October, 1943), 270–73, 303; Margaret S. Lewisohn and Agnes E. Benedict, "A New Design for Public Elementary Schools," *School and Society*, LXI (June 23, 1945), 412–14; *The Public and the Schools*, No. 433, December 28, 1943; No. 434, January 25, 1944; No. 441, December 26, 1944.

[37] New York City, Board of Education, *Extended Services Through the All-Day Neighborhood Schools*, p. 2; New York City, Board of Education, *The First Fifty Years*, pp. 157–58; PEA, *Annual Report*, 1945, pp. 11–15.

achieved. Now the PEA girded itself for the long job of spreading the
idea that the All-Day Neighborhood Schools were "the schools of
tomorrow." It disbanded its old All-Day Neighborhood School Committee and began to lay plans for the formation of a city-wide citizens
group "with a chairman who has a big public following to act as a
pressure or public relations committee" for the extension of the All-Day
Neighborhood School idea.[38]

In 1952 the PEA brought into existence the City-Wide Citizens
Committee for the All-Day Neighborhood Schools.[39] A few years later
this group became the Independent Citizens for the All-Day Neighborhood Schools, but the PEA retained close ties with it. Among the
officials of the Citizens for the All-Day Neighborhood Schools are
Mrs. Milton K. Breslauer, president, and Mrs. Broadus Mitchell and
Frank Karelsen, honorary presidents. It has a long list of distinguished sponsors and is very well financed. It has its own organ, the
"ADNS Newsletter," and an extensive program of publications of the
pamphlet variety.[40] It sponsors Citizens Committees in each All-Day
Neighborhood School, and provides these schools with volunteer help
of all sorts. It leaves few stones unturned in its efforts to educate taxpayers and the Board of Estimate that All-Day Neighborhood Schools
are not an expense but an investment in the prevention of juvenile
delinquency.[41]

III

Although the PEA, in the sphere of public elementary education,
has been oblivious to the ideal of the public school as a vehicle through
which the children of the poor can rise in the world, in the sphere of
public higher education, it has, at least since 1942, fought energetically
and effectively to make this ideal a reality.[42]

Throughout the forties the PEA urged the establishment of state-
aided community or junior colleges. Also, the PEA led the drive to

[38] Minutes of the Board of Trustees of the PEA, May 3, 1945; PEA, *Annual
Report*, 1945, pp. 14–15.
[39] *The Public and the Schools*, No. 475, January, 1952.
[40] From a collection of Citizens for the ADNS publications in the files of the
PEA.
[41] In November, 1960, Citizens for the All-Day Neighborhood Schools became a regular part of the PEA organization. PEA, *Report Card*, December, 1960.
[42] The College Committee, organized in 1942 under Mrs. Richard O. Loengard,
has been the spearhead in the PEA's efforts to broaden educational opportunities
for New Yorkers.

persuade Governor Thomas E. Dewey and the state legislature to provide state aid for the teacher-training programs of the city's municipal colleges.[43] Finally, the PEA played a prominent role in the sharp struggle to establish a state university. It early joined forces with civil liberties and minority groups in the city that initiated the state university movement. It lobbied actively itself, and lined up the support of most of the groups on its Co-Ordinating Committee in the fight to secure the legislation which, in 1948, finally created the New York State University. Subsequently, the PEA played a vital role in the organization of the "Committee to Save the State University" which successfully fought off the attempts of the Board of Regents to gain control of the new institution.[44] These aforementioned efforts on behalf of public higher education mark the most important innovation in PEA program and policy since 1914.

IV

"Today we are going to make the great New York City public the interested public." [45] As stated by Mrs. Lewisohn in 1940, this old PEA and good government objective was to be one of the major innovations in PEA policy. During Mrs. Lewisohn's reign, however, with few exceptions, the PEA made no real effort to expand considerably the public which would respond to educational questions. The PEA's strategy was rather, by the avoidance of publicity, to keep the size of the interested public small, and to wage an intensive propaganda effort within this limited public. The most important exception to this strategy of restricting the size of the interested public in education was in the area of school finance.

The PEA's major effort during the period 1940–1954 was its "Save the Schools" crusade of 1947–48. The intensive, well-publicized drive was undertaken for several reasons: a strong minority group within the PEA's inner core of leadership was demanding that PEA act more aggressively; school support was a basic PEA concern; and, finally, the times were propitious for a school aid campaign. The downward trend in school enrollment in the city which began in the mid-1930's, and which saw the average day school register drop from about 1,105,000 in 1936 to 827,000 in 1946, came finally to a halt in the postwar period.

[43] PEA, *Annual Reports,* 1942–1948.
[44] Oliver C. Carmichael, Jr., *New York Establishes a State University* (Nashville, Tenn., 1955), pp. 73, 79, 98, 279, 284ff; PEA, *Annual Reports,* 1946–1949.
[45] Minutes of the Board of Trustees of the PEA, April 25, 1940.

The school year 1946–47 witnessed the first increase in school register in more than a decade, an increase of about 3,000.[46] To school officials in 1947 this event, together with a dramatic increase in the birth rate, the continuing influx of Negroes and Puerto Ricans into the city, plus the fact that school construction had been suspended during the war, heralded an impending school crisis.[47] The spiraling postwar inflation helped to heighten the sense of imminent crisis.

Beginning in 1941, because of the declining school enrollment, Mayor La Guardia began to cut back on school appropriations. The school budget for operating expenses for the year 1944–45, $134,700,000, was back at Depression levels. It began to rise again after the war, reaching $178,000,000 in 1947–48, but not quickly enough to keep pace with the rampant inflation which began after the war.[48] To add to the school's plight, a trend had set in, also because of declining enrollment, of reduced state aid for the city schools. Furthermore, the Friedsam Formula, upon which state aid was based, stood unrevised, inflation or not, since its enactment in the mid-twenties. For all of these reasons, if PEA had to make a public show of its leadership it seemed wisest to do so in the area of school finance.

On December 8, 1947, the PEA issued a well-publicized exposé of disgraceful conditions in many of the city's schools. In strong language the PEA asserted that more than 200,000 school children "spend their lives in educational slums." The PEA called for an immediate $140,000,-000 school building, modernization, and repair program, $100,000,000 to come from the city and the rest from the state. Thus the PEA kicked off its "Save the Schools" crusade.[49] It was a crusade waged at state and local levels.

In 1947 the PEA, in collaboration with the New York State Educational Conference Board, sponsored a series of highly technical surveys

[46] New York City, Board of Education, *Fifty-Sixth Annual Report of the Superintendent of Schools, 1953–1954,* Statistical Section, pp. 1–5, 34.

[47] New York City, Board of Education, *The First Fifty Years,* pp. 189, 193–94, 201–02; *New York Times,* December 23, 1945, Sec. IV, article by Benjamin Fine. School officials anticipated that by 1953 elementary school enrollment would be 35 per cent greater than in 1947.

[48] New York City, Board of Education, *The First Fifty Years,* p. x; Garrett, *op. cit.,* p. 204. In 1951 the government announced that the purchasing power of the dollar was worth 59.3 cents as compared with 1939, and its value was still shrinking. Goldman, *op. cit.,* pp. 20, 25–26, 46–47, 186.

[49] *New York Times,* December 9, 10, 13, 1947; *New York Times,* December 13, 1947, ed.; *Newsweek,* XXX (December 22, 1947), 79–80; *Fiscal Policy for Public Education in the State of New York: Report of a Joint Committee Representing the New York State Educational Conference Board and the Public Education Association of New York City* (New York, 1947).

of state and local fiscal policy by a team of experts under Professor
Paul R. Mort of Teachers College. As a result of the studies, in late
1947 the PEA recommended an immediate $103,000,000 increase in
state support beyond 1947 levels, $40,000,000 of which was to go to
New York City.[50] Subsequently the Young–Milmoe bill, drafted by
the PEA and the Educational Conference Board and granting this
amount of new state aid, was introduced into the 1948 legislative session.[51] The PEA's Committee on School Administration and Legislation, its strongest committee, led the fight in Albany on behalf of the
bill. David M. Freudenthal was the committee chairman. The committee also included Winthrop Rockefeller, Newbold Morris, Joseph Mc-
Goldrick, Robert Benjamin, Frank E. Karelsen, Bethuel M. Webster,
Francis A. Truslow, and William B. Nichols.[52] But Mason Bigelow,
long associated with PEA activity in the field of school legislation, then
president-elect of the New York State Bar Association, was absent from
the fight. He informed the board that he could not engage in activities
that had "political overtones" and submitted his resignation.[53]

Indeed there were "political overtones" to the PEA's activities. In
the gubernatorial election of 1942, Republicans elected a Governor for
the first time since 1920. From 1942 to 1954 Thomas E. Dewey and
successive Republican legislatures dominated the state government.[54]
Dewey, in the tradition of his Democratic predecessors in Executive
Mansion in Albany, carried out substantial educational reforms.[55] But
1948 was a presidential election year, and Dewey, a presidential aspirant,
was embarrassed by the importunate pleas coming from New York City
virtually to double state aid to education. However, he saw the need for
adjusting the state's foundation program and, in late January, several
weeks after the Young–Milmoe proposal was introduced, submitted his
own legislation providing for an emergency $30,000,000 increase in state
aid of which $6,000,000 would go to the city.[56] Now the stage was set
for a short but interesting legislative battle.

[50] *New York Times*, December 9, 1947; *Fiscal Policy for Public Education in
the State of New York . . .* , p. ix; *ibid.*, Staff Study #6, *A Program for Meeting the Needs of New York City Schools*, prepared by Stanton F. Leggett and
William S. Vincent (New York, 1947), p. 2.

[51] *New York Times*, January 13, 1948; Minutes of the Board of Trustees of
the PEA, December 4, 1947; PEA, *Annual Report*, 1948, pp. 17–19.

[52] PEA, *Annual Report*, 1948, p. 28.

[53] Minutes of the Board of Trustees of the PEA, December 4, 1947.

[54] David M. Ellis, *et al.*, *A Short History of New York State* (New York,
1957), Chap. XXXIII, "Republican Rule in War and Peace"; Warren Moscow,
Politics in the Empire State (New York, 1948), pp. 32–35.

[55] Ellis, *op. cit.*, pp. 443–45.

[56] *New York Times*, January 30, 1948.

Democrats, casting about for some issue with which to challenge Dewey, seized upon state aid and rushed to the support of the Young–Milmoe bill. A small group of upstate Republicans, chafing under Dewey's domination of the legislature, also came out for the Young–Milmoe measure.[57] The PEA's Co-Ordinating Committee was strenuously active in Albany, while its Publicity Committee poured oil on the flames with a publicity blitzkreig in New York.[58] All for naught. In mid-February Dewey cracked the whip. On February 18th his state-aid bill was overwhelmingly approved by the legislature. Not one Republican in either chamber opposed it.[59]

The PEA attacked the Governor for making a "political football" out of public education, while its Co-Ordinating Committee changed hats and became a "Save Our Schools Committtee," pledged to wage an unrelenting fight for increased state aid until victory was secured.[60] In the 1949 legislative session the PEA and its allies were successful. The Governor asked for a $40,000,000 rise in state aid over the amount required by the existing formula, and recommended the revision upward of that formula. The legislature duly approved the Feinberg–Milmoe bill embodying the Governor's recommendations. New York City's share of the new grant amounted to $23,600,000. With this increment, the state subvention to education in the city for 1949–50 came to about $72,000,000.[61]

The PEA's campaign for increased school support was as well aimed at the Mayor and Board of Estimate as it was at the Governor and state legislature. The PEA was no less successful in the city. For 1947–48 city school appropriations amounted to $178,100,000. In late January 1948, when the PEA's school aid campaign reached its peak, the Board of Estimate approved a $209,000,000 school budget, the largest to then in the city's history.[62]

Between 1948 and 1954, despite the fact that the increase in city public school enrollment has been nowhere near 1947 estimates, the city school budget mounted at an accelerated rate. For 1952–53 the

[57] *New York Times*, various issues January 13–February 18, 1948.

[58] The PEA popularized and distributed in large quantity its fiscal surveys; distributed more than 100,000 copies of "Let's Close the Schools," a pamphlet describing the plight of the city's schools; produced a movie short, "These are Your Schools," starring Henry Fonda, Jinx Falkenberg, and Tex McCrary, which was shown in thirty-three theaters in the city; and organized a citizens rally at Hunter College in support of the Young–Milmoe Bill. PEA, *Annual Report*, 1948, pp. 3–5, 17–19, 21–23; *New York Times*, January 27, 1948.

[59] *New York Times*, February 19, 1948.

[60] *New York Times*, February 19, 20, 1948; PEA, *Annual Report*, 1948, p. 19.

[61] *New York Times*, January 25, 26, 1949, March 31, April 7, 1949.

[62] *New York Times*, January 23, 1948.

figure for operating expenses reached almost $251,000,000.[63] The steep climb in school expenditures was the result of, among other reasons, persistent inflation, the heightened need for special services and specially trained personnel due to the problems posed by the growing number of Negro and Puerto Rican students, the need to erect new buildings to keep up with the growth and movement of the city's school population, and the increasing effectiveness of organized teacher groups in the city. But something must also be said for the persistent and effective agitation of many of the city's civic groups.

The PEA has worked quietly since 1948, but with great perseverance, especially within its Co-Ordinating Committee, to educate the city's influentials to the need for generous school support. It has been, with the United Parents Associations, the leader of the city's "service-demanding" groups in the sphere of public education. It is one of the most liberal of all the non-governmental groups in the city in its conception of school needs. In 1949 the PEA asked the city for a $500,000,-000 school building program.[64] Two years later it urged that per-pupil city school expenditures be raised from $300 to $450.[65]

The PEA has a simple formula for answering all the criticism and for solving all the ills of the city's public schools. To quote Mrs. Lewisohn, "We get just what we pay for." [66] In the PEA argument, the sole difference between the Lincoln School or the Horace Mann School and any public school in New York City is a monetary one. If school appropriations were increased, again to quote Mrs. Lewisohn, "the public school system would be able to give our youngsters the education that only a fortunate few are receiving." [67] The PEA's positive, easy solution for the complex problems besetting the city school system rings with a beguiling plausibility and has gained widespread acceptance in the city.

V

Several other aspects of the school program, besides those having to do with questions of money, curriculum, and methods of teaching

[63] In the period 1947–1953 the school's average daily register increased about 62,000, from 831,000 to 893,000. Among the reasons why the increase was less than anticipated were the flight of middle-class parents with school-age children to the suburbs and the rise in Catholic parochial school enrollment. New York City, Board of Education, *Fifty-Sixth Annual Report of the Superintendent of Schools, 1953–1954*, pp. 28–29, 31.

[64] *New York Times*, November 1, 1949.

[65] *New York Times*, May 6, 1951, Sec. IV.

[66] *Ibid.*

[67] *New York Times*, December 9, 1947.

and learning, elicited continuing controversy in New York City as in the nation during the period with which this chapter deals. They had to do with the role of religion in the public schools, the closely related question of federal aid to education, and loyalty oaths and efforts to discover and oust Communists from the teaching profession. The PEA met the religious issue head-on, avoided the federal aid dispute, and, moving hesitatingly, ultimately joined the academic freedom debate.

After the abortive attempt during the Gary School War of 1915–1917 to introduce a public school program of released time for religious education into the city, the issue remained long quiescent. Then in the late 1930's there came mounting demands that the public schools foster the religious education of the young, either by the direct teaching of religion or by the release of children to receive such instruction. In 1938 and 1939 a number of bills providing for religious instruction in the public schools were unsuccessfully introduced into the New York state legislature.[68] But in 1940 the Coudert–McLaughlin bill permitting public schools to release children for a period of one hour a week for purposes of religious instruction, such instruction to be given off school premises, was enacted into law. In 1941 a released-time program was started in New York City.[69]

The PEA opposed the Coudert–McLaughlin bill when it was before the legislature, but found itself seriously divided on what steps to take, if any, now that it was law. One faction, led by Mrs. Lewisohn and Karelsen, strongly favored coming out for repeal. Another faction, led by Mason Bigelow, urged a wait-and-see attitude.[70] While it continued to debate the question, in 1942 the Board of Trustees set up a special Committee on Released Time under Dr. Vivian T. Thayer, one of the nation's most articulate defenders of a strict interpretation of the principle of separation of church and state, to study the operation of the city's released-time program.[71]

[68] The Public and the Schools, No. 389, March 29, 1938; No. 396, February 28, 1939.

[69] Leo Pfeffer, Church, State and Freedom (Boston, 1953), pp. 316–17, 354–55; PEA, Released Time for Religious Education in New York City Schools: A Research Study by the Center for Field Services, New York University, Dan Dodson, Director (New York, 1949), p. 1.

[70] Minutes of the Board of Trustees of the PEA, January 30, June 5, 1941; Minutes of the Executive Committee of the PEA, February 13, April 3, 1941.

[71] PEA, Annual Report, 1943, pp. 8–10. See the following books by Thayer: American Education Under Fire (New York, 1944), Chap. VI; Religion in Public Education (New York, 1947); and The Attack Upon the American Secular School (Boston, 1951).

Thayer's committee issued reports in both 1943 and 1945.[72] The 1945 report found that as of May of that year more than 110,000 children were participating in the released-time program, about 80 per cent of them of the Roman Catholic faith.[73] The report stated that as the program grew, school personnel—principals, teachers, and clerks—became increasingly involved in the program; that there was an increase in truancy on the afternoons set aside for the program; and that the participant schools were confused about what to do with those children who did not wish to take advantage of the program.[74] The PEA criticized the released-time program as "ill-advised" and called for the severance, as far as possible, of school involvment in it; but it did not bring up the constitutional issue, or call for the program's discontinuance.

The PEA did not pursue the matter any further until the spring of 1948. Then on March 8, 1948, the Supreme Court ruled that the released-time plan in Champaign, Illinois, under which children were released for religious instruction on school premises, was unconstitutional because it violated the First Amendment and was in effect an establishment of religion.[75] That same day the PEA released a statement to the press lauding the decision and predicting court action soon against New York City's released-time program.[76] Two months later the PEA, in cooperation with the American Civil Liberties Union, the United Parents Associations, the American Jewish Congress, and several other Jewish groups, instituted suit against the program in the Brooklyn Supreme Court.[77] While the suit was in progress, the PEA published another released-time survey, essentially similar to that of 1945, but now urging outright the discontinuance of the program.[78]

The Brooklyn court upheld the constitutionality of the city's released-time program. This decision was subsequently affirmed in the Appellate Division, and then in the Court of Appeals. Finally the PEA

[72] PEA, *Released Time for Religious Education in New York City's Schools* (New York, 1945), pp. 3–4.
[73] *Ibid.*
[74] *Ibid.*, pp. 17–18.
[75] *McCollum v. Board of Education*, 330 U.S. 203 (1948). For a discussion of this case see R. Freeman Butts, *The American Tradition in Religion and Education* (Boston, 1950), pp. 201–05; Pfeffer, *op. cit.*, pp. 342–53; R. Freeman Butts and Lawrence A. Cremin, *A History of Education in American Culture* (New York, 1953), p. 547.
[76] *New York Times*, March 9, 1948.
[77] *New York Times*, May 6, 24, July 29, 1948.
[78] PEA, *Released Time* . . . (New York, 1949); *New York Times*, June 14, 15, 1949.

and its allies took the appeal to the United States Supreme Court, where it was decided in April 1952. In a six-to-three decision the Court held that the New York system was unlike the Champaign system and was, therefore, permissible because the schools did not aid the religious groups to promote their religious instruction in the school buildings and did not spend public funds for the purpose.[79]

Now the PEA, split on the wisdom of having gone to court in the first place, dropped the issue completely. The upshot of its decade-long efforts to shore up the "wall of separation" between church and state was that not only did it fail to achieve this aim but it also incurred the wrath of *The Tablet*, the official organ of the Catholic diocese of Brooklyn.[80] Unwillingness to become any further embroiled with Roman Catholic groups is possibly the major reason why the PEA refrained from taking any public stand during the bitter disputes of the late 1940's and early 1950's over federal aid to education.[81]

During the McCarthy Era the problem of academic freedom came under close scrutiny and public debate. One of the most contentious issues of the time was whether the fact of Communist party membership was sufficient grounds to disqualify or dismiss school or college teachers. The academic community was split sharply on the issue.[82] But there was general unanimity of opposition to the Feinberg law, the latest and most drastic in the steadily growing list of New York State legislative responses to the recurrent alarums over internal subversion.[83] The PEA, like the teaching profession and the academic community, found itself deeply divided on whether Communist party membership was sufficient basis for ousting teachers from the public school system. For years the Board of Trustees debated the thorny problem without reaching any agreement. The PEA did not want Communist teachers in the schools. This much was agreed upon. The stumbling block was

[79] *Zorach and Gluck v. Board of Education*, 343 U.S. 306 (1952). For more on this case see Pfeffer, *op. cit.*, pp. 353–76; Butts and Cremin, *op. cit.*, p. 548.

[80] N.d. [1956], article by V. S. Cassidy, in a collection of newspaper clippings in "Folder No. 1," files of the PEA.

[81] The controversy over Federal aid reached the greatest intensity during the debate over the Barden Bill in 1949, and spilled over into 1950. Francis Cardinal Spellman's attack on Mrs. Eleanor Roosevelt, especially, caused a great uproar in the city. Pfeffer, *op. cit.*, pp. 487–94, and see, in general, Butts and Cremin, *op. cit.*, pp. 534–38.

[82] Robert W. Iversen, *The Communists and the Schools* (New York, 1959), pp. 333–34; Butts and Cremin, *op. cit.*, pp. 551–55.

[83] Lawrence H. Chamberlain, *Loyalty and Legislative Action: A Survey of Activity by the New York State Legislature, 1919–1949* (New York, 1951), Chap. V; Iversen, *op. cit.*, pp. 263ff; Butts and Cremin, *op. cit.*, pp. 555–56.

how to identify and eliminate them.[84] But the PEA, with other civil liberties groups in the city, actively opposed the Feinberg law because of the danger of witch-hunting inherent in the measure.[85]

In 1951 the PEA broke with its traditional policy that public school teachers were entitled to enjoy full liberty of belief and opinion. The "bounds of freedom" it had defined in 1936 were now to be somewhat more circumscribed. The PEA was now agreed that Communist party membership was of itself sufficient basis for disqualifying or dismissing public school teachers.[86] In this position the PEA was in basic agreement with the city's Board of Education. The PEA subsequently supported Superintendent William Jansen's investigation of public school faculties and the Board of Education's policy of discharging teachers who declined to answer the questions of the Superintendent regarding alleged Communist affiliation.[87]

The PEA was more solicitous of academic freedom in the field of public higher education. William B. Nichols issued a sharply worded rejoinder when Joseph Cavallaro, chairman of the city's Board of Higher Education, announced that he would welcome a congressional investigation of subversives on the faculties of the municipal colleges. Nichols expressed apprehension that the board might be turned into an "inquisitional group similar to the McCarthy Committee, for which Mr. Cavallaro has expressed his admiration." [88] Mr. Cavallaro retorted that this smacked strongly of the *Daily Worker*.[89]

Thus the PEA continued to play a part in the debate over how to deal most effectively with Communist teachers and how to preserve academic freedom but, like many other progressive groups, as the cold war became more menacing, not so forcefully nor so confidently as it had in the past. Still the PEA has not been able to escape criticism. In 1956, *The Tablet* bitterly denounced the PEA's record for the period 1949–1956 as soft on Communism, as well as hostile to religion.[90]

[84] Minutes of the Board of Trustees of the PEA, June 3, December 2, 1948, April 7, 1949; PEA, *Annual Report*, 1949, pp. 4–5; PEA, *Annual Report*, 1950, p. 6; *New York Times*, November 1, 1949.
[85] Chamberlain, *op. cit.*, p. 194; PEA, *Annual Report*, 1949, pp. 5, 13; PEA, *Annual Report*, 1950, p. 6.
[86] PEA, *Up-Hill Journey: A Report on the Activities of the Public Education Association for the Years 1951–1953*, p. 19.
[87] *Ibid.*, pp. 19–21; PEA, *Up-Hill Journey: Annual Report of the Public Education Association for the Year 1953–1954*, pp. 30–32.
[88] PEA, *Up-Hill Journey* . . . *1951–1953*, pp. 21–24.
[89] *Ibid.*
[90] N.d. [1956], article by V. S. Cassidy, "Folder No. 1."

VI

Over the years one of the most frequently articulated goals of the PEA has been that of getting "politics" out of the management of the public schools. During the thirties the PEA shelved this concern, at least overtly, as it concentrated on cultivating ties with the La Guardia administration. It will be recalled that in 1940, at the reorganization meeting, Mrs. Lewisohn had declared that the fight to keep the schools of New York City free from politics was less necessary because school appointments were mostly nonpolitical. But then in 1943 the PEA announced: "we will continue our efforts to keep our schools out of politics and politics out of our schools." [91] As usual the PEA shift in policy and strategy was dictated by its assessment of the occupant of City Hall.

As the thirties went by, and as second term became third term, the PEA became increasingly disillusioned with Mayor La Guardia. The Mayor gave PEA no preferential treatment. He continued the tradition of balanced religious group representation on the Board of Education.[92] And he was no respecter of sacred cows. La Guardia curtailed school appropriations as school enrollment dropped. He more or less openly treated school officials and school administrative employees like political appointees. The Mayor also attempted to integrate the business side of the school system into the city's Purchase Department and, through the exercise of his budgetary power, to eliminate teaching and school administrative posts.[93] By 1943 La Guardia had gone so far in open

[91] PEA, *Annual Report*, 1943, p. 3.

[92] The politics of group representation on the Board was simplified in the spring of 1948, during William O'Dwyer's administration as Mayor, when legislation was passed with little publicity and almost no controversy enlarging the Board from seven to nine, its present size. *New York Times*, January 14, February 24, March 4, and April 6, 1948; New York City, Board of Education, *The First Fifty Years*, p. 195.

[93] See the *New York Times Index* for 1940–1943 for the almost constant scrapping between the Mayor and the Board of Education, the Board of Superintendents, and teachers' organizations. And see also Rose Naomi Cohen, *The Financial Control of Education in the Consolidated City of New York* (New York, 1948), pp. 1–5; and Garrett, *op. cit.*, pp. 201–03. Professor Garrett takes a dim view of La Guardia's actions in the school department: "Though Newbold Morris often told him that the Board of Education was mainly supposed to be a body independent of city control, La Guardia persisted in regarding education as very much his business and the Board of Education as a department under the city's jurisdiction." *Ibid.*, p. 201.

violation of PEA ideological commitments that the PEA, in one of its rare public criticisms of the Mayor, called upon the citizenry of New York to fight his "dangerously growing desire to control the Board of Education." [94] It was not the PEA, however, but the city's organized teacher groups which called down upon La Guardia's head the famous investigation of the N.E.A.'s National Committee for the Defense of Democracy through Education which found the Mayor guilty of "Interferences with the Independence of the New York City Board of Education." [95]

This was the context in which the PEA in 1943 again took up its longtime goal of divorcing the schools from politics. Political developments in the city subsequent to 1943 were not such as to weaken the PEA's commitment to this policy. In October 1945 came the brief, violent squabble between La Guardia and Frank E. Karelsen, Jr., vice-president of the PEA, brought on by the latter's resignation as chairman of the Board of Education's Advisory Committee on Human Relations and his well-publicized parting blast that school conditions in the city were "chaotic and inexcusable." [96] Of more consequence, in November 1945 the Democratic party, with William O'Dwyer heading its slate, recaptured City Hall. Tammany, after twelve years as the "outs," was back.[97] Although Tammany's power was no longer what it used to be, to the PEA this made little difference. The PEA's relations with Mayor O'Dwyer were cool; its relations with Vincent Impellitteri, who succeeded O'Dwyer upon the latter's precipitate resignation in 1950, frigid. Mayor Impellitteri, "Impie," supposedly an independent, was quite as inaccessible to the PEA as Mayor Hylan had been. He ab-

[94] *New York Times*, May 19, 1943.

[95] National Education Association, National Committee for the Defense of Democracy through Education, *Report of an Investigation: Interferences with the Independence of the New York City Board of Education* (Washington, D.C., 1944); *New York Times*, February 7, 1944. See also Garrett, *op. cit.*, p. 203; Cohen, *op. cit.*, pp. 5–6. One of the humorous by-products of the NEA investigation occurred when the Board of Education itself dissented from the findings. *New York Times*, March 4, 1944.

[96] *New York Times*, October 18, 1945, and the *Times* for the remainder of October. Garrett describes the incident well but unaccountably ignores the political context in which Karelsen's resignation came; that is, mid-October 1945, less than one month before the municipal election. *Op. cit.*, pp. 122, 205–06.

[97] Accounts of New York City politics in the forties and fifties may be found in Garrett, *op. cit.*, Chaps. XIV–XV; Wallace S. Sayre and Herbert Kaufman, *Governing New York City: Politics in the Metropolis* (New York, 1960), *passim*; and the brief but admirable *New York Politics*, by Frank J. Munger and Ralph A. Straetz (New York, 1960).

solutely refused to have anything to do with the PEA or the PEA's Co-Ordinating Committee.[98]

In 1944 the PEA posed for itself a problem: how to develop means of minimizing "interference" by municipal authorities in the Board of Education and the Board of Superintendents.[99] Since then, the PEA has devoted much of its energies to the solution of this problem. The solution the PEA offered in 1944 was one it had abandoned two decades before as hopelessly controversial and doomed to failure—"fiscal independence." [100] This school reform formula is still anathema to the Citizens Union, the City Club, and the Citizens Budget Commission, as well as to academic students of public administration.[101] Nevertheless in recent years, thanks chiefly to PEA's intensive propaganda within its own membership and within its Co-Ordinating Committee, it has increasingly been getting a hearing in the city.[102] In 1950 the Citizens Budget Commission, in favor of integrated as well as economical city government, was roused to publish a refutation of fiscal independence aimed directly at "the spearhead of fiscal independence for education in New York City . . . the Public Education Association." [103]

Fiscal independence, however, was only one of the strategies the PEA employed to advance its goal of divorcing the schools from politics. How members of the Board of Education should be chosen was much

[98] *New York Times*, December 10, 11, 1951; *New York Times*, December 11, 1951, ed.; PEA, *Up-Hill Journey* . . . *1951–1953*, pp. 12–13.

[99] PEA, *Annual Report*, 1944, p. 7.

[100] *Ibid.*

[101] Educators and political scientists are still gravely divided over the question of city–school relations. For a review of the continuing controversy, see Robert L. Morlan, "Toward City–School Rapprochement," *Public Administration Review*, XVIII (Spring, 1958), 113–17.

[102] PEA, *Annual Reports*, 1944–1954; Frederick C. McLaughlin, *Fiscal and Administrative Control of City School Systems*, Staff Study No. 4 of the Fiscal Policy for Public Education in New York State, Under the Auspices of the New York State Educational Conference Board and the Public Education Association (New York, 1949).

[103] Citizens Budget Commission, *Should New York City Adopt Fiscal Independence for Education?* (New York, 1950), p. 5. In 1951 the Education Management Survey of the Mayor's Committee on Management Survey, directed by George D. Strayer and Louis Yavner, recommended fiscal independence. New York City, Mayor's Committee on Management Survey, *Administrative Management of the School System of New York City* (2 vols., 1951), Vol. II, p. 44. This proposal was rejected, however, by the full Committee. New York City, Mayor's Committee on Management Survey, *Modern Management for the City of New York* (2 vols., 1953), Vol. I, p. 245; Vol. II, pp. 31, 84–85, 492–96, 498, *New York Times*, April 17, 1952; "School Board Status Debated in New York," *National Municipal Review*, XLI (February, 1952), 93–94.

debated by the PEA in the 1940's. The PEA was, as it had always been,
unalterably opposed to paid boards and popular election of board members.[104] In 1946 it reaffirmed its support of the traditional method of
choosing members of the Board of Education: appointment by the
Mayor.[105] Then in 1950 the PEA took a new tack and began to press
for the appointment of a citizen advisory council which would propose
candidates for openings on the board, and from which the Mayor would
make his selection of board members.[106] The PEA also endeavored to
minimize the influence of city officials in the schools through the
formula of the concentration of power and authority in the City
School Superintendent and the Board of Superintendents. The PEA
fought for two decades for the so-called Superintendent's Bill, increasing the power of the City School Superintendent, which was finally
passed by the State Legislature and signed into law by Governor Dewey
in 1944.[107] It has continued, since 1944, to press for the still greater
concentration of responsibilities in the hands of the City School Superintendent and his colleagues.[108] In short, by a variety of means the PEA
attempted to make the city school system a "non-political agency," to
use the Sayre and Kaufman term for a governmental unit insulated by
rule or custom from intervention by party leaders or supervision by
elected officials.[109]

The PEA was not altogether unaware of the costs, in terms of good
government, of this development. From time to time it criticized the
"hypercentralization" of educational authority in the city, the im-
potence of local school boards, and the Board of Education's reluctance

[104] PEA, *Annual Report*, 1944, p. 7.
[105] *Ibid.*
[106] PEA, *Annual Report*, 1950, p. 6; *New York Times*, December 18, 1952;
PEA, *Up-Hill Journey . . . 1951–1953*, p. 8. In 1952 the Mayor's Management
Survey Committee threw its weight behind a similar proposal. New York City, Mayor's
Committee on Management Survey, *Modern Management for the City of New
York*, II, 498. The PEA had proposed something quite similar in 1922, in its
Meyer–Ullman bill.
[107] *New York Times*, January 13, 26, February 23, March 21, 1944; Cohen,
op. cit., pp. 135–37. La Guardia, despite his campaign pledge, opposed the bill.
Garrett, *op. cit.*, p. 374.
[108] PEA, *Annual Reports*, 1944–1945.
[109] *Op. cit.*, pp. 732–33. In pursuit of this objective the PEA is frequently
obliged by politicians themselves. Thus in 1945 the three Mayoralty candidates
—Newbold Morris, the No Deal candidate; Judge Jonah J. Goldstein, the Fusion,
Liberal, and Republican candidate; and William O'Dwyer, the Democratic and
American Labor Party candidate—speaking at the PEA, each pledged if elected to
protect the schools from all political interference. *New York Times*, October 23,
1945.

to take the public into its confidence.[110] And in 1949 the PEA added another to its long list of pioneering school experiments going back to 1896 and recreation centers, when, in cooperation with the Board of Education, Teachers College, and the Metropolitan School Study Council, it sponsored an experiment in local school government in the Bronx Park area of the city. The stated objectives of the new experiment, known as the Bronx Park Community Project, were to work out methods of decentralized school control, to increase citizen participation in the schools, and to adapt the Bronx Park schools to the needs of the community.[111] When the experiment ended three years later, an ingenious plan had been worked out by school authorities, community leaders, and the PEA. The plan called first for the creation of a special Bronx Park Community School District. Next, the citizenry of this district were to elect 108 "area representatives." Finally, the 108 area representatives in turn were to elect a "community school committee" of nine (a local "Board of Education"). The local school committee was granted limited advisory powers and the power to report back to the community.[112] It cannot be said of the Bronx Park Project that it was a great success. At the end of three years of study groups, community studies, lectures, and speeches, and two elections, little was changed. As the PEA's director commented drily: "The experiment was limited in scope because it had to be carried out without basic changes in the school administrative setup. . . ." [113]

School officials are resourceful in techniques of maintaining their essential autonomy, but something must also be said of the PEA's ambivalence towards the Bronx Park Project from the first. The PEA enjoyed privileged access to school officials. And, as Truman observes, once a political interest group has established access, it will exert tremendous efforts to retain the structural arrangements that have given it advantage.[114] It would appear that the PEA cried "hypercentraliza-

[110] *New York Times*, December 9, 1942, March 25, 1944, December 9, 1947; PEA, *Annual Reports*, 1944–1949.

[111] John W. Polley, Joseph G. Loretan, and Clara F. Blitzer, *Community Action for Education: The Story of the Bronx Park Community Project of New York City* (New York, 1953); New York City, Board of Education, *Our Public Schools, Report of the Superintendent of Schools, 1948–1950*, Part II, pp. 5–10; PEA, *Annual Reports*, 1949–1953.

[112] Polley, *et al.*, *op. cit.*, pp. 91–99; *New York Times*, February 18, 1952; August 23, 1953, Sec. IV; PEA, *Up-Hill Journey* . . . 1951–1953, pp. 10–11.

[113] PEA, *Up-Hill Journey* . . . 1951–1953, p. 9.

[114] David B. Truman, *The Governmental Process: Political Interests and Public Opinion* (New York, 1951), p. 327.

tion" and sponsored the Bronx Park Project to keep up its membership
in good standing as an organization dedicated to "good school administration," knowning full well that no real alterations in school structure
would ensue.

VII

The Public Education Association was born of protest. It was a product
of certain clubs organized to fight the evils of Tammany Hall. It reversed
its policy on becoming an independent organization. It freed itself from its
critical attitude to become the counsellor and friend of the Board [of Educa-
tion]; to become almost as its lay arm.[115]

Thus begins a PEA Golden Jubilee pamphlet. This is less a piece of
PEA history (the last two sentences, at any rate) than a description of
what the PEA was becoming in 1945.

One of the strategies of the contestants in New York City's political
contest, Sayre and Kaufman point out, is to shape the rules governing
the contest. In turn, the rules help shape the strategy and tactics of
the contestants.[116] So it was with the PEA. The main thrust of its governmental reform program was in the direction of enhancing the
power and influence of the City School Superintendent and the Board
of Superintendents, and minimizing the power and influence of the
Mayor, political leaders, and the Board of Education. Subsequently, the
PEA made the top-level school professionals the main target for the
exercise of its influence.

The high status of the PEA's officials, leaders, and fellow-travelers,
the prestige that went with such status, and the routinized set of relationships established over the years with the highest officials of the
school system ensured the PEA a measure of influence in the system.
This was considerably supplemented by the PEA's policy of close collaboration with school officials. The PEA threw its weight behind their
aspirations for expansion and autonomy and influenced its allies to do
the same. The PEA's formal and publicized objective continued to be
that of informing the public, and it continued to refer to itself as the
"watchdog" of the public schools; nevertheless in the 1940's, with the
notable exception of its state aid crusade, the PEA refrained from overt
criticism of the school system or school officials and from acts that
might have shown the school system or its leaders in an unfavorable

[115] Agnes E. Benedict, *Education on the March: Fifty Years with the Public
Education Association of New York City* (New York, 1945).

[116] *Op. cit.,* p. 112.

light.[117] But as the Board of Trustees was increased in size the leadership found it increasingly difficult to keep the new activists in line. The Advisory Council proved its utility here.

In 1944, at the behest of Mrs. Lewisohn and the Council, the board appointed an Evaluation Committee to help it make plans for the postwar period. The Committee was led by Dr. Eduard C. Lindeman; dominated by members of the Advisory Council. [118] It reported in 1945. "All of its deliberations seemed to stem," we are told, "from one important premise, namely that the Association, while retaining its 'watchdog' function should move steadily in the direction of closer collaboration with the Board of Education and the School and College Administrations." Its major recommendations were that the PEA should strive for an enlarged and more active membership and an increased budget, and that it should employ a professional educational director.[119]

The PEA was already moving in the directions recommended by the Lindeman Committee, whose report simply spurred it on. From 1941 to 1944 PEA expenditures rose from $8,000 to $15,500. By 1952–53 its budget was almost $57,000. Although the PEA remained heavily dependent on foundation grants, benefit art exhibits and theater parties, and large individual benefactions, a dramatic increase in membership helped contribute to its new affluence. In 1941 the PEA had 258 dues-paying members. In the wake of a membership drive in 1945, its Golden Jubilee year, membership rose to an all-time high of 2,000.[120] In the late forties membership levelled off at about 1,000, still a figure greater than it had ever known before 1945.

[117] The case in point here is the PEA's behavior during the Karelsen–La Guardia affair, the most publicized school explosion since the twenties. It was the United Parents Associations that rushed to Karelsen's support, while the PEA issued several guarded press releases and then discreetly called for an impartial investigation of the bitter charges and countercharges. *New York Times*, November 10, 21, December 12, 1945; *The Public and the Schools*, No. 447, October 30, 1945; No. 448, November 27, 1945; No. 449, December 31, 1945; PEA, *Annual Report*, 1946, p. 14.

[118] Minutes of a Joint Meeting of the Board of Trustees and Advisory Council of the PEA, June 1, 1944; *The Public and the Schools*, No. 446, May 29, 1945; PEA, *Fiftieth Annual Report*, 1945, p. 24. The Evaluation Committee included, in addition to Lindeman, William B. Nichols, several other members of the board, and also the following: Dr. Leona Baumgartner, Winifred Fisher, Lawrence K. Frank, Alice V. Keliher, William Heard Kilpatrick, V. T. Thayer, Caroline Zachry, Frederick Ernst, William Hannig, and William Jansen.

[119] Eduard C. Lindeman, "Evaluation Report," 1945, mimeographed, in the files of the PEA; also PEA, *Fiftieth Annual Report*, 1945, pp. 19–20.

[120] PEA, *Annual Financial Reports*, 1940–1953, typewritten, in the files of the PEA; PEA, *Annual Reports*, 1943–1953.

Mrs. Lewisohn's goal of encouraging greater participation on the part of PEA officials and members was also stimulated by the Lindeman report. In the late 1940's the PEA had more committees active than at any other time since 1911. Two of the committees, Childhood Education and Youth Education, were field committees. With their organization, the PEA once again, after an interlude also dating back to 1911, when it disbanded its old School Visiting Committee, had firsthand contact with the public schools.[121] In line also with the recommendations of the Evaluation Committee, Frederick T. Rope of the New York State Education Department was appointed director of the PEA.[122] He was shortly replaced by Frederick C. McLaughlin, an expert in school finance and administration, who ably filled the position until his resignation in late 1951. The PEA's return to a professional director and staff had little real significance. Mrs. Lewisohn, as chairman of the board, together with a handful of trustees, continued to run the PEA, but, after 1945, not with as free a hand as before.

Expansion brought both advantages and disadvantages to the PEA. It strengthened the PEA's program and influence, but it also raised the spectre of disunity. Throughout the forties there was a persistent undertow of irritation and dissatisfaction within the PEA over questions of program, strategy, and tactics. There was a serious breach between the old-guard oligarchy and a more militant group of newcomers. The old guard, led by Mrs. Lewisohn and backed by the Advisory Council, wished to move the PEA "steadily in the direction of closer collaboration" with school authorities. They thought primarily of protecting the PEA's established position and policies through informal contacts and concessions to school officials and intensive cultivation of civic and organizational leaders in the city—who, as group leaders and respected individuals, could influence important sectors of public thinking and activity. Enjoying their intimate role in school decision-making, and with the memory of Hylan, Walker, and O'Shea still green, they shunned engaging PEA in controversy—in a "watchdog" function. They preferred to work behind the scenes. On the other hand, a dissident group, composed of newly recruited activists led by Mrs. Richard Rodgers, wanted the PEA to emphasize, or live up to, its publicized image—that of watchdog of the schools. They thought of the PEA in terms of an

[121] The committees active throughout the latter part of the 1940's were the College, Childhood Education, Youth Education, School Administration and Legislation, Public Relations, and Modern School Building Needs.

[122] At this same time the PEA moved into new enlarged quarters in Freedom House, Wendell Wilkie Memorial Building, 20 West 40th St., which it still occupies.

aggressive pressure group, creating news, making its own issues, and appealing to public support as the chief means of influencing the decisions of school officials. The tension between the old guard and the dissidents eased during the Save the Schools crusade of 1947–48, but then rose to a new pitch of intensity as the PEA, in 1948, once again withdrew from publicized activity.

The gravity of the PEA's internal crisis was etched sharply in a report prepared in 1950 by the Public Relations Committee, one of its new committees.[123] The PEA's school crusade of 1947–48, the report began, awakened the citizens of the city to the basic facts of school needs and created tremendous potential support for the Association. Subsequently, the report continued, the PEA returned to an academic program of interest primarily to professionals. Now, the Public Relations Committee asserted, it felt itself increasingly impotent. The committee had two main criticisms of PEA policy and program. In the first place, it was difficult to relate the PEA's program to the educated layman's interest in his child or his society. It seemed to the committee that only a "connoisseur" of school affairs could take an intelligent interest in legal and fiscal questions and technical problems of school administration. In the second place, "it was difficult if not impossible to conduct a public relations program so long as we are not allowed to call honest attention to existing conditions in the schools."

The PEA was becoming "less and less a 'public' association and more and more a 'trade' association—a sort of seminar for educators." It seemed to the committee that the PEA owed a responsibility to the public: "We strongly urge that PEA return to its role as a citizen group." The past history of the PEA, the report continued, was richly suggestive of a program of more general interest: malpractices of administration, poor appointments, overcrowding and split sessions, inadequate teaching, bad plant, building blocks, and teacher-training deficiencies. Any one of these would lend itself to an effective public relations program "if a strong position were taken, backed by facts, and by a willingness to publicize the facts." The report concluded: "If the Trustees feel that PEA's program should be for educators and specialists—removed from the lay citizen and his interests and support—then there is no need for a Public Relations Committee."

After a thorough ventilation of this sharp critique, the Board of

[123] "Memorandum to the Board of Trustees from the Public Relations Committee, April 1950," mimeographed, in the files of the PEA. The report was signed by Mrs. Alvan T. Barach, Mrs. Donald Hunt, Mrs. Richard Plant, Mrs. Richard Rodgers, Mrs. Arthur Stanton, Jerry Mason, and Charles Schlaifer.

Trustees took steps to appease the insurgents.[124] Beginning in the fall
of 1950 and culminating in late 1953, the PEA assumed a more critical
stance toward the Board of Education and a more active, publicized
role in the city's political life. That there was continuing tension within
the PEA during this period, however, is implicitly revealed by the turnover of its professional directors. In 1951 Hubert C. Armstrong of
Harvard University's Graduate School of Education replaced Frederick
McLaughlin, who had held the post since 1946. In 1953 Armstrong was
replaced by Joseph P. Lyford, a community relations expert.[125]

The PEA's biannual report for the years 1951–1953, a 78-page
booklet significantly entitled *Up-Hill Journey*, is the main source of
documentary evidence for the PEA's shift in policy and strategy.[126]
Up-Hill Journey is in the best muckraking tradition. It provides a unique
glimpse of the PEA in a return to a role it forsook in the late 1920's,
that of "watchdog" of the public schools. *Up-Hill Journey* raked over
Mayor Impellitteri, the Board of Estimate, the Board of Education,
the Board of Examiners, the Superintendent, and the Board of Superintendents.

Mayor Impellitteri was attacked for his failure to reappoint James
Marshall to the Board of Education and Dean Harry Carman to the
Board of Higher Education, and for his failure to discuss school appointments with the PEA or with its Co-Ordinating Committee. The Board
of Estimate was attacked for its arbitrary school budget reductions and
for using a portion of state aid monies to service the municipal debt.
The Board of Education was accused of taking action at public meetings
on matters not on the calendar. The board was also criticized for faulty
planning and red tape in school construction, maintenance, and operation. Nor did the PEA neglect the school system's professional leaders.
Up-Hill Journey described the superintendent's annual report for 1952
as "designed chiefly to advertise the theories and successes of school
administration rather than to present a balanced report on strengths
and weaknesses." [127]

Up-Hill Journey also carried accounts of the investigations by several
of the PEA's committees. The Youth Education Committee reported
"glaring inadequacies" in high school guidance services, with teachers
"clearly unsuited" for the work often handling guidance responsibilities.
The Committee on Teacher Training criticized the testing methods and

---

[124] Minutes of the Board of Trustees of the PEA, April 13, May 4, 1950.
[125] McLaughlin returned as PEA director in September, 1960.
[126] PEA, *Up-Hill Journey* . . . 1951–1953, *passim*.
[127] *Ibid.*, pp. 12–18.

selection procedures of the Board of Examiners. It expressed curiosity as to what happened to those candidates who failed teacher-licencing examinations as well as to those who passed. It called attention to the fact that, although in theory misfits could be eliminated during the three-year probationary period, during the period 1948–1952 only seven teachers out of 7,000 holding temporary teacher licences failed to receive permanent tenure because of an unsatisfactory rating.[128]

Up-Hill Journey also carried a summary of the investigation, by the Childhood Education Committee, of the five "600" day public schools, the special schools set up to deal with the most seriously maladjusted children in the city public schools. The committee reported serious defects in almost every important administrative and educational phase of the "600" school program: inadequate curriculum, lack of properly trained teachers, inferior building facilities, and "ineffective administrative leadership of the program." The "600" schools were called "custodial" rather than "therapeutic." Finally, the Childhood Education Committee urged that the "600" school program not be extended, that no new "600" schools be established, and that "immediate steps be taken to correct the weakness in the present program." [129]

Up-Hill Journey was placed in the mail in late October 1953. The aftermath was not long in coming. School officials were displeased with the tone and content of the entire report, but it was the inclusion in the report of the excerpts from the "600" school investigation that triggered an explosion that rocked the PEA to its foundations. The PEA's leadership apparently realized that the "600" report was dynamite and took every precaution with it. The Board of Trustees carefully went over the report itself and appointed a special study committee of four to examine it further. Subsequently a digest of the report was sent to Superintendent Frank J. O'Brien of the Bureau of Child Guidance and the principals in charge of the "600" schools, while the report itself was given a "confidential" classification, the usual fate since the 1920's of a

---

128 *Ibid.*, pp. 12–15, 16, 17–18, 29–32, 37–40, 46–47. See also the *New York Times*, July 1, October 13, 1950, January 2, 17, April 17, 25, May 6, December 10, 1951, May 7, 1952; and *The Public and the Schools*, No. 484, March 13, 1953. I. L. Kandel called the PEA's Teacher-Training Committee report an "attack on the Board of Examiners." "The Selection of Teachers," *School and Society*, LXXV (May 17, 1952), 315. Interestingly, the PEA responded that its purpose was not to "attack" but "to venture a recommendation and raise a series of questions." *Up-Hill Journey . . . 1951–1953*, p. 47. Several years later, Dr. Harold Fields, an examiner for twenty years, also charged that the school system failed to weed out unfit teachers. *New York Times*, September 20, 1960.

129 PEA, *Up-Hill Journey . . . 1951–1953*, pp. 33–36; *New York World-Telegram and Sun*, October 26, 1953.

PEA study critical of one or another aspect of school practices or procedures.[130] No public release was made of the report except for the account that appeared in *Up-Hill Journey*, and that was subsequently summarized in the *World-Telegram and Sun*. So far as school officials were concerned, this was two places too many. Unaccustomed to having their programs and practices critically reviewed or evaluated, shock soon turned to outraged bluster.

When the news of official displeasure at Board of Education headquarters reached the PEA, there followed the most turbulent meeting in PEA history. PEA trustees were informed that at a meeting between top PEA officials and top school officials, City School Superintendent Jansen had questioned the competence of the Childhood Education Committee to pass judgment on "technical" matters, and that O'Brien had questioned whether non-professionals should or could evaluate any kind of professional work. One PEA trustee reported that the PEA was now *persona non grata* at the Board of Education. Lyford, who as director prepared *Up-Hill Journey*, Mrs. Shirley C. Fisk, chairman of the Childhood Education Committee, and Mrs. Trude Lash were ready to stand up to school officials, but they found little support. Mrs. Blitzer urged that the PEA cooperate with rather than criticize the Board of Education. Nichols, with several other longtime leaders of the PEA, expressed displeasure over the way the whole "600" affair had been handled. Finally, Mrs. Lewisohn said that Nichols, Lyford, and she would see Jansen and Andrew Clauson, President of the Board of Education, to discuss the whole controversy. The "600" report, she said, would be backed all the way.[131]

The meeting between the PEA and school leaders took place on November 10, 1953. The PEA agreed that in the future, PEA reports which were to be made public would be shown to Jansen before release. But, he was informed, "PEA will retain its autonomy." The School Superintendent would be given an opportunity to discuss, but not to alter, PEA reports. The PEA also agreed to send the full Childhood Education Committee report to the five "600" school principals with a covering letter "apologizing for the distorted impression" its biannual report gave because it omitted the good work done by the "600" schools.[132]

[130] *Ibid.*, p. 36.
[131] Minutes of the Board of Trustees of the PEA, November 5, 1953.
[132] Minutes of the Board of Trustees of the PEA, December 3, 1953. The PEA's evaluation of the "600" schools was later borne out by the city's Juvenile Delinquency Evaluation Project directed by Robert M. MacIver, and by the State Education Department investigation. *New York Times*, May 28, 1957, August 6, 1958.

In the midst of this furor, Mrs. Lewisohn called for yet another appraisal of the troubled PEA. A new Evaluation Committee was set up, this one headed by Dr. Alonzo Grace, Dean of the School of Education of New York University. The Grace Committee reported in 1954, recommending that the PEA create a special information and public relations program in order to reach a broader public, employ a professional educator with a national reputation as director, and enlarge the Board of Trustees. The committee also stated that:

the PEA must preserve its own independence and disinterestedness, while seeking as much as possible to cooperate with the administration and teaching personnel in the school system.[133]

The chief significance of the Grace Committee report lies not in its recommendations, which are strikingly similar to those of the 1945 evaluating committee, but in the fact that it was signed by most of the members of the PEA's Public Relations Committee. The Grace Committee reported early in 1954. In mid-1954 Lyford resigned. Later that year the Public Relations Committtee was disbanded.

The aforementioned events happened but recently. Perspective is still lacking. But all signs indicate that with the "600" affair, the PEA reached a critical point in its history. The Association affirmed that it would retain its "autonomy." Yet it is hard to avoid the conclusion that, at the first sound of fire, the Association abjectly surrendered to school officials. To protect its preferential access to the Board of Education, the Association made the humiliating journey to Canossa. The question was answered, at least for the time being, of whether the PEA would continue along the road of emphasizing a "watch-dog" function or move towards closer partnership with school officials.

VIII

On May 6, 1954, Mrs. Lewisohn excitedly confided to the Board of Trustees that she was working on a new project—a new attempt to bridge the gap between the citizens and the schools.[134] But Mrs. Lewisohn was not destined to elaborate her new plan. Six weeks later she was dead, killed in an auto accident.[135]

Mrs. Lewisohn has been described by those who knew her as a

---

[133] Alonzo G. Grace, "Evaluation Report," 1954, mimeographed, in the files of the PEA; also PEA, *Up-Hill Journey. Annual Report for the Year 1953-1954*, p. 6.
[134] Minutes of the Board of Trustees of the PEA, May 6, 1954.
[135] *New York Times*, June 15, 1954.

person dedicated to the cause of education.[136] In the content of her commitment, no less than in its intensity, she was so much like the avant-garde pedagogues of the 1920's. As a young woman she learned that the education of the "whole child" was the key to bringing up emotionally secure, happy, and creative children; that such an education also served the community by preventing social maladjustment; and that if the public schools were only taken out of the hands of elected officials and politicians all would be well. Evidently nothing happened after the 1920's to cause her to doubt these teachings of her youth. Mrs. Lewisohn turned away all adverse criticism of progressive education as the work of enemies of democracy and cranks. And the thought that the insulation of school officials from ordinary political processes might be a violation of democratic polity, or that the professional school hierarchy might be using the PEA to further its own ends, seemed not to have occurred to her. For Mrs. Lewisohn there was never anything to regret. Nothing was wrong with the public schools that money couldn't cure.

For more than fourteen years, since April 1940 when she announced her willingness to become the full-time director of the PEA, Mrs. Lewisohn had placed her energies, her wealth, and her personal influence at the service of the PEA. When she took personal charge of the PEA in 1940, it did not possess a corporal's guard of members; by 1954 it had a respectable 1,000 dues-paying members. In 1940 the PEA budget was less than $8,000; by 1954 it amounted to more than $45,000. In 1940 the PEA was becoming defunct as a civic group; by 1954 it had re-occupied its position as the city's leading civic group in the field of public education.

Under Mrs. Lewisohn's aegis, the PEA, with great skill, furthered its aim of divorcing politics from the schools, strengthened its ties with school leaders, and successfully defended progressive education. As an illustration of how skillful PEA leadership in the 1940's and early 1950's was, compare the PEA's fortunes with those of an organization with which it had the closest links—the Progressive Education Association. Of course, the political problems both organizations faced were of a different magnitude, but they both aimed to preserve themselves, to defend the same educational practices and procedures, and by the same strategies. In the 1940's and 1950's it was all downhill for the Progressive Education Association. In 1954 it was dying. (It finally expired in 1955.) In 1954 the PEA was approaching another peak in its fortunes.

[136] William B. Nichols, Interview, September 29, 1959, New York City; Frederick C. McLaughlin, Interview, August 26, 1958, New York City; *New York Times*, "Margaret Lewisohn," June 16, 1954, ed.

Chapter 7

RETROSPECT AND CONCLUSIONS

THE PEA WAS THE OFFSPRING of the great New York City reform movement of 1894. Leading reformers of the day presided at its birth; considerations of political strategy dictated its organization. The PEA was the child of Nicholas Murray Butler and Good Government Club E. It was brought into existence to serve a specific purpose: to advance the cause of reform in the city public school system. Like the broader reform movement of which it was part and parcel, public school reform had its social phase. The East Side, the home of myriads of immigrants from Southern and Eastern Europe and the burgeoning tenement slum, was the major focus of city reform efforts; it was the major focus of school reform. The school's functions were to be expanded in order to help the city cope with that "peculiar environment" below Fourteenth Street. And like the broader reform movement, school reform had its good government phase. Tammany Hall was to be ousted from its strongholds in city school government, the machinery of school administration was to be reformed along the lines of efficiency and expertise, the schools were to be "taken out of politics." The PEA's basic core policy subsequently became oriented to extending and expanding these concepts.

I

The PEA's school reform program has always reflected ideas inherited from earlier periods, changes in the city, and changes in broader currents of progressivism. Its career epitomizes the changing content and meaning of progressive education.

The PEA was brought into existence to help the reform party shape a school system to cope with the urgent and baffling problems posed

213

by the East Side. In pursuit of this objective, in the decade 1895–1905, the PEA took its tone from Mrs. Schuyler Van Rensselaer and the University Settlement, its chief source of inspiration and ideas in these early years. It advocated a school reform program which was limited, specific, and immediately attainable: kindergartens; manual training; school playgrounds; clean, safe, and attractive school buildings; "a seat for every child"; and, the frontier of *fin dè siecle* school reform, the transformation of the public schools into neighborhood social centers. This school reform program clearly was part and parcel of contemporary "municipalism," clearly part of the broader movement of social reform and social amelioration of the time. It was also progressive education. Taken up by the City Club, the Good Government Clubs, the Citizens Union, and then Tammany Hall, endorsed by the electorate in municipal elections, progressive education won a series of quick victories. "The silly old regime," Jacob Riis announced in 1902, "is dead." [1] Now progressives in New York set to work to build a new regime.

During the Progressive Era the influx of new immigrants to the United States reached flood tide. By 1910, of New York City's population of some 4.8 million, 1.9 million were foreign-born, another 1.8 million were children of foreign-born parents. They spilled out of lower Manhattan into Brooklyn and the Bronx. The East Side, Julia Richman explained to a group of school reformers in 1907, was no longer a geographic concept but a sociological concept—wherever you had immigrants or housing problems you had the East Side. [2] The immigrant and the slum seemed to be everywhere. And in the early 1900's New Yorkers were less confident of the city's ability to cope with the "immigrant problem" than they had been in the 1890's. The more despairing of the adult immigrant and the more despairing of city conditions they became, the more intense became their concern for the "tenement child" and the more radical became their demands upon the public school. In one of the seminal works of progressive education, *Poverty*, Robert Hunter demanded that the public school "take as its responsibility, the entire problem of child life and master it." [3] Social workers, Social Gospelers, child labor reformers, municipal reformers, professors of education, progressives of every stripe agreed. The PEA, under Mrs. Van Rensselaer's successor, Mrs. Miriam Sutro Price, and then under Charles P. Howland, fell into line also. The PEA's chief objective in the period from 1905 to 1917 became, indeed its chief objective in the period from

[1] *The Battle with the Slum* (New York, 1902), p. 347.
[2] "Opportunities of the East Side," *The School Journal*, LXXIII (1907), 406.
[3] New York, 1904, p. 209.

1905 to the present has been, to convince the city school system why it should, and to demonstrate how it could, "take as its responsibility, the entire problem of child life and master it."

In retrospect the years 1905–1914 were essentially transitional years for the PEA. It had outgrown its earlier, "incipient" phase of organization; it was not yet in the "organizational" phase. In this decade the PEA's self-image was still that of an auxiliary to other reformist groups in the city: the organized charities, the Association of Neighborhood Workers, the New York Child Labor Committee, and the National Society for the Promotion of Industrial Education. Active in many areas —compulsory education, vocational education, vocational guidance, school lunches, sex education, the education of mentally and physically defective children, and the visiting teacher—its activities were largely haphazard and ineffective. By 1915, however, the PEA had taken on a radically different look.

The reorganization of 1911–1914, carried out by Charles P. Howland with the aid of Abraham Flexner and others, against a background of mounting public school crisis in the city, was the decisive event. The PEA emerged from the reorganization with its elite character fixed, its long-range goal formulated. Its new inner circle of leadership comprised a small group of eminent corporation lawyers, respected financiers and merchants, philanthropy-minded society women, and executives of a handful of the new foundations: the Carnegie Foundation, the Russell Sage Foundation, the New York Foundation, and the Rockefeller Foundation. The basic school objective on behalf of which the leadership lent their names, and on behalf of which they gave their money, was revealed when Harriet Johnson, in the course of a description of the Association's visiting teacher project, explained:

> The work of the visiting teacher is not radically new, but rather a very natural extension of the public schools as a child welfare agency, adapted to meet the social needs of children in a large municipal organization.[4]

Here was the culmination of trends which began with the opening of the schools for purposes other than formal instruction. Here was the signpost for the future. The die was cast. The PEA's long-range goal would undergo no substantial change. There would be further developments, to be sure. But these would be little more than modifications of the basic goal: the transformation of the public schools into child welfare agencies. The reorganization completed, its basic goal decided

[4] *The Visiting Teacher in New York City* (New York, 1916), p. 1.

upon, now the PEA was ready to take charge of the growing impatience of progressive elements in New York with half-measures of school reform that seemed to be getting nowhere, and to direct it into the proper channels. In 1915 the PEA assumed civic leadership of the drive to install the Gary School Plan in the city. The Gary Plan was the apogee of pre-World War I progressive education.

For the PEA the Gary School War of 1915–1917 was a decisive event: decisive in the sense that it determined that the PEA would go ahead with its basic core objective of transforming the schools into effective centers of social service. True, the Gary Plan had been rejected by the electorate. But there would be no turning back. Not when the whole enlightened, progressive community of New York City and beyond—the community represented by the Mitchel Administration, the *New York Times*, the *New Republic*, the *Survey*, the Woman's Municipal League, and such—was behind the school reform blueprint that embodied this objective. The Gary School War was decisive also in the sense that it determined the main strategy the PEA would subsequently use to forward its basic school objectives. The Gary affair taught the PEA a lesson: so far as winning any large public support was concerned, reform of school methods and curricula had gone about as far as it could go. In the future, to gain its school reform ends, the PEA would rely upon the methods of demonstration and publicity, behind-the-scenes bargaining, and the quiet, intensive education of the city's lay influentials, organizational leaders, and school officials in pedagogical progressivism.

The 1920's were a period of serious division and divisiveness in American life.[5] In a quest for security and homogeneity some Americans, the one-hundred-per-centers and the Ku Kluxers, turned to the techniques of restriction, repression, and violence. Other, equally perplexed and fearful Americans, including an important segment of progressive thinkers and progressive organizations, turned to behavior control through the more benign techniques of psychology and the social sciences as the key to a new integration. As usual, all paths led progressives to the schools. "There is no panacea for all our social ills," *The Public and the Schools* admitted in 1919. But "many of us believe that through a wholesome education from the earliest years the irreducible minimum of social maladjustment can be secured." "Our motto is,"

[5] Arthur Mann, *La Guardia: A Fighter Against His Times, 1882–1933* (Philadelphia, 1959), pp. 181–83; William E. Leuchtenburg, *The Perils of Prosperity, 1914–1932* (Chicago, 1958); Henry F. May, "Shifting Perspectives on the 1920's," *Mississippi Valley Historical Review*, XLIII (December, 1956), 425–26.

the PEA's newsletter declared, "Never Reform To-Morrow What You Can Educate To-Day." [6] These words struck the keynote of the PEA's school reform program in the 1920's.

If the public school were to prevent "delinquency and other social problems," then non-promotion, failure, and truancy, deemed by psychologists, social workers, and leaders in the field of mental hygiene to be critical factors in the etiology of delinquency, would at all costs have to be prevented. The solution was to minimize courses of study, eliminate academic standards or set them at the lowest level, and educate the public school staff in the principles and precepts of mental hygiene. This cluster of assumptions and convictions was translated into action in two extremely significant PEA projects in the 1920's: its nationwide visiting teacher demonstration and its Little Red School House experiment. The chief objective of the PEA's visiting teacher demonstration, which found the PEA in alliance with the Commonwealth Fund, the National Committee for Mental Hygiene, and the New York School of Social Work, was to educate the regular public school staff in the "social point of view." The chief objective of the Little Red School House experiment, which found the PEA in alliance with the Progressive Education Association, was to incorporate mental health principles into public school curricula and teaching methods. The alliance between the PEA and the Progressive Education Association is noteworthy. The Little Red School House was the embodiment of philanthropy and social work, non-education by traditional definition, or custom, and as such limited in its acceptability. But the progressive thinkers were not to fail the progressive activists. Progressive education and the Progressive Education Association, with its rhetoric of high principle, provided the PEA with the perfect legitimation of its social work ethos.[7]

In the mid-1930's, with the adoption of the "activity program" by the New York City school system, the PEA's decades-old dream of the public school as a legatee institution was nearer fulfillment than ever before. The PEA was not very active in the thirties. But in the thirties it was not necessary for the PEA to be very active. It had done its promotional spade work well in the previous decade. And now there was the Great Depression. With its burden of confusion, insecurity, and

[6] No. 13, February 22, 1919.

[7] It might prove interesting to analyze progressive education in terms of symbols and propaganda techniques. See the discussion of the uses of propaganda in Harold D. Lasswell, *Politics: Who Gets What, When, How* (New York, 1936), Chap. II.

demoralization, the depression gave great impetus to the growing recognition of the responsibility of the school for the "whole child." Now more than ever, as *The Public and the Schools* pointed out in the winter of 1932, was the time to turn to the schools.[8] The State Education Department, the *New York Times*, the New York City Board of Education, the United Parents Associations, the bar and the bench, Teachers College, and New York University concurred; city school officials would not have inaugurated the activity program unless assured of strong civic support.

In the 1940's and 1950's, now under Mrs. Samuel A. Lewisohn's astute leadership, the PEA devoted itself to educating a new generation of civic leaders and school officials in the city in progressive education, to forwarding its unique modification of the activity program—the All-Day Neighborhood School, and to fighting off counterprogressive educational tendencies. The influx of Negroes and Puerto Ricans into the city beginning in the 1940's and the increasingly serious problems these newest immigrants posed as their numbers swelled, as well as the juvenile unrest and tension accompanying World War II and the Korean War, helped keep strong the PEA's conception of the school as a legatee institution and strategic center for the prevention of juvenile delinquency and social maladjustment.

II

Like the progressives described by Mowry,[9] the PEA's leaders see themselves as wholly divorced from any special interest. The PEA presents itself to the public as an altruistic group of citizens who "have no axe to grind . . . no vested interest," who have "only one goal—to see that the best possible education is offered to the youth of the City of New York." The bulk of the evidence says otherwise. It has represented a single class interest. Over the years the PEA has taken its tone from a small, relatively homogeneous inner core leadership of wealthy, upper-class, well-educated Yankee Protestants and Germans Jews. Typically, the PEA's leadership has been composed of a coalition of Wall Street lawyers and financiers, business leaders and merchants, and philanthropy-minded socialites, with a small sprinkling of civic leaders and professional educators. And special note should be made of the PEA's longtime alliance with the philanthropic foundations. The New

[8] No. 345, November 22, 1932.
[9] George E. Mowry, *The California Progressives* (Berkeley, Calif., 1951), pp. 87–104.

York Foundation, the Hofheimer Foundation, the Rockefeller Foundation, and others have provided the PEA with its most reliable source of income and enabled it to maintain its elite character.[10]

The PEA is a Manhattan-bound, "elite organization of limited membership," as Sayre and Kaufman succinctly characterize it.[11] Its leaders, with very few exceptions, neither sent their children to the public schools nor attended public schools themselves. The PEA is then a surrogate group twice removed from the groups directly affected by its school policy. True, the PEA's Board of Trustees and Executive Committee were expanded somewhat in the forties and fifties to include representatives of the city's newly rising middle classes, children of the old Jewish immigration for the most part, and to include more representatives of the city's most important civic, social, and philanthropic agencies. But this has not significantly altered the PEA's elite character, its oligarchic leadership structure, or its special interests.

Reflecting the makeup of its leadership and constituency, the PEA has, at least since the early twenties, demonstrated a persistent concern with such issues as academic freedom and separation of church and state. But these have been incidental to the PEA's main concern. The PEA's main concern, at least since 1914 or 1915, has been the preservation of social order and social stability. The PEA's basic concern is manifest in Jane Culbert's assertion, in the early 1920's, that the public school is "the logical agency from which to work for the prevention of juvenile delinquency and other social problems." [12] And again, twenty years later, by Mrs. Samuel A. Lewisohn:

the only possible solution of the problem [of juvenile delinquency] is prevention and the logical center of prevention is the public school, in which we taxpayers already have so large an investment.[13]

True, as Howard Nudd pointed out in 1937, on the occasion of the PEA's "School Child and Crime Prevention" conference, the PEA has

[10] E.g., in the period 1909–1949 the New York Foundation made grants to the PEA of $106,200. The foundation's appropriations in this period totalled about $7,891,000. New York Foundation, *Forty Year Report, 1909–1949* (New York, 1950), pp. 50, 55, 63.

[11] Wallace S. Sayre and Herbert Kaufman, *Governing New York City: Politics in the Metropolis* (New York, 1960), p. 284. In its leadership structure, as well as its constituency, the PEA is very similar to the Citizens Unions, the Men's and Women's City Clubs, and the newer Citizens Committee for Children. *Ibid.*, pp. 497–508. See also the depiction of the PEA by former PEA director John Bartky in his *Social Issues in Education* (Boston, 1963), p. 280.

[12] "The Visiting Teacher," *The Annals*, XCVIII (November, 1921), 82.

[13] *New York Times*, November 1, 1942, Sec. IV.

always been concerned with the prevention of delinquency. This was one of the chief reasons why the PEA fought for more and decent schools, playgrounds, and school social centers in its first decade. But there is a difference. In these early years the PEA's school reform program could be characterized as reformist and relatively indifferent to the school's role in the formal instruction of children. By 1914, however, the PEA's reformist bent had been sloughed off, while its program had become no longer merely indifferent to the school's role in the training of intelligence, but hostile to it. Since 1914 priority in the PEA's school reform program has gone to social adjustment and emotional development. In pursuit of these vague complexities the PEA has urged the city to adopt a school program best described, to borrow a phrase from Jacques Barzun, as "education without instruction." [14] It is questionable whether this is "the best possible education" for the great numbers of lower-class or underprivileged children who attend the public schools of New York City.

More is involved, however, in the PEA's basic school program than a quest for security. Compassion is present also. The PEA suffered for the child laborer, the mentally disabled child and the physically disabled child, the undernourished and the underprivileged child, the unhappy and the "unadjusted" child. It turned to the schools as strategic centers for humanitarian effort. Finally, there is the utopian element in the PEA's activities which must be reckoned with. The chiliastic hopes that once characterized movements for social reform in the Progressive Era, hopes thought by many to have perished with World War I, have survived in education. Through progressive education the PEA hopes to secure the final abolition of unhappiness; the final extirpation of all social problems. The public school, Elisabeth Irwin declared, has this much to gain from an alliance with mental hygiene: "happiness in education need not remain a pious hope but may be translated into a technique of living." [15] Through progressive education "every child [is] to become a happy, well adjusted, productive individual and a valuable social asset." [16] "No Child Need Be Lost," the title of a magazine article describing a mental hygiene project with five-year-olds at the PEA's All-Day Neighborhood School experiment, well summarizes the PEA's point of view.[17] If this utopian side of the PEA's character is overlooked,

[14] *The House of Intellect* (New York, 1959), p. 88.
[15] Elisabeth Irwin and Louis Marks, *Fitting the School to the Child* (New York, 1924), p. 131
[16] *The Public and the Schools*, No. 320, December 11, 1930.
[17] Evelyn Seeley, "No Child Need Be Lost," *Survey Graphic*, XXXVI (November, 1947), 579–83.

then the consistency with which the PEA has, at least since 1915, pursued its fundamental objectives cannot be understood.

One of the PEA's proudest legacies from the past is its concern with child welfare: its role in getting all the children into the public school; its role in broadening the community's sense of responsibility toward the child in the school. As La Guardia's Board of Education put it, "All the Children Means All the Children." [18] But the success of the PEA in succoring the "underdog" and in helping the city to cope with its social problems has helped the PEA to ignore, or conceal from itself, the adverse consequences in terms of the ideal of equality of educational opportunity inherent in the program it has been urging upon the city for the past half-century.

If these conclusions are valid, then both the praise and the reproach belong not alone to the PEA but to an influential and strategic element of progressivism in general. For the PEA has always kept the best progressive company.

III

From the circumstances of its birth the PEA inherited a heterogeneous legacy. The PEA was born of protest against a rigid and formalistic conception of public education: school organization, curricula, and procedures were to be reformed along progressive lines. But the PEA was also born of protest against favoritism, incompetency, and inefficiency in the management of the city school system. The Department of Education, no less than the other branches of city government, was to be reformed: merit was to be extended; efficiency procedures installed; and the power and authority of the School Superintendents, the "Board of Experts," enhanced. By means of this reform formula the schools were to be "taken out of politics." The informed public and the bright light of publicity would constitute the ambient air in which the schools would be kept accountable to the people. This school reform program is clearly recognizable as the application to the city school system of contemporary municipal progressivism; the movement for reform of the management of the city schools clearly was part of the general political reform movement of the time.

More was involved in the New York City school reform movement of 1894, however, than questions of progressive theory or a concern for

[18] Rebecca B. Rankin, ed., *New York Advancing. World's Fair Edition: The Result of Five Years of Progressive Administration in the City of New York, F. H. La Guardia, Mayor* (New York, 1939), pp. 141ff.

scientific school management. Also importantly involved were questions of group power and group influence: the control of educational policy-making in the city was one of the chief stakes for which Butler and the other leaders of the school reform movement were playing. Tammany Hall, the symbol of venality and turbulence; Tammany Hall, the symbol of vulgar, ignorant, vaguely menacing Irish Catholic dominance in city politics, was to be ousted from its strongholds in the city school system and, so far as possible, kept out. Control of the schools was to be lodged in the hands of the "good people" or the "better element," the city's educated, cultured, civic-minded community, the old stock Yankee Protestants and the wealthy, assimilated German Jews (just then beginning to join their uptown, Christian neighbors in reform efforts), or their spokesmen or representatives—the "experts." The good government credo was admirably suited to serve this group interest.

The issue then was not one of keeping all "politics" out of the public schools. The reformers' objective was to keep all politics except their own kind of politics out of the schools. Their slogan, "Take the schools out of politics," was an effective battle cry with which to influence the Mayor's selection of school board members, reduce the influence of the city's political leaders, and enhance their own influence. As a hedge against the propensity of the city electorate to vote Democratic, the reform element, where the city school system was concerned, sacrificed their cherished principle of "home rule" and insisted that the state remain a privileged participant in city school affairs. In short, the question of school administration was more than a question of administrative theory. It was a question of political strategy; a question of the distribution of power and influence. Nicholas Murray Butler and the reform party understood this full well.

Thus the PEA inherited a program in which the demands of good government and the demands of group strategy were held in a more or less precarious state of tension. Up to 1917, the PEA's program and policy left this tension undisturbed. After 1917, however, the balance began to be weighed down in favor of considerations of group strategy: what is good for the PEA "improves" the school system; good politics became good government. And, paradoxically, this occurred even while the Association, with some critical exceptions to be sure, was to cling to the orthodox good government tenets of the 1890's.

Until 1917 the PEA played its part in stimulating public interest in the schools with vigor and robustness. Until 1917, thanks to the PEA and thanks also, of course, to other reform groups in the city, notably the Citizens Union, questions of public school policy were very much in the public eye, while the reformers scored, with the aid of a large and interested public, school victory after school victory. But the Gary School War of 1915–1917 and the rejection of the Gary Plan by the city in the mayoralty election of 1917 taught the PEA a lesson: never again to let matters of school policy in the sphere of curriculum practices and procedures be decided by elected officials, political leaders, or the electorate. After the Gary affair the PEA's strategy became to limit the size of the interested public on questions of school policy to school officials, lay influentials, and key civic organizations, and to wage intensive propaganda for further school innovations within this limited public.[19] The Association's strategy was remarkably successful. In the period 1917–1954, except in the area of school finance, in New York City no great questions of educational policy were brought before the public for debate. The case in point is the inauguration of the "activity program" in 1935.[20]

The PEA kept alive the legacy of the founders somewhat longer regarding the school "watchdog" ideal. For instance, in the 1920's— a decade of Tammany monopoly of the city government—school appointments in the city and school building conditions were more exposed to public scrutiny than at any other time in the city's history, thanks chiefly to the PEA and the *New York Times*. But by the end of the decade the PEA found itself caught on the horns of a dilemma: its efforts to influence the school system from the outside, via well-publicized watchdog tactics, and its efforts to influence the schools from the inside, via behind-the-scenes negotiations with school officials, seemed to be mutually exclusive. Thus, on the one hand, thanks largely to the PEA's muckraking, the value of the public schools as spoils of politics had become, by the end of the twenties, distinctly limited, and the schools had been kept largely free of the scandals which tainted Mayor Walker's administration. But, on the other hand, the PEA's open and continuous opposition to the city administration and leaders of the

[19] The strategy and tactics employed by the PEA in pursuit of its objectives are not peculiar to the PEA but are drawn from the armory of techniques available to interest groups concerned with influencing governmental decisions in general. For the techniques of influence, see Sayre and Kaufman, *op. cit.*, Chap. XIII; David B. Truman, *The Governmental Process: Political Interests and Public Opinion* (New York, 1951), Part III; Henry W. Ehrmann, ed., *Interests Groups on Four Continents* (Pittsburgh, 1958); V. O. Key, Jr., *Politics, Parties, and Pressure Groups* (New York, 1952), Part I.

[20] However, it should be pointed out that the PEA's *The Status of the Public School Education of Negro and Puerto Rican Children in New York City* (1955) brought into the open an issue which has since then dominated the educational scene in the city.

school system cost it dearly in terms of influence. By the end of the decade the Association found its access to school leaders severely restricted, the success of its basic school objectives jeopardized, and its very existence threatened by the rise of the United Parents Associations, which did not have the PEA's record of political partisanship to contend against.

By 1930 the PEA found itself faced with the choice of expanding its base of support significantly, reducing its aspirations for leadership in the city in the field of school policy-making, or de-emphasizing its role as civic "watchdog" of the schools. The PEA decided to retain its elite character and de-emphasize its muckraking activities. To enhance its position in the school system and to protect and further its basic school objectives, the PEA decided to pursue a strategy of cultivating ties with school officialdom. This strategy of collaboration has been the one the PEA has largely followed since 1930. Although the PEA continued to refer to itself as the "watchdog" of the public schools, after 1930 the light of publicity on the school system became weak indeed. This was the burden of the critique of the PEA by its own Public Relations Committee in 1950. And this is the context—of the abandonment by the PEA of the progressive ideal of the informed and interested public—in which the Association's proposals for school management reform must be appraised.[21]

Between 1896 and 1922 the PEA was largely indifferent to the question of good school government or proper city–school relations. Through the administrations of Mayors Strong, Van Wyck, Low, McClellan, Gaynor, Mitchel, and through Mayor Hylan's first term in office, the PEA was largely satisfied with the City School Law and with its own role and position in the city school system. And when the Association did intervene in the sphere of school law reform, as it did in 1896 and again in 1917, its view of city school government and its reform program

[21] At that, the PEA has been through the years a more constant friend of the ideal of the interested and informed public, as well as a more constant friend of the "watchdog" ideal, than any other reform or civic group in the city. The City Club and the Citizens Union, for instance, set a precedent for the PEA's strategy and tactics. Furthermore, characteristically, reform or civic groups never considered it necessary to watchdog reform or fusion administrations. The fate of the City Affairs Committee is palpable evidence: "It died," said the Reverend John Haynes Holmes, "because in the administration of La Guardia, we felt that our cause had been largely won." Holmes to Charles Garrett, April 6, 1954, quoted in Garrett, *The La Guardia Years: Machine and Reform Politics in New York City* (New York, 1961), p. 314. With the inauguration of La Guardia, the PEA's hard line toward the city administration and city school officials would have automatically softened. The PEA simply decided that in the future it would pursue the soft line no matter who the occupant of City Hall was.

were in a direct line with progressive trends. Then, in 1922, after Hylan's re-election as Mayor, the PEA stepped forward as the most vociferous and zealous protagonist, at least among the city's non-governmental groups, of the "removal of the schools from politics and politics from the schools." Since the early 1920's the PEA has sought to remove the schools from "politics" by every means available to a skilled and resourceful participant in New York City politics: appeals to the electorate; raising the "hue and cry"; appeals to the Governor and state legislature for school investigations; and, especially in recent decades, proposals to change the city school law in the direction of enhancing the authority of the school professionals. In this struggle to make the schools a "nonpolitical" agency, the PEA has been joined by reformist groups like the Civil Service Reform Association, the *New York Times*, and, of course, the organized school groups themselves. The PEA and its allies have been remarkably effective in winning acceptance of their reform proposals. Through the years control of school affairs has been lodged more and more in the hands of the school experts. This harmonizes neatly with the PEA's own interests. Working behind the scenes with school leaders, throwing its weight behind their aspirations for expansion and autonomy and influencing its allies to do the same, and using its resources of experience and prestige with great skill, the PEA has become an intimate part of the machinery of educational decision-making in the city, especially in the crucial sphere of curriculum policy, and has established itself as the city's dominant non-governmental group, exclusive of the religious groups, in the public school field.

But the consequences of the acceptance in the city of the notion that the public schools should be a "nonpolitical" agency for the ideal of good government have been, to say the least, mixed. The consequences have included not only an increase in conventional rationality and competence in the administration of the schools, but the creation of a school "island of power." The school bureaucracy, deeply involved in questions of policy and value, has won a peculiar freedom from democratic controls. "The two school boards [the Board of Education and the Board of Superintendents] each operate in an environment of low visibility approaching complete privacy." [22] It is only during budget sessions that school officials are reminded that ordinary democratic political procedures apply to them also:

For the moment, the isolation and autonomy of the school system is pierced and its officials are held accountable for some of their actions to someone other than themselves. But the moment is brief and the scrutiny

[22] Sayre and Kaufman, *op. cit.*, pp. 280–81.

is inescapably limited in scope. The self-governing status of the school officialdom is only mildly impaired.[23]

Although it is difficult to avoid the conclusion that to maintain or increase its own influence ranks first among the hierarchy of values which have spurred the PEA to insist so zealously, and for so long, that the schools must be taken out of politics, there is something else importantly involved here. Implicit in the PEA's core program for city school reform is a certain conception of the city population and its political leaders, a conception indissolubly tied to a complex of antipathetic feelings and attitudes evoked by Tammany Hall.

Tammany's power and influence in the city have grown and waned with the political tide since Tweed days, and its style and method of operation have been equally inconsistent. Yet through all its cycles, the opprobrium which was Tammany's in the days of Lord Bryce and E. L. Godkin has endured in the hearts and minds of New York's civic leaders from that day to this. A chronic distrust of the city electorate, their elected officials, and political leaders, runs through the PEA's program and strategy for city school reform. This, too, is a legacy from progressivism.

To summarize, study of the PEA leads strongly to the conclusion that progressive education is simply one facet of American progressivism writ large; that, like the broader progressive movement, progressive education has an unsavory side as well as a beneficent side; that educational policy is inevitably value-loaded, and that in any appraisal of public school reform a critical question to ask is: "Whose interests are served?"; and, finally, that the processes whereby public school policy is made are deserving of the most careful scrutiny. The PEA likes to be thought above politics. Regardless of the impression it prefers to foster, the PEA has been throughout its career deeply involved in politics. Its chief *raison d'être* has been to influence the decisions of a department of the New York City government—the Department of Education.[24] In its efforts to influence decision-making in the New York City school system, the PEA has employed all the strategies and tactics available to a skilled and resourceful interest group in city politics. It has been remarkably successful in winning acceptance of its basic pro-

---

[23] *Ibid.*, p. 283.
[24] The PEA obviously falls into the class of groups defined by Sayre and Kaufman as having "functional" interests; groups characterized by high persistence and frequent intervention in a relatively narrow range of governmental decisions. *Ibid.*, pp. 76–80.

gram. Clearly, decision-making in public education reflects something more than the unalloyed wisdom of school officials (or school officials and professors of education). That the role and influence of the PEA and its allies is largely ignored by both defenders and critics of New York's public school system highlights the need for a more sophisticated analysis of the political matrix, or "field of forces," in which educational policy in the city is formulated.[25]

[25] A tentative description of the "field of forces" is set forth in Wallace S. Sayre, "Additional Observations on the Study of Administration," *Teachers College Record*, LX (November, 1958), 73–76.

NOTE ON SOURCES

In the preparation of this study I have read all documents in the files of the Public Education Association, 20 W. 40th St., New York, as of the spring of 1959. I have also read all books and pamphlets published by the PEA during the period 1895–1959 and all books and articles published during this same period by PEA officials or activists that might possibly have been relevant to this study.

The files of the PEA were indispensable. Among other materials, the files contain Minutes of the Board of Trustees, 1910–1917, incomplete; Minutes of the Board of Trustees, 1921–1959, complete; Minutes of the Executive Committee, 1910–1917, incomplete; Minutes of the Executive Committee, 1921–1959, complete; and Minutes of various PEA committees, 1910–1959, incomplete. "The PEA at Work," a mimeographed resumé submitted annually to the Board of Trustees by the PEA's director during the years 1932–1940, was helpful as were the several scrapbook collections of newspaper clippings, pamphlets, leaflets, and letters. The "Margaret S. Lewisohn" folders, containing copies or drafts of many of Mrs. Lewisohn's speeches and articles, were very useful, especially for the 1940's and 1950's. The collection of manuscript materials on the Chelsea School Project, later renamed the All-Day Neighborhood School Project, also in the possession of the PEA, contributed greatly to this study.

The PEA's published *Annual Reports*, 1895–1913 and 1943 to date, were invaluable. For a more limited span of years, the same might be said of the *PEA Bulletin*, which made its appearance in October 1912. Thirty-one numbers of the *Bulletin* appeared, irregularly, before it ceased publication in September 1918. Indispensable, of course, was the PEA's official organ, *The Public and the Schools*, which first appeared on November 23, 1918, and has appeared irregularly ever since (weekly until October 1925; bi-weekly to October 1928; monthly to October 1929; and bi-weekly to October 1931, when it became a monthly again). The PEA has probably the only complete file of *The Public and the Schools*.

The collection of manuscript materials concerning the PEA's Little Red School House experiment, in the possession of the Little Red School

House, 196 Bleecker Street, New York, added significantly to this study. Other extremely important manuscript or document collections are: "Citizens Committee of One Hundred on Public School Reform," and "The Fight for School Reform in the City of New York: 1889–1896," both at Teachers College Library, Teachers College, Columbia University; and "The School War: Correspondence in Re New York Schools, 1895–1897," and Nicholas Murray Butler Papers, both in Columbiana Collection, Low Memorial Library, Columbia University. The Minutes of the Women's Conference of the Society for Ethical Culture, March 29, 1893, to April 24, 1899, incomplete, at New York Ethical Culture Society headquarters, 2 W. 64th St., New York, helped shed light on the PEA's earliest years.

The collected papers of Howard Nudd, in the possession of Howard Nudd, Jr., of Foxboro, Mass., as well as those of Charles P. Howland, in Historical Manuscripts Collection, Sterling Memorial Library, Yale University, proved empty of value for this study. The collection of papers relating to Mrs. Schuyler Van Rensselaer's life and career, in the possession of Mr. George Griswold, Jr., of New York City is, unfortunately, not yet available for research. Nor are the important archives of the City and Country School in New York open for study. The Abraham Flexner Papers, in the possession of the Library of Congress, are closed until July 1, 1965. The James B. Reynolds Correspondence, at the University Settlement Society, was out on loan and unavailable during the entire time this study was in preparation.

Marilyn D. Ranschburg's "An Appraisal of the Impact of the Public Education Association on New York City's Schools, 1953–1961," a Master of Science in Education thesis (Queens College, New York, 1962), is lacking in sophistication, but covers the main facts on the PEA's more recent program of activities.

For biographical data on PEA activists, *Who's Who in New York, Who's Who in America, Dictionary of American Biography, National Cyclopedia of American Biography, Who's Who in American Jewry, New York Social Register*, and the news columns and obituary columns of the *New York Times* were indispensable, especially for the men. There is a great gap on the reference shelves with regard to women which, hopefully, Radcliffe College's forthcoming *Notable American Women, 1607–1950*, will fill. In the meantime the aforementioned works, together with *American Women, Woman's Who's Who in America, 1914–1915*, and Mrs. John A. Logan, *The Part Taken by Women in American History* (1912) had to suffice. The latter two volumes especially must be used with caution.

The interviews and manuscripts gathered by the Oral History Project at Columbia University contain much helpful material. The "Reminiscences" of the following New Yorkers were most pertinent: Charles C. Burlingham, Louis H. Pink, William A. Prendergast, Henry W. Bruere, William H. Allen, William Jay Schieffelin, and Genevieve B. Earle. The "Reminiscences" of Jeremiah T. Mahoney, a member of the Board of Education during the La Guardia years, are not yet open for research.

The *New York Times*, because of its published index (beginning in 1912) and because it took a special interest in the PEA, was most valuable. The interest of periodicals in civic reform or educational reform has varied through the years. In general, most helpful for this study were the following: *Educational Review, School and Society, Outlook, World's Work, Municipal Affairs, The Annals, Survey, New Republic,* and *Progressive Education.*

For perspective and background, the activities of the PEA's allies and rivals, and sometime allies, sometime rivals, had to be kept in mind. At different stages of the PEA's career, the annual reports and other relevant publications of the following organizations were consulted: University Settlement Society, College Settlements Association, Ethical Culture Society, Children's Aid Society, City Club, Citizens Union, Woman's Municipal League, Women's City Club, United Parents Associations, Citizens Committee on Children, Rockefeller Foundation, New York Foundation, General Education Board, and Commonwealth Fund.

A few books have been especially valuable for this study. Lawrence A. Cremin's pioneering *The Transformation of the School: Progressivism in American Education, 1876–1957* (1961) places progressive education squarely in the context of American progressivism writ large. A splendid guide through the history, politics, and government of New York City is Wallace S. Sayre and Herbert Kaufman's *Governing New York City: Politics in the Metropolis* (1960). Many insights were gleaned from David S. Truman's *The Governmental Process: Political Interests and Public Opinion* (1951). In addition to the excellence of their texts, the Cremin and Truman volumes contain very useful bibliographical essays. A comprehensive, annotated bibliography on all aspects of New York City politics and government can be found in *Governing New York City: Politics in the Metropolis* following each chapter.

Of the recent and relevant literature, Robert H. Beck pays homage to Felix Adler, Caroline Pratt, and Margaret Naumberg in "Progressive Education and American Progressivism," *Teachers College Record,* LX (1958–59), 77–89, 129–137, 198–208. Raymond Callahan's *Education and the Cult of Efficiency* (1962) is an interesting history of school administrative reform. Timothy L. Smith, "Progressivism in American Education, 1880–1900," *Harvard Educational Review,* XXXI (Spring, 1961), 168–193, is a thorough survey. Rush Welter's *Popular Education and Democratic Thought in America* (1962) is a welcome addition to the scholarly literature in American educational history. The chapter on education in Blake McKelvey's *The Urbanization of America, 1860–1915* (1963) is insightful.

A comprehensive history of New York City politics is sadly needed. Dealing with a limited period, Charles Garrett's *The La Guardia Years: Machine and Reform Politics in New York City* (1961), while helpful, is written from the orthodox good government point of view. Arthur Mann's *La Guardia: A Fighter Against His Times, 1882–1933* (1959) is a model of sophisticated political and social history. The brief but admirable Frank J. Munger and Ralph A. Straetz's *New York Politics* (1960) brings New York City (and New York State) politics up to date. The best overview of the political history of New York City is still Allan Nevins and John A. Krout, eds., *The Greater City: New York, 1898–1948* (1948).

For New York State history and politics, David M. Ellis and others, *A Short History of New York State* (1957), is a superb example of history writing as a joint enterprise. Lynton K. Caldwell's *The Government and Administration of New York* (1954) is excellent in its specialized field. Warren Moscow, *Politics in the Empire State* (1948), deals extensively with many aspects of New York government and politics. So does Allan Nevins, *Herbert H. Lehman and His Era* (1963).

A history of public education in the Greater City is lacking. In the meantime three books should be consulted: A. Emerson Palmer, *The New York Public School* (1905); and New York City, Board of Education, City School Superintendent, *The First Fifty Years, 1898–1948: Fifieth Annual Report*, are the only comprehensive histories of the New York public schools extant; Rose Naomi Cohen's *The Financial Control of Education in the Consolidated City of New York* (1948) is very good on the interrelationships among the school system, the city government, and the state in the period 1898–1944. The annual reports of the City Superintendent of Schools are, of course, indispensable. H. H. Horner, ed., *Education in New York State, 1784–1954* (1954), is a prosaic survey.

The history of progressive education is still very much the historians' unfinished business. Although the following works neglect public school reform, they contain extremely valuable and often brilliant insights into the progressive mind: Richard Hofstadter, *The Age of Reform: From Bryan to F.D.R.* (1955); Eric F. Goldman, *Rendezvous with Destiny* (1952); Morton G. White, *The Revolt Against Formalism* (1949); Louis Hartz, *The Liberal Tradition in America* (1954); Arthur Ekirch, Jr., *The Decline of American Liberalism* (1956); George E. Mowry, *The California Progressives* (1952); and Rowland Berthoff, "The American Social Order: A Conservative Hypothesis," *American Historical Review*, LXV (April, 1960), 495–513.

Since American urban history is still a largely unexplored field, perhaps it is not surprising that progressive education has been overlooked. Among the better of the urban histories are Charles Hirschfeld, *Baltimore, 1870–1900* (1941), which never forgets education, and Blake McKelvey, *Rochester: The Quest for Quality, 1890–1925* (1956), the concluding volume of McKelvey's three-volume history of Rochester, which likewise emphasizes school developments. And not to be overlooked is McKelvey's *Urbanization of America, 1860–1915*. There are pertinent insights for the historian of education in Arthur M. Schlesinger, "The City in American History," *Mississippi Valley Historical Review*, XXVII (1940), 43–66, and W. Stull Holt, "Some Consequences of the Urban Movement in American History," *Pacific Historical Review*, XXII (November, 1953), 337–51. Anyone digging into urban history should first read the warnings in R. Richard Wohl, "Urbanism, Urbanity, and the Historian," *University of Kansas City Review*, XXII (Autumn, 1955), 53–61; and Eric E. Lampard, "American Historians and the Study of Urbanization," *American Historical Review*, LXVII (October, 1961), 49–61. Roy F. Nichols' call for a more sophisticated analysis of political behavior on the part of historians is also pertinent: "Unfinished Business," *Pennsylvania Magazine of History and Biography*, LXXII (April, 1948), 109–115.

Political scientists have been almost as neglectful of the public school field as historians. Arthur F. Bentley's 1908 classic, *The Process of Government: A Study of Social Pressures,* called for a more sophisticated approach to the matter of decision-making in public education (pp. 377–78). Yet it is only within the last decade or so that political scientists and students of public administration have begun to treat seriously the question of the politics and government of public education. Oliver Cromwell Carmichael, Jr., *New York Establishes a State University* (1955), is a unique case study of educational policy-making at the state level. Theodore Powell, *The School Bus Law: A Case Study in Education, Religion, and Politics* (1960), deals with a hot issue in Connecticut educational politics. Robert A. Dahl's brilliant *Who Governs? Democracy and Power in an American City* (1961) contains a brief but exemplary chapter on the politics of education in New Haven (Chap. XI). Two older studies are still notable excursions into city–school relationships: Nelson B. Henry and Jerome G. Kerwin, *Schools and City Government* (1938), and John A. Vieg, *The Government of Education in Metropolitan Chicago* (1939).

Wallace S. Sayre, "Additional Observations on the Study of Administration," *Teachers College Record,* LX (November, 1958), 73–76, is the most incisive analysis in print of the realities of educational organization. No other book or article attempts anything like Thomas H. Eliot's "Toward an Understanding of Public School Politics," *American Political Science Review,* XIII (December, 1959), 1032–51, reprinted as "Public School Politics" in Edward C. Banfield, ed., *Urban Government: A Reader in Administration and Politics* (1959), 515–535. The new "Economics and Politics of Public Education Series" of Syracuse University Press apparently intends to make up for the past years of neglect. For example, see Roscoe C. Martin, *Government and the Suburban School* (1962), and Stephen K. Bailey and others, *Schoolmen and Politics: A Study of State Aid to Education in the Northeast* (1961).

Educationists have not been slow to see that public education is a field for the play of diverse pressures and interests but, with some notable exceptions, have been unable to view this fact with any kind of detachment. The literature is mostly of the exposé variety; e.g., Bruce Raup, *Education and Organized Interests in America* (1936); Bessie Louise Pierce, *Citizens Organizations and the Civic Training of Youth* (1933); and William Gellerman, *The American Legion as Educator* (1938). *Who Runs Our Schools* (1958), by Harvard sociologist Neal Gross, belongs in this category. In a class by itself is George S. Counts, *School and Society in Chicago* (1928), the first major study of the relations between interest groups and educational policy-making. Two volumes in the Teachers College, Columbia University, series "Contributions to Education" are, despite their titles, quite informative: Walter Albert Jessup, *The Social Factors Affecting Special Supervision in the Public Schools of the United States* (1911); and Philo T. Farnsworth, *Adaptation Processes in Public School Systems* (1940).

Merle Curti's classic, *The Social Ideas of American Educators* (1935), effectively examines the social and political functions of public education. And V. O. Key, Jr., *Politics, Parties, and Pressure Groups* (1952), contains a unique discussion of the political function of education (Chap. XXIV).

But on the whole, sociologists have been quicker than historians or political scientists to see education in its broadest implications. The place to start is Orville G. Brim, Jr., *Sociology and the Field of Education* (1958), an excellent review of sociological research in the field of education in the '40's and '50's. The following works should also be consulted: A. H. Halsey, Jean Floud, and C. Arnold Anderson, *Education, Economy and Society: A Reader in the Sociology of Education* (1961); H. Otto Dahlke, *Values in Culture and Classroom* (1958); and Robert J. Havighurst and Bernice L. Neugarten, *Society and Education* (1957).

The presuppositions and underlying assumptions of the theory and practice of American public education need to be thoroughly reexamined. Contemporary critiques of the social sciences should be the models for such reappraisal; e.g., Bernard C. Crick, *The American Science of Politics: Its Origins and Conditions* (1959); Leon Bramson, *The Political Context of Sociology* (1961); Loren Baritz, *The Servants of Power: A History of the Use of Social Science in American Industry* (1960); and Thomas S. Szasz, *The Myth of Mental Illness* (1961). An older study, extremely relevant for the student of education, is C. Wright Mills, "The Professional Ideology of Social Pathologists," *American Journal of Sociology*, XIL (September, 1943), 165–180.

CHAPTER 1, 1880-1895

Dealing with the general aspects of the Progressive Movement, among the best works are Harold U. Faulkner, *Politics, Reform, and Expansion, 1890–1900* (1959); Samuel P. Hays, *The Response to Industrialism, 1885– 1914* (1957); and Henry Steele Commager, *The American Mind: An Interpretation of American Thought and Culture since the 1880's* (1952). Still helpful are three older volumes in the History of American Life Series: Allan Nevins, *The Emergence of Modern America, 1865–1878* (1932); Arthur M. Schlesinger, *The Rise of the City, 1878–1898* (1933); and Harold U. Faulkner, *The Quest for Social Justice, 1898–1914* (1931).

No really good study of the crusade for municipal reform exists. The oft-cited Clifford W. Patton, *The Battle for Municipal Reform: Mobilization and Attack, 1875–1900* (1940), is disappointly slight. Frank Mann Stewart, *A Half Century of Municipal Reform: The National Municipal League* (1950), Chaps. I–II, adds little. But contemporary sources are plentiful. Among the most important are William Howe Tolman, *Municipal Reform Movements in the United States* (1895); Albert Shaw, "Our Civic Renaissance," *Review of Reviews*, XI (April, 1898), 415–27; "The National Conference for Good City Government," *The Annals*, IV (May, 1894), 850–56; Herbert Welch, "A Definite Step Towards Municipal Reform," *Forum*, XVII (March, 1894), 181–84; and Alfred R. Conkling, *City Government in the United States* (1894). Banfield's criticism of the good government ideology, *Urban Government* (pp. 209–12), is relevant here.

An objective history of Tammany Hall is needed. The standard sources, Gustavus Myers, *The History of Tammany Hall* (1917), and Morris R.

Werner, *Tammany Hall* (1928), paint the Organization in hues too black. For the New York City reform movement of 1894, the place to start is the compendious *Triumph of Reform: A History of the Great Political Revolution, November Sixth, Eighteen Hundred and Ninety-Four* (1895). William H. Tolman, *Handbook of Social Reform for New York* (1894), and William H. Tolman and William I. Hull, *Handbook of Sociological Information with Especial Reference to New York City* (1894), should also be consulted. New York City politics in the 1890's and later are described in many excellent and famous memoirs. Charles H. Parkhurst has two books: *Our Fight with Tammany* (1895), and *My Forty Years in New York* (1923). Not to be overlooked are Theodore Roosevelt, *An Autobiography* (1913); Everett P. Wheeler, *Sixty Years of American Life* (1917); Charles Edward Russell, *Bare Hands and Stone Walls: The Confessions of a Sideline Reformer* (1933); Richard B. Hovey, *John Jay Chapman—An American Mind* (1959); Richard Welling, *As the Twig Is Bent* (1942); Gregory Weinstein, *The Ardent Eighties and After* (1949); and, of course, Lincoln Steffens' masterful *Autobiography* (1931).

The schools do not operate in a political or social vacuum, regardless of the impression they have sometimes given. The full-blown anti-Tammany sentiment of the "better element" in New York in the nineties is epitomized in the following articles by E. L. Godkin: "The Problems of Municipal Government," *The Annals*, IV (May, 1894), 857–82; "Criminal Politics," *North American Review*, CL (June, 1890), 706–10; and "New York City," *Encyclopaedia Britannica* (1881), p. 462. Allan Nevins, *The Evening Post: A Century of Journalism* (1922), Chap. XXII, is relevant, as is Nevins' *Abram S. Hewitt, With Some Account of Peter Cooper* (1935), pp. 510–515. *The Religious Condition of New York City: Addresses Made at a Christian Conference Held in Chickering Hall, New York City, December 3, 4, and 5, 1888* (1888) is an important document in the history of anti-Irish Catholic nativism.

The role of the public schools as a factor in the anti-Catholic feeling rife in New York in the late 1880's is documented in the aforementioned *The Religious Condition of New York City*. Important here, and for many other aspects of New York's political and social life, are two memoirs by a leading figure in reform Protestantism, the Rev. William S. Rainsford: *The Story of a Varied Life* (1922) and *A Preacher's Story of His Work* (1904).

For the milieu of city problems to which progressive education was the response, there is a profusion of sources. Among the most important are: New York State Legislature, Assembly, *Report of the Tenement House Committee* (1895); Robert W. DeForest and Lawrence Veiller, eds., *The Tenement House Problem* (two vols., 1903); and Kate Holladay Claghorn, "The Foreign Immigrant in New York City," U.S. Industrial Commission, *Report of the Industrial Commission on Immigration and Education* (19 vols., 1900–1902), Vol. XV, Chap. IX. Moses Rischin, *The Promised City: New York's Jews, 1870–1914* (1962) is a fine contribution to New York's social history, and supports the thesis that the city's newest immigrants and the East Side became the major focus of city reform efforts. Roy Lubove's admirable *The Progressives and the Slums: Tenement House Reform in*

New York City, 1890–1917 (1962) contains valuable insights and also supports this thesis. Robert H. Bremner's unique study, *From the Depths: The Discovery of Poverty in the United States* (1956), is also relevant.

The Jewish "invasion" of the public schools of the city was the subject of much remark around the turn of the century by Jews and non-Jews alike: James K. Paulding, "Educational Influences: New York," in Charles S. Bernheimer, ed., *The Russian Jew in the United States* (1905), pp. 184–99; Abraham Cahan, "The Russian Jew in the United States," *ibid.*, pp. 32–33; Hutchins Hapgood, *The Spirit of the Ghetto* (1902), pp. 9, 36–37; Jacob Riis, *The Children of the Poor* (1892), p. 47; Claghorn, "The Foreign Immigrant in New York City," p. 478; and Myra Kelly's sweet, fictional account, *Little Citizens: The Humors of School Life* (1903). Estimates of the number of Jewish children in the city's public schools are found in Paulding, "Educational Influences: New York," p. 185; and Alexander M. Dushkin, *Jewish Education in New York City* (1918), p. 150. See also United States Government, Reports of the Immigration Commission, 1907–1910, *The Children of Immigrants in Schools* (5 vols., 1911), Vol. IV, pp. 610–15.

Of seminal importance for all aspects of reform in New York City are two books by Jacob A. Riis: *How the Other Half Lives* (1890), and *The Children of the Poor* (1892). Not to be overlooked is Riis's "Special Needs of the Poor in New York," *Forum*, XIV (December, 1892), 492–502. *The Making of an American* (1904), Riis's autobiography, is also important.

A skilful depiction of Riis's life and work is Lubove's *The Progressives and the Slums*, Chap. III. Consult also the guardedly critical Emma Louise Ware, *Jacob A. Riis: Police Reporter, Reformer, Useful Citizen* (1939). John Haynes Holmes, "Jacob August Riis," *Dictionary of American Biography*, XV (1935), and Steffens, *Autobiography*, pp. 203–07, are worshipful. For a contemporary critique of Riis, consult the review of *How the Other Half Lives* in *The Critic*, XIV (December 27, 1890), 332.

Other expressions of hostility towards the new immigrant appear in *The Religious Condition of New York City* and George Haven Putnam, *Memories of a Publisher, 1865–1915* (1915), p. 169. The attitude of German Jews in New York to their East European co-religionist in the 1880's and 1890's may be sampled in Arthur Garfield Hays, *City Lawyer* (1942), p. 24. Consult also Rischin, *The Promised City*, Chap. VI; Oscar Handlin, *Adventure in Freedom: Three Hundred Years of Jewish Life in America* (1954), pp. 95, 103–106, 143–147; and Samuel Joseph, *History of the Baron De Hirsch Fund: The Americanization of the Jewish Immigrant* (1935).

Indispensable for the general background out of which school reform emerges is John Higham, *Strangers in the Land: Patterns of American Nativism, 1860–1925* (1955). Maldwyn Allen Jones' thesis in *American Immigration* (1960) that "immigration . . . has been the most pervasive influence in her [America's] development" supports my own. But in his otherwise excellent history Jones overlooks the impact of immigration on American public education.

The buoyant optimism with which pioneer settlement residents greeted the city's newcomers in the nineties emerges clearly in Gaylord S. White,

"The Social Settlement after Twenty-Five Years," *Harvard Theological Review*, IV (January, 1911), 47–70; Helen Rand Thayer, "Blazing the Settlement Trail," *Smith Alumnae Quarterly*, II (April, 1911), 130–37; and Jane E. Robbins, "First Years at College Settlement," *Survey*, XXVII (February 24, 1912), 1800–02.

For the social settlements and public school reform three memoirs are germane: Mary Kingsbury Simkhovitch, *Neighborhood, My Story of Greenwich House* (1938); and Lillian Wald's *The House on Henry Street* (1915), and *Windows on Henry Street* (1934). Two older volumes by Robert A. Woods and Albert J. Kennedy are still standard: *The Settlement Horizon* (1922) and *A Handbook of Social Settlements* (1911). Morris I. Berger's "The Immigrant, the Settlement, and the Public School" (Teachers College, Columbia University, 1956) is also helpful.

The response of the public schools to the challenge of the city ran remarkably parallel to that of the liberalized Protestant churches. In fact, the schools became "socialized" somewhat later than did the church. The relationship between the two movements, progressive education and the Social Gospel, bears further investigation. In this connection, see the following works by the Reverend William S. Rainsford: *The Story of a Varied Life*, Chap. XVI; *A Preacher's Story of His Work*, pp. 118, 126, 151, 165–67. An early formulation of progressive education may be found in Richard T. Ely, "The Needs of the City," in *National Needs and Remedies: The Discussions of the General Christian Conference Held in Boston, Mass., December 4th, 5th and 6th, 1889, Under the Auspices and Direction of the Evangelical Alliance for the United States* (1890), pp. 51–52. Basic for the emergence of reform Protestantism are three works: Aaron I. Abell, *The Urban Impact on American Protestantism, 1865–1900* (1943); Charles H. Hopkins, *The Rise of the Social Gospel in American Protestantism, 1865–1919* (1940); and Henry F. May, *Protestant Churches and Industrial America* (1949). These studies should be taken as models for social and intellectual histories of education.

The annual reports and other publications of the Children's Aid Society, the New York Kindergarten Association, the Industrial Education Association, and the Association for Improving the Condition of the Poor reveal the organized charities in New York City as an important source of progressive education. See, for example, Children's Aid Society, *The Children's Aid Society of New York: Its History, Plans and Results* (1893); also Children's Aid Society, *The Crusade for Children: A Review of Child Life in New York During 75 Years, 1853–1928* (1928). *The Dangerous Classes of New York* (1872), by Charles Loring Brace, the founder of the Children's Aid Society, and *The Jukes* (1877), by Robert L. Dugdale, are pertinent and provocative. Felix Adler's pamphlet, *The Workingman's School* (1881), and Ethical Culture Society, *Report of the Workingman's School* (1880), are revealing. Lawrence A. Cremin, David A. Shannon, and Mary Evelyn Townsend, *A History of Teachers College, Columbia University* (1954), Chaps. I–III, examines the strands of philanthropy, social service, and professionalism that went into the preparation of the new teacher.

CHAPTER 2, 1895-1905

The political history of New York City at this time is sketched well in Nevins and Krout, eds., *The Greater City: New York, 1898–1948*, pp. 61–73; and Garrett, *The La Guardia Years: Machine and Reform Politics in New York*, pp. 38–41. Most of the memoirs cited in Chap. I are appropriate here. For New York State politics, see Ellis and others, *A Short History of New York State*, Chap. XXIX.

There is no good, general study of the contribution of the "new woman" to the civic renaissance. Mann, *Yankee Reformers in the Urban Age*, Chap. IX, is valuable for Boston. A recent survey of the emergence of the American woman into public life in general is Eleanor Flexner, *Century of Struggle* (1959). One has to depend mostly on biographies, memoirs, and contemporary sources; e.g., Maud Nathan, *Once Upon a Time and Today* (1933); Abbie Graham, *Grace H. Dodge: Merchant of Dreams* (1926); William Rhinelander Stewart, *The Philanthropic Work of Josephine Shaw Lowell* (1911); Mrs. Joseph P. Mumford, "The Relation of Women to Municipal Reform," *Proceedings*, National Conference for Good City Government (1894), pp. 134–43; Lillian W. Betts, "The New Woman," *Outlook*, LII (October 12, 1895), 587; Tolman, *Municipal Reform Movements in the United States*, Part IV.

A full-scale biography of Nicholas Murray Butler is still wanting, as is a study of Butler as public school reformer. Richard Whittemore, "Nicholas Murray Butler and Public Education, 1862–1911" (Teachers College, Columbia University, 1962), is a start. Butler's *Across the Busy Years: Recollections and Reflections* (two vols., 1939) is of special value. Cremin and others, *A History of Teachers College, Columbia University* (pp. 18–27) provides a good overview of Butler as school reformer. So does Richard Whittemore, "Nicholas Murray Butler and the Teaching Profession," *History of Education Quarterly*, I (September, 1961), 22–35. Horace Coon takes a sceptical view of "Nicholas the Miraculous" in *Columbia, Colossus on the Hudson* (1947), pp. 101–04.

The PEA's *Annual Reports*, 1895–1905, are an important source of information about early Association policy and program. So are the publications of Good Government Club E for the years 1894–1896. These sources were supplemented by Mariana Griswold Van Rensselaer, "The Public Education Association of New York," *Educational Review*, XVI (October, 1898), 209–19, and by two articles by Lillian W. Betts: "Women and Public Education," *Outlook*, LIII (March 21, 1896), 512; and "In the Interests of Education," *ibid.*, LI (June 1, 1895), 911. The PEA's ties with the University Settlement Society are documented in the *Annual Reports* of the latter for the years 1894–1898. The PEA's ties with the New York Ethical Culture Society are documented in the Minutes of the Women's Conference of the New York Society for Ethical Culture, 1893–1897, incomplete, at Ethical Culture Society headquarters, 2 W. 64th St., New York. Also the *Annual Reports* of the Women's Conference of the New

York Society for Ethical Culture, 1894–1897, and Women's Conference of the New York Society for Ethical Culture, *65 Years of Study, Service, Friendship: 1893–1958* (1958), p. 3.

When publisher Henry Holt asked Mrs. Van Rensselaer to write her memoirs, she refused, saying, "What could I possibly have to say?" Holt, *Garrulities of an Octogenarian Editor* (1923), p. 433. It is regrettable that Mr. Holt could not persuade Mrs. Van Rensselaer to change her mind. But Mrs. Van Rensselaer wrote much. For her social thought consult "Places in New York," *Century*, LIII (February, 1897), 511–15; "People in New York, *ibid.*, XLIX (February, 1895), 534–48; and "Midsummer in New York," *ibid.*, LXIII (August, 1901), 483–501. Not to be overlooked are Mrs. Van Rensselaer's short stories about life on the East Side: "The Lustigs" and "Corinna's Fiammetta," both in her collection of short stories, *One Man Who Was Content* (1897). Mrs. Van Rensselaer's educational views are stated in "Our Public Schools: A Reply," *North American Review*, CLXIX (July, 1899), 77–89; and "The Public Education Association of New York," *Educational Review*; and Conference of Eastern Public Education Associations, *Bulletin No. 1* (1902), pp. 3–6. For Mrs. Van Rensselaer's life, the best source is Talbot Faulkner Hamlin, "Mariana Griswold Van Rensselaer," *Dictionary of American Biography*, XIX (1936).

Manuscript and document collections were invaluable for the "school war." Teachers College Library, Teachers College, Columbia University, has "The Fight for School Reform in the City of New York: Documents, 1889–1896"; and "Citizens Committee of One Hundred on Public School Reform." Columbiana Collection, Low Memorial Library, Columbia University, has "The School War: Correspondence in Re New York Schools, 1895–1897"; and the Nicholas Murray Butler Papers.

Although the view is a lop-sided one, the "school war" can best be followed in the editorial pages of the *Educational Review* for 1895 and 1896. The *Outlook* also paid a good deal of attention to the struggle. The *Times, Herald, Tribune,* and *World* were also helpful. For the upstate slant on the school war, see Harold F. Gosnell, *Boss Platt and His New York Machine* (1924), pp. 230–31; Louis J. Lang, comp. and ed., *The Autobiography of Thomas Collier Platt* (1916), Chap. XV; De Alva Stanwood Alexander, *Four Famous New Yorkers: The Political Careers of Cleveland, Platt, Hill and Roosevelt* (1923), pp. 230–36. Robert McElroy, *Levi Parsons Morton: Banker, Diplomat and Statesman* (1930), pp. 244–45, exaggerates Governor Morton's role in the fight for school reform.

One of the important manifestations of political progressivism in the late nineties was in the field of city school management. An early, classic statement of the orthodox good government view is Joseph Mayer Rice, *The Public School System of the United States* (1894), pp. 26–27. Also Truman A. DeWeese, "Better City School Administration," *Educational Review*, XX (June, 1920), 61–71; and Dorman B. Eaton, *The Government of Municipalities* (1899), pp. 398–407. A less doctrinaire position is taken by James T. Young, "The Administration of City Schools," *The Annals*, XV (March, 1900), 171–85.

Municipal Government (1910), by Columbia University professor and

City Club activist Frank J. Goodnow, urges a pragmatic approach to the entire question of city governmental reform. Another Columbia University professor, Frank Rollins, in *School Administration in Municipal Government* (1902), applies this approach to the schools. The school reform program of the New York "reform party" can be reconstructed if Rollins' work is placed next to a work which carries the imprimatur of Nicholas Murray Butler: Samuel Train Dutton and David Snedden, *The Administration of Public Education in the United States* (1908), Chaps. VIII–IX. The political reality of the "rules of the game" and the political reality involved in demands for changing same are brilliantly analyzed in Sayre and Kaufman, *Governing New York City: Politics in the Metropolis*, pp. 105–08. Godkin, "New York City," views legislative enactments with considerable sophistication, or candor. The history of the New York City School Law before 1896 is detailed in Palmer, *The New York Public School*, Chaps. XIX–XX, and Cohen, *The Financial Control of Education in the Consolidated City of New York*, Chap. I.

That the school awakening of the mid-nineties was nationwide is indicated by Robert L. McCaul, "Dewey's Chicago," *The School Review*, LXVII (Summer, 1959), 268–73; McKelvey, *Rochester: The Quest for Quality, 1890–1925*, pp. 74, 82–85, 192–204; his *Urbanization of America, 1860–1915*, Chap. XII; Hirschfeld's *Baltimore, 1870–1900*, Chap. III; and Bayrd Still, *Milwaukee: The History of a City* (1948), p. 416.

The "socialized" school was one of the progressives' key answers to the urban welfare problem. Of special importance for New York City are Citizens Union, *More and Better Schools* (1897); and "The New York Campaign. What Reform Has Done for Children," *Outlook*, LXXV (September 26, 1903), 201–02. Two works by Jacob Riis describing reform accomplishments in New York are virtually treatises on public school reform: *The Battle with the Slum* (1900) and *A Ten Years War* (1902). Consult also Mrs. Vladimir Simkhovitch, "The Enlarged Function of the Public School," *Proceedings*, National Conference of Charities and Correction (1904); Winifred Buck, "Work and Play in the Public Schools," *Outlook*, LXXX (July 22, 1905), 725–32; and Lillian W. Betts, "The Child Out of School Hours," *ibid.*, LXXV (September 26, 1903), 209–16.

Of broader scope, two extremely important books by Charles Zueblin, *American Municipal Progress* (1902) and *American Civic Progress* (1905), locate the extension of school activities squarely within the context of contemporary municipal reform. See also the following: Frederick C. Howe, *The City, the Hope of Democracy* (1906), pp. 230–32, 283; Milo Roy Maltbie, "Municipal Functions: A Study of the Development, Scope and Tendency of Municipal Socialism," *Municipal Affairs*, II (December, 1898), 565–57, 683–84; Charles R. Woodruff, "Expansion of Municipal Activities," *Arena*, XXXIII (January, 1905), 132; and Edgar J. Levey, "Municipal Socialism and Its Economic Limitations," *Political Science Quarterly*, XXIV (March, 1909), 35–36. A fine recent appraisal of "municipalism" in general is Roy Lubove, "The Twentieth Century City: The Progressive as Municipal Reformer," *Mid-America*, XLI (October, 1959), 195–209.

For contemporary educational progressivism in the major cities of

Europe, an important source of influence upon American school reformers, there are a handful of important books: Robert Archey Woods, *English Social Movements* (1891); Albert Shaw, *Municipal Government in Continental Europe* (1895), the same author's *Municipal Government in Great Britain* (1904); and two books by Frederick C. Howe: *The British City: The Beginnings of Democracy* (1907) and *European Cities at Work* (1913). Arthur Mann's perceptive "British Social Thought and American Reformers of the Progressive Era," *Mississsippi Valley Historical Review*, XLII (March, 1956), 685–87, contains much of relevance for the student of education.

The Conference of Eastern Public Education Associations is best approached through the *Annual Reports* of the PEA of New York, 1898–1905; the *Annual Reports* of the PEA of Philadelphia, for the same years; and Mrs. William E. D. Scott's "The Aims and Work of the Conference of Public Education Associations," *The Annals*, XXV (April, 1905), 371–374. Not to be overlooked is the important issue of *The School Journal*, LXXIV (April 20, 1907). Contemporary sources describing the aims and work of civic groups in the public school field are plentiful. Among the most enlightening are Zueblin, *American Municipal Progress*; Elsa Denison, *Helping School Children: Suggestions for Efficient Cooperation with the Public Schools* (1912); and Ella Lyman Cabot, *Volunteer Help to the Schools* (1914). Lewis R. Harley, *A Generation of Progress in Our Public Schools, 1881–1912: A History of the Public Education Association of Philadelphia* (1912), indicates that the PEA of Philadelphia was quite influential in that city. An Englishman comments on the role of citizen groups in United States educational reform in the late 1890's in H. Thistleton Mark, *Individuality and the Moral Aim in American Education* (1901), pp. 203–05, 210–23. The larger context of the rise of citizen action groups in America at the turn of the century may be sampled in "The Activities of Civic Organizations for Municipal Improvement in the United States," a symposium in *The Annals*, XXV (April, 1905); and Clinton Rogers Woodruff, "The Nationalization of Municipal Movements," *ibid.*, XXI (1903), 252–60.

CHAPTER 3, 1905-1917

There is a large and still growing literature on pre-World War I progressivism. For purposes of this study, the following works were most helpful: Hofstadter, *The Age of Reform*; George E. Mowry, *The Era of Theodore Roosevelt, 1900–1912* (1958); and the older Faulkner, *The Quest for Social Justice, 1898–1914*. Henry May, *The End of American Innocence: The First Years of Our Own Time, 1912–1917* (1959), examines a brief but important span of years with great virtuosity. Berthoff's "The American Social Order: A Conservative Hypothesis" is highly suggestive. Of contemporary sources the following are germane: Benjamin Parke DeWitt, *The Progressive Movement* (1915); William Allen White, *The Old Order Changeth: A View of American Democracy* (1910); and Walter E. Weyl, *The New Democracy* (1912).

Indispensable for progressivism in the cities, and not only because they are importantly concerned with public school developments, are Charles A. Beard, *American City Government: A Survey of Newer Tendencies* (1912); Charles Zueblin, *American Municipal Progress* (rev. ed., 1916); and William Bennet Munroe's authoritative *Bibliography of Municipal Government in the United States* (1915).

Wheeler, *Sixty Years of American Life*, Chap. XIV, is an appreciation of two Tammany Mayors, McClellan and Gaynor, by a veteran New York reformer. Not to be overlooked is Harold C. Syrett, ed., *The Gentleman and the Tiger: The Autobiography of George B. McClellan, Jr.* (1956). Mayor McClellan's reminiscences include important material (pp. 242–43) on politics in the Board of Education. Herbert H. Rosenthal, "The Progressive Movement in New York State, 1906–1914" (Harvard University, 1957), is thorough.

For a sense of the increasing despair generated among New Yorkers in the Progressive Era by the unceasing flow of immigration and the burgeoning slums, a despair which greatly hastened the pace of city school reform, the starting place is Robert Hunter, *Poverty* (1904). Also important are John Spargo, *The Bitter Cry of the Children* (1906); Lawrence Veiller, *Housing Reform* (1910), pp. 10–11; Edward T. Devine, "Immigration as a Relief Problem," *Charities*, XII (February 6, 1904), 129–33; and F. H. Ainsworth, "Are We Shouldering Europe's Burden?" *ibid.*, pp. 134–35. Two autobiographies of relevance are Raymond B. Fosdick, *Chronicle of a Generation: An Autobiography* (1959), pp. 58–59, 69–74; Ernest Poole, *The Bridge* (1940), Chaps. VII–VIII. James B. Reynolds, ed., *Civic Bibliography for Greater New York* (1911), is also relevant. Higham, *Strangers in the Land: Patterns of American Nativism*, Chap. VII, "The Loss of Confidence," is indispensable for background.

A seminal work in the history of progressive education is Hunter's *Poverty*, especially Chap. V. Comparison of Hunter's educational views with those of Riis, a decade earlier, is very instructive. John Spargo, *The Bitter Cry of the Children* (1906), supplements and supports the school reforms urged by Hunter, his friend and Socialist party comrade. The contemporary literature on the school-as-social-welfare-agency, or "legatee" institution, is vast. The following works sample the progressive spectrum: Wald, *The House on Henry Street*, and the same author's *Windows on Henry Street*; Jane E. Robbins, "The Settlement and the Public School," *Outlook*, XCV (August 6, 1910), 785–87; Howard Woolston, "Socialized Education in the Public Schools," *Charities*, XVI (September 1, 1906), 570–78; Stuart B. Queen, *Social Work in the Light of History* (1922), pp. 59–61, 160–61; Edward T. Devine, "Education and Social Economy," *Proceedings*, National Education Association (1914), pp. 142–50; John Lewis Gillin, *Poverty and Dependency* (1931), Chap. XXXIII; George B. Mangold, *Child Problems* (1910), and *Problems of Child Welfare* (1914); Ellwood Cubberley, *Changing Conceptions of Education* (1909), Part II, and his *Public Education in the United States* (1919), Chaps. XI–XIII; Dutton and Snedden, *The Administration of Public Education in the United States*, Chaps. XXII–XXIII; two volumes by Irving King: *Social*

Aspects of Education (1912), and *Education for Social Efficiency* (1915); Goodnow, *Municipal Government*, pp. 41–42; Delos Wilcox, *The American City* (1924), pp. 91–117; Beard, *American City Government*, pp. 263, 275–79, 312–24; Washington Gladden, *Social Salvation* (1902), Chap. VI; and Walter Rauschenbusch, *Christianizing the Social Order* (1912), p. 442.

One of the most powerful of progressive movements in the pre-World War I decade was the child labor movement. Hand in hand with the child labor movement went the compulsory education movement. The impact of the former on the latter, and on school reform in general, would repay exhaustive investigation. For the influential New York Child Labor Committee, investigators should start with "Child Labor Reform in New York," *Survey*, X (January 10, 1903), 52–56; New York Child Labor Committee, 1903–1908, *A Five Years Fight for New York's Children* (1908); and Fred S. Hall, *Forty Years, 1902–1942, The Work of the New York Child Labor Committee* (1942). A biography of special value for this whole subject is Josephine Goldmark, *Impatient Crusader: Florence Kelley's Life Story* (1953). The following articles should also be consulted: Felix Adler, "Child Labor in the United States and Its Great Attendant Evils," *The Annals*, XXV (May, 1905), 417–29; Samuel McCune Lindsay, "Child Labor and the Public Schools," *ibid.*, XXIX (January, 1907), 104–09; and Lewis M. Parker, "Compulsory Education, the Solution of the Child Labor Problem," *ibid.*, XXXII (July, 1908), 40–56. For general aspects, see Mary Stevenson Calcott, *Child Labor Legislation in New York* (1931), and Forest Chester Ensign, *Compulsory School Attendance and Child Labor* (1921).

The PEA-sponsored study *Colored School Children in New York* (1915) by Frances Blascoer is a classic. Other and relevant phases of the Negro problem are dealt with in Mary White Ovington, *Half a Man: The Status of the Negro in New York* (1911), and George E. Haynes, *The Negro at Work in New York City* (1912).

For the school lunch movement an important document is "Shall the Schools Serve Lunches?" *PEA Bulletin*, No. 10, February 25, 1913. There is a thorough discussion of the matter in Paul Kennaday and Burton J. Hendrick, "Three-Cent Lunches for School Children," *McClure's*, V (October, 1913), 125–32.

The Progressive Era was much concerned with the problem of mentally defective children. The PEA contributed the following articles by Elisabeth Irwin of its staff: "Work for Mentally Defective Children in New York City," *PEA Bulletin*, No. 8, January 20, 1913; and "A Study of the Feeble-Minded in a West Side School in New York City," *ibid.*, No. 21, December 8, 1913. Also Anne Moore, *The Feeble-Minded in New York: A Report Prepared for the Public Education Association of New York* (1911). Henry H. Goddard's alarmist *School Training of Defective Children* (1914) and his equally alarmist "Ungraded Classes," in New York City, Board of Estimate and Apportionment, *Report of the Committee of School Inquiry* (3 vols., 1913), Vol. I, are both very important. Stanley Powell Davies, *Social Control of the Feeble-Minded* (1923) is good for background. Rudolph J. Vecoli, "Sterilization: A Progressive Measure?" *Wisconsin Magazine of History*, XLIII (Spring, 1960), 190–202, is pertinent.

Alice P. Barrows, "Report of the Vocational Guidance Survey," *PEA Bulletin*, No. 9 [1912], is an important contribution to an important progressive movement. In connection with Miss Barrows' study, Robert Coit Chapin, *The Standard of Living Among Workingmen's Families in New York City* (1909), is required reading. The vocational education and vocational guidance movements are criticized by the Socialist William English Walling, *Progressivism—and After* (1914), pp. 106–20, 213–17. John M. Brewer, *History of Vocational Guidance: Origins and Early Developments* (1942), errs when he denies the connection between the vocational education and vocational guidance movements, as a careful reading of his own text proves. The general history of the vocational education movement is well told in Cremin, *The Transformation of the School*, Chap. II.

Although it is outdated, and although it must be used with caution, especially so far as the PEA's involvment is concerned, the best general history of the visiting teacher movement is Julius John Oppenheimer, *The Visiting Teacher Movement* (1924), a study subsidized by the PEA and the Commonwealth Fund. A note of millenarianism, heretofore a minor note in progressive education, emerges clearly in the literature of the visiting teacher movement. Important here are PEA staff member Eleanor Hope Johnson's "Social Service and the Public Schools," *Survey*, XXX (May 3, 1913), 173–78; and convinced supporter Julia Richman's "A Social Need of the Public School," *Forum*, XLIII (February, 1910), 161–69.

For the background of changing emphasis in social work in the Progressive Era, consult two classic works by Mary C. Richmond: *Social Diagnosis* (1917), and *What Is Social Case Work?* (1922). These should be supplemented by Virginia C. Robinson, *A Changing Psychology in Social Case Work* (1930); and Frank J. Bruno, *Trends in Social Work, 1874–1956: A History Based on the Proceedings of the National Conference of Social Work* (1957), Chap. XIX. Not to be overlooked is John Chynoweth Burnham, "Psychiatry, Psychology and the Progressive Movement," *American Quarterly*, XII (Winter, 1960), 457–65. *Social Work in the American Tradition* (1958), by social worker Nathan Edward Cohen, is the best general history of social work in America extant, which is not to say that a history of social work is not badly needed. The newer *From Charity to Social Work in England and the United States* (1962), by Kathleen Woodroofe, helps fill some of the gaps.

The most explicit statement of the radical educational implications of the Gary Plan comes from the PEA's director, Howard Nudd: "The Gary Plan and Its Social Bearing," *Proceedings*, National Conference of Charities and Corrections (1916), p. 559. Equally revealing is the hard-to-locate PEA, *Official Wirt Reports to the Board of Education of New York City* (1916); and William A. Wirt, "The Place of the Public School in a Community Program of Child Welfare," *The Child*, I (July, 1912), 11–15.

Contemporary accounts in *School and Society, Elementary School Journal*, and *Survey* were helpful for the Gary School War in New York.

The *New York Times*, because of its role as one of the important observers of and one of the chief actors in the struggle, was invaluable. A critical study of the educational attitudes and policies of the *Times* since the formation of the Greater City would be worthwhile. The *New Republic* was an important participant in the Gary Affair. See, for example, the series of five eulogistic articles on the schools of Gary by Randolph Bourne which the *New Republic* carried in 1915, and which were later reprinted in Bourne's *The Gary Schools* (1916). These same articles, plus some others in the same vein by Bourne which the *New Republic* ran in late 1915 and 1916, are reprinted in Bourne's *Education and Living* (1917), Chaps. XIV–XVIII, XXII. See also "The School Situation in New York," *New Republic*, VI (February 5, 1916), 8; and "Politics Against the Schools," *ibid.*, VI (February 12, 1916), 32–33. Louis Filler comments provocatively on Bourne's role in progressive education in *Randolph Bourne* (1943), pp. 63–70. Cremin describes the Gary Plan as the apogee of pre-World War I educational progressivism in *The Transformation of the School*, pp. 154–58. The sharp critique of the Gary Plan on its home grounds in Abraham Flexner and Frank P. Bachman, *The Gary Schools: A General Account* (1918), should be read. The full story of the progressives' assault on culture in the pre-World War I decade has yet to be told, but a brilliant start has been made by Henry F. May, *The End of American Innocence: The First Years of Our Own Time, 1912–1917*.

In his brief career as a PEA official, Willard Straight attended committee meetings, helped PEA raise funds, and suggested programs for the PEA. Given the ties between Straight and the Association, and given the role of the *New Republic* in the Gary School War, the discerning analysis of the elitism of the *New Republic* and its editors in Charles Forcey, *The Crossroads of Liberalism: Croly, Weyl, Lippmann and the Progressive Era, 1900–1925* (1961), pp. 175, 178, 182, is relevant. Straight's interest in "social education" is documented in a fine biography by Herbert Croly, *Willard Straight* (1925), p. 471. Edwin Lewinson's thoughtful "John Purroy Mitchel, Symbol of Reform" (Columbia University, 1961), documents similarly the elitism of the city administration and is likewise relevant to this chapter.

Abraham Flexner's *I Remember* (1940) is remarkable more for what it leaves out than for what it includes. Included is a brief but incisive discussion of the Gary Plan and schoolmen generally (pp. 253–56). Omitted are any mention of Flexner's service on the Board of Education or his connection with the PEA. Also ignored are the Bureau of Municipal Research, William H. Allen, John Purroy Mitchel and New York politics, the Gary School War in New York City, and the contemporary criticisms of the General Education Board and himself. Perhaps Mr. Flexner's Papers, in the possession of the Library of Congress and closed until July 1, 1965, will shed some light on some or all of these matters.

A biography of William H. Maxwell would shed light on a crucial era of New York City educational history. Samuel P. Abelow, *Dr. William H. Maxwell* (1934), is slight. John S. Brubacher, "William Henry Maxwell," *Dictionary of American Biography*, XII (1933), is helpful as far as it goes. Mary I. McDonald, "Dr. Maxwell as an Educator" (New York University, 1923), is almost worthless.

The literature concerning the influence of philanthropic foundations upon American public education is scant, and what there is treats mostly of the education of the Negro in the South, and rural education. A study of foundation policy, with regard to urban education generally, is needed. For the General Education Board and reconstruction of the South through education, consult General Education Board, *General Education Board: An Account of Its Activities 1902–1914* (1915); Louis R. Harlan. *Separate and Unequal* (1958), Chap. III; and Charles W. Dabney, *Universal Education in the South* (two vols., 1936), Vol. II. For the General Education Board, Abraham Flexner, and the experimental Lincoln School of New York, consult Cremin and others, *A History of Teachers College, Columbia University*, pp. 110–11; and Cremin, *The Transformation of the School*, pp. 280–82. For the principals, principles, and activities of the New York Foundation, see New York Foundation, *Forty Year Report, 1909–1949* (1950).

The Russell Sage Foundation was extremely active in the Progressive Era in the sphere of socialized education. See, for example, the following studies published by the Foundation: Clarence Arthur Perry, *Wider Use of School Plant* (1910); M. Louise Greene, *Among School Gardens* (1911); Leonard P. Ayres, *Laggards in Our Schools: A Study of Retardation and Elimination* (1909); and Luther H. Gulick and Leonard P. Ayres, *Medical Inspection in Schools* (1910). See also John M. Glenn, Lillian Brandt, and F. Emerson Andrews, *The Russell Sage Foundation: 1907–1946* (two vols., 1947), especially Vol. II.

The extant literature on foundations is written for the most part by foundation personnel and is largely descriptive and non-critical. The latest, Raymond B. Fosdick, *Adventure in Giving: The Story of the General Education Board* (1962), is one of the best. Not to be overlooked is the brief, incisive discussion of foundations as a "power structure" in higher education in Frederick Rudolph, *The American College and University: A History* (1962), pp. 430–34. An older, general critique, Eduard C. Lindeman, *Wealth and Culture* (1936), pp. 11–12, is still well worth reading.

CHAPTER 4, 1917-1932

There are several excellent general histories of the 1920's. John D. Hicks, *Republican Ascendency, 1921–1933* (1960), is mostly political history, but contains a thorough bibliographical essay. More helpful for this study were the vividly written William E. Leuchtenburg, *The Perils of Prosperity, 1914–1932* (1958); and Arthur M. Schlesinger, Jr.'s fine *The Crisis of the Old Order, 1919–1933* (1957), Vol. I of his *The Age of Roosevelt*. The older William Preston Slosson, *The Great Crusade and After, 1914–1928* (1930) is still useful.

Arthur Link's observation, in "What Happened to the Progressive Movement in the 1920's?" *American Historical Review*, LXIV (July, 1959), 838–50, that research is needed on the survival of progressivism in the

'20's, the forms in which it survived, and the degree of its vigor, bears repetition. Not to be overlooked is Henry May's provocative "Shifting Perspectives on the 1920's," *Mississippi Valley Historical Review*, XLIII (December, 1956), 405–27.

Tammany hegemony in New York City politics in the 1920's is documented in Sayre and Kaufman, *Governing New York City: Politics in the Metropolis*, p. 175; Garrett, *The La Guardia Years: Machine and Reform Politics in New York City*, Chap. III. Mann's masterful *La Guardia: A Fighter Against His Times, 1882–1933*, illuminates many phases of New York life and thought, and goes beyond New York. Two relevant memoirs are: Henry H. Curran, *Pillar to Post* (1941), and Gene Fowler's affectionately critical *The Life and Times of Jimmy Walker, Beau James* (1949). Theodore Lowi's study of ethnic and nationality factors in the appointment process, "At the Pleasure of the Mayor: A Study of Appointment Politics in New York City, 1898–1958" (Yale University, 1961), especially pp. 61–62, is pertinent.

New York State politics in the twenties is the story of Al Smith. There is a large body of literature about the Governor. For general purposes, Ellis and others, *A Short History of New York State*, Chap. XXX, is eminently satisfactory. Al Smith's fight against the Lusk Laws is well known; his championship of public education in the state virtually unknown. But see William C. Bagley, "Alfred E. Smith's Record in the Promotion of Public Education," *School and Society*, LX (October 14, 1944), 243–44; Ellis and others, *A Short History of New York State*, pp. 402–03; Alfred E. Smith, *Up to Now: An Autobiography* (1929), pp. 276–79. Two books written in the '20's broke new ground in work on state aid to education: George D. Strayer and Robert M. Haig, *The Financing of Education in the State of New York* (1923); and Paul R. Mort, *State Support for Public Schools* (1926).

The whole body of literature on the Red Scare and the academic freedom crisis of the postwar period deals importantly with the situation in New York City. Standard is Robert K. Murray, *Red Scare: A Study in National Hysteria, 1919–1920* (1955). Consult also Harold M. Hyman, *To Try Men's Souls: Loyalty Tests in American History* (1959), pp. 317–20. Dealing only with the crisis in higher education is Richard Hofstadter and Walter P. Metzger, *The Development of Academic Freedom in the United States* (1955), pp. 495–506. Robert W. Iversen's unique *The Communists and the Schools* (1959) might well be subtitled "New York City." The whole issue of academic freedom in New York City was complicated by the aggressive tactics of the New York Teachers Union. See, for example, a typical broadside, Teachers Union, *Toward the New Education: The Case Against Autocracy in Our Public Schools* (1918). Although it needs qualification in some respects, the standard source for the anti-radical activities of the New York State legislature is Lawrence H. Chamberlain, *Loyalty and Legislative Action: A Study of Activity by the New York State Legislature, 1919–1949* (1951). Of the older works, Zachariah Chafee, Jr., *Freedom of Speech* (1940), is still valuable. Howard K. Beale, *Are American Teachers Free?* (1936) is meandering and unenlightening. The same might be said of Bessie Louise Pierce, *Public Opinion and the Teaching of History in the United States* (1926).

The talks delivered at the PEA-sponsored debate, "Freedom and Initiative in the Schools," are as relevant today as they were in 1919. There is a summary in the *New York Times*, April 27, 1919. All the addresses are reprinted in *The Public and the Schools*: No. 23, May 3, 1919; No. 25, May 17, 1919; and No. 26, May 24, 1919. The same holds true for the PEA-sponsored debate, "Should Teachers Affiliate with Organized Labor?" There is a summary in the *New York Times*, February 15, 1920. For the complete text of the addresses, consult *The Public and the Schools*: No. 56, February 28, 1920; No. 57, March 6, 1920; and No. 60, March 27, 1920.

With regard to the growing split amongst progressives on the issue of city–school relationships, the educationist view is epitomized in Ellwood P. Cubberley, *Public School Administration* (1929), pp. 188–89. The political scientists are represented by William Anderson, *American City Government* (1925), pp. 90–96; and Thomas Harrison Reed, *Municipal Government in the United States* (1926), pp. 296–98.

For the 1920's as a seriously divisive moment in U.S. history, important background for educational developments in the twenties, see Leuchtenburg, *The Perils of Prosperity, 1914–1932*; May, "Shifting Perspectives on the 1920's," pp. 425–26; Higham, *Strangers in the Land: Patterns of American Nativism, 1860–1925*, Chaps. VIII–XI; Mann, *La Guardia: A Fighter Against His Times, 1882–1933*, pp. 181–83. Nathan Glazer's revisionist "The Integration of American Immigrants," *Law and Contemporary Problems*, XXI (Spring, 1956), 256–59, is also pertinent. For relevant contemporary sources consult Ross L. Finney, *Causes and Cures for the Social Unrest* (1922); Ben B. Lindsay and Wainwright Evans, *The Revolt of Modern Youth* (1925); Walter Lippmann, *A Preface to Morals* (1929); and Joseph Wood Krutch, *The Modern Temper* (1929).

Juvenile delinquency emerged as a major symptom of urban unrest in the 1920's, with important implications for school reform. The literature turned out by the New York State Crime Commission, Sub-Commission on Causes and Effects of Crime, are in effect treatises on education. The following works by the Crime Commission are of especial importance: *From Truancy to Crime—A Study of 251 Adolescents* (1928); *A Study of Problem Boys and Their Brothers* (1929); *Crime and the Community: A Study of Trends in Crime Prevention* (1930); and a summary volume, *A Special Summary of the Work of the Crime Commission*. Finally, not to be overlooked in the history of progressive education is the report of the White House Conference on Child Health and Delinquency, *The Delinquent Child* (1932), pp. 38–41, 99–133.

A history of the mental health movement as a social movement would prove enlightening. Nina Ridenouer's *Mental Health in the United States: A Fifty-Year History* (1961) is of the inspirational genre. The impact of the mental health movement on American public education would repay exhaustive study. Such a study might begin with William A. White, "Childhood: The Golden Period for Mental Hygiene," *The Annals*, XCVIII (November, 1921), 54–67, and the same author's *The Mental Hygiene of*

Childhood (1919); Jessie Taft, "The Relation of the School to the Mental Health of the Average Child," *Mental Hygiene,* VII (October, 1923), 673–87; William H. Burnham, *The Normal Mind* (1924); and Jonathan Clark, "The Educational Ideas of Adolf Meyer" (Teachers College, Columbia University, 1960). In the 1920's scarcely an issue of *Mental Hygiene* went by without an article on education. The annual *Proceedings* of the National Conference of Social Work for the 1920's should also be examined.

The social case work and mental health point of view is ubiquitous in the writings of PEA staff members in the twenties. The aspirations of social workers are given notable statement in Jane F. Culbert, "The Public School as a Factor in the Training of the Socially Handicapped Child," *Proceedings,* National Conference of Social Work (1921), pp. 95–98, and "The Visiting Teacher," *The Annals,* XCVIII (November, 1921), 81–89. Howard Nudd's articles, "The School and Social Work," *Proceedings,* National Conference of Social Work (1927), pp. 37–45; "Social Case Work as Applied to the Schools," *ibid.* (1923), pp. 422–25; and "Social Work Enters the Schools," *Survey Graphic,* LIV (April, 1925), 30–34, are also extremely important.

The Commonwealth Fund's *Fourth Annual Report* (1922), announcing the inception of the Fund's "Program for the Prevention of Juvenile Delinquency," is an extremely important document. With some slight changes the announcement is reprinted in Barry C. Smith, "The Commonwealth Fund Program for the Prevention of Delinquency," *Proceedings,* National Conference of Social Work (1922). Consult also Commonwealth Fund, Program for the Prevention of Delinquency, *Progress Report* (1925). A highly significant progressive innovation is described in W. Carson Ryan, Jr., "The Preparation of Teachers for Dealing with Behavior Problem Children," *School and Society,* XXVIII (August 18, 1928), 208–15. The trends of a decade in school reform are importantly surveyed in William I. Thomas and Dorothy S. Thomas, *The Child in America: Behavior Problems and Programs* (1928), Chap. V; and Lois Meredith, "Education and Social Work," *Social Work Yearbook* (1933), pp. 137–42.

In connection with the social work and mental health movements, Sol W. Ginsburg's brilliant critique, "The Mental Health Movement. Its Theoretical Assumptions," in Ruth Kotinsky and Helen Witmer, eds., *Community Programs for Mental Health* (1955), pp. 1–29, should be read. The following works are also extremely helpful: Robert M. MacIver, *The Contributions of Sociology to Social Work* (1931); Kingsley Davis, "Mental Hygiene and the Class Structure," *Psychiatry,* I (February, 1938), 55–65; and C. Wright Mills, "The Professional Ideology of Social Pathologists," *American Journal of Sociology,* XIL (September, 1943), 165–80. Raymond A. Bauer's *The New Man in Soviet Psychology* (1952) has broad implications.

The PEA's experiment in the education of "superior" children received wide publicity: Louise F. Specht, "Terman Classes in Public School No. 64, Manhattan: An Experiment in Selecting, Grouping and Training a Number of Children of Very Superior Intelligence," *School and Society,* IX (March 29, 1919), 393; and "Experiments in Education," *World's Work,* XLIII

(February, 1922), 353. Not to be overlooked is the classic Elisabeth A. Irwin and Louis Marks description of the PEA's P.S. 64 experiment, *Fitting the School to the Child* (1924).

In the background of experiments such as the aforementioned lurked the I.Q. movement. Lewis M. Terman, *The Intelligence of School Children* (1919), was very influential. Also widely discussed were Henry S. Pritchett, "Are Our Universities Overcrowded?" *Scribner's Magazine,* LXXIII (1923), 556–60; and Cornelia J. Cannon, "American Misgivings," *Atlantic Monthly,* CXXIX (February, 1922), 145–57. Of special relevance for New York is New York City, Board of Education, Bureau of Reference, Research and Statistics, Publication No. 19, *Pupils' Progress through the Grades* (1922), and City Superintendent of Schools William L. Ettinger's lugubrious "Facing the Facts," *School and Society,* XVI (November 4, 1922), 505–12. The controversy which raged in the early 1920's over educational restrictionism based on I.Q. is well told in Cremin, *The Transformation of the School,* pp. 188–91.

For the story of the PEA's Little Red School House Experiment, I owe much to the manuscript collection at the Little Red School House, 196 Bleecker St., New York. The pedagogical views of Elisabeth Irwin as well as the principles and practices of the Little Red School House can be reconstructed from the work Miss Irwin co-authored with Louis Marks, *Fitting the School to the Child* (1924), a goldmine of contemporary pedagogical progressivism, and a handful of articles Miss Irwin wrote in the twenties: "Personal Education," *New Republic,* XL (November 12, 1924), 7–9; "The Youngest Intellectuals," *ibid.,* XLVIII (November 10, 1926), 339–41; "We Watch Them Grow," *Survey,* LX (June 1, 1928), 273–76; and "The Teacher Steps Out," *ibid.,* LXIII (December 15, 1929), 340. The above-mentioned articles should be compared with articles which Miss Irwin wrote at an earlier phase of her career: "Lace Workers of the Italian Quarter of New York," *Craftsman,* XII (July, 1907), 404–09; "Where the Players Are Marionettes—A Little Italian Theatre on Mulberry Street," *ibid.,* XII (September, 1907), 667–69; and "Little Gardens of the East Side," *ibid.,* XIV (July, 1908), 404–06. Miss Irwin is eulogized in Lucy Sprague Mitchell, "A Tribute to a Pioneer," *Progressive Education,* XX (February, 1943), 65.

Important for the Little Red School House as well as for educational progressivism in general are Agnes De Lima, *Our Enemy the Child* (1926), and Agnes De Lima with others, *The Little Red School House* (1942). Two autobiographies of extreme value are Caroline Pratt, *I Learn from Children* (1948); and Lucy Sprague Mitchell, *Two Lives: The Story of Wesley Clair Mitchell and Myself* (1953). Of great help was sociologist Caroline Ware's extraordinary study, *Greenwich Village, 1920–1930: A Comment on American Civilization in the Post-War Years* (1935). For progressive education in the 1920's in general, Cremin, *The Transformation of the School,* pp. 179–224, 240–50, is authoritative.

If progressive education were to make headway in the public schools, the support of middle-class parents was essential. In this connection Margaret A. Lighty and LeRoy E. Bowman, *Parenthood in a Democracy*

(1939), a history and horizontal study of the United Parents Associations of New York City, is extremely revealing. The Child Study Association of America and the National Committee for Mental Hygiene were also importantly engaged in parent education; e.g.: Dorothy Canfield Fisher and Sidonie Matsner Gruenberg, *Our Children: A Handbook for Parents* (1932); White House Conference on Child Health and Protection, Report of the Subcommittee on Types of Parent Education, Content and Method, Sidonie M. Gruenberg, Chairman, *Parent Education: Types, Content, Method* (1932). Consult also V. F. Calverton, ed., *The New Generation: The Intimate Problems of Modern Parents and Children* (1930); Sidonie M. Gruenberg, "What Should Parents Know?" *New Republic*, XLVII (July 14, 1926), 221–22; Flora M. Thurston, "What's Ahead for Parents," *Progressive Education*, VI (January–March, 1929), 40–44; and Franklin E. Williams, "What Are Parents For?" *Survey*, LVII (December 1, 1926), 307–09, 335.

CHAPTER 5, 1932-1940

Many aspects of the history of the thirties are covered in the monumental *Age of Roosevelt*, by Arthur M. Schlesinger, Jr., three volumes of which have appeared: Vol. I, *The Crisis of the Old Order, 1919–1933* (1957), Chaps. XXX–XXXV; Vol. II, *The Coming of the New Deal* (1959); and Vol. III, *The Politics of Upheaval* (1960). David A. Shannon, ed., *The Great Depression* (1960), documents the insecurity and tension of the time. Dixon Wecter, *The Age of the Great Depression, 1929–1941* (1948), is standard.

We shall have to await Mann's second and concluding volume of his biography of La Guardia for a truly satisfactory account of the election of 1933 and the Little Flower's subsequent career as Mayor. In the meantime Garrett, *The La Guardia Years: Machine and Reform Politics in New York City*, should be consulted. Charles Belous, *Faith in Fusion* (1951), contains the views of a die-hard reformer. So does Newbold Morris, *Let the Chips Fall: My Battles Against Corruption* (1955). Important sources of information about the La Guardia years, albeit they must be used with caution, are three works edited by Rebecca Rankin: *New York Advancing: A Scientific Approach to Municipal Government . . . 1934–1935* (1936); *New York Advancing, World's Fair Edition: The Result of Five Years of Progressive Administration in the City of New York* (1939); and *New York Advancing, Victory Edition: Seven More Years of Progressive Administration in the City of New York, 1939–1945* (1945). The old curmudgeon, William H. Allen, complains about civic quietism during La Guardia's first two terms in *Why Tammany's Revive: La Guardia's Mis-Guard* (1937), pp. 22, 34–36. See also the aforementioned work by Garrett, pp. 313ff.

Nevins, *Herbert H. Lehman and His Era*, has filled an important gap. See also Ellis and others, *A Short History of New York State*, Chap. XXXII; Moscow, *Politics in the Empire State*, pp. 19–23; and Charles W. Van Devander, *The Big Bosses* (1944), Chap. II.

William F. Whyte, *Financing New York City* (1935), illuminates a subject badly in need of illumination. Also important for the 1932–1934 economy drive in the city are the following: Joseph D. McGoldrick, "Storm Warnings in New York City's Finances," *National Municipal Review*, XXI (February, 1932), 168–75; and William C. Beyer, "Financial Dictators Replace Political Boss," *ibid.*, XXII (April, 1933), 162–67. Consult also two articles by Margaret I. Tanzer: "New York City's Economy Bill," *National Municipal Review*, XXIII (May, 1934), 287–88; and "The Situation in New York City," *ibid.*, XXIII (March, 1934), 190. "A Year of La Guardia," *Nation*, CXL (January 16, 1935), 61, is critical of the Mayor's fiscal policy. And, in general, consult Garrett, *The La Guardia Years: Machine and Reform Politics in New York City*, pp. 143–45.

New York State, Special Report of the State Tax Commission No. 13, *The Fiscal Aspect of State and Local Relationships in New York* (1937), by Paul E. Malone, is very good on state aid to education. The background of depression in the state and Governor Roosevelt's pioneering attempts to cope with the disaster are treated in three important works: Bernard Bellush, *Franklin Delano Roosevelt as Governor of New York* (1955), Chap. VII; Frank Freidel, *Franklin D. Roosevelt: The Triumph* (1956), Chap. XV; and Schlesinger, *The Crisis of the Old Order, 1919–1933*, pp. 391–93.

The powerful New York teachers' lobby is studied in Belle Zeller, *Politics in New York: A Study of Group Representation before the Legislature* (1938), pp. 115–20. Dayton McKean, *Pressures on the Legislature of New Jersey* (1938), pp. 115–20; and Arnold E. Weiss, *Some Major Influences on Recent Educational Legislation in Pennsylvania* (1940), Chaps. III–IV, catch the teachers' lobby in action in other states. For the schools and the depression in general, consult the following: Eunice Langdon, "The Teacher and the Depression," *Nation*, CXXXVII (August 16, 1933), 182–85; Avis D. Carlson, "Deflating the Schools," *Harper's Magazine*, CLXVII (November, 1933), 705–13; and Wayne W. Parrish, "The Plight of Our School System," *Literary Digest*, CXVI (September 23, 1933), 32.

The full impact of PWA and, more importantly, WPA on the public schools—indeed, on the cultural life of the nation—is still to be calculated. Perhaps a future volume of Schlesinger's *Age of Roosevelt* will fill the gap. In the meantime Carl Degler, *Out of Our Past: The Forces that Shaped Modern America* (1959), pp. 389–90, is helpful. For New York City two works are important: John D. Millett, *The Works Progress Administration in New York City* (1958), pp. 110–13; Alexander Leopold Radomski, *Work Relief in New York State, 1931–1935* (1947), pp. 246–299. In general, see Doak S. Campbell, Frederick H. Bair, and Oswald L. Harvey, *Educational Activities of the WPA* (1939). Cremin has some thoughtful comments on the New Deal and progressive educationists in *The Transformation of the School*, pp. 318–24. Helpful also is Harry Zeitlin, "Federal Relations in American Education, 1933–1944: A Study of New Deal Efforts and Innovations" (Columbia University, 1958).

Iversen, *The Communists and the Schools*, although it misses the ferment in the high school in the '30's, is indispensable for the Communist seizure of the New York Teachers Union, for the Communist infiltration of youth movements, and for college student radicalism in general. The depression background of radicalism among American youth is stressed by Celeste Strack, "The Student Movement in the United States," *The Communist*, XVI (February, 1937), 142–60. Communist youth groups are described in Bessie Louise Pierce, *Citizens Organizations and the Civic Training of Youth* (1933), pp. 226–34. The peace movement of the '30's is described by a partisan in Merle Curti, *Peace or War: The American Struggle, 1636–1936* (1936), Chap. IX. The discontents of youth are discussed sympathetically in George Philip Rawick, "The New Deal and Youth: The Civilian Conservation Corps, the National Youth Administration, and the American Youth Congress" (University of Wisconsin, 1957). Chamberlain, *Loyalty and Legislative Action . . .* , Chap. II, is standard for the anti-radical measures of the New York State Legislature.

Oscar Handlin, *The Newcomers: Negroes and Puerto Ricans in a Changing Metropolis* (1959), pp. 43–52, is basic for the changing composition of New York's population in the thirties. Ira De A. Reid, *The Negro Immigrant, His Background Characteristics and Social Adjustment, 1899–1937* (1939), is a pioneering study of foreign-born Negroes, chiefly from the British West Indies, chiefly residing in New York City. Not to be overlooked is the sceptical "The Melting Pot," *Fortune*, XX (July, 1939), 72–76, 171–77. Jones, *American Immigration*, Chap. X, discusses the "new immigration" of 1924–1959 with discernment.

For upstate pedagogical progressivism the following are important: New York State University, Department of Education, *Twenty-Fifth Annual Report* (1928) and, especially, from the same source, *Cardinal Objectives in Elementary Education* (1928).

Two documents of major importance for the history of education in New York City are New York State University, Department of Education, *Report of a Study of New York City Schools, Part I: The Administrative-Supervisory Organization; Part II: Evaluation of Achievement*, by Frank Pierrepont Graves (1933); and New York State University, Department of Education, *The Activity Program: The Report of a Survey of the Curriculum Experiment with the Activity Program in the Elementary Schools of the City of New York by the State Education Department, under the Direction of J. Cayce Morrison* (1941).

The principles and practices of the city's activity program are best approached in the writings of New York City school officials. City School Superintendent Campbell reveals the activity program to the city in *New York Times*, June 27, 1934. Consult also the Superintendent's "Grade System Changed," *New York Times*, June 30, 1935, feature article, Sec. IX; and the same author's "Why a New School Plan," *New York Times*, July 1, 1934, feature article, Sec. IX. Also revealing are the following magazine articles by John J. Loftus, at the time an Assistant School Superintendent: "New York's Large Scale Experimentation with an Activity Program," *Progressive Education*, XVII (February, 1940), 116–24; and "Learning Comes to Life," *ibid.*, XXI (April, 1944), 186–89. Consult also the *Annual Reports* of the City School Superintendent during the later '30's, also the *Annual Reports* of the District Superintendents for the same period. The

Board of Education takes credit for the activity program in several volumes edited by Rebecca Rankin: *New York Advancing: A Scientific Approach to Municipal Government* . . . *1934–1935,* Chap. V; and *New York Advancing, World's Fair Edition: The Result of Five Years of Progressive Administration in the City of New York* (1939), Chap. V. A highly relevant work, which must be used with caution, however, is Wayne Wrightstone, *Appraisal of Newer Elementary School Practices* (1938).

The activity program was clearly a branch of progressive education. See, for example, National Society for the Study of Education, Thirty-Third Yearbook, Part II, *The Activity Movement* (1934); A. Gordon Melvin, "The Nature of True Activities," *Progressive Education,* XIII (January, 1936), 46–48; and F. C. Borgeson, "What Makes an Activity Program," *ibid.,* 50–52. Guy M. Whipple, "The Activity Movement from an Adverse Point of View," *Progressive Education,* XI (October, 1934), 340–45, should also be consulted.

La Guardia's remarks at the PEA's "The School Child and Crime Prevention" conference provide a revealing glimpse of the progressive as social reformer: *New York Times,* January 17, 1937, Sec. II. The PEA's rebuttal is an important statement of a radically different approach: *The Public and the Schools,* No. 379, January 26, 1937.

For the PEA's Chelsea School Project, manuscript sources in the files of the PEA, especially "Leila V. Stott to Director [Howard Nudd] [May 12, 1937]," mimeographed, and "Proposed Plan for the City and Country School Extension Service in P.S. 33. A Memorandum Submitted to the Director [Nudd] by Mrs. Moses Blitzer and Miss Adele Franklin, May 21, 1937," mimeographed, were indispensable. The same might be said for Miss Franklin's mimeographed semi-annual and annual reports of the Chelsea School Project, in the "Chelsea School Project" and "All-Day Neighborhood School" files at the PEA. Ruth Gillette Hardy, "School Services," *Progressive Education,* XVII (October, 1940), 418, is extremely revealing. So is Adele Franklin, "The All-Day Neighborhood School Plan," *The Nervous Child,* III (July, 1944), 350–58; and the aptly titled New York City, Board of Education, *Extended School Services through the All-Day Neighborhood Schools,* Curriculum Bulletin, 1947–1948 Series (1948). Caroline Pratt acknowledges P.S. 33 as an offspring of the City and Country School in *I Learn from Children,* pp. 137, 181. Unfortunately the important files of the City and Country School are still closed.

The socio-economic diagnosis of mental ability was popular in the thirties. Often cited was Julius B. Maller, "Economic and Social Correlations of School Progress in New York City," *Teachers College Record,* XXXIV (May, 1933), 655–70. J. L. Gray, "Blood Won't Tell," *New Republic,* XIX (July 22, 1933), 313–15, is critical of this procedure. The poignant complaint of long-time New York school principal Leonard Covello, *The Heart is the Teacher* (1958), p. 203, is pertinent.

CHAPTER 6, 1940-1954

The disquieting background in domestic and international affairs against which the school crisis of the '40's and '50's was played is well described by Eric F. Goldman, *The Crucial Decade: America, 1945–1955* (1956). Best for the general history of American education in the last quarter-century is R. Freeman Butts and Lawrence A. Cremin, *A History of Education in American Culture* (1953), Part IV. Consult also Merle Curti's essay, "The Last Twenty-Five Years," in his revised *Social Ideas of American Educators* (1959).

A very adequate account of New York City politics in the '40's and '50's is that in Garrett, *The La Guardia Years: Machine and Reform Politics in New York City*, Chaps. XIV–XVI. *New York Politics* (1960), by Frank S. Munger and Ralph A. Straetz, is excellent. For New York State politics in this period, largely the Thomas E. Dewey story, consult the last-named work. Also Ellis and others, *A Short History of New York State*, Chap. XXXIII, and Moscow, *Politics in the Empire State*, pp. 32–35.

Garrett views La Guardia's acts in the school sphere very much as the PEA does: *The La Guardia Years: Machine and Reform Politics in New York City*, pp. 200–06. There is a firsthand account of La Guardia in action in school affairs in John Gunther, *Inside U.S.A.* (1947), pp. 583–84. The orthodox educationist view is set forth in National Education Association, Committee for the Defense of Democracy through Education, *Report of an Investigation: Interferences with the Independence of the New York City Board of Education* (1944).

The split between educationists and political scientists and students of public administration on the issue of city–school relations deepened in the '40's and '50's. W. G. Fordyce, "The Independent School Board," *School and Society*, LXXV (April 5, 1952), 214–16; Edward M. Tuttle, *School Board Leadership in America* (1958); the aforementioned N.E.A. report; and an article by the PEA's Frederick C. McLaughlin, "Local Government and School Control," *School and Society*, LXXV (April 5, 1952), 211–14, present the educationist point of view. Educationists pick up support from Harvard sociologist Neal Gross, *Who Runs Our Schools?* (1958), and Washington University historian Raymond E. Callahan, *Education and the Cult of Efficiency* (1962). Political scientists counter in Ernest A. Engelbert, "Educational Administration and Responsible Government," *School and Society*, LXXV (January 19, 1952), 33–36; and Eldon L. Johnson, "Co-Ordination: The Viewpoint of a Political Scientist," *The Annals*, CCCII (November, 1955), 136–42; *Civic Victories: The Story of an Unfinished Revolution* (1952), Chap. XXII, by veteran New York civic reformer Richard S. Childs, is also pertinent. Robert L. Morlan's *Intergovernmental Relations in Education* (1950), although dealing only with Minnesota, has more than local significance. Two older studies of city–school relations are still valuable: Henry and Kerwin, *Schools and City Government*, and Vieg, *The Government of Education in Metropolitan Chicago*. Harvey C. Mansfield and Fritz Morstein Marx, "Fiscal Accountability," in Fritz Morstein Marx, ed., *Elements of Public Administration* (1946), although not dealing with education, is highly relevant.

The controversy between educationists and political scientists is epitomized in two studies of particular importance for the city. New York City, Mayor's Committee on Management Survey, *Administrative Management of the Schools of New York City* (1951), by George D. Strayer and Louis E. Yavner, calls for "fiscal independence" for the city schools. This proposal is rejected in the full New York City, Mayor's Committee on Management Survey, *Modern Management for the City of New York* (two vols., 1953), Vol. I, p. 245; Vol. II, pp. 30–33, 84–85, and Chap. XIII. Both are reviewed in "School Board Status Debated in New York," *National Municipal Review*, XLI (February, 1952), 93–94. Citizens Budget Commission, *Should New York City Adopt Fiscal Independence for Education?* (1950), aimed at the PEA, answers "no," and gives many reasons.

An important source of the "defense of democracy" argument used in behalf of progressive education in the '40's and '50's were the studies on social climates by Kurt Lewin, Ronald O. Lippitt, and Ralph K. White, which first appeared in 1938 and 1939 in *American Journal of Sociology*, *Journal of Social Psychology*, and *Sociometry*, and which have recently been gathered together in Ralph K. White and Ronald O. Lippitt, *Autocracy and Democracy: An Experimental Inquiry* (1960). Goodwin Watson, "What Are the Effects of a Democratic Atmosphere on Children," *Progressive Education*, XVII (May, 1940), 336–42, is a pioneer application of the Lewin, Lippitt, and White studies to education. Other aspects of the progressives' strategy in meeting "attacks on modern education" are well revealed in Margaret S. Lewisohn, "The Battle for Modern Education," *Progressive Education*, XXI (January, 1944), 29–31; Edward L. Bernays, "Speak Up for Public Education," *ibid.*, XVIII (February, 1941), 111–23; Ronald O. Lippitt, "Attacks on the Schools: How to Develop Preventive Strength," *ibid.*, XXVIII (May, 1951), 217–18; and Gordon McCloskey, "Meeting Attacks on Education," *ibid.*, XXIX (January, 1952), 119–121.

Albert Lynd, "Who Wants Progressive Education?" *Atlantic Monthly*, CXCII (April, 1953), 29–34, characteristically overemphasizes the influence of John Dewey and educationists in general on progressive school innovations. Much more sophisticated is PEA director Frederick C. McLaughlin, "Control of Education in Public Schools," *Teachers College Record*, LV (March, 1954), 293–300.

The leadership, policy, and strategy of the National Citizens Commission for the Public Schools (which became the National Citizens Council for Better Schools in 1956) needs investigation. The existing literature on the Commission, and on the citizens' movement in education in the '50's in general, is of the inspirational genre; e.g.: National Society for the Study of Education, Fifty-Third Yearbook, Part I, *Citizen Cooperation for Better Schools* (1954); and Herbert M. Hamlin, "Organized Citizen Interest in the Public Schools," *Review of Educational Research*, XXIII (October, 1953), 346–52. An exception is Fred Hechinger's feature article on the Citizens Council in *New York Times*, June 14, 1959. Authoritative on the attacks on progressive education and the demise of the Progressive Education

Association is Cremin, *The Transformation of the School*, pp. 250–73 and Chap. IX.

That the "legatee" concept of the school, despite the torrent of criticism, is still firmly entrenched is evidenced by the following works: U.S. Children's Bureau, Publication 272, *White House Conference on Children in a Democracy, Final Report* (1940); Helen Leland Witmer and Ruth Kotinsky, eds., *Personality in the Making: The Fact-Finding Report of the Mid-Century White House Conference on Children and Youth* (1952), Chap. XI; Hazel Fredericksen, *The Child and His Welfare* (1948), Chap. IX; and "The Public Schools and Other Community Services," *The Annals*, CCCII (November, 1955), 1–73. Nationwide concern with the problem of juvenile delinquency in the postwar period focused attention on the schools, with familiar results: National Society for the Study of Education, Committee on Juvenile Delinquency and the Schools, *Juvenile Delinquency and the Schools* (1948); U.S. Department of Health, Education, and Welfare, *Report on the National Conference on Juvenile Delinquency* (1954), pp. 18–23. Education as "character prophylaxis" is called for in Sheldon and Eleanor Glueck, *Unraveling Juvenile Delinquency* (1950), p. 288. See also the Gluecks' *Delinquents in the Making* (1952), pp. 199–206. Two books by William C. Kvaraceus are important: *Juvenile Delinquency and the School* (1945) and *The Community and the Delinquent* (1948), Chap. X. An older article by the PEA's Adele Franklin, "Is Delinquency the School's Business?" *Progressive Education*, XX (October, 1943), 270–73, 303, is relevant. And see also Dorothy Rogers, *Mental Hygiene and Elementary Education* (1957), and National Society for the Study of Education, Fifty-fourth Yearbook, Part II, *Mental Health in Modern Education* (1955).

The PEA studies of released time: *Released Time for Religious Education in New York City's Schools* (1943, 1945) and *Released Time for Religious Education in New York City Schools: A Research Study by the Center for Field Services, New York University, Dan Dodson, Director* (1949) have more than local significance. Agnes E. Meyer, "The Clerical Challenge to the Schools," *Atlantic Monthly*, CLXXXIX (March, 1952), 42–46, expresses a sentiment widely shared in progressive quarters. Leo Pfeffer, *Church, State and Freedom* (1953), is extremely thorough and extremely partisan. The most scholarly work in this contentious area is R. Freeman Butts, *The American Tradition in Religion and Education* (1950). The interest of many Protestant church groups in providing some form of religious education in the public schools is reflected in two important books written in the thirties: William A. Brown, *Church and State in Contemporary America* (1936), pp. 118–23; F. Ernest Johnson, *Study of Religion in the Public Schools* (1939).

Consult Chamberlain, *Loyalty and Legislative Action . . .* , Chap. V, for New York State's Feinberg Law. All phases of the academic freedom crisis of the early '50's, with special attention to New York, are well discussed in Iversen, *The Communists and the Schools*. The best overall account of the various controversies which raged around the schools in the '40's and early '50's is Butts and Cremin, *A History of Education in American Culture*, Chap. XV.

The literature about the PEA's novel Bronx Park Community Project is surprisingly scarce. If read carefully, John W. Polley, Joseph O. Loretan, and Clara F. Blitzer, *Community Action for Education: The Story of the Bronx Park Community of New York City* (1953), is revealing. PEA, *Up-Hill Journey: An Account of Two Years Work, 1951–1953* (1953), pp. 9–11, is cautiously critical. Of general relevance is Richard C. Lonsdale, *The School's Role in Metropolitan Area Development* (1960).

Oliver C. Carmichael, Jr., *New York Establishes a State University* (1955) documents the PEA's efforts in the State University fight. It is also a unique case study of the politics of educational decision-making. On the same subject, disappointingly formal and conventional is Frank C. Abbott, *Governmental Policy and Higher Education: A Study of the Regents of the State of New York, 1784–1949* (1958), Chaps. X–XI.

PEA, *Up-Hill Journey: An Account of Two Years Work, 1951–1953* (1953), is extremely valuable for this chapter. Also of extreme importance are the following documents, all in the files of the PEA: "Memorandum to the Board of Trustees [of the PEA] from the Public Relations Committee, April 1950," mimeographed; Eduard Lindeman, "Evaluation Report" (1945), mimeographed; and Alonzo G. Grace, "Evaluation Report" (1953), mimeographed.

Going beyond the period with which this study is concerned, but too significant to be overlooked, is the PEA's path-breaking *The Status of the Public School Education of Negro and Puerto Rican Children in New York City* (1955). The changing patterns and problems of group life in New York are excellently discussed in Handlin, *The Newcomers: Negroes and Puerto Ricans in a Changing Metropolis*, Chaps. IV–V. The ecology of the city is provocatively examined in Edgar M. Hoover and Raymond Vernon, *Anatomy of a Metropolis* (1959). Vernon's look into the future, *Metropolis, 1985* (1960), contains much food for thought. On Puerto Rican immigration there is a rapidly growing body of literature. C. Wright Mills and others, *The Puerto Rican Journey* (1950), although outdated in some respects, is a well-informed study. Elena Padilla's *Up From Puerto Rico* (1958) is an intensive study of a New York Puerto Rican community by an anthropologist. Christopher Rand's *The Puerto Ricans* (1958) and Dan Wakefield's *Island in the City* (1959) are sharply observed pieces of reporting originally published in the form of magazine articles. *The Impact of Puerto Rican Migration on Governmental Services in New York City* (1957), Martin B. Dworkis, ed., a careful piece of research, contains a chapter on education (Chap. V).

The estimate of mental health in Leo Srole and others, *Mental Health in the Metropolis: The Midtown Manhattan Study* (1962), has broad implications for public education in the city.

Nathan Glazer writes with great discernment about New York's problems in a recent series of magazine articles: "New York's Puerto Ricans," *Commentary*, XXVI (December, 1958), 469–78; "Is 'Integration' Possible in the New York Schools?" *ibid.*, XXX (September, 1960), 185–95; and "Is New York City Ungovernable?" *ibid.*, XXXII (September, 1961), 185–93.

INDEX

                              Index

munity Project, 203; goal to preserve or enhance its access, 203–04; and Lindeman evaluation, 205; new vigor, late 1940's, 205–06; internal crisis over strategy and tactics, 206–07; criticized by its Public Relations Committee as a "trade" association, 207; assumes more aggressive stance toward school officials, 1951–1953, 208–10; "600" school crisis, 209–10; retreat to behind-the-scenes strategy, 210–11; death of Mrs. Lewisohn, 211–12; appraisal of under Mrs. Lewisohn's leadership, 212; summary and conclusions, 213–27; chief objective to solve problem of child life in city, 214–15; alliance with foundations, 215, 218–19; alliance with social welfare agencies, 217; alliance with Progressive Education Association, 217; ultimate success in activity program, 217; as educator of civic leaders and school officials in progressive education, 218; as opponent of counter-progressive educational tendencies, 218; as elite special interest group, 218–19; and security, humanitarianism, and utopianism, 220; inheritor of school reform program balancing good government and group interest, 221–22; good politics becomes good government, 222–24; appraisal of as interest group, 225–27

Public Education Association of Philadelphia, 57, 58
Public School Neighborhood Associations, 98
Public School Society, 26
PWA and city schools, 152, 173
Puerto Ricans, 157, 186, 187, 188, 194, 223n

Rainsford, Mrs. William S., 1–2, 38, 43, 46–47, 62
Rainsford, Rev. William S., 9, 14, 22, 33; *see also* St. George's Episcopal Church
"Red scare," 103–05
Redefer, Frederick L., 180, 181n
Reed, Mrs. Horace G., 175
"Reform party," Butler on, 34–35; *New York World* on, 37n
Reformers, New York City, 4, 86, 87; school reform as objective, 4; and

schools as solution for East Side, 8; and school as Americanizing agent, 12; and school and slum reform, 12–13; and kindergartens and manual training, 13–14; and school law revision, 21, 24; and "school war," 1895–1896, 34–43; criticized, 40; on "popular control" of schools, 41; on home rule, 41–42; as pragmatists, not ideologists, 41–42; insist on state playing leading role in city schools, 42, 222; gain control of school system, 43, 44; and school crisis in 1914, 86–87; and uses of good government credo, 221–22; and schools as non-political agency, 225

Released time, and Gary Plan, 92, 195; and Coudert-McLaughlin bill, 195; controversy in city, 195–97; PEA investigates, 196; PEA tests constitutionality of, 196–97

Republican party, New York City, election of 1917, 96, 99n, 102, 109; criticizes city schools, 154

Republicans, New York State, 35, 38, 39, 192

Revised City Charter of 1901, school provisions, 93

Reynolds, James B., 3, 12, 33, 37n, 49, 52, 62; *see also* University Settlement

Rice, Joseph Mayer, 21n, 40n

Richman, Julia, 37n, 68, 75, 76, 214

Richmond Hill House, 75

Riegelman, Mrs. Charles, 181

Riis, Jacob A., 6–11, 13, 20, 25, 30, 31, 33, 34n, 37n, 45, 48n, 50, 52, 53, 214

Robbins, Jane E., 12, 65, 83, 124

Robinson, Charles Mulford, 59

Rockefeller, John D., 79, 82, 85n, 96, 97

Rockefeller, John D., Jr., 134n

Rockefeller, Winthrop, 181, 192

Rockefeller Foundation, 82, 85, 96, 215, 219

Rodgers, Mrs. Richard, 181, 206, 207n

Rogers, Henry H., 44

Roosevelt, Franklin D., 145, 149n, 155

Root, Elihu, 37n

Rope, Frederick T., 206

Rosenman, Mrs. Samuel I., 181

Round Table, 59

Runkle, Mrs. Charles A., 2, 45

Russell, Mrs. Isaac Franklin, 108n

Russell, William F., 156n, 161n

Russell Sage Foundation, 77, 83, 84, 215
Ryan, George J., 108n, 111, 154

St. George's Episcopal Church, 2, 14; *see also* Rainsford, Rev. William S.
Schlaifer, Charles, 207n
Schmuck, Mrs. Thomas K., 102, 133n, 139, 175
School evening play centers, 49–50
The School Inquiry, *see* Hanus Survey
School lunches, 72
School playgrounds, 10, 11n
School reform movement, N.Y.C., overarching objective of, 10; as anti-Catholic crusade, 22; in platform of Committee of Seventy, 23; *see also* Reformers, N.Y.C.; Schools, N.Y.C.
School social worker, *see* Visiting teacher
School Survey Committee, 161
"School war," 1895–1896, 34–43; as power struggle, 39–40; *see also* Butler, Nicholas Murray; Compromise School Bill; Good Government Club E; PEA; Reformers, N.Y.C.; Tammany Hall
Schools, N.Y.C., central role in reform, 4, 8; and philanthropic tradition, 11; control by Tammany, 17; control by Catholic Church, 17; as issue, election of 1894, 20–23; progressive reforms in, 30–31, 44, 51, 53, 79; decorated with pictures and casts by PEA, 55; attendance, 61n, 86; and education of Negro children, 70; description, 86–87; appropriations, 87; demands for economy, 87; and Lusk Laws, 103–05; and teacher salaries, 105–07; as election issue in 1921, 109; attendance and appropriations in 1920's, 112n; free from scandal, 137; acceptance of mental hygiene point of view, 138; during Depression, 144–52; and PWA and WPA, 152; progressive education triumphs in, 153, 162–63; criticized by Republicans, 154; investigation of and report on by Graves, 158–59; Campbell inaugurates activity program, 160–62; and radicalism in 1930's, 171–72; attendance and appropriations in 1940's, 190–91; attendance and appropriations in 1950's, 193–94; and released-time controversy, 195–97; and Communist teachers, 197–98; investigation

by PEA, 200; as nonpolitical agency, 225–26
Schussler, Amy, 73
Scott, Mrs. William E. D., 58, 59
Sex education, 72, 125n, 175n
Shapiro, Mrs. Morris, 181
Shaw, Edward, 3
Sheehan, Joseph, 144
Simkhovitch, Mary, 52
Simon, Robert E., 137n, 156n, 161n; *see also* United Parents Associations
Simpson, Kenneth M., 102, 141
"600" schools, 209–10
Smith, Al, 105, 106n, 112, 115, 145
Smith, Eugene Randolph, 127n
Snedden, David S., 104n
Social adjustment as goal of progressive education, 118
Social case work, *see* Social work
Social Gospel, *see* "Institutional church"
Social settlements, responsive to neighborhood needs, 12; respect for immigrant, 12; and school reform, 12; and Americanization, 12; and school social center movement, 49, 52; and visiting teacher movement, 74–75; *see also* College Settlement; Reynolds, James B.; University Settlement
Social work, and progressive education, 75–76, 101, 103, 135–36; and Commonwealth Fund's Program for the Prevention of Juvenile Delinquency, 119–23
Socialized education, 52, 87
Society for the Promotion of Industrial Education, 78
Somers, Arthur S., 108n
Sons of the American Revolution, 184n
Spencer, Mrs. Lorillard, 2, 38
Speyer School, 52n
Sprague, Henry L., 24
Stanton, Mrs. Arthur, 207n
State aid to education, PEA fights for in 1920's, 106; Friedsam Commission, 106n; in early 1930's, 145; PEA fights for, 147–49; Lehman fights for, 148–49; and PEA and Dewey, 191–93
Stern, M. Samuel, 129
Stevenson, George S., 181n
Stimson, Rev. Henry D., 40
Stix, Regina, 132
Stott, Leila V., 166, 167
Stover, Charles, 51

Wald, Lillian, 149
Walker, James J., 107, 112–13, 117, 136, 138, 154
Warburg, Felix M., 66, 84n, 106, 129
Warburg, Mrs. Felix M., 144
Warner, Emily Smith, 181
Webster, Bethuel M., 181, 192
Weet, Herbert S., 156n
Welfare and Health Council of New York City, 181n, 182n
Welsey, Frank D., 108n
Wendell, Mrs. Gordon, 38
Whalen, John, 93n
White, Gaylord S., 53, 66
Whitney, Dorothy, 66, 77, 83, 84
Wile, Ira S., 73, 89, 93n, 98, 127n
Willard, David, 54
Willcox, William G., 93n
Williams, Elizabeth S., 51, 73
Wilsey, Frank D., 96n, 99n
Winthrop, Egerton L., Jr., 66
Winthrop, Mrs. Egerton L., Jr., 67n, 84n
Wirt, William A., 87–88, 91, 99; *see also* Gary Plan; Gary School War
Wise, Rabbi Stephen S., 106
Withers, John W., 156n, 161n

Woman's Association for Improving the Public Schools, origins, 2, 26–27; becomes PEA, 2, 28, 29
Woman's Auxiliary of the University Settlement, 49
Woman's Municipal League, 3, 33, 45, 61, 90, 216
Women Principal's Association, 68n
Women's City Club, 111, 116n, 137n, 175n, 182n, 219n
Women's Conference of the New York Ethical Culture Society, 45
Women's Educational Association of Boston, 57, 76n
Women's Trade Union League, 182n
Woodruff, Clinton Rogers, 58, 59
Woods, Robert A., 53
Work-Study-Play School, *see* Gary Plan
WPA and New York schools, 152–53, 166, 170n, 173

Yeska, Joseph, 108n
Young, James T., 115
Young-Milmoe bill, 192–93; *see also* State aid to education

Zachry, Caroline, 181n, 205n